The Book of Illumination
Kitāb al-Tanwīr fī Isqāṭ al-Tadbīr

with

Sign of Success on the Spiritual Path
ᶜUnwān al-Tawfīq fī Adab al-Ṭarīq

IBN ʿAṬĀʾ ALLAH AL-ISKANDARĪ

Kitāb al-Tanwīr fī Isqāṭ al-Tadbīr
The Book of Illumination

TRANSLATED FROM THE ARABIC

WITH AND INTRODUCTION AND NOTES BY

Scott A. Kugle

along with

ʿUnwān al-Tawfīq fī Adab al-Ṭarīq
Sign of Success on the Spiritual Path

FONS VITAE

First published in 2005 by
Fons Vitae
49 Mockingbird Valley Drive
Louisville, KY 40207
http://www.fonsvitae.com
Email: fonsvitaeky@aol.com

Library of Congress Control Number: 2004115749

ISBN 1-887752-62-5

With gratitude to L. Cadavid,
C. Goddard and S. Kugle for
the illustrations and map.

This book was typeset by Neville Blakemore, Jr.
Printed in Canada

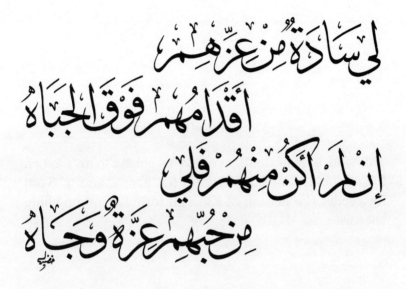

I have masters full of power and might—my forehead is at
    their feet;
Though I'm not of them, let me love them—I might good
    fortune meet.

~ an anonymous poet quoted by Ibn ʿAtaʾ Allah al-Iskandari
    in *ʿUnwān al-Tawfīq fi Adab al-Ṭarīq*
    (*Sign of Success on the Spiritual Path*)

DEDICATION

This work is dedicated to two beloved guides: to my mother, Lynn Kugle, for being nothing but happy, and to Syed Rasheedul Hasan Jeeli-ul-Kaleemi for relying on nothing but trust.

CONTENTS

ACKNOWLEDGEMENTS

This work has accompanied me for several years, and it is with some sadness that I call it complete. The project of translating The Book of Illumination has been like a faithful travel companion on many journeys, and like a good companion it has helped me to see the world differently. Countless hands have urged along the translation; it is difficult to name and thank everyone who either touched my reading of the text or touched me as I was working on it. My teachers in Morocco include Professor Kenneth Honerkamp and Ustadh ᶜAli al-Filali, under whose guidance I began this translation. At Duke University, Professors Rkia Cornell and Vincent Cornell encouraged me to investigate the rich resources of North African Sufism, and pointed to sign-posts along the way. Nutfa, ᶜAlaqa and Madgha did their feline best to reveal the inner wisdom of the text with their own utter dependence, while the example of Imam Faisal Abd al-Rauf cast subtle light upon it. Many thanks go also to Gray Henry at Fons Vitae and Omid Safi on the editorial board for lending their provocative enthusiasm for the project. I am also grateful to my students at Swarthmore College, Joanna Taylor, Noor Ali, and Bradley Phillips, for giving me creative criticism while the manuscript was still ripening. From all of you I beg forbearance with my shortcomings, as naturally all errors or oversights in the translation are my own responsibility entirely.

The transliteration system used throughout this book to represent the sounds of the Arabic alphabet is as follows: ᵓ (*hamza*), b, t, th, j, ḥ, kh, d, dh, r, z, ṣ, ḍ, ṭ, ẓ, ᶜ (*ayn*), gh, f, q, k, l, m, n, h, w, y.

The short vowels are represented as: a (*fatha*), i (*kasra*), u (*dumma*).

The long vowels are represented as: ā, ī, ū.

Diphthongs are represented as *ay* and *aw*, as in the common words *khayr* and *yawm*.

The definite article *al-* is not changed according to pronunciation, for ease of visual recognition; for instance "the sun" is *al-shams* rather than *ash-shams*.

The *tāᵓ marbūṭa* is represented as pronounced: as a final *-a*, unless the word is part of an *iḍāfa* phrase, in which case it is represented as *-at*.

The first time Arabic proper names are mentioned in the text, they are transliterated with full diacritics and exact vowels. Thereafter they are represented in a more simplified way, so as to ease reading of the text in English.

In the translation, Arabic terms are given in (parentheses) for accuracy, while explanations of the translator are given in [brackets] for clarity.

A Parable
The Straying Servant

A person who is concerned for himself is like a servant whose master has dispatched him on a mission. The master has sent him to some land that the master owns in order to procure some cloth there for him. When the servant arrives in that place, he begins to say to himself, "Where will I reside? Whom will I marry?" He gets preoccupied with these questions, expending all his energy on anxiety about these concerns, until he is delinquent in executing the commands for which his master had sent him. When his master calls on him, his reward from the master will be that the master cuts him off and separates himself from the servant, since he was totally preoccupied by his own affairs rather than observing the prerogatives and rights of his master.

So it is with you, my fellow believer. The true One has dispatched you to this world and commanded you to serve in it faithfully, and has undertaken to support and sustain your existence contingent on your service. If you become engrossed in worrying about your own concerns for yourself and neglect the rights held over you by your master, then you have turned aside from the path of right guidance and slid down the low road to ruin.

This book is about one concept encapsulated in a single Arabic word: *tadbīr*. *Tadbīr* literally means "arranging," yet it is a very complex idea, encompassing many diverse terms. In today's colloquial English, we might say that tadbīr means "taking care of business."

While studying Arabic language and literature in Morocco, I first encountered the polysemic term, *tadbīr*. While taking care of my needs in the market or making decisions with friends, the colloquial phrase, *dabbir raʾsak* kept coming to my ears. *Dabbir raʾsak* is a colorful phrase, literally rendered "Manage yourself," that means "Do what you please." It sounds positive, as if you have permission to do what's best for you. At least, that is how I heard it at first. But with time, I began to understand its negative connotations: "Do what you please" also means, "You bear the consequences!" In Morocco, this is what you say to someone who is about to do something potentially harmfully who won't be dissuaded by you. With the pithy ambiguity that characterizes Moroccan colloquial Arabic, it is both permission and chastisement at the same time! Plan to do what seems best for you, but the consequence will fall on your own head.

Of course, our planning ahead and doing what seems best to us never actually works out, at least not the way we project that it will. Such insight is not particular to Moroccan Arabic or even Arabic. In Urdu, the acclaimed love poet with Sufi orientations, Mīr Taqī Mīr, expresses the same idea with characteristic grace using the same profound word, *tadbīr*.

1

Overturned lie all my plans, all my cures fail to mend
Told you so, this heart sickness completes its job
    in the end[1]

In an inner sense, it refers to what one thinks in one's head
in planning ahead to get ahead: reasoning, calculating, setting goals, imagining outcomes, prioritizing values and laying down strategies. In an outer sense, it refers to what one
does in the world of actions, objects and relations to bring
our goals into reality: planning, plotting, implementing,
working and, finally, consuming. I have tried to bring together all these activities, mental, imaginal and physical,
together in one term by translating *tadbīr* as "selfish calculation."

As such, *tadbīr* refers to the full range of our work in
the world, through which we struggle to maintain our being and assert ourselves against the material and social forces
around us. "Selfish calculation" is the very activity base of
the ego. The title of the book translated here, *Kitāb al-Tanwīr
fī Isqāṭ al-Tadbīr*, might be rendered into English as "The
Book of Illumination for Desisting from Selfish Calculation" though an exact English translation is hard to devise
for its abstract and rhyming conciseness. Other possible
translations indicate further levels of nuance. For example,
one could say "Illumination on the Riddance of Self Pre-
Occupation," or "Illumination on Abandonning Over-Con-
cern for One's Welfare," or even "Illumination on the Limits of Self-Reliance," or "Illumination on Understanding
the Futility of Personal Initiative." The author was a medieval Muslim mystic, or Sufi master, named Ibn ʿAṭāʾ Allah
al-Iskandarī. This treatise examines the spirituality of our
ego economics: how we earn, save, consume and plan. It
explains how these activities reinforce the ego that drives

them. Of course, the title of the book indicates its moral stance. The goal is not just to understand "selfish calculation" but rather to desist from it and drop all claims of right to it. The author's basic insight is really very simple. Investing energy in the anxiety of perpetuating egoistic self-determination is an investment that is worse than wasted— it is corrosive to the soul. Rather, the author argues, rely on nothing other than God, not even yourself. The refusal to engage in what your reason urges you to do, to take care of yourself and manage your own affairs, opens up space in the heart for the light of wisdom to shine, illuminating the world with a different, deeper kind vision. This is the connection that Ibn ᶜAtaᵓ Allah makes between relinquishing selfish calculation and receiving spiritual illlumination; these two terms, calculation and illumination, happily rhyme in Arabic as *tanwīr* and *tadbīr*, creating a tangible link between two otherwise abstract concepts.

Approaching the Text

While I was living in Morocco, I also first encountered *The Book of Illumination*. My Arabic teacher placed it before me as "the starting place for anyone who wants to read anything about Sufism." Little did I know that a lesson in Arabic would turn into a lesson in life. I soon discovered that the cultural ambivalence in contemporary Morocco surrounding "planning for oneself" reflects a much older and deeper religious sensibility among North African Muslims, as expressed more clearly through the oral Sufi teachings that they deeply revere and its written traces. "If you must plan, and how can you not plan, then plan only for how not to plan!" admonished Abū al-Ḥasan al-Shādhilī, a spiritual teacher from Morocco whose mystical way deeply shaped Sufi thought and popular Islamic culture across North Africa. The first Sufi follower of al-Shadhili to systematically explain the master's teachings in writing was Ibn ᶜAṭāʾillah, the author of *The Book of Illumination*, who lived in Egypt from 1252-1309 CE. Ibn ᶜAtaʾ Allah follows to its logical extreme the ramifications of the belief that God has created the world, and is the only sustainer of the world. He questions our penchant for erecting false idols of inviolability around the notion that the ego is self-sustaining. He does this by inquiring of us how it is that we consume, work and save, how we conduct the very basic activities of sustaining life that we would rather conveniently ignore.

It is certainly true that human beings, in constructing civilizations (whether based on institutionalized religion or on institutionalized ideology), tend to articulate ideals which lead our vision away from, rather than toward, examining our mode of livelihood. Yet our labors in work and our patterns of consumption are major factors that affect our spiritual condition and are affected by it. The Austrian journalist and Middle East correspondent, Leopold Weiss, articulated this fact in a way that will resonate with contemporary readers in the Anglophone world of post-industrial plenty.

One day—it was in September 1926—Elsa and I found ourselves traveling in the Berlin subway. It was an upper-class compartment. My eye fell casually on a well-dressed man opposite me, apparently a well-to-do businessman, with a beautiful briefcase on his knees and a large diamond ring on his hand…But when I looked at his face, I did not seem to be looking at a happy face. He appeared to be worried: and not merely worried but acutely unhappy, with eyes staring vacantly ahead and the corners of his mouth drawn in as if in pain—but not in bodily pain...Then I began to look around at all the other faces in the compartment—faces belonging without exception to well-dressed, well-fed people: and in almost every one of them I could discern an expression of hidden suffering, so hidden that the owner of the face seemed to be quite unaware of it.[2]

Shocked by the transformation of a routine train-ride into a moral vision, he shared this experience with his wife, Elsa. She also looked around with new eyes, and said, "You are right. They all look as though they were suffering torments of hell...I wonder, do they know themselves what is going on in them?" When he returned home, he chanced upon his copy of the Qur°an, which had fallen open to the 102nd chapter, called "Hoarding."

> You are obsessed by greed for more and more
> Until you go down to your graves
> Nay, but you will come to know.
> Nay, but you will come to know!
> Nay, if you but only knew it with the knowledge
> of certainty
> You would indeed see the hell you are in.
> In time, indeed, you shall see it with the eye
> of certainty.
> On that day you will be asked what you've done
> with the boon of life.[3]

Leopold Weiss was shocked by his vision of people who were "taking care of themselves" in the fires of anxiety juxtaposed with the voice of God as it speaks through the Qur°an trying to reach such people. He went on to become Europe's most famous convert to Islam, Muhammad Asad.[4]

He found in the Qurʾan a voice that addressed the particular obsession of his age (which is still our age, despite our intellectuals' pretension to be not just "post-modern" but also "post-contemporary").

> Although it [the Qurʾan] had been placed before man over thirteen centuries ago, it clearly anticipated something that could have become true only in this complicated, mechanized, phantom-ridden age of ours. At all times, people have known greed: but at no time before this had greed outgrown a mere eagerness to acquire things and become an obsession that blurred the sight of everything else: an irresistible craving to get, to do, to contrive more and more—more today than yesterday, and more tomorrow than today: a demon riding on the necks of men and whipping their hearts forward toward goals that tauntingly glitter in this distance but dissolve into contemptible nothingness as soon as they are reached, always holding out the promise of new goals ahead.[5]

The author of *The Book of Illumination* addresses this same obsession: the craving "to get, to do, to contrive more and more." This craving is universally human, yet also particularly aggravated in our present system of social, economic, and political relationships. Even though this work by Ibn ʿAtaʾ Allah was written six centuries ago, an English translation of it is extraordinarily timely for us, wherever our societies are contrived to increase and intensify our craving while we find fewer and fewer resource that teach us to reduce and refrain. This English translation may be timely for us in the "Economic North" (of the English-speaking zones of North America, Europe and Australia) as well as in societies where Muslims predominate demographically.

Ibn ᶜAtaᵓ Allah invites us gently on a journey into self-critique, in order to reduce our needs and restrain our craving. The landmarks along the road are verses from the Qurᵓan. The signposts along the way are teachings reported from of the Prophet Muhammad. The Sufi master offers himself as our companion on the journey, telling us stories, challenging us with parables, and offering interpretations. He does this to knock our habitual egoism off balance in the hopes that we might see ourselves, the world, and our grasping at the world in a different light—in a more illuminating light.

In the conclusion of *The Book of Illumination*, the author imagines a conversation in which God addresses each person personally, in a voice that seems to answer the shock and horror of that sensitive and adventurous journalist on the subway train in Berlin. It is a voice that can resonate with the spiritual condition of each listener. Ibn ᶜAtaᵓ Allah counsels:

O my servant, examine carefully the relationship between your being and all the dimensions of my cosmic creation. Don't you see that you are an inextricable part of its evanescence that is destined to dissipation? Can't you see the relation of every created thing (and you, too) to what will never dissipate, never fade and never decay? You have come to peace with me as the One who establishes all my creation, so quit contesting my mastery and desist, through your competing with me in arranging your own affairs, from opposing my essential divinity...O my servant, whenever I have made you seem necessary to yourself, it is to test your mettle and

7

see what you're made of. Whenever you take anything other than me from my cosmos as a sufficient means to the exclusion of me, that will begin to consume you and corrode you.

Such a book is especially significant in this age, when we are beginning to realize how inextricably connected are the powerful field of politics and economics to the deeper field of religion and spirituality. These fields were once imagined to be separate, as "infrastructure" and "superstructure." However, now we are forced by the world we have made to revise this view, and see them united in a very complex single structure. The forces that increasingly shape our world, like ecological degradation, technological manipulation, and the threat of mutual annihilation through weapons of mass destruction, all point to the inter-relation between spirituality (whether conceived of as religion or ethics) and the exercise of power (through politics and economics).

For this reason, I hope that the audience for this book will be wide. Of course, *The Book of Illumination* will be of intense fascination to those with specialized interest in Sufism and Islamic thought. It will offer deep insights to anyone interested in mysticism from any religious tradition. Those interested in comparative religion will find provocative ideas about the this-worldly immanence of hell and heaven, analyses of how human craving shapes our mode of existence that echo Buddhist notions of the cycle of desire and suffering. *Illumination* contains surprising interpretations of familiar Prophets: Adam and Eve in the garden, Abraham in the fiery furnace, Moses in the Sinai desert, Mary in the throes of pregnancy with Jesus.

More generally, this book can offer guidance to all spiritual seekers, especially those interested in the practice of radical simplicity. Beyond the common conception of ascetic renunciation, this text offers guidelines for living and working in this world in ways that minimize our grasping urge, that reduce our sense of need, and question our unlimited ambition. These are guidelines that, if put into practice, can have great economic and political implications in our current global economy. Finally, for general Muslim readers, this text offers the spiritual blueprint of an "Islamic work ethic" that will be useful as Muslims integrate further into developed societies (as immigrants to the "Economic North") and into the global network (as elites within their own nation-states).[6] It may serve to further the cause of progressive Islam, and might further re-engage the insights of Sufism into the ethical activism of Islamic law and juridical reasoning.[7]

CONTEXTUALIZING THE TEXT'S TRANSLATION

The need for a revitalized "work ethic" that embraces spiritual growth and inculcates self-restraint has never been greater. It is a factor that can contribute to countering the depredations of the current world order. This issue needs to be addressed from all religious traditions, and *The Book of Illumination* offers an Islamic (specifically Sufi) approach that can resonate with and reinforce approaches from other traditions. Contemporary people of faith must look deeply and self-critically at the way resources are used and needs are fabricated, for these shape our very conception of ourselves. Ecological realism reveals to us that the current world order is not sustainable. Current patterns of production, transportation and consumption in the "Economic North" do not establish an inviolable buffer of comfort and luxury around us, as our leaders promise us. Rather, current practices increasingly require the theft of resources from others, destruction of natural environments, and economic slavery of the "two-thirds world" of people who do not control the global market and its reorganization of wealth, resources and organizational infrastructures to benefit the few.[8]

This shocking reality is illustrated by a visit to the tomb of the author, Ibn ᶜAtaᵓ Allah. The Qarāfa cemetery is a vast burial ground that was formerly outside the city of Cairo. It had been a spacious mortuary park that contained not only the bodies of rulers, Sufi masters and scholars but also housed masterpieces of Islamic architecture that encased them. However, the cemetery now is overcome by the city itself, which has expanded wildly over the past half-century since Egypt achieved nominal independence. Often called "the city of the dead," the cemetery has itself become a city within a city, as rural poverty pushes people and hope for scarce resources pulls people into the city in what has become a global phenomenon throughout the developing world.[9] In this world of new Cairene districts, there are more thirsty mouths than there is water, more ambitious minds than there are schools, and more tombs made into homes than actual houses. As Ibn ᶜAtaᵓ Allah forcefully argues, God does not bring anyone into the world without providing the means of sustenance for that person. The ethical conclusion from this theological idea is that, if there is degrading and dehumanizing poverty, some people are consuming what does not rightfully belong to them thereby unjustly depriving others of their divinely ordained sustenance.

People of faith from various religions have begun to articulate critiques of current globalization that threatens to destroy the ecological balance that all people rely upon for sustainable existence. The Christian theologian, Julio de Santa Ana, has written that this situation depends upon the "complacent and comfortable [who] passively allow the market to assume the properties and dimensions of God in their imaginations and behavior."[10] The question is how to cultivate self-restraint. From a Jewish theological perspective, Rabbi Jonathan Sacks argues that "reverence, restraint, humility, a sense of limits, the ability to listen and respond to human distress—these are not virtues produced by the market, yet they are attributes we will need if our global civilization is to survive and they are an essential part of the religious imagination."[11] Our new technologies allow us a global reach and power to dominate the world in ways that are both promising and terribly frightening. They are especially frightening when such technologies are coupled with an economic ideology that portrays self-interest, acquisitiveness and greed as positive forces that drive "the market" and promise "progress and freedom."

All thoughtful people acknowledge that civilization can thrive when based upon the cultivation of self-restraint. But in our world, based on the free play of desires immediately fulfilled, where will we find resources to relearn the benefits of cultivating self-restraint? Muslims, along with Christians and Jews like the ones quoted above, insist that their religious traditions offer indispensable resources for the cultivation of self-restraint. Many are circling back to religious traditions to see what resources they can offer in the form of "ancient wisdom" that might restore a lost sense of simplicity, tranquility and meaningful destiny to our lives.

This new-age search for ancient wisdom and spirituality is a reaction to very real pain, disillusionment and hopelessness. But it is usually just as indulgent as the consumerist lifestyle that incites it. Any search for religious consolation must lead to a pragmatic assessment of our selfish drive to consume, control and hoard; it must be radical in being characterized by psychological depth, political acuteness, and ecological realism. Anything less is just seeking consolation from propitiating idols that can never offer an authentic and powerful confrontation with the divine. The creation of idols complements an economic system of domination in which a few control resources that they refuse to share with the many. This was true among the Arab aristocracy during the time of the Prophet Muhammad; protesting against this economic idolatry was a major theme of his preaching of radical monotheism, as illustrated most forcefully in the Qurʾan, in such chapters like "Hoarding," cited above.[12] It may be a universal human trait that the greed of an empowered few constructs both a social system of dominance as well as a religious projection in the form of idols. Such a trait is certainly central to our own situation in the "Economic North" where it is hoped this translation will circulate among readers of English.

In *The Book of Illumination*, Ibn ᶜAtaʾ Allah presents a mystical and theological analysis of our human urge to create idols for ourselves and out of ourselves. As a medieval author, he is most attentive to the subtle psychological working of our human ego. He marshals resources from his religious tradition, Islam, that can confront and overcome it. This is the key to understanding the three key terms that make up the Arabic title of his work, *al-Tanwīr fī Isqāṭ al-Tadbīr.* By relying on our own control, we deny the control that only rightly belongs to God, the only force in the cosmos with true ability to arrange affairs (*tadbīr*) on any scale. In view of this reality, he argues, we should drop (*isqāṭ*) any claim we make to control our own affairs according the prompting of our egoistic motivations, the same way we would drop a false claim in court in the face of evidence

12

that contradicts it. The result of desisting from claiming as our right and ability what is clearly beyond our control is illumination (*tanwīr*) of the heart, clarity of the mind and tranquility of the soul.

The goal of Ibn ᶜAtaʾ Allah's discussion is that we achieve this inner illumination of the heart, which is close to the sense of "enlightenment" that has become common in English language discussions of spirituality and gnosis. However, as contemporary readers, we must not limit his insights to some ethereal realm of spirituality. We must be attentive to the powerful societal ramifications of the egoism he critiques, and struggle to draw out the connections between Ibn ᶜAtaʾ Allah's provocative mystical theology and our own concrete work in this world. We cannot help but read this text, on "Illumination for Desisting from Selfish Calculation," in our present context. Reading it engaged with the present might prompt us to rename the title "Rumination for Resisting any Arrogant Exploitation." Reading it with an eye to the future, we might call it "Clarification for Subsisting without Systemic Degradation." To facilitate this shift in perspective between a text from the past and a context in the present, I have endeavored to translate the text in a simple style. It has as few technical terms, devotional formulas, and theological abstractions as possible while retaining the ideas, insights and texture of the original classical Arabic.

CONCEIVING OF THE TEXT'S AGENDA

The texture of the classical Arabic is very rich and variegated. Through a range of discursive modes, Ibn ᶜAtaʾ Allah conveys his message: that investing anxious energy in perpetuating egoistic self-determination is an investment that is corrosive to the soul. His writing weaves together poetic couplets, rhymed prose, gentle advice, chiding admonition, scriptural interpretation, legal disputation, and allegorical parables. It is the wide range of discourses that makes the text so enjoyable to read and so challenging to translate. This variety of discourses has two principle sources: the voice of Divine Speech rendered in scripture (Qurʾan) and the inner voice of the Sufi master's own experiential intuitive knowledge (maʿrifa). In Ibn ʿAtaʾ Allah's experience, these two sources resonate in harmony with each other in a hermeneutic circle. The Qurʾanic recitation sparks the Sufi's intuitive understanding, and this knowledge honed through ethics gives the Sufi the necessary insight to interpret the Qurʾan.

Ibn ʿAtaʾ Allah asserts that if we really listened to the Divine Speech of the Qurʾan, we would generate the self-restraint to stop calculating selfishly for our own benefit. His exposition of this idea follows the etymological force of the Arabic verbal root, d-b-r. Ibn ʿAtaʾ Allah wants us to acknowledge that God alone arranges our affairs (tadbīr), yet we turn our backs (idbār) on such beneficial blessing. He wants us to overcome our ineffectual urge to plan for ourselves (tadbīr) by leaving behind (istidbār) our own ability to calculate, control and plan. What motivates us to do this psychologically difficult task is deep attention and apt action (tadabbur), especially deep attention to the Qurʾan and apt action in assimilating the Prophet's virtues. *What, they still don't pay deep attention to the Qurʾan—or are there locks upon their hearts?* asks the Qurʾan of its listeners.[13] In his prose, Ibn ʿAtaʾ Allah asks this of us.

Such intricate rhetorical plays on Arabic verbal roots in their many forms and meanings is the backbone of this text, like many other Sufi masterworks in classical Arabic. When mentioning a word like tadbīr, Ibn ʿAtaʾ Allah takes for granted that his audience will intuitively grasp the verbal root and its possible expanding forms. He also takes for granted that his audience will know the variety of ways in which that word or its root appears in the Qurʾan. This accounts for the power of his rhetoric to move the audience deeply with a pithy sentence. However, a contemporary English reading audience cannot be expected to know the Qurʾan so fully (if at all), and an English translation obscures the resonance of Arabic roots and rhymes. It is therefore necessary to give a brief introduction to the word *tadbīr* and the many levels of its resonance in the Qurʾan.

The Qurʾan never uses the term *tadbīr* to describe human activity. The term is carefully reserved for descriptions of God in the role of creator, fashioner, originator, controller and maintainer of the cosmos. *Tadbīr* is God's activity alone.

> Your Lord is God who created the heavens
> and the earth in six days
> Then ascended, settling firmly and uprightly
> upon the throne
> Overseeing and regulating all affairs (*yudabbir al-ʾamr*)
>
> There is no intercessor except
> with the permission of God.
> This divinity is your Lord,
> therefore serve God worshipfully
> Will you not bear this constantly in mind?[14]

In fact, the Qurʾan never uses *tadbīr* as an abstract verbal noun at all, but rather uses the verb from which it is derived. Arranging, controlling, and maintaining what exists are always actions, not abstractions. They are actions that the Qurʾan associates with a height beyond the sky. After

15

the act of creation, which implies an immediate, intimate and close contact with the material world, God is depicted as "ascended, settling firmly upon the throne." The Throne represents authority and command, the position from which acts of control and planning take place.

> God is the One who raised the heavens
> without any perceptible supports
> Then ascended, settling firmly and uprightly
> on the throne
> And subjected the sun and the moon
> to their courses
> Each runs its course
> in its designated time.
> God oversees and regulates all affairs
> and clearly elaborates all signs
> That you may believe with firm certainty
> in the meeting of your Lord.[15]

One of the most important skyward "signs" of God's arrangements for this world is the rain. It is a material sign of the divine presence that sustains all life in rain or rivers, coursing in channels to nourish plants and animals, sustaining human livelihood from sources beyond our routine consciousness. Understanding these signs in the material world around us is the key to understanding signs of the life to come. God's care in arranging provision and sustenance from the skies down to the earth must be mirrored by our care in rising above or ascending back to the divine presence, through keeping mindful, giving thanks, and guarding each other's well-being.

> God is the One who created the heavens
>   and the earth
> And all the lies between,
>   in six days.
> Then ascended, settling firmly and uprightly
>   on the throne.
> Other than God, you have no one to protect you
>   or intercede for you.
> Therefore, will you not bear God
>   constantly in mind?
> God oversees all affairs
>   from the sky to the earth.
> All affairs will go up to God
>   on a day (of reckoning)
> The length of which is one thousand years
>   as you perceive their number.
> This is the One who knows all things
>   hidden or displayed
> The One exalted in power,
>   the compassionate One.[16]

But in general, people do not ponder God's arrangement of divine signs and beneficial processes in the natural order. We take it for granted, or worse we take it in our own hands as if we possess the right to arrange for ourselves. By doing this, people turn their backs on divine arrangement and stoke the fires of arrogant possessiveness.

> All in vain, for the blazing fire
> Stripping off the burned outer layer
> Encompasses those who turn their backs,
>   who turn away
> Taking shelter in what they gather and hoard.

For the human being is by nature agitated with greed:
When brushed by harm, in loss lamenting
When brushed by benefit, miserly in clutching.
Except for those who pray
And keep steadfast in their prayer
Who keep aside, from what they own,
A portion for others who ask and those prevented
Who believe in the day of reckoning.[17]

Reflecting on these Qurʾanic exhortations, Ibn ʿAtaʾ Allah embarks on his address. He aims to teach us how overcome our human penchant to be "agitated with greed." Giving time and attention to God in prayer and giving material and support to others from what we own is certainly the goal, but how do we get there? It is not enough to perform these actions through command-and-obedience. Rather, the actions should flow from us through sincerity and love.

For this reason, this text is not merely a theological interpretation of the Qurʾan; it is also a book about how to embody virtues and implement them in practical affairs. Ibn ʿAtaʾ Allah's argument is complex because the human psyche rears up, in open rebellion or in subtle subversion, against the idea of being at peace. Being at peace means being at one with one's surroundings by acting as a vessel for another's will rather than asserting one's own will. This is especially hard when we are confronted with material scarcity that prods us (either through its actual rigors or through our imagined fear of them) to start calculating how to work, earn, save, and arrange our lives for our own benefit.

Tadbīr, then, is an abstract noun that describes a human activity that we could think of as "taking care of business for oneself." Victor Danner, the scholar who first translated one of Ibn ᶜAtaᵓ Allah's writings into English, defined the term like this:

> *Tadbīr* implies egocentric concern for one's direction in life, and more particularly in one's daily existence, to the point where it blots out the obligations due God. In that case, which is self-direction, the tadbir is negative and should be eliminated. But if the planning or direction is in conjunction with God's directives, then it is positive and not an obstacle in the Path, in which case it is not self-direction but Self-direction.[18]

This term is rooted in the Qurᵓan without being used in the Qurᵓan. It is the genius of Sufi literature to find skillful means to draw out resonant references from the Qurᵓan that weave seamlessly into every-day human life: into how we treat our bodies, how we use our imaginations, or how we interact with others in the marketplace of work.

In finding the skillful means to convince us, Ibn ᶜAtaᵓ Allah sets forth two strategies. On the one hand, he invokes God's overwhelming power, through God's attributes of being the One who enforces, the One who destines and the One who owns (*al-qahhār, al-qadīr, al-mālik*); these qualities grant us no right to presume control over our own affairs. On the other hand, Ibn ᶜAtaᵓ Allah invokes God's care and attention, through God's attributes of being the One who helps, the One who provides, the One who is subtly aware and ever sustaining (*al-muᶜīn, al-razzāq, al-laṭīf, al-qayyūm*); these qualities preclude us from any need to care for our own affairs. These two facets of divine treatment are the "two hands" of God as described by the Qurᵓan. Sufis understand "the left hand" to be mighty wrath and power (*jalāl*) that enforces all the overwhelming attributes, and "the right hand" to be beauty and grace (*jamāl*) that enacts all the caring and supporting attributes. Ibn ᶜAtaʾ Allah wrote in his *Sufi Aphorisms*: "When God gives you a gift, it is so that you become aware of divine kindness; when God deprives you, it is so that you become aware of divine power."[19] In being nurtured with both hands, Sufis understand that the human being is one, as God describes, *whom I have created by my two hands*. God's two hands knead the clay of our material nature between the power and care of these two hands while blowing into it the animating force of divine breath.[20] Creation is not something achieved by divine fiat in the past, but something that we experience continuously in each moment. Just as we never plotted and planned for ourselves in anxiety over our futures while being created, why should we plot and plan with selfish calculation now, while our creation and continual sustenance is not yet complete?

We can think of Ibn ᶜAtaʾ Allah's perspective as radical monotheism. It would be easy for English readers in the "Economic North" to dismiss this as encouraging passive acceptance of fate and abdicating freewill. However, a careful reading of Ibn ᶜAtaʾ Allah reveals that he advocates a delicate balance between accepting divine acts without willful assertion and acting effectively in society with full confidence that one's actions are in accord with divine will. The analyst of Andalusian Islamic culture, Lenn Goodman, makes an acute observation:

Strange as it may seem at first, radical monotheism does not demand rejection of free will. The same determinism which we associate perhaps with "middle eastern fatalism and lassitude" may equally have been the spark that powered the industrial revolution. What makes the difference between fatalism and the kind of determinism that inspired the Puritan work ethic is the extent to which subjective identification is achieved with the divine purpose. Islam may be interpreted to mean resignation to the will of God; but if that will remains no longer other, but is accepted by the consciousness as self, then the I can expect of itself the ability to move mountains.[21]

It might even be that Islam shares these qualities with Puritan Christianity, qualities that make up the Puritan notion of "the calling" that led, under special circumstances, to modern capitalism and industrial production. The sociologist of religion, Max Weber, observed that the Puritan revolution provided a religious element of culture that was instrumental in sparking the development of capitalist industry. If Weber had known more about Islam, and about Ibn ᶜAtaᵓ Allah's brand of Shadhili Sufism, he might not have attributed these qualities uniquely to Puritans in Europe and North America.

The Puritan wanted to work in a calling; we are forced to do so. For when asceticism was carried out of monastic cells into everyday life, and began to dominate worldly morality, it did its part in building the tremendous cosmos of the modern economic order. This order is now bound to the technical and economic conditions of machine production which to-day determine the lives of all the individuals who are born into this mechanism, not only those directly concerned with economic acquisition, with irresistible force. Perhaps it will so determine them until the last ton of fossilized coal is burnt. In Baxter's [the Puritan theologian's] view the care for external goods should only lie on the shoulders of the saint "like a light cloak, which can be thrown aside at any moment." But fate decreed that the cloak should become an iron cage.[22]

If Weber had known more about Islam, he might have noted that the symbolism of "the cloak" is potent in Sufi communities; it acts as a symbol of initiation into a spiritual discipline, of struggling to live in the world without being of the world.

Yet in Puritan Protestantism, the cloak has become a cage. Weber observes, with some note of nostalgia and regret, how spirituality fueled these revolutionary changes in society, which quickly overran and expelled spirituality. In a rare moment of prognostication, he looks forward to the moment when members of capitalist societies, locked into the cage of technical manipulation, will have lost consciousness in their own "petrifaction" and "self-importance." This is, perhaps, the present moment. From the present, we can look forward to the inevitable moment when the last fossil fuels are burnt, a moment which opens the door to other alternate ways of seeing the world and acting in it, other ways to which *The Book of Illumination* may act as a guide. Weber concludes this passage by saying: "No one knows who will live in this cage in the future, or whether at the end of this tremendous development entirely new prophets will arise, or there will be a great rebirth of old ideas and ideals, or, if neither, mechanized petrifaction, embellished with a sort of convulsive self-importance."[23] By reading Ibn ʿAtaʾ Allah's text attentively, we can discern the outlines of an Islamic conception of "the calling" that Weber attributes uniquely to Protestant Northern Europe and North America. Yet the Islamic version of "the calling" is to work diligently, act sincerely, and acquire scrupulously, work that is restrained by a suspicion of hoarding or multiplying one's own wealth at the expense of others' welfare. Perhaps as ecological limitations reveal our current economic and political system as unsustainable, despite its "convulsive self-importance," Ibn ᶜAtaʾ Allah's writing can contribute to a "great rebirth of old ideas and ideals" of a fuller humanity, side by side with pre-modern intellectuals from other religious and cultural traditions.

UNDERSTANDING THE TEXT'S AUTHOR

As mentioned above, some of Ibn ᶜAtaʾ Allah's many writings have already been translated into English in the skillful hands of Victor Danner and Mary-Ann Koury Danner. The book before you is one in the series of translations, forthcoming from Fons Vitae Press, that should encompass the author's remaining *oeuvre* in the near future. To further this goal, this book includes an appendix with a translation of Ibn ᶜAtaʾ Allah's short work, *Sign of Success on the Spiritual Path* (ᶜ*Unwān al-Tawfīq fī Adab al-Ṭarīq*), which complements *The Book of Illumination*. In what follows, I will give a brief introduction to Ibn ᶜAtaʾ Allah to assess his important place among Sufis in North Africa, specifically in his role as the third axial saint (*quṭb*) in the Shadhili Sufi community that grew to predominate across that region.

The Shadhili Sufi community later spread into the Near East, Central Asia and Southern Asia, before finally reaching Europe and North America during the twentieth century.[24] But it first grew in the fertile ground between two cultural regions of the Arab-Islamic world: the extreme West which consists of Morocco and Southern Spain (*al-maghrib al-aqṣā*) and Nilotic Egypt, part of the Eastern Arab lands

23

(*al-mashriq*). The cities of Tunis and Alexandria were cosmopolitan urban centers that connected these two regions, participating in the culture of both without being dominated by either. These four locations are the geographical points where early masters of the Shadhili community lived and taught.

The first axial saint of the Shadhili community, Abū al-Ḥasan al-Shādhilī, hailed from Ghumāra in Northern Morocco. His charismatic personality attracted able disciples, awed local political rulers, and fueled the jealousy of detractors among literalist jurists and scholars. He was born into a *Sharīf* family that claimed biological descent from the Prophet Muhammad (through his grandson, Imām Ḥassan). Shaykh al-Shadhili's spiritual master in Morocco, Shaykh Ibn Mashīsh, was also a *Sharīf*, and the two cultivated a style of Sufi spirituality that centered on devotion to the Prophet's outward commands (in scripture and law) and inward character (through ascetic virtue and visionary boldness). In *The Book of Illumination*, Ibn ᶜAtaᵓ Allah tells the story of how the master met his future disciple and gave him his first lesson. The local cultural climate in Northern Morocco was not immediately receptive to their teachings, and it appears that Shaykh al-Shadhili was Ibn Mashish's only disciple. It may even be that Ibn Mashish was assassinated by a faction involved in local tribal politics, possibly because of his outspoken advocacy of the spiritual leadership of *Sharīf* families.[25]

In any case, Shaykh al-Shadhili moved to a small town outside of Tunis, called Shādhila. In this region he took on the nickname by which he and his community of followers would be known until today—"al-Shādhilī." Here, he found a place receptive to his teachings and he founded his first *zāwiya*, or devotional center, in Tunis in 1227 CE. The cave to which he would retreat for devotions (*maqām*) still exists on a mountaintop outside the city, and has become the foundation of a large mosque. In Tunis, he drew together a large and vibrant body of followers. Here, a young man joined him, who would become his primary follower and the inheritor of his spiritual station, Abū al-ᶜAbbās al-Mursī.

Like Shaykh al-Shadhili, Shaykh al-Mursi was from the extreme West, but from the opposite shore of that region: from the refined and urbane port of Murcia in Southern Spain rather than from the rough and rugged mountains of Northern Morocco. He was a scholarly young man who left home to travel East toward Egypt in search of intellectual learning. However, during a port call in Tunis, he was drawn to Shaykh al-Shadhili's charismatic way of combining outer allegiance to Islamic law with inner visionary experience. Ibn ᶜAtaᵓ Allah himself recorded the oral traditions in which al-Mursi described how he met his Shaykh: "When I was staying in Tunisia after coming from Murcia—at which time I was a young man—I heard mention of Shaykh Abu al-Hasan al-Shadhili (may God be pleased with him). A man said to me, 'Will you come with me to see him?' I replied, 'Once I have sought God for guidance in the matter.' As I slept that night, I saw a man on a mountain donned in a green robe. He was seated, with a man to his right and a man to his right. I looked at him and he said to me, 'You have found the vice-regent of the age.' I awoke, and after the dawn prayer, the man who had invited me to visit the shaykh with him came to me, and I went with him. When we went in to see the shaykh, I was astounded to find him seated on the very bench I had seen on top of the mountain. The shaykh said to me, 'You have found the vice-regent of the age. What is your name?' So I told him my name and my line of descent. He said to me, 'You were lifted up to me ten years ago.'"²⁶ Al-Musri perceived no need for other teachers and soon abandoned his previous goals in order to live with and learn from his Shaykh.

Shaykh al-Shadhili had a vision commanding him to move East. He took Shaykh al-Mursi and some close followers to Alexandria where he built a new devotional center, while leaving other followers to perpetuate the community in Tunis. Shortly before he died in 1258 CE, Shaykh al-Shadhili delegated both his spiritual and communal authority to Shaykh al-Mursi, who was recognized as the second axial saint (*quṭb*) of the Shadhili lineage. Authority was delegated in an outward dimension. However, in an inward dimension, al-Mursi had so assimilated his Shaykh's personality that no distinction was made between them. According to Ibn ᶜAtaᵓ Allah, "Shaykh al-Shadhili said, 'Abu al-ᶜAbbas, I only took you as my companion in order for you to be me, and me, you." Others in the early Shadhili community perceived this fusion of personalities in a more graphic way. In a vision, one of them saw Shaykh al-Shadhili descending from the sky while Shaykh al-Mursi was waiting for him, his feet planted firmly on the ground, "until Abu al-Hasan [al-Shadhili] descended upon him and disappeared into his head."²⁷

After the death of Shaykh al-Shadhili, the new community in Alexandria was largely shaped by the personality of Shaykh al-Mursi, who combined a gentle, scholarly demeanor with penetrating spiritual insight. Like his master, Shaykh al-Mursi wrote no books, but left a large body of oral teachings, some powerful litanies of invocation that his followers used in devotional exercises, and the personalities of disciples who were stamped by his spiritual presence. He shunned the political elite and took on the role of a teacher of Islamic knowledge in a local mosque. According to Ibn ᶜAtaᵓ Allah, it was al-Mursi who "circulated the knowledge of Shaykh Abu al-Hasan, spreading the light of this knowledge and revealing its secrets...until the shaykh's fields of knowledge were disclosed on people's lips and through their written words."[28] Of course, it was Ibn ᶜAtaˀ Allah himself who was primarily responsible for setting into written words the teachings and biographies of his master, and his master's master in the Shadhili lineage.

It was in his role as a teacher and preacher in the mosque that Shaykh al-Mursi met Ibn ᶜAtaˀ Allah, who was a precocious youth who excelled in the intellectual field of Islamic jurisprudence.[29] After completing his madrasa education, he had already gained renown, and seemed destined to rise to fame as a jurist (faqīh) in the Mālikī method of jurisprudence. In his youth, Ibn ᶜAtaˀ Allah was suspicious and possibly hostile to Sufis. He believed that Muslims required nothing beyond knowledge of scripture and obedience to law, not needing spiritual development through Sufism. This was, perhaps, a form of rebellion against his father, who was a devoted follower of Shaykh al-Mursi in Alexandria, and in sympathy for his grandfather, who apparently disapproved of the Shadhili circle. However, while arguing with some fellow students about Sufi teachings, he admitted that he had never actually heard Shaykh al-Mursi speak and was invited along to hear one of the Shaykh's public discourses. He later recorded this experience:

Then I came to the Shaykh's gathering and I found him speaking about aims that the law-giver ordered us to achieve. He said, 'The first aim is submission (islām), the second is faith (īmān) and the third is doing what is beautiful (iḥsān). Or you could say the first is worship (ᶜibāda), the second is servanthood (ᶜubūdīya), and the third is selfless service (ᶜubūda). Or you could say the

27

first is following religious law (*sharīᶜa*), the second is comprehending spiritual reality (*ḥaqīqa*), and the third is becoming spiritually realized (*taḥaqquq*).' He continued to speak, saying 'And if you like, you could say this...or you could say that' until my reason was bedazzled. This man was drawing out spoonfuls of the overflowing ocean of divinity! Thus did God dispel the doubts that I had had about him.[30]

After this experience, perhaps at this very gathering, Ibn ᶜAtaᵓ Allah put aside his former reservations and placed himself in the spiritual training of Shaykh al-Mursi, who assured him that taking on Sufi discipline did not require one to abandon studying or teaching jurisprudence. Shaykh al-Mursi later said, "...the Messenger of God patiently endured the unbelief of the Quraysh, in hopeful anticipation of their [believing] descendents. And we, likewise, patiently enduring this jurist's grandfather for the sake of his grandson," referring to Ibn ᶜAtaᵓ Allah.[31]

However, it was not so easy for the young Ibn ᶜAtaᵓ Allah to balance the demands of Islamic law and Sufi devotion, at least at first. He was overcome by the urge to leave the study of Islamic law in favor of single-minded devotion to Sufism. In longing to grow closer to al-Mursi, he once commented to a fellow disciple, "I would like the Shaykh to regard me with solicitude and grant me a special place in his thoughts." Al-Mursi later answered him, "Demand not that the shaykh grant you a special place in his thoughts. Rather, require yourselves to grant the shaykh a special place in your thoughts. For, to the degree that you revere the shaykh, he will revere you."[32] Yet as he grew closer to Shaykh al-Mursi by placing the shaykh in his single-minded concentration, he feared that he would loose hold of studying and practicing law. He writes that he heard some students of the outward religious sciences (like scriptural interpretation and law) say that those who keep company with the shaykhs acquire nothing in the realm of outward sciences. "It distressed me to think of missing the opportunity to acquire such knowledge; however, it also distressed me to think of losing the shaykh's companionship, may God be pleased with him."[33] Reading his thoughts, al-Mursi assured him that he never demands anyone leave his occupation in order to join the Sufi circle, whether the disciple is a merchant, craftsperson or student of the law. "We do not tell a student: abandon your pursuit of knowledge and come. Rather, we confirm everyone in that in which God has established him, and whatever portion he receives through us will be his as well."[34]

However, for the young Ibn ᶜAtaᵓ Allah the law was not merely an occupation, it was a preoccupation. He writes of his youth, "I used to have frequent obsessive doubts as to whether I was in a state of ritual purity. When word of this reached Shaykh Abu al-Hasan [al-Shadhili], he said to me, 'I've heard that you are prone to obsessive doubts as to whether you've performed your ablutions or not.' 'Yes, I am,' I replied. Then he said (may God be pleased with him), 'This group of ours calls the shots with Satan, not the other way around.' Several days passed and I went in to see him again. 'How are you doing with your obsessive doubts?' he asked. 'There hasn't been any change,' I replied. He said, 'If you don't abandon this obsessive preoccupation, don't come back to see me again!' What the Shaykh had said caused me such anguish that from that time forward, God delivered me from my inward tormentor."[35] With such tough treatment, the Shadhili masters lovingly weaned Ibn ᶜAtaᵓ Allah from his legalistic narcissism.

As if in response to this growing spiritual resolve, the young Ibn ᶜAtaᵓ Allah again veered towards abandoning his outward employment and family profession in religious law. However, Shaykh al-Mursi slyly steered him away from that path, in a gracefully indirect way that contrasts with the more direct, confrontational style of Shaykh al-Shadhili.

When I was younger, I determined for myself to lead a life of utter dependence on God by refusing to work. So I went to visit Shaykh al-Mursi, after making this decision. I said to myself, "It is better to arrive at God's presence through a reclusive life than through a life busied with studying religious tradition and law, teaching it to others, and getting all mixed up with people and their problems." Without my revealing any of these thoughts, Shaykh al-Mursi said to the assembly, "Once a man used to keep company with me. He was always busy studying and teaching the outer religious disciplines of knowledge. In fact, he was a leading religious authority in our town. Then he experienced a little spirituality on this Sufi path—just a taste. He immediately came to me and said, 'O master, I'm leaving the life I had been leading and I'm devoting all my time to sitting with you.' I told him, 'Mind your own business! Abide with the condition in which you find yourself, for whatever God has appointed for you [of spiritual insight] that comes to you through my agency will come to you—your work is no obstacle to that!'" Having relayed this story, Shaykh al-Mursi looked directly at me and said, "The sincere ones are like that. They leave nothing by their own devices and choices until the true One governs their leaving one situation and moving on to the next."[36]

30

Upon leaving the Shaykh's presence, Ibn ʿAtaʾ Allah found that God "had washed my heart clean of all those misleading thoughts." In Shaykh al-Mursi, Ibn ʿAtaʾ Allah found a model for the Sufi master who was also a teacher of religious knowledge. In living with his master for twelve years, Ibn ʿAtaʾ Allah himself later perfected this delicate balance of allegiance to the inner and outer legacy of the Prophet Muhammad. Al-Mursi predicted that Ibn ʿAtaʾ Allah would be appointed to the position once occupied by his grandfather, the leading jurist of Cairo. He said, "The jurist [who appoints you] will sit on one side, and I will sit on the other, while you, if God wills, will speak to us of both outward and inward knowledge."[37]

This balance of inward insight and outward knowledge was the remarkable characteristic of Ibn ʿAtaʾ Allah's personality. It was this balance that allowed him to write down the Shadhili masters' teachings without reducing their complexity and force, while weaving their wisdom into the fabric of Islamic scriptural and legal knowledge. This was in strong contrast to Shaykh al-Shadhili, who focused his full attention on the inward spiritual condition of his followers; Shaykh al-Mursi followed him in this inward attention, but explained why he never wrote anything by saying, "My companions are my books."

After Shaykh al-Mursi's death in 1288 CE, Ibn ʿAtaʾ Allah lived out his life in Cairo, the capital city of the Mamlūk dynastic empire. He led a professional life as a jurist and professor in the leading religious-intellectual institutions of his time, like the madrasas of al-Azhar and al-Manṣūrīya. He also preached in public, where his voice reached a huge audience in the capital. In his more private role as a Sufi master, he founded a *zawiya* in Cairo while continuing to train disciples in Alexandria. In the Shadhili community in Egypt, he was regarded as the third axial saint in the lineage. In the public life of medieval Egypt under Mamluk rule, he was regarded as the principle spokesman for Sufism, and was called upon to defend Sufi practices in 1307 CE, when challenged in public debate by the puritanical literalist and political rabble-rouser, Ibn Taymīya. It seems that this defense was effective, since the Sultan refused to enforce Ibn Taymiya's protests. In 1309 CE, while in the midst of giving a lesson in jurisprudence, Ibn ᶜAtaᵓ Allah breathed his last and passed beyond the fabric of material existence.

Appreciating the Author's Works

Ibn ᶜAtaᵓ Allah left a dual legacy that is both spiritual and literary, and these two dimensions are integrally related. Spiritually, he absorbed and then transmitted the teachings of the early Shadhili masters, as refracted through his own personality as an intellectual and jurist. He trained a wide community of disciples and oversaw the continuing expansion of the Shadhili community in Egypt and Arabia, and across the urban centers of North Africa. He advocated a distinct style of Sufism that integrated juridical training and Sufi insight, which would become a characteristic of the later Shadhili community. The Shaykhs al-Mursi and Ibn ᶜAtaᵓ Allah can be called Sufi-jurists in the Mālikī tradition. They conceived of Imām Mālik, the famous eighth-century jurist and preserver of the traditions attributed to Muhammad, not only as the founder of their legal system but also as a founder of Sufism. They asserted that Imam Malik was the first to encourage an integral synthesis between Sufi spiritual striving and legal rigor, and recorded Malik as having pronounced: "The one who takes up jurisprudence without Sufism is hollow. The one who takes up

Sufism without jurisprudence is hypocritical. The one who takes up both in balance has realized the truth."[38]

The text you have before you is a beautiful example of this approach to Sufism. It takes jurisprudence as the starting point and indispensable foundation for spiritual insight. After exhorting his audience to persevere in obligatory ritual acts of worship, Ibn ᶜAtaᵓ Allah writes:

> Don't be self-satisfied with fulfilling only the acts of worship that God has made obligatory for you. Rather, give rise to love by committing yourself to interacting with God in everything you do beyond obligatory acts of worship. If you die and find in the scales of your balance only the bare minimum of fulfilling obligatory acts and avoiding forbidden acts, you will have missed goodness and subtle gifts that are beyond enumerating and assessing. Glory be to the One who opens for us the gates of continual interaction with God in everything we do...[39]

This is the voice of the Sufi-jurist. However, Ibn ᶜAtaᵓ Allah also cultivated a more interior kind of spirituality, akin to what specialists in Religious Studies call "monism." That is the systematic cultivation of states of mind that perceive the phenomenal world to have no existence of its own and to persist only because of "the oneness of being" with the divinity. In Sufi circles, this type of spirituality is most closely associated with Ibn ᶜArabī (1165-1240 CE). Although Ibn ᶜAtaᵓ Allah does not discuss Ibn ᶜArabi by name and does not adopt his highly technical philosophical approach, he does show an aptitude (even a reliance) upon the basic concept of Ibn ᶜArabī's system. That is that God is *al-ḥaqq,* the true One and the only real existence upon which all material or phenomenal things depend and outside of which nothing really exists at all.[40] In the period following Ibn ʿAtaʾ Allah's death, his followers, especially ʿAlī Wafāʾ and his circle, actively cultivated the thought of Ibn ʿArabī.[41] This circle of followers introduced an element of speculative boldness and poetic license to the Shadhili community as it developed around Ibn ʿAtaʾ Allah in Cairo (characteristics that later Moroccan Sufis would see as typically Egyptian or *Mashriqī*).

In addition to training disciples, Ibn ʿAtaʾ Allah was the first master of the Shadhili community to write books. This is another powerful indication of his integration of the roles of spiritual guide and scholarly teacher. His reputation as a spiritual guide spread more widely through his writings than through his followers, and some Sufis became known as "Shadhilis" through their dedication to teaching his written works rather than through their outward pledge of initiation to a living master. He preserved in writing the oral teachings and biographical anecdotes about Shaykh al-Shadhili and Shaykh al-Mursi. In addition, his own writings (of which seven texts currently exist while others have seemingly been lost) display his powerful personality very clearly in poetry and prose.

Of all his texts, Ibn ʿAtaʾ Allah gained fame for his short collection of pithy wisdom sayings, in which he offered a gem-like aphorism (*ḥikma*), subtle and iridescent, for each of the many stages or situations that a mystic might pass through. By the fifteenth century CE, it had become a devotional custom (*sunnat al-ṭarīqa*) for a Sufi master of the Shadhili community to write a commentary on this collection of *Sufi Aphorisms*. In Morocco, Shaykh Ibn ʿAbbād al-Rundī began this persistent commentary tradition, and Shaykh Aḥmad Zarruq spread it by writing numerous commentaries (perhaps as many as twenty of them) during his long travels across the wide network of North African cities, from Fes to Cairo.[42] In the Shadhili community, disciples advanced through reading the aphorisms, committing them to memory, reciting them and reflecting on them. It is almost as if committing their insight about the aphorisms to paper was the mark of an advanced disciple having become a venerable master. It is understandable, even appropriate, that the *Sufi Aphorisms* would be the first work of Ibn ʿAtaʾ Allah to be translated into English.

However, the *Sufi Aphorisms*, despite its wide renown and masterful literary craftsmanship, is a very difficult book. It was written for advanced Sufi disciples who were already deeply immersed in spiritual training under the committed guidance of a Sufi master. Beyond being "esoteric" (as most everything associated with mysticism is labeled), the work is almost obtuse: its texture is very delicate, its terminology highly abstract, and its meaning playfully elusive. It is certainly not meant to introduce the general reader to Ibn ʿAtaʾ Allah's thoughts and guidance, or to Sufism in general. Ibn ʿAtaʾ Allah himself went on to write six other books, weaving the gossamer threads of his insight into the fabric of more expository prose. In this sense, it is unfortunate that the *Sufi Aphorisms* remained for many years the only work of his that had been rendered into English. Subsequently, Mary-Ann Koury Danner has produced a wonderful translation of Ibn ʿAtaʾ Allah's important book on meditation (*dhikr*), entitled *The Key to Salvation*. Yet again, this work is mainly relevant to committed Sufis who already have a high degree of facility with devotional practices and Sufi concepts, especially those with allegiance to the Shadhili community.

There is a grave need for a translation of Ibn ᶜAtaᵓ Allah's guidance for beginners. The category of "beginners" would include skeptics who see no value in esoteric practices (for whom overwrought terms like "mystic," "gnosis" or "the oneness of being" would be obstacles to insight rather than incentives to understanding). Beginners would also include spiritual seekers who may not have previous exposure to Islam or the cultivation of Islamic spirituality through Sufism. Beginners would include people with an interest in Sufism or even allegiance to Sufi practice, but who find themselves struggling with the basic values and floundering in a muddle of how to balance high ideals with the murky reality of everyday life. I admit freely that I am a perpetual beginner, striving to translate this work for fellow beginners. I first read *The Book of Illumination* while just beginning my study of Arabic literature, and its greatest impact upon me was that it revealed me to myself as someone stumbling, perplexed and not fully in control.

It is clear that Ibn ᶜAtaᵓ Allah intended this book to be an introduction to his Sufi method, to prepare disciples in the basics before they might move on to his more famous but concentrated works, like the *Sufi Aphorisms*. If fact, the whole text is an extended commentary on one of Ibn ᶜAtaᵓ Allah's aphorisms: "Rest yourself from self-direction (*tadbīr*), for what someone else has carried out on your behalf, do not you yourself undertake to do it."[43] This aphorism is the fourth in a series of 262 aphorisms. Commentators have long debated whether there is a distinct order to the aphorisms: that is, whether they follow one after the other in a progression that mirrors the spiritual growth of the disciple. Whether or not this is true for the whole collection, the first few aphorisms (numbers 2 through 7) have the common theme of "desisting from selfish calculation"

36

in contradiction to what being at peace with God provides for you. In the *Sufi Aphorisms*, it is implied that the first obstacle to spiritual development is "selfish calculation" in managing your affairs. Naturally, as an introduction to Sufi method, *The Book of Illumination* would act as an extended commentary upon this series of initial aphorisms to get the beginner over the first set of hurdles.

Victor Danner wrote that "[the book of *Sufi Aphorisms*] itself, when properly understood and assimilated, ends up by being its own best commentary."[44] This phrasing could have the effect of relegating Ibn ᶜAtaᵓ Allah's other writings to an inferior status, as works that merely open up "further angles of insight." In particular, this statement obscures the importance of *The Book of Illumination*. Ibn ᶜAtaᵓ Allah must have thought that his aphorisms needed further commentary beyond the *Book of Sufi Aphorisms* itself in order to unfold their meaning more systematically and elucidate their ramifications more clearly. In a contrasting assessment of *The Book of Illumination*, Victor Danner calls it a "companion piece" to the *Sufi Aphorisms*, and Mary-Ann Koury Danner expands upon this more complimentary view, noting that it "is a kind of commentary" on the *Sufi Aphorisms*. In fact, *The Book of Illumination* specifically explicates the aphorisms that deal with planning and plotting in one's own life, as noted by the sixteenth-century Sufi scholar from India, ᶜAlī Muttaqī.[45] These are key nuggets of wisdom, indispensable for the initial stages of growth on the Sufi path. They guide the novice Sufi through the minefield of self-concern, without which there is no ascent to the higher stages of mystical experience and wise insight. Ibn ᶜAtaᵓ Allah may have observed that his own followers ran into obstacles overcoming the practical reasoning of routine that prevents one from truly relying on God.

In observing this, he undertook to dictate his teachings about overcoming self-direction and relying on God's provision, as a systematic guide to properly understanding and assimilating the initial wisdom sayings in the popular text.

In practice, Sufis in the Shadhili community used *The Book of Illumination* as an introduction to Sufism; it comprised their initial training before they could contemplate the *Sufi Aphorisms*. This is because it is about practicing virtues, whereas the *Sufi Aphorisms* is concerned with cultivating insight. Basic virtues like patience, trust, and sincerity are necessary to open the door of spiritual insight and knowledge. This sequence reflects Ibn ᶜAtaᵓ Allah's intent, as a Maliki jurist who became a Sufi master, to emphasize the necessity of outward practice as the foundation for the support of inward illumination.

However, the label "companion piece" to the *Sufi Aphorisms* does not adequately describe the importance of *The Book of Illumination*. Ibn ᶜAtaᵓ Allah says that, far from being just an "extended commentary" on the first series of *Sufi Aphorisms*, *The Book of Illumination* guides the reader to achieve the key virtues that open the aspirant up to spiritual progress.

There are nine levels in realizing faithful certainty. These nine levels are repenting, renouncing, enduring patiently, giving thanks, standing in fearful awe, being content, actively hoping, entirely trusting, and intimately loving. Consider carefully how none of these levels of faith is sound and whole without the necessary condition of desisting from selfish calculation, caring for your own concerns, and choosing in competition with God.

Desisting from selfish calculation is the foundational principle for spiritual progress through all the stations recognized by Sufi theoreticians. Without it, reading any of the aphorisms, initial or advanced, would be just tinkling bells and clashing cymbals.

For this reason, this text is more that just a late text of passing interest—it is rather an epitome of Sufi writings. Ibn ᶜAbbād of Ronda, the earliest and arguably most insightful commentator on Ibn ᶜAtaᵓ Allah's *Sufi Aphorisms*, described it so in one of his letters directed to a beloved beginner:

> I suggest that the book that you have by Ibn ᶜAtaᵓ Allah, [*The Book of Illumination*], is the epitome of all the books, long or short, on Sufism. And it combines completeness with conciseness. The way in which it leads the traveler is the road of the acknowledgement of God's unity, a path that admits no one who denies the Oneness of God...If you add to that a study of the *Sufi Aphorisms*, so famous and so widely used, and strive to come to grips with it and assimilate it, you will have no need of any other renowned writings.[46]

In further confirmation of this opinion, Ibn ᶜAbbad makes explicit reference to *The Book of Illumination* while writing his own famed commentary on the *Sufi Aphorisms*, to the point of quoting long passages from it verbatim. If the *Sufi Aphorisms* were their own best commentary, then why did the master commentators on the aphorisms turn to *The Book of Illumination* to interpret the first series of aphorisms? In fact, disciples in the Shadhili community always studied the two texts together in a series: *Illumination* was their introduction to Sufism and *Sufi Aphorisms* was their subsequent guide along the changing stations of their ongoing spiritual progress. For instance, in late-medieval Morocco, Shaykh Aḥmad Zarrūq notes explicitly that his teacher and spiritual master, Shaykh Muḥammad al-Qūrī, taught him *The Book of Illumination* first and then set him to memorizing and meditating on the *Sufi Aphorisms*.[47] Shaykh al-Quri was following in the footsteps of Ibn ᶜAbbad, who had introduced these texts into Moroccan Sufi circles and whose followers perpetuated his tradition of juridical Sufism (based on the model of Ibn ᶜAtaᵓ Allah) in Moroccan cities like Fes and Meknes. Zarruq passed along this admonition to all later Shadhili Sufis: "You must rely upon the principles of Sufism, from among the sound principles found in the books of the masters. From those addressing the inner spiritual realms, there are the works of Ibn ᶜAtaᵓ Allah, especially *The Book of Illumination*, and from those addressing the outer legal realms, there is the Introduction (*Madkhal*) written by Ibn Ḥajj."[48]

In a similar way, this text serves as an introduction to Ibn ᶜAtaᵓ Allah's other texts, like *The Key to Salvation* (*Miftāḥ al-Falāḥ fī Miṣbāḥ al-Arwāḥ*). *The Book of Illumination* argues succinctly for the need of having structured meditation (*dhikr*) in order to recollect the nature of God (*tadhakkur*) and to concentrate the soul on cleaving to the presence of God. In contrast, *The Key to Salvation* provides a detailed guide to the practice of meditation, highlighting its spiritual subtleties and demonstrating its Islamic authenticity. It is also intimately related to Ibn ᶜAtaᵓ Allah's well-known work, *Subtle Blessings in the Saintly Lives* (*Lataᵓif al-Minan*), which presents a biographical and doctrinal sketch of his spiritual guides, Shaykh al-Mursi and Shaykh al-Shadhili. Many anecdotes recorded in *Subtle Blessings* in a documentary manner are deployed in *The Book of Illumination* in an expository manner. In addition, Ibn ᶜAtaᵓ Allah gives detailed interpretations of passages from the litanies of Shaykh al-Shadhili and Shaykh al-Mursi, litanies that are recorded in full in *Subtle Blessings* but not interpreted. In this way, it complements the biographical *Subtle Blessings*, giving us glimpses into the profound depth of the devotional material of the early masters of the Shadhili community, through the lens of the spiritual insight of Ibn ᶜAtaʾ Allah. Many of these glimpses are not found elsewhere in his body of writings.

TRANSLATING THE TEXT

In translating *Kitāb al-Tanwīr fī Isqāṭ al-Tadbīr* into English, I am continuing a tradition. The text has been recently translated into Spanish and French.[49] These translations were primarily by and for disciples in the Shadhili Sufi community, which has spread widely among Europeans due to the charismatic personality of Shaykh al-ᶜAlawī al-Darqāwī, an Algerian Sufi master of the early twentieth century. However, it is little known that the late-medieval Sufi scholar from India, Shaykh ᶜAlī Muttaqī, translated *The Book of Illumination* into Persian in the sixteenth century. He found this text so useful that he translated parts of it (especially from the first chapter) in order to spread its message through the far eastern Islamic world, where Persian was the common language. He entitled his translation *Means of Conveyance to True Faith and Absolute Reliance* (*Kitāb al-Tawaṣṣul fīʾl-Yaqīn waʾl-Tawakkul*), and it exists in manuscript form in several archives in India and Pakistan, though it has never been published.[50]

The first modern Arabic publication of this text was by lithographic press, in Cairo in 1883. It has been subsequently reprinted many times, in cheap "yellow paper" editions common for theological and Sufi literature in Egypt. This translation is based on such a printed edition.[51] A recent reprint, from a publisher near al-Azhar University, contains

41

the hard work of an anonymous editor who provided useful details for the scriptural references in the text.[52] These printed editions, however, contain many typographical errors, and are at variance in some details from manuscripts of the text. To my knowledge, there has been no carefully edited publication of the text that works directly from the archival, hand-written manuscripts. Some minor corrections were made to the printed versions of the text through reference to manuscript sources housed at the library of al-Qarawiyyīn mosque in Fes (where this work was begun).[53] However, it must be stressed that this present book is a translation that hopes to convey the ideas in the text to a wider audience; it is not an edited edition that strives to create a single standard text from the earliest authentic copies. It is hoped that in the future another dedicated scholar will be inspired to live up the demands of editing such a text.

The goal of this work is to present the English reader with an authentic translation that is not trapped in a literalist rendering of words from one language to another. The text in Arabic has many textures. It consists mainly of discursive prose, punctuated with poetry. This translation tries to capture the feeling of the poetry as well as its meaning, and occasionally manages to recreate a rhyme that echoes the original (especially in the longer *qasīda* poems that Ibn ᶜAtaʾ Allah himself composed). The prose often accelerates and intensifies into *sajaᶜ*, a classical Arabic style of "rhyming prose" wherein sentences will end on a rhymed phrase or balance between two rhymed elements, without being formally weighted with meter as in poetry. This translation tries to follow Ibn ᶜAtaʾ Allah's skillful use of *sajaᶜ*, through which he adds emotional intensity and urgency to his reasoned discourse.

Those who have read the original work in Arabic will recognize some changes that have happened through the

42

act of translation. Acknowledging these changes is important, as it highlights how translation is not a simple act of moving a text from one language to another, but a complex act of moving a text from one culture to another. Every effort was made to translate Arabic terms (which are sometimes highly technical in mystical or legal terminology) into colloquial English that might be easily understood by readers who are not specialists.

These changes range from small to large. This translation has removed devotional formulas that, in Arabic and Islamic discourse, come after the mention of a revered person's name: prophets, saints, respected teachers or beloved friends. Muslim readers will gain the merit of supplying blessings on the Prophets and benedictions on past Sufi masters for themselves, without the translation having to remind them in print. Non-Muslims will gain the ability to absorb the concepts and principles of the book without being distracted by devotional interjections that seem to interrupt the flow of the prose. Let it be said at the outset that, if the author did not respect and revere these masters, he would not have read the original or dedicated many hours of hard work to translate it. You might say that the best way to respect and revere these masters is to understand their ideals and put them into practice. It is hoped that removing the written benedictions, which can become a bit opaque and cumbersome in English, will more clearly express these Sufi master's ideals and facilitate the readers' putting them into practice in what ever way they are capable.

Deeper changes were made to the original. This translation respects the basic division of the text: it begins with an introductory invocation (*dibāja*), has a body of two chapters (*faṣl*), and concludes with a prayer (*munajāt wa duᶜā*). However, in translating the text, I have created new sectional divisions within these two longer chapters; these divisions make clear the organization of the content of each chapter, mainly reflecting breaks or topical shifts in the original text. New headings that are not part of the original were given to these sections. The headings are derived from the ideas or phrasings present in that section. Such additions help organize a medieval Arabic text in such a way as to facilitate the contemporary English readers' understanding of it and ability to utilize its counsel.

Other changes involve quotation from and discussion of the Qurᵓan. The original text quotes strings of Qurᵓanic verses in tandem, trusting that the readers have already committed the scripture to memory and can intuitively grasp the common thread between the quotations, which are often fragments of a single verse. This translation has not literally reproduced such dense quotations of the Qurᵓan; rather the quoted verses are given in the context of the prose that comments upon them, and are repeated each time the prose turns to interpreting a word or phrase in them. This translation also provides, in boxed text, longer quotations from the Qurᵓan that are not given in the original text, but which the readers are assumed to already know. This will give contemporary English readers the ability to see the depth of Ibn ᶜAtaᵓ Allah's interpretations in the wider context of the verses he discusses. It may also encourage readers to refer back to the Qurᵓan in a fuller way so as to understand the origin and force of the ideas that Ibn ᶜAtaᵓ Allah proposes.

The presentation of parables has also changed from that in the Arabic text. In the original, the parables are appended to the end of the work in a list without titles, just after the expository chapters and before the concluding prayer. I felt that the parables had a stronger impact when read within the text rather than at the end in a list. For this reason, this translation presents the parables at various points where I felt their impact resonates with Ibn ᶜAtaᵓ Allah's prose, to serve to illustrate his expository idea. In all, there are twenty-six parables from the appended chapter that, in this translation, are set within the prose and announced by the rubric, "A Parable." These augment several parables that occur within the original text of the two chapters that were not set apart in the final appendix; these were simply translated as part of the prose and are not set off by any heading.

Other changes are in the field of gender. The original text was written for an audience that was assumed to be male. There were women who were highly literate in medieval Arab societies, and there were certainly women active in the Shadhili community across North Africa.[54] However, out of social convention Ibn ᶜAtaᵓ Allah addresses his reader as a single male person, with various addresses like, "My dear brother (ākhī)," or "my dear believer (muᵓmin)," or "my dear fellow servant (ᶜabd)." This was not a conscious decision on the part of Ibn ᶜAtaᵓ Allah, but was rather a pre-conscious decision shaped by the author's social environment in medieval Cairo. There is no reason to slavishly replicate this gender bias in a contemporary English translation, where the audience can be assumed to include women and men on roughly equal terms. This translation has adopted a simple strategy to be gender-inclusive: it renders the Arabic singular male subject into an English plural subject in which gender remains ambiguous. Where the original Arabic might read, "The heart of the believer (male) is pure," this English translation reads, "The hearts of the believers are pure." The same idea is conveyed in slightly modified grammatical form that is free from gendered social conventions which might distract a contemporary English reader from understanding and absorbing the deeper message of the text. Where the singularity of the subject is important to preserve, this translation favors the use of "a person" or "one" without pre-determining the gender of the subject. This strategy is in harmony with the Qurʾan's voice, which is revolutionary in addressing female believers and male believers as spiritual equals.[55] This translation renders Qurʾanic verses in such a way as to maintain gender neutrality when they address "the human being (*insān*)" which many previous scholars have translated as "man" or "mankind." Readers who would like to know more about obstacles of grammatical and patriarchal gender can refer to Appendix Two, which discusses in detail the assumed gender of the audience and the projected gender of God. That appendix also presents a short passage of *The Book of Illumination* which preserves the more literal male gender, so that readers can compare this to the translation offered here and gain a deeper understanding of the subtle challenges faced by any translator.

Another difference between this translation and other English translations of Ibn ʿAtaʾ Allah's works is the use of capitalization. Victor Danner and Mary-Ann Koury Danner make liberal use of capital letters to set off references to God from other references, as do many scholars of Sufism. Victor Danner's definition of the term *tadbīr*, quoted above, provides an interesting example of this: "If the planning or direction is in conjunction with God's directives, then it is positive and not an obstacle in the Path, in which case it is not self-direction but Self-direction." This translation avoids such capitalization. While capitalization of nouns occurred in medieval and early-modern English, it no longer plays a functional role in contemporary English. Readers might find such a use of capitals, as regressions to medieval models of English, to appear slightly pompous. As a translation of Arabic, such capitalization is utterly anachronistic, since Arabic has no equivalent of a capital letter, neither to highlight a noun nor to signify the start of a sentence.

This translation minimizes the use of capital letters, reserving them to refer to proper names only. God is capitalized as a proper name of the divinity and "One" has been capitalized in translations of the ninety-nine names of God. The most frequent instance of this is Ibn ᶜAtaᵓ Allah's denoting the divinity with the name *al-ḥaqq*, the true One.[56] Arabic prose manages to clearly describe God and divine attributes without recourse to any capitalization, mainly through the context of the sentence itself, while preserving moments of creative tension where the reference is not clearly determined to be God or a human being.[57] Such moments of creative tension and deliberate indeterminacy are, of course, crucial to Sufi discourse and can spark moments of spiritual insight in attentive and attuned readers. This English translation tries to replicate this rhetorical strategy by limiting the use of capitalization to proper nouns, such as "God" or "the One." Similarly, capitalization sets off the translation of the proper name of the Qurᵓan; though literally Qurᵓan means "the ever-recited Recitation" it is here translated conceptually as Divine Speech.

Enough of my own voice! By now, after reading a few pages of introduction, you may have tired of it. The translator's true role is to step into the background and suppress her or his own voice while speaking as another. So let me be silent now, and speak in the voice of Shaykh Ibn ᶜAtaᵓ Allah. In the name of God...

The screened enclosure above the place where Ibn
ᶜAtaᵓ Allah (d. 1309) is buried at the foot of the
Muqattam Hills in Cairo.

INVOCATION

In the name of God, the compassionate One, the One who cares.

Praise belongs to God who alone deserves praise. God is unique in the act of creation and is uniquely concerned for each being's direction. God is singular in the power of decision and execution. God is the incomparable sovereign, for *there is nothing similar to God, the most acute of hearing, the most penetrating of vision,*[1] whose sovereignty requires no mediator to oversee its dominion. God is the ruler, from whose jurisdiction nothing escapes at all, whether great or small. God is the One hallowed, whose perfect qualities exceed comparison or competition. God is the One transcendent, whose perfect essence is beyond likeness or depiction. *Do they not know who created them, the infinitely subtle, the ever aware?*[2] God is the One who knows, whose knowledge encompasses each thing's beginning and ending. God is the One who hears, whose acuteness admits no difference between whispering and resounding. God is the One who provides, blessing created beings by leading them to their sources of nourishing. God is the One who establishes, steadfastly supporting them in their changing states of flourishing. God is the One who bestows, freely giving all souls their existence in living. God is the One who decrees, calling all things to return after the completion of their passing. And God is the One who recounts, repaying them on that fateful day when they present their good acting and wayward erring.

Praise be to the One who freely bestows upon all people benevolence, even before their worldly existence. Praise be to the One who undertakes to sustain them, whether they act toward divine will with compliance or resistance. Praise be to the One who extends support to every thing living through the prior existence of divine giving. Praise be to the One whose being safeguards the being of all creation with its self-sustaining effusion. Praise be to the One who appears in the world through traces of wisdom's subtlety, who manifests in the heavens by evidence of power's potency.

I witness that there is no god but God, the singular One, who shares in no partnership. These words of witness come from a person who has handed over all his concerns and cares to God's deciding, who has peacefully submitted to the current of God's decreeing and executing. I witness that Muhammad is God's worshipful servant and messenger, that Muhammad is preferred over all the rest of God's many prophets who preceded him, and that he is especially selected by the bounty of the virtues and gifts bestowed upon him. Muhammad is both the opener and the closer, which are qualities that none of the other prophets share with him.[3] Muhammad is the intercessor when the true One gathers all souls to divide them in judgment, when they all will turn to him. May God bless him, with all the other prophets, and preserve him. May God bless his family and his companions who adhere to his benevolent presence and follow him. May God multiply blessings upon them all.

OPENING ADDRESS

My brothers and sisters, you are made to experience God's love. You have been granted the rare gift of nearness to God's being. God has offered you a taste of the liquor sipped by the people of divine intimacy. God's continual intimate connection to you has been safeguarded from any chance of opposition or termination. God has made you the followers of those people who are chosen to bear divine messages. Their hearts break with longing when they realize that their vision cannot perceive God—then their broken hearts are strengthened through insight as God becomes actual in their lives, bestowing upon them light. God has opened for them the gardens of divine nearness, stirred up from this garden the fragrance of God's indwelling presence, wafted its inspirations over their hearts, and showed them the depth of God's prior concern for their well-being. Then God could reveal the subtlest of artful actions through which their lives are sustained, and they desisted from resistance and obstinate self-will.

In this way, they have fully submitted themselves to divine care and completely entrusted it to oversee all their concerns, for they know that nobody reaches the goal of satisfying God except through being completely satisfied with God. They acknowledge that nobody arrives at the purest sincerity except by the fullest inner submission to divine dictates and decrees. Thus their disposition is never sullied by the murk of distraction, as one from among them has said poetically:

Fluctuations in time never beguile them in vain
   In the most intense trial, they keep hold of the rein

Divine decrees flow over them, and they act aptly. They react with respect for its might and allow themselves to be led by its powerful currents.

> Divine acts flow over your anxious self
> Bowing down the head of your concern

Whoever seeks an intimate connection with God must realize that it is actualized by divine agency [not by the seeker's desire]. Achieving this connection comes by means of God's own devising [not by the seeker's effort]. In traveling this path, beware of being concerned for your own interests and rebelling against the conditions the divine has decreed for you![4] This is the most important obstacle to be avoided, from which you should abstain and keep pure. I have composed this book in order to clarify this single crucial point, and to make explicit all the subtleties within it. I have entitled it "The Book of Illumination" so that the title would perfectly reflect the book's contents, so that its words would communicate its intended meaning.

I beseech God, the generous One, by virtue of divine all-embracing comprehensiveness, to accept this work as sincere. And I entreat God to allow this book to benefit the specialist, who has chosen the path of becoming a Sufi, as well as the common seeker. I ask all this for the sake of the Prophet Muhammad, may he be blessed and preserved. Surely God executes whatever is divine will, and fulfills whatever need there is to fill.

CHAPTER ONE: DESISTING FROM SELFISH CALCULATION

SECTION ONE: RECOGNIZING SELFISH CALCULATION

We can recognize selfish calculation through the many moments of Divine Speech (*Qur'ān*) that address the necessity of desisting from anxious concern and struggle against the decrees of God, and in the teachings of the Prophet Muhammad (*ḥadīth*). In some cases the words indicate this meaning clearly; in other cases they allude to it subtly. In what follows, we will discuss three moments from Divine Speech in detail. Resonating with them, the Prophet is reported to have said, "Those people who are satisfied with God as their Lord, with Islam as their religious path, and with Muhammad as their Prophet have tasted the nourishment of true faith." The Prophet Muhammad is also reported to have said, "Worship God by being satisfied and content, and if you are incapable of such worshipful contentment, then know that there is great benefit for you in patiently bearing what you loath to bear."

In considering these moments from Divine Speech and the teachings of the Prophet about desisting from selfish calculation, some of the people of intimate experiential knowledge (*ma'rifa*) have said "Those people who do not care for themselves will be cared for." Shaykh Abū al-Ḥasan al-Shādhilī has said, "If you must plan, and how can you not plan, then plan only for how not to plan!" The Shaykh has also said, "Make no choice upon your own authority in anything. Choose not to choose. Flee from that choice, from your flight and from everything to God, for *God has created what God wills and chooses for them.*"[5]

Let us turn to the first moment of Divine Speech. God says, *No indeed, by your Lord, they do not believe unless they turn to you (The Prophet) for your decision in whatever they quarrel over and further, unless they find themselves free of anguish and anxiety in regard to what you have decided for them, and resign themselves with complete resignation.*[6]

This verse indicates that only the people who turn to God and to the Prophet to decide matters for them have true faith. *They do not believe unless they turn to you for your*

Women
Surat al-Nisā° 4:60-68

Have you not considered those who assert that they believe
    in the revelation that has come to you
    and those that have come before you?
They desire to resort to the evil one for judgment in what they dispute
    even though they were ordered to deny him.
The tempter desires to mislead them far from the right way. (60)
When it is said to them,
    'Come to what God has sent down and to the Messenger,'
    you see the hypocrites avert their faces from you in disgust. (61)
How then do they act when seized by misfortune
    because of what their deeds produced?
Then they come to you swearing by God,
    'We wanted only good-will and accord!' (62)
Those people! God knows what is in their hearts
    so turn away and admonish them.
Say to them a word that will reach the depth of their very selves. (63)
We have not sent any Messenger except to be obeyed
    in accord with the will of God.
If only they had come to you, when they oppressed their own selves
    with misdeeds, and asked God to forgive them
    and the Messenger had asked God to forgive them.
Then they would have found God ever clement, most merciful. (64)
No indeed, by your Lord, they do not believe unless they turn to you
    for your decision in whatever they quarrel over
    and further unless they find themselves free of anguish and anxiety
    in regard to what you have decided for them
    and resign themselves with complete resignation. (65)
If we (God) had obliged them to sacrifice their lives or leave their homes
    they would not have done it—except for a few of them!
If they had done what they were exhorted to do
    it would have been better for them
    and would have established them more firmly. (66)
And therefore we would have given them
    from our presence a great reward! (67)
And we would have led them to a straight way. (68)

decision in whatever they quarrel over, whether in matters of speech, of action, of what they accept or leave aside, and of what they love or despise. Deciding their matters for them includes decisions of how to take upon oneself obligatory actions (*taklīf*) and also decisions of how to come to right knowledge (*ta'rīf*). Deciding their matters for them necessitates their fullest internal acceptance of both types of decision about acting and knowing. To be bound by both kinds of divine decisions is necessary for every believer (*mu'min*). Decisions of obligatory action are enjoinders and prohibitions relating to gaining merit through acts of worship. Decisions of coming to know rightly refers to what insights God causes to appear to you from your experience of being overpowered by God's divine presence. True faith cannot be realized except through these two complementary acts of submission: by modeling one's behavior in accord with divine decisions, and by the fullest inner submission to the overpowering force that decides them.

Furthermore, this moment of Divine Speech clarifies that God is not content to simply deny the shallow faith of those people who do not turn to God and to the Prophet to decide for them. It also denies the faith of those who turn to God but find themselves constricted and fail to accept what was decided for them. Beyond simply denying the shallow faith of such people, Divine Speech swears by the name of lordship: *No indeed, by your Lord.* The Prophet Muhammad specially comprehended this lordship in its subtle and all-pervading qualities: its comprehensive care, its allotment of what is required for him at each shifting moment, its singling him out as special, and its safeguarding him from error. This is evident because Divine Speech does not swear by stating "No indeed, by the Lord," but rather swears specifically *No indeed, by your Lord, they do not believe un-*

*less they turn to you for your decision in whatever they quar-
rel over.* In this oath, the one who swears is specified [as
the Lord] while the one sworn to is also specified [to you,
Muhammad, *by your Lord*]. This is so that each soul might
know that unfolding within it is the divine love that will
overpower it and the divine aid that will insure its victory,
regardless of whether God's decisions seem to be for or
against it [at any particular moment].

This oath also demonstrates the Lord's all-comprehen-
sive care for the Prophet Muhammad, for God has made
divine decrees into Prophetic decrees and has made divine
decisions into Prophetic decisions. Therefore, all people
must submit themselves with tranquility to the Prophet's
decisions and follow what he enjoins. Indeed, their faith is
not accepted until they accept the decisions of God's Prophet
within their innermost selves. This is because the Prophet
is just as Divine Speech describes him: *He does not speak
from his own selfish desires, rather his speech is nothing
but inspired inspiration.*[7] Therefore [though he is human]
the Prophet decided what are truly God's decisions and
decreed what are truly God's decrees. Divine Speech clarifies this by saying, *Surely those who pledge allegiance to
you pledge allegiance to God.*[8] This point is repeated for
emphasis and certified [in the phrase that follows]: *The hand
of God is upon their hands.*

If you listen closely to the moment of Divine Speech
first mentioned, you will find that it alludes to the greatness
of the Prophet's power of executing judgments and the forceful pronouncement of his enjoinders. The subtle allusion is
in the phrasing of Divine Speech, *No indeed, by your Lord.*
In this oath, the speaker [God] has attached the name of
divine lordship to the possessive pronoun indicating the
Prophet's person [in saying *your Lord*]. This same phrase

56

is pronounced in a separate verse in a way that gives a contrasting meaning. *Kaf ha ya ayn sad... This is a reminder of the mercy of your Lord to God's servant, Zakaria.*[9] The true One attached the name of the Lord to the pronoun indicating Muhammad [*the mercy of your Lord*]. In contrast, the true One attached the pronoun indicating God to the person of Zakaria [*to God's servant, Zakaria*]. Divine Speech specified these possessive pronouns for a subtle reason. It is so that all people might know and acknowledge the difference between the levels of dignity possessed by these two prophets. Although both are prophets, Muhammad is granted closer proximity to the divine lordship through the specification, *by your Lord.*

Now let's return to the moment of Divine Speech first mentioned. *No indeed, by your Lord, they do not believe unless they turn to you for your decision in whatever they quarrel over and further unless they find themselves free of anguish and anxiety in regard to what you have decided for them.* God does not stop with enjoining believers to turn to the Prophet for decisions at the level of apparent action only, so that they qualify as true believers. Rather, Divine Speech elaborates by setting out the condition that they should be free of discontent in accepting these decisions. What is discontent? It is that feeling within the soul of being constricted or limited when accepting the Prophet's decisions, regardless of whether the decision agrees with one's personal desires or goes against them. This feeling of constriction in the soul is the result of a lack of illumination and the alienating presence in the heart of others [objects of worship or desires in competition with God]. Because of the darkness of obscuring otherness in the heart, the soul feels constricted and discontent. It chafes at being limited or bounded by divine decrees.

The true believer's soul, however, does not feel this constriction and discontent, since believers' hearts are filled with the light of true faith. Their ears are expansive and open. They are made expansive by the light of the faith in the expansive One, the One who knows (*al-wāsi^c al-^calīm*). Support is extended to their hearts through the unbounded bounty of God. Their hearts are opened, rendered receptive to incoming divine decrees and made strong enough to hand over all cares and preoccupations to God; they never think twice about the possibility of appeal or repeal of such decisions.

TEN WAYS TOWARD WISDOM

This brings up a crucial point that is worth a digression. Let me elaborate on it for a moment. You should know that if the true One desires to strengthen people to bear what divine decrees come over them, God clothes them in the illuminations of divine attributes and qualities, enrobing them with divine gifts and blessings. Know that God sends down decrees upon them and at the same time conveys to them illuminations [helping them to bear the decrees]. The ability to bear such decrees is from the Lord, not from within the people themselves! Thus, people are strengthened under every hardship and are able to endure every difficulty.

To cut to the pith, you could say that the dawning of inner light helps make for us destiny's weight light. You could say this so many different ways! You could say, opening the door of insight helps us bear divine decrees' might. Or you could say, the advent of subtle gifts helps us bear affliction's rifts. Or you could say, acknowledging how wholesome is God's choice empowers us to bear divine decrees' force. Or you could say, knowing that God knows our condition gives us patience with God's decision. Or you could say, God's unveiling divine beauty eases our facing God's actions with humane duty. Or you could say, knowing that patience leads to contentment lets us bear our fate without resentment. Or you could say, lifting the veils of alienation helps us endure divine decrees without agitation. Or you could say, granting us the secrets of intimacy strengthens us to bear obligation's gravity. Or you could say, knowing divine goodness' subtleties hidden in every difficulty gives us patience in high degrees to endure all divine decrees.[10]

These are ten ways of saying the same thing. They are ten means toward a single goal. Each way requires your patience and unflinching constancy in facing the Lord's decrees, calling for strength when such decrees impact your life. God is the generous giver of all these qualities from endless divine bounty (*faḍl*). God bestows support to those people who can discern, in confronting divine decrees, the more subtle divine concern. Let's now turn our attention to each of these ten means one by one, so that all the benefits latent in each of them might come to fruition and that you might, by realizing their different levels, advance along the path of understanding and intuition.

The dawning of inner light helps make for us destiny's weight light. This is because illumination, when it appears glowing from within, reveals the intimate closeness of the true One to the bearer of difficult decrees. Such illumination reveals that these decrees have come from the true One directly. Knowledge that such decrees have come from the Lord gives a person consolation and provides a way to patiently bear such decrees. Have you not listened to the Divine Speech when God spoke to the Prophet, saying *Patiently hold firm under the decree of your Lord, for surely you are under the observance of our gaze.*[11] This means that there is no source engendering decrees other than God, for which you should become anxious; rather, each decree that you experience is from your Lord, each is established on the firm foundation of God's wholesome care for your needs. I present a couplet that expresses the same point:

You have lightened what burdens I toil to bear
    For you're the one who tries me and knows if I'm able.
There is no one to alter God's decision,
    Of improving God's provision no one is capable

To grasp this reality, imagine that you are standing in a darkened room. Someone else in the room clobbers you with a powerful blow and you reel, not knowing who has struck you. However, when a light begins to illumine the room, you see clearly who has struck you. If it turns out to be your venerated teacher, your respected father or your mighty ruler, then you clearly perceive the need to bear such a blow with patience. Illuminating knowledge effortlessly evokes such patient endurance.

A Parable
Groping in the Dark

Anyone who is anxious despite God's attentive supervision is like a child traveling with her father in a long caravan. As night falls, the father keeps watch over his child from a distance, out of compassionate concern for her welfare. Yet the child cannot see her father because of the terrible darkness that has descended between them. The child may be wracked by anxiety about her own concerns; how will she ever secure all her needs by herself? Yet when the moon rises luminous in the night sky, the child can see her father's actual intimacy. Therefore, her anxiety settles and her fear subsides, since she can sense her father's comforting proximity.

In this way, children are enriched by the care they receive from another. They are relieved of needing to care for their own needs by their own means. Those who are anxious for their own concerns despite the concern of God for them only plot anxiously because they are engulfed in the dark night of separation. They do not witness the intimate proximity of God to them. If only the luminous moon of bearing witness to God's unity (*tawhīd*) or the brilliant sun of experiential knowledge (*maʿrifa*) of the divine presence would rise over them, they would see the intimacy of the true One to them. Then they would be ashamed of plotting or planning in competition with God. They would consider themselves enriched by the divine concern that encircles them and would rise above plotting for their own wellbeing.

Opening the door of insight helps us bear divine decrees' might. You should realize that, when God sends down a decree upon someone, God opens the door of insight for that person through bearing such a decree. Understand that God desires that you ascribe every decree to its divine originator. Such understanding leads your attention back to God, urges you toward God's presence, and impels you to entrust your security to God alone. Divine Speech reveals that *whoever entrusts to God their every need, surely God is sufficient for them.*[12] In other words, God alone is sufficient for people, and God's presence is abundant in relation to their needs. God is their only aid in vanquishing other-ness from the heart and God watches over them, protecting them. For understanding God from God (*fahm biʾllah ʿan Allah*) discloses for you the secret of true worshipful servanthood that lies potential within you. As Divine Speech points out: *Is not God alone sufficient for God's worshipful servant?*[13] In reality, each of these ten different sayings de-scribed above leads back to understanding God from God. Each saying is a single variegated facet of this return.

The advent of subtle gifts helps us bear affliction's rifts. All of the secret gifts that have come down to you from God prior to this moment remind you of their giver's con-stant presence, and this reminder helps to bolster you to bear what God has decreed for you in the present. As you recollect all that God has granted you which you have de-sired for yourself, so you should endure patiently with God in that through which God desires to try you. Have you listened to Divine Speech questioning: *What? When a di-saster befalls you [will you question God's providence] even though you had earlier been granted a victory twice as great?*[14] Thus God consoles people in what afflicts them by reminding them of the victories and advantages granted to them previously. These are the subtle prior gifts alluded to above.

At the very moment when affliction strikes, there ac-companies it those reminders that lighten the burden for those who must bear it. This brings people closer to God, disclosing to them the great reward that God has stored up for them for the sake of their patiently bearing this afflic-tion. From this treasury of rewards come the affirmation and tranquility that God rains down upon their hearts, along with the refined and subtle graces that God showers upon them. [So potent are these secret gifts] that some of the

Prophet's companions, when an illness afflicted them, used to say "Tighten your strangle-hold!" [In tasting these gifts] someone endowed with intimate experiential knowledge has said, "I was afflicted with an illness, yet desired that it not pass away until the subtle aid of God had sprung up within me, revealing to me the presence of the unseen!" In-depth discussion of such sayings is another topic for another time.[15]

Acknowledging how wholesome is God's choice empowers us to bear divine decrees' force. This is because, when people witness the wholesome care that suffuses what God chooses for them, they know that the true One never intends to cause them unnecessary pain, for God is the One who cares (*raḥīm*). *And God is full of mercy toward those who believe*.[16] Once the Prophet saw a woman with her young child; [he turned to those accompanying him] and said, "Can you imagine this woman hurling her child into the fire?" They all cried out, "No, O messenger of God!" So he explained to them, "God is far more caring with one who believes than even a mother with her child."

Despite the fact that God might decree circumstances for you that cause you pain, this pain is also the occasion for granting you favors and blessings. Have you not listened to Divine Speech recite: *Surely the recompense for those who persevere is ample, indeed incalculable!*[17] If God delegates to people the authority to make their own choices, then they are forbidden access to divine graces and prevented from entering paradise. For God alone deserves praise for making wholesome choices. Have you not listened carefully to Divine Speech: *It may be that you loath something that is beneficial for you, and it may be that you love something that is harmful for you.*[18]

Surely a compassionate father who makes his son undergo the rigors of the surgeon never intends to inflict his son with pain! Likewise, a doctor may advise a remedy for your health calling for razor-sharp scalpels, even though it may cause you intense pain. If you followed your own choice, you would avoid the treatment altogether! But you would only get sicker.

In contrast, consider those who have been deprived of their own choice and realize that this limitation is really an act of compassion upon them. For such people this apparent limitation of having been deprived is really a great gift. This is analogous to a mother's forbidding her child to eat too much, for she fears that the child might suffer indigestion. In this same vein, Shaykh al-Shadhili has said, "You should realize that when God forbids you something, God never forbids out of stinginess or ill-will, but rather only forbids out of compassion for you." In reality, your being prevented from choosing what you want is a great gift! However, nobody understands the benefits in being thwarted except for those who are purely sincere (*ṣiddīq*) toward God. I have set down and verified all of the discussion above in another book, saying

What relieves for you the pain of bearing afflictions
    is that you know God is the one who afflicts you
For the one who sets divine decrees heading your way
    is the one who makes the best choices
    for your well-being.[19]

Knowing that God knows our condition gives us patience with God's decision. Being aware that God is watchful over all people's responses to what afflicts them eases for them the chaffing difficulties of the affliction. Have you not listened to Divine Speech saying, *Patiently hold firm under the decree of your Lord, for surely you are under the observation of our gaze.*[20] It is as if God were saying, 'O Muhammad, none of the resistance and deceit you have encountered from the Quraysh [aristocracy of Mecca] who deny your message is hidden from us.' Listen to this famous story about a man being lashed in punishment. During the first ninety-nine lashes, he never let loose even one moan of pain, but when he was lashed with the final hundredth stroke, he moaned in deep agony. The people who had gathered around asked him about this strange behavior. The man replied, "During the first ninety-nine lashes, the beloved one for whose sake I have been lashed was present near me in the circle of on-lookers; only when he turned away from me [at the moment of the final stroke] did I suddenly feel pain!"

God's unveiling divine beauty eases our facing God's actions with humane duty. At the moment that people taste the bitterness of being overrun by affliction, God manifests divine beauty in their eyes. Witnessing this beauty takes away their burning pain by giving them a taste of the sweetness of the divine's dazzling manifestation. Perhaps this rapture will even transport them beyond any feeling of pain at all! One moment of Divine Speech is enough to illustrate this point [by describing the effects of the Prophet Joseph's beauty]: *When the women saw him, they were astonished and extolled him and cut their hands.*[21]

Knowing that patience leads to contentment lets us bear our fate without resentment. The patience of people who bear God's decrees that weigh heavily upon them leads God to grant them contentment. They endure the burning pain as a request for God to be satisfied with them, just as you swallow bitter medicine hoping for curative results.

Lifting the veils of separation and alienation helps us endure divine decrees without agitation. If God desires to help people bear the burdens imposed upon them, God lifts the obscuring veil [of separation] from their vision. God shows them that the divine presence is unspeakably near to them. The intimacy of this close presence eclipses any perception of pain.

If the true One would ever manifest divine beauty in all its splendor and perfection before the souls tormented in the fires of hell, this would totally eclipse their any perception of horrible punishments. Likewise, if God would obscure the divine presence from those souls in paradise they would experience as tortuous punishment all the wholesome blessings that are ripened and offered to them. Surely painful punishment is the existence of alienation from the divine presence, and the varieties of punishment [in descriptions of hell] are the various textures of this veil of separation. Likewise, blessings and rewards are really nothing but divine self-disclosure and the manifestation of divine presence, and the varieties described in depictions of paradise are the various appearances this manifestation could take.[22]

Granting us knowledge of the secrets of intimacy (*ta°rīf*) strengthens us to bear obligation's gravity (*taklīf*).[23] The obligations of worshipful servitude placed upon people are weighty, requiring hard work and constant vigilance. These obligations include carrying out all commands and refraining from all prohibitions, as well as bearing patiently all decisions imposed and giving thanks for any blessings. Thus, there are four possible circumstances in regard to your aptly performing obligations toward God: responding with obedience, responding with rebellion, being blessed, or being tried with affliction.[24] These four conditions comprehensively sum up all possible spiritual circumstances; there is no fifth possibility. In each of these four conditions, you must adhere to the goal of worshipful servitude in deference to God's absolute lordship.

God claims rights over you in your obedience: that you acknowledge the freely given gifts that God has bestowed upon you through your acts of obedience. God claims rights over you in your rebelliousness: that you ask forgiveness for what you have wasted through your acts of heedless obstinacy. God claims rights over you in your afflictions: that you patiently endure with God in bearing your trials. God claims rights over you in your being blessed: that you profusely offer thanks in enjoying your blessings. Understanding the fluctuation of these four conditions [and your worshipful response in each] will ease for you the difficulty of bearing divine decrees. For understanding that acts of obedience are gifts freely given to you which confer to you great benefits helps you patiently endeavor to obey without swerving. Knowing that headstrong persistence in acts of rebellion will result in punishment from God in the next life as well as diminishing faith's light in this life would cause you to desist from rebelliousness. If you knew that patient endurance will accrue for you its beneficial fruits and attract toward you its blessings, you would firmly intend to practice patience and plunge into it deeply. If you knew that giving thanks invokes the promise that God will provide you with exponentially more, as declared by Divine Speech, *If you give thanks, surely I multiply for you the favor,* you would give thanks continually and be roused to the task.[25] We will expand on the discussion of these four conditions at the end of this work, dealing with each one in a distinct section, if God wills.

Knowing divine goodness' subtleties hidden in every difficulty gives us patience in high degrees to endure all divine decrees. God has placed secret subtle graces in what you loath. Have you not listened to Divine Speech warn, *It may be that you loathe something that is good for you.*[26] This is confirmed by the saying of the Prophet, "Paradise is surrounded by things you loathe, while hell is surrounded by things you crave." Surely there are secret subtle graces hidden in trials, afflictions and poverty. Only those with keen insight can grasp such graces. Don't you see that facing trials trains your ego to serve? Facing trials humbles it and keeps it off guard, preventing it from always claiming its share [in the world]. Humbling the ego comes through facing trials; in turn, through humbling yourself comes divine aid to vanquish otherness from the heart. *God had aided you to victory at Badr when you were humble.*[27] This is a crucial point, but expanding on this discussion will take us outside the main goal of this book.

TRANSCENDING DISCONTENT

Let us return now to the previous trajectory of the discussion by continuing to look at the first moment of Divine Speech: *No indeed, by your Lord, they do not believe unless they turn to you for your decision in whatever they quarrel over, and further, unless they find themselves free of anguish and anxiety in regard to what you have decided for them, and resign themselves with complete resignation.* It should be clear to you that these words specify three distinct states: the state before deferring to the Prophet for a decision, the state during this act of deference, and the state following the decision. As for the first state, the criterion for aspiring to worshipful servitude is that people turn to the Prophet to decide their affairs for them. As for the state during the deciding and after, the criterion for aspiring to worshipful servitude is that people not harbor any feelings of discontent in the settlement of their affairs.

Someone might raise the objection that transcending discontent is required by the revealed words *until they turn to you for a decision.* However, not all who turn to a higher authority to decide for them are totally free of discontent. Some may turn with deference only in outward appearance, while loathing still exists within them. So it is absolutely necessary for the words *until they turn to you* to be followed successively by the condition that they find themselves free of discontent and full of tranquility after the decision. Someone might further object that, if those who subject themselves to the Prophet's decision do not experience the anxiety of discontent, they have resigned themselves with complete resignation. The objector might ask what is the point of Divine Speech continuing to state *and resign themselves with complete resignation* after already stating that being free of anxious discontent is a required condition for the acceptance of the Prophet's decision, acceptance which has as a necessary attribute their being confirmed in acceptance? The answer to this objection is that Divine Speech saying *and resign themselves with complete resignation* means that their resignation is in all affairs in totality, rather than just in the affair over which they may have quarreled, prompting them to seek a decision. Someone might continue to object that this generality is required from the first condition, *until they turn to you for a decision.* The answer to this objection is that the first condition, to defer to the Prophet's authority, is not generalized but rather is specific and limited to *whatever they quarrel over,* rather than the general, holistic meaning alluded to above.[28]

This moment of Divine Speech as a whole contains three crucial points. The first is that people turn to a higher authority in whatever they differ over amongst themselves. The second is their need to be free from feeling the anxiety of discontent in the act of subjecting themselves to this decision. The third is their need for absolute resignation to the decisions of the highest authority in what they quarrel over and in all circumstances that come down upon them from above, both between themselves and within themselves. Therefore, the Divine Speech has both a limited, specified intent followed by a far more general, absolute intent. So ponder its depths!

The second moment of Divine Speech that deals with this topic is when God says, *By your Lord, God creates whatever God wills and chooses for them. They have no power of choice in themselves. And praise be to God, exalted be God, far beyond what others associate with God!*[29]

This moment of Divine Speech contains signs that point out every person's need to desist from presuming self-concern and to leave their care with God. For if God creates whatever God wills, then God also arranges the affairs for all creation as God wills. Whoever has not created has no ability to arrange their concerns! *Is one who creates like one who never creates? Will you then not bear this in mind?*[30] When Divine Speech says that God *chooses*, it conveys this profound meaning: that God is unique in being able to choose. God's acts are neither based on compulsion nor limited by necessity. Rather divine acts flow effortlessly from the qualities of divine will and choice.[31] This ultimate reality requires every person to desist from calculating their concerns and asserting their choices in competition with God, since qualities that belong solely to God should not belong to you!

In this moment of Divine Speech, the phrase, *they have no power of choice in themselves* conveys two meanings.

The Narration
Surat al-Qaṣaṣ 28:61-70

Is the person to whom we (God) have made a good promise
    and who meets its fulfillment
    equal to the person to whom we have given
    the pleasurable things of this life for a short respite
    after which he, on the day of resurrection, is among those
    ushered into my presence? (61)
That day they are called, 'Where are my partners, those you asserted?' (62)
Those against whom the charge is justly laid say,
    'Our Lord! It is these who led us astray.
We deceived them as we were ourselves deceived.
We renounce them in your presence. They never served us well!' (63)
It is said to them, 'Petition those you asserted as partners with me!'
So they call upon them and they never answer.
They will see the punishment—
    if only they had been rightly guided. (64)
That day they will be called,
    'How did you answer the Messengers?' (65)
Then the sequence of events will be darkened to their senses.
Then they will not be able
    to question each other [to establish the narrative]. (66)
Yet any who have repented and believed and performed good deeds
    might be among those achieving success. (67)
By your Lord, God creates whatever God wills and chooses for them.
They have no power of choice in themselves.
Praise be to God, exalted be God, far beyond what others associate
    with God. (68)
Your Lord knows what their chests conceal and what they reveal. (69)
For God it is—there is no god but God.
To God is all praise, in the first and in the last.
With God is the power to decide and to God you all return. (70)

First, people should exercise no scope of choice or volition, through which they might consider themselves more deserving of choice than God. The second meaning of *they have no power of choice in themselves* is that God has not given them the power of choice or entitled them to all that lies within the power of choice. This moment of Divine Speech continues with *praise be to God, exalted be God, far beyond what others associate with God!* This indicates that God is incomparably transcendent—it is inconceivable that we could assert choice in association or competition with God. These words make clear that those who assert their choice or preference in partnership with God are among the idolaters and those who associate [who ascribe divinity to anything other than God]. Such hypocrites lay claim to exercising lordship with the tongue of their spiritual condition, even if they assert that God is the Lord in their verbal testimony.

There is a third moment of Divine Speech that relates to this topic. *Should people have just what they fancy? To God belong the beginning and the ending.*[32] These words reveal your need to desist from arranging your own affairs in competition with God. The opening phrase, *Should people have just what they fancy* means that 'people don't have just what they want nor should they, for we [God] have not made them for this purpose.' This meaning is reaffirmed by the phrase that follows, *For to God belong the beginning and the ending.* This phrase, too, states the need for people to stop looking after their own concerns in competition with God's concern for them. In other words, if to God belong the beginning and ending, then nothing in either realm [this world and the next] really belongs to any other, including us. In reality, the only one who should look after any concern at all in either of the two worlds is the owner of both of them! That owner is God alone.

THE PROPHET'S TEACHING ABOUT CONTENTMENT

I mentioned in the introduction the tradition that is reported of the Prophet Muhammad. He has said, "Those who are satisfied with God as their Lord, with Islam as their religious path, and with Muhammad as their Prophet have tasted the nourishment of true faith." From this it is clear that whoever is not content [with these three guides] has not found the sweetness of true faith or tasted of its delight. Such a person's faith is like a form with no spirit enlivening it. It is like an image with no substance or like an outward tracing with no inner reality. However, hearts that are wholesome, safe from the diseases of heedlessness and selfish desire, are blessed with savory spiritual nourishment, just as our sensual selves feast on sumptuous meals. Only those who are satisfied with God as Lord taste of true faith.

When one is satisfied with God as Lord, one resigns oneself to God and allows oneself to be led by God's decrees. One hands over the reins to God and leaves aside anxiously arranging one's own concerns and choosing one's own direction. Instead, trust in God's wholesome concern and careful selection, and discover the delicious taste of true living and the peace of mind attained by handing over all cares [to their rightful owner]. Those who are satisfied with God as Lord find that God is also content with them; this is revealed in the Divine Speech, *God is satisfied with them, and they are satisfied with God.*[33] If God expresses satisfaction in regard to them, then God makes manifest to them the sweetness of satisfaction, causing them to know

73

all that God has freely bestowed upon them and God's benevolent proficiency toward them.

Satisfaction with God comes only through understanding. Understanding comes only through illumination. Illumination comes only through intimacy to the source of light. Intimacy comes only through the care and concern by which God regards you. Thus, when divine care proceeds you at every step, gifts are presented to you from the treasuries of divine graces. When the graceful help and illuminating lights extended by God reach you, then the heart is cleansed of all diseases and ailments.[34] One's perception becomes clear and sound, and one can perceive the delicious sweetness of faith that keeps perception sound and taste keen. If the heart were to fall sick through heedlessness or forgetfulness, then perception of this sustaining sweetness would be cut off. This is like the case of a person suffering from a fever who finds the taste of sugar bitter, even though sugar is really not bitter! Likewise, when disease falls away from the heart, one perceives things as they truly are: one tastes the sweetness of faith, the savoriness of worshipful obedience, and the repellent bitterness of separation and contrariness.

Tasting the sweetness of true faith [for just a moment] necessitates aspiring to always taste of it. This leads the heart to witness the subtle gifts that God gives freely through this taste of sweetness. This makes necessary finding the means to preserve faith and draw closer to it. Tasting the delicious aroma of worshipful obedience obliges one to persevere in its practice by keeping one's eyes on the subtle gifts that God bestows upon the heart. Tasting the bitterness of ungrateful infidelity and contrariness necessitates leaving them both, shunning them after leaving them, and never ever inclining toward them. Leaving infidelity and contrariness depends on desisting from committing any

74

wrongful deeds and never feeling curiosity or attraction toward wrongful attitudes. Just as some people are attracted
to committing wrong and then do it, some people refuse to
commit a wrong but are still attracted to the deed! Your
desisting from wrongdoing must be complete [in action and
intention] because the illumination of insight reveals that
acting contrarily [to God's decrees] and heedlessly are poi-
sons deadly to the heart. Therefore, the hearts of believers
completely avoid contradicting God, just as you avoid contact with poisoned food.

In this tradition, the Prophet continued to propose a second condition: "those who are satisfied with Islam as their
religious path (*dīn*)." If people are satisfied with Islam as
their path of religious obligation, then they are satisfied with
what satisfies their Lord and what God has chosen for them.
This is according to two moments of Divine Speech that
declare *Truly the religious obligation in God's regard is
submission (islām)* and *Those who take upon themselves
anything other than submission (islām), it will not accepted
from them.*[35] In addition, the Divine Speech points out that
*Surely God has selected for you your path of religious obli-
gation, so do not die as anything other than being those
who submit (muslimūn).*[36] If one is satisfied with Islam as a
path of religious obligation, then it is necessary to perform
all duties and avoid all prohibitions, to enjoin others to act
according to the sanctified path and to forbid others what
has been disavowed along this path. If you see someone
trying to actively lead others astray from this path, then you
must dispute their injecting into the path what is really not
of it. You must shatter them with clear proofs and restrain
them with cogent illustrations.[37]

In this tradition, the Prophet continued to propose a third
condition, "and those who are satisfied with Muhammad as

their Prophet." It is necessary for those who are satisfied with Muhammad as their Prophet to act as his authoritative representative and intimate friend (*walī*). They must culti- vate their comportment by means of Muhammad's example. They must embody his virtuous qualities by minimizing their dependence on the world, leaving aside worldly means, turning away from committing evil acts, and freeing them- selves from what leads to harm. They must embrace all other means through which they can actualize following the Prophet in word and deed, in what is taken and what is left aside, in what is loved and what is loathed, in what is exter- nally visible and what is internally manifest.

Thus whoever is satisfied with God is tranquil and re- signed before God, whoever is satisfied with Islam works at practicing it, and whoever is satisfied with Muhammad follows his example. There cannot be one of these satisfac- tions without all three of them. It is impossible to be satis- fied with God as Lord and yet be unsatisfied with Islam as a path of religious obligation. It is impossible to be satis- fied with Islam yet be unsatisfied with Muhammad as Prophet. You must understand this [necessary relationship] with clarity.

SPIRITUAL PROGRESS MEANS DESISTING FROM SELFISH CALCULATION

Once this relationship between contentment and the sweet taste of faith has become clear to you, consider that there are nine levels in realizing faithful certainty. These nine lev- els are repenting, renouncing, enduring patiently, giving thanks, standing in fearful awe, being content, actively hop- ing, entirely trusting, and intimately loving. Consider care- fully how none of these levels of faith is sound and whole

76

without the necessary condition of desisting from selfish calculation, caring for your own concerns, and choosing in competition with God.

Consider repenting (*tawba*). Just as repentant people must repent of their wrong deeds, they must also repent of having looked after their own cares. This is because being concerned for yourself and choosing your own direction are two of the gravest sins of the heart, and persistence in these dangerous activities is opposition against God. In reality, repenting is turning back to God, turning away from everything in yourself with which God is not satisfied. God is certainly not satisfied with your appropriating for yourself oversight of your own concerns, because such appropriation amounts to infidelity and associating partners with God's lordship.[38] By appropriating this oversight to yourself, you disavow the blessed gift of reason and discernment, and God is never satisfied with people's disavowal and disbelief. How could anyone deem wholesome the repentance of people who are still anxiously engrossed in self-concern for their own cares and heedless of the excellent supervision of the One who protects them?

Likewise, renunciation and minimizing your dependence on the world's means (*zuhd*) is only sound if you also depart from attending to your own cares. Among the things you are enjoined to leave aside and renounce is attachment to your own concerns. This is because renunciation actually consists of two dimensions: outer renunciation and inner renunciation. The outer dimension consists of refusing anything more than is barely necessary of sanctified types of food, clothing and the like. The inner dimension consists of refusing to grasp for power or to crave for recognition. Included within this inner dimension is refusing to look after your own concerns in deference to God's concern for you.

Likewise, neither patient endurance (*ṣabr*) nor grateful thanksgiving (*shukr*) can be sound without also leaving your own concerns and cares to God. Patient people are those who resist rushing headlong into reactions in ways that are not loved by God, and it is clear that God does not love for people to aspire to control their own affairs or choose their own direction. Patience is of many kinds: patience in resisting what is forbidden, patience in enduring what is enjoined, and patience in asserting your own concerns and choices. Or you could rephrase this by saying, patience in resisting your human impulses' claim upon you, and patience in enduring the necessary steps toward embodying worshipful servitude. One from among these necessary steps is desisting from attending to your own concerns in competition with God's concern for you.

Likewise, giving thanks can never be sound or sincere without such desisting. Junayd of Baghdad defined giving thanks most aptly when he said, "One gives thanks by not opposing God with respect to divine blessings."[39] Understand that you could never aspire to care for your own concerns while disregarding God if it were not for your power of reason (*ʿaql*). God endowed you with the power of reason so that you could oversee your animal nature; God has made this endowment of reason the cause of your potential self-perfection. Look closely! Inanimate objects and animals do not plot and plan for their own benefit beyond what God has given them, since they lack the power of reason which can discern the ultimate outcomes of different means and judge the importance of these outcomes.[40]

The levels of fearful awe (*khawf*) and active hope (*rajāʾ*) are also incomplete if sullied by self-concern. When the overwhelming forces of fear [of God's dissatisfaction] seize the heart, it prevents you from finding any ease or security in arranging your own affairs. Active hope [for God's satisfaction] also excludes self-concern, since hopeful people's hearts are completely filled with joy in regarding God, and their time is completely filled with the activities that God enjoins. So when is there a spare moment to be engrossed in your own cares in disregard to God's care for you?

The level of trust (*tawakkul*) is also infirm with the distraction of self-concern. Those who entrust to God all their concerns pass to God the reins of control and rely on God alone in every affair. Entrusting God requires you to empty yourself of concern for your own cares and to fill yourself with tranquil resignation under the currents of divine decrees. The direct [mutually exclusive] relationship between self-concern and this level of trusting contentment is clearer than the relation between self-concern and all the other levels.

Self-concern also weakens the level of intimate loving (*maḥabba*). The lover is completely engrossed in adoring the beloved. Leaving aside willful desires in deference to the beloved is the very essence of love's goal. Lovers do not have a moment of empty time to assert their self-concern in regard to God, because their intimate love for God has totally distracted them from their own demands, enrapturing them completely. Therefore some have said that those who have tasted even slightly of the pure love for God are distracted by this taste to the point of being oblivious to anything other than God.

The level of contentment (*riḍā*) is also incapacitated by one's self-concern, and this is unambiguously clear. Those who are content are completely satisfied by how God has cared for them in all that came before. They consider God's care absolutely sufficient. How could you ever imagine that people could look after their own concerns while being content with God's concern for them? Do you not realize that the illuminating light of contentment cleanses from their hearts the obscuring scum of self-concern? For those who are content, God amplifies the illumination of contentment under divine decrees.[41] Thus they never meddle in anxious self-concern in competition with God, and consider whatever God chooses for them as perfectly sufficient for their needs. Ponder all of this deeply.

SECTION TWO: RESISTING SELFISH CALCULATION

There are several strategies that may lead you to stop taking care of your own concerns and choosing for yourself in competition with God. The first is acknowledging all the nuances of how God has taken care of you in the past. For you must know that God was looking after your concerns before you ever looked after them yourself. Before your worldly existence, God provided for all your needs and there was no trace of your self-concern to contradict this divine care. Likewise, God is the One who oversees and the One who cares for your needs after your existence in this world unravels. Therefore, be with God now as you were with God then, so that God might look after you now as fully as God looked after you then! To this end, al-Ḥusayn al-Ḥallāj prayed to God, "Be for me now as you were for me when I had not yet begun to be!"[42] Al-Ḥallāj was asking God to be with him, to oversee his affairs and take over all his cares after his worldly existence just as God had overseen them and taken care of him before he even began his worldly existence.

Before people come into this world, their every need is overseen by the apt and actualizing knowledge of God, even though they have not yet passed into worldly existence. [After this passage] people presume to claim oversight for their own concerns for themselves, falling into disappointment and despair. Someone might object that al-Ḥallāj was in a state of non-being during the time signified by "when I had not yet begun to be," so how could God have provided for and overseen his needs? Know that all things exist in the knowledge of God even when they yet have no existence in and of themselves.[43] In this state, the true One takes responsibility for overseeing their every need, since they exist solely in divine knowledge. Although there is no place in this work to discuss it fully, it is a topic for deep contemplation and searching meditation.

WHAT WERE YOU BEFORE YOU BEGAN TO BE?

You should realize that the real One has taken charge of caring for your every need through every stage of your development. God has undertaken to bring you through each stage into your worldly existence, and began this careful oversight on the Day of Destinies.[44] This is the moment when God created all the souls that would ever exist and questioned them *Am I not your Lord?* All souls answered in unison *Indeed, we have testified.*

It was from divine care for all your needs that, on that day, God allowed you to know the divine as your Lord—thus you first acknowledged God. At that time, God manifested to your senses and you were able to witness the divine. God urged you to speak for yourself, and inspired you to pronounce your agreement with divine lordship—thus you pronounced God your single Lord. Then God made of your soul a tiny spermazoid safeguarded in the loins of your ancestors and fulfilled all your needs with divine concern

The Heights
Surat al-Aᶜraf, 7:172-174

When your Lord took out from the children of Adam
Their descendents from their loins
    and made them bear witness
    concerning themselves
'Am I not your Lord?'
They answered, 'Indeed, we have testified.'
In case you should say, on the Day of Reckoning,
'We certainly had been heedless and forgetful!' (172)
Or in case you should say,
'Our ancestors were idolatrous before us,
Whereas we are descended from them,
So will you destroy us because of the errant deeds
Of people who came before?' (173)
For this reason we expound the signs in detail
That they might return. (174)

while you rested there. God protected you, and protected all your ancestors who carried you as a spermazoid, dispatching divine nourishment and aid to support you by means of all those people who carried you within them, back to your very first forefather, Adam. Then God cast you into the womb of your mother and took charge of all your needs while you were there, making her womb accept you like fertile ground accepts a sprouting seed. God protected you there, giving you life in her womb. God caused to join together two spermazoids [one from the father, and one from the mother] that became intimate and loved each other and melded into one. You exist from this union, built upon the divine wisdom that all of existence is based on the secret principle of bringing forth unity from duality. From a spermazoid, God transformed you into a mucus clot, soft and receptive to the qualities and destinies that God desired to transmit to you. After you became a clot, God transformed you into a fleshy lump. Then God divided and expanded the flesh, shaping it into your likeness and establishing your physical form. Then God breathed into you the spirit and nourished you with the blood of the uterus in the womb of your mother and made flow to you your sustenance before you ever emerged into independent existence.

God kept you in the womb of your mother until your bodily organs were adequate and your supports were firm, in order to prepare you for your coming out into the world, the world consisting of all apportioned for you and against you. You emerged into a realm that you can come to know and experience through God's bounteousness and evenhandedness. When you descended into the world, God knew that you were incapable of eating the raw and rough food of the world, for you had no teeth or digestive powers to make use of what you might eat. So God caused breasts to flow with gentle and refined nourishment. God empowered the compassion harbored in your mother's heart to incite the breasts: every time they stopped excreting milk, they were urged to begin anew by the compassion for you sparked in your mother's heart. In this way, the flow of milk is ever renewed, never slacking, with fullness imbued.

Then God set your mother and father to work, procuring for you all you might need and looking after you with the eye of intimate parental care. What is this care except the care that God has poured out for you, as for all people, in the guise of mothers and fathers, in order that you come to know tender love? In reality, nothing has cared for you except God's lordship. Nothing has raised you except God's presence with you. God obliged your father to provide for you until you reached a mature age, in order that you might be cared for through him. Then the burden of responsibility was suspended for you until the time when your powers of understanding are complete, at the time of puberty.

A PARABLE
A CHILD IN THE FIRE

A person in this world is dependent on God like a child is dependent on its mother. No mother would ever neglect her child's needs or leave her child unattended. The believer is dependent like this in relation to God, who undertakes to care for the believers. God pours forth subtle gifts for them and protects them in their trials. It is reported that, "The Messenger of God saw a woman with her child, sitting beside a campfire. He said to his companions, 'Can you imagine this woman throwing her child into a fire?' They answered 'No, certainly not!' So

the Messenger replied, 'God is even more compassionate with those servants who believe in God than
this woman is with her infant child.'"

Then up through the time when you become middle-aged,
God never stops bestowing generously. God never stops
caring for you even as you reach old age and your life draws
to a close, and as you return to God and are assembled [with
all other souls] before God's presence and are stood upright and alone between God's hands. Likewise, God may
keep you safe from punishments and allow you to enter the
realm of divine reward, lifting away the veils of separation
and alienation from the divine presence and seating you in
the company of intimate beloved ones. Divine Speech states,
*Surely those who are righteous and act with wary conscious-
ness of God are in the place of gardens and rivers, in meet-
ings of purest sincerity with a sovereign all-powerful.*[45] How
could you give thanks to God for such a benefit bestowed
upon you? How could you ever recount such blessings and
enumerate such rewards? Listen to the expressions of Divine Speech: *You experience no blessing except that which
comes from God.*[46] You have never been devoid of God's
benevolent acts on your behalf, nor will you ever be devoid
of them! God's abundant generosity and subtle unearned
gifts will never abandon you.

A PARABLE
THE PLACE PREPARED FOR YOU

Here is an analogy of the relationship of God to
people in this world. Imagine that a father sows many
fields of crops and builds a spacious home. When
asked, "For whom did you do all this?" the father
answers, "For a child that might yet be born to me

85

in the future." The would-be father provides for his child everything necessary even before the child comes into existence, simply out of loving devotion to him. Think about it! If the father works so hard to provide for a child who is not yet born, will he refuse to meet the child's needs after the child's birth? In an analogous way, God prepares for people subtle gifts and appoints their provision even before their creation and emergence into this worldly realm. Indeed, how many divine gifts have preceded your very existence, if only you had the insight to understand! Can you perceive what all God gave to you in your very existence and the great gift of God's causing you to appear in this world? God provided for you in pre-eternal potentiality before you existed as a discrete being and before you could perform any service or obedience. All that God has measured out for you and appointed for you and stored up for you would never be refused to you. How could it be that God, who creates you and prepares a place for you in the world even before your existence, would neglect your provision once you come into existence?

If you desire clear proof of these changing states that you passed through in coming into the world, then listen to these expressions of Divine Speech: *We surely created the human being from an essence of clay. Then we made the clay into a miniscule sperm in a place of safe repose. Then we transformed the sperm into a mucus-like clot. Then we fashioned this clot into a soft fleshy lump. Then we created firm bones within the flesh and clothed the bones with muscle. Then we devised for it another creation [breathing life into it]. Blessed be God, the best of creators! Then after your*

86

creation you will all surely die. Then after death you will all surely be raised on the Day of Reckoning.[47] Let these expressions' flashing illuminations appear to you, and let their penetrating light expand over you. For in this speech, my fellow servant, are expressions that require you to completely resign yourself before God and entrust all your affairs to God. They require you to drop your self-concern and empty yourself of struggle against divine dictates, for God grants success to those who cooperate with currents of divine will.

DOORS AND FOUNDATIONS FOR BUILDING GOOD LIFE

Here is a second point to consider which may spur you to desist from selfish calculation. If you think for a moment, you will see that concern and direction of your affairs for your own sake is willful ignorance of how to aptly look after your well-being. Believers know that when they leave aside anxious concern for themselves in deference to God, they enjoy the wholesome care that comes from God. This is according to the words of Divine Speech, *For those who trust completely in God, God alone is sufficient.*[48] Their acute self-concern transforms into desisting from self-concern, just as their taking care of themselves aptly transforms into leaving aside looking after their own cares. In this regard, consider the Divine Speech, *Enter houses by their proper doors.*[49] Surely, the proper door through which to enter into God's oversight of your concerns for you is your refusing to be anxiously concerned on behalf of yourself!

Here is another point to consider. Examine carefully how destiny does not flow according to what you plot and plan for yourself. Rather, how much of what happens is what you never plan, and how little happens because you planned it and oversaw its actualization! The person with keen discernment does not plan a building on a weak foundation. For when you try to realize the building, shifting fortune will topple it and you will be prevented from ever completing it. There is a poem illustrating this:

> When will the building
> ever reach its completion
> If you undertake its construction
> and another its destruction?

A Parable
Castles in the Sand

The person who plots and plans for him or her self despite God is like one who builds a house on the seashore. Each time she or he struggles to build it up, the waves rise higher and rush over what is built, collapsing its walls one upon the other. So it is that a people struggle to build their houses of self-concern independent of God. They always collapse under the inexorable pressure of incoming divine decrees. This is the meaning of the proverb, "The schemer may scheme while fate just laughs."

As you carefully plan while divine decrees contradict all your plans, what is the benefit of all your anxious concerns if God does not aid you with accord and support? Rather, the right to plot and plan should be deferred to the One who controls potential destiny and actualizing decrees. To this point, it has been said:

When I saw destiny cascading
with no uncertainty or hesitation,
I entrusted all rights to my creator
and threw myself into the current.

ANOTHER PARABLE
A FIRM FOUNDATION

People who plot and plan for themselves despite God
are like a man who builds his house on sand dunes.
When the storm winds blow, the terrain of the sands
shifts completely. Everything he built on such an
unsure foundation collapses to the ground. Just as it
has been sung in Arabian poetry:

Their familiarity with the sands
has passed into oblivion
Just like all that is built
on a foundation of sand.

YOUR PLACE IN THE COSMIC ORDER

From another angle, consider that God, the exalted One, is
in charge of taking care of everything within divine dominion, from the highest zenith of the loftiest affairs to the lowest nadir of the most mundane, from those things unseen to
all that is visible. Just as you hand over to God the right to
oversee the divine throne and dais, and the right to regulate
the heavens and the earth, you should also hand over to
God the right to look after your own personal existence in
this world. Look carefully at your existence in comparison
to the wide world and it will reveal a relation that necessitates your personal annihilation in insignificance. Similarly,
if you compare the relation of the seven celestial heavens
and the seven terrestrial worlds to the divine dais you will

find them to be as insignificant as a small ring hurled into a vast, empty plain. Further, if you compare the entire cosmos of the divine dais plus the celestial and terrestrial to the divine throne, you will find them to be like a tiny earring tossed in a trackless desert. So who are you within the vast scope of God's dominion, that you should give any anxious thought to arranging your own affairs?

Your planning for yourself is thus willful ignorance of God. However, in reality, the situation is as Divine Speech describes: *People have not estimated God's worth and power in its just estimation.*[50] For if people really knew God, they would be ashamed to presume to plan in competition with God's planning for them. Only if these had veiled themselves against God's presence would people plunge headlong into the raging sea of anxious self-concern. Those who have a firm and certain knowledge of what has been unveiled before the insight of their hearts have witnessed that they are cared-for rather than able to care for themselves, acted-upon rather than able to act aptly themselves, and directed rather than moving by their own volition.

Those beings who live in the loftiest celestial realms constantly witness the manifesting of potential power and the willful acuteness of divine decision. They clearly see the relation between divine power and the motion it empowers, just as they see the relation between divine will and the aims it achieves. The appearances [of worldly cause-and-effect] are far removed from these beings' vision. Therefore, they are kept pure from the presumption that they could care for themselves, because they are overpowered by their eye-witnessing and their single-minded orientation toward the divine. To certify this, the Divine Speech pronounces, *Surely it is we who inherit the earth and all that is upon it. To us they all are led back.*[51] This pronouncement refers to the purity of the angels, indicating that they never claim rights to any qualities that have been endowed to them. They never ascribe to themselves that which has been granted to them. If angels were to do this, then the Divine Speech would pronounce, "Surely it is we who inherit the earth and the heavens." However, in contrast, the angels' clear relation to God, their awe-filled awareness of God, and their deferent humility toward God's might prevent them from relying on anything other than God. Therefore, just as you have surrendered to God oversight of the heavens and management of the earth, pass back to God your anxious concerns for your own personal existence. *For surely the creation of the heavens and the earth is more demanding that the creation of humankind.*[52]

A PARABLE
BE A TREE

Imagine a tree that is planted by a gardener who desired that it grow, flourish and bear fruit. The tree knows, or can sense in the way that we people have knowledge, that the one who planted it would never deny it the water it needs to grow. How could the gardener neglect to water the tree when he had planted it, intent on its bearing fruit? And you, my fellow believer, are just like the tree. God has planted you and waters you continuously by providing you with nourishment and provision. God would never have taken the effort to root the tree of your existence and then subsequently refuse you water after placing you in the soil, for God is never careless or negligent.

Own up to What You Really Own

While you are at it, consider how you are owned by God. You have no right to direct the future concerns of what belongs to someone other than you. [It is commonly known that] you do not have shares in the direction of what you don't own. My fellow servant, consider how you don't quarrel over or worry about objects that do not belong to you. Consider how you own only what has been granted to you in ownership by another. You have no real ownership in and of yourself. Ownership is actually just a term of legal relations. Relations between people require that ownership be specified and regulated, rather than ownership being some right established in you by any quality inherent in your person that entitles you to consider yourself an "owner." From these considerations, you should realize that it is best for you and most befitting for you to not meddle in what truly belongs to God as the only One who owns. Divine Speech relates, *Indeed God has purchased from the believers their souls and their goods, so that they might have paradise.*[53]

After selling an object, you should not meddle in the future direction of what is sold or quarrel over the rights of ownership. You are obliged to resign your concerns over anything that you sell, rather than entertain rights over it. Presuming to exercise direction over something that you have sold is an infringement against the contract of sale!

A Parable
All Sales are Final

Imagine that someone who plans for himself is a man who has sold a house or a slave. Imagine that, after the completion of the sale, the seller goes up

92

Repentance
Surat al-Tawba 9:109-111

Which is best? The one who lays a foundation
    Upon wary consciousness of God and what satisfies God?
Or the one who lays a foundation
    Upon the edge of a precipice, eaten away from below, about
    to collapse?
Then it will collapse from beneath into the fires of hell.
God does not guide people who act oppressively. (109)
The foundations of those who build like this
    Have doubt and suspicion in their hearts
    Until their hearts fall into fragments.
And God is the wise One, the One who knows all things. (110)
Indeed God has purchased from the believers
their souls and their goods, that they might have paradise.
They fight in the cause of God, they slay and are slain
    for the sake of a pledge binding upon God
    a truthful right in the Torah, the Gospel, and the Qurʾan.
And who is more faithful to their pledge than God?
So rejoice in the sale that you have contracted with God
    For that is the supreme success. (111)

to the new owner who bought the house. Imagine that the seller begins to tell the new owner to build a certain addition, to tear down specific walls, or to make particular changes and alterations. The one who bought the house will tell him, "You have sold this building and after the sale you have no right to dispose of it, change it, or make use of what you sold!" Clearly, we can't wrangle and haggle after a sale. God has said in revelation: *Indeed God has purchased from the believers their souls and their goods, that they might have paradise.* Therefore, the believer must resign herself and all that is associated with her self to God's use, for God alone has created that self and has purchased it. Resignation before God requires you to leave aside planning for yourself since you are resigned to the plans of the One who truly owns.

One day, I entered the presence of my Shaykh, Abū al-ᶜAbbās al-Mursī, and complained about some matters concerning me. He said to me, "If your self were your own, then you could act with it in any way you please. But you will never be able to do this, ever! If you lay no claim on yourself, then resign yourself to God to act with you as God wills." Then he said to me, "The peace of resignation toward God and of leaving aside self-concern in competition with God—this alone is true worshipful servanthood." Ibrāhīm ibn Adham[54] has said, "One night I fell asleep and failed to perform the nightly devotion that I had voluntarily taken upon myself. When I awoke I was so filled with regret that I slept for the entire following three days, neglecting all the obligatory prayers. Then, when I awoke, I heard a voice calling out to me:

'Everything is forgiven for you
except turning away from us
We have excused what slipped from you
What remains is what you passed up from us.'

Then the voice said to me, 'Ibrahim, be a true servant!' Since then, I have been serving and have found true peace."[55]

Consider that you are a guest of God's hospitality, since the world is the house owned by God and you are just staying in it temporarily under divine care. It is the right and duty of guests to not give a single thought to feeding or sustaining themselves in competition to the Lord of the house. Once, someone asked Shaykh Abu Madyan, "Sir, what should we make of the fact that we see other great Sufi masters getting involved in worldly means [to extract their livelihoods] but you don't get involved in these means?" Abu Madyan answered, "My brother, I have considered the world to be the house of God, and we are only the Lord's guests. Surely the Prophet has said, 'The period of staying as a guest is three days. Therefore we have only three days' period as guests of God. Surely Divine Speech says, *A single day in regard to your Lord is like a thousand years as you count time.*[56] Therefore we have, in God's regard, three thousand years of staying as guests under the care of God. From this period is the short duration of our residence in this world. The remainder is in the next world, by divine bounty, and above and beyond this period [God gives us] eternal abiding."

A PARABLE
PROVISION IS NONE OF YOUR BUSINESS

There was once a servant who worked in a house. The master of the house told him to stay in the house and stand at attention in order to serve. The master would not command service without also arranging for the servant to receive food, drink, clothing, and shelter. No, the master who commands will give every manner of provision to care for his every need (*kifāya*) and watch over him (*ri'āya*). Likewise, God has ordered people to obey and act in accord with divine commands in this world and has therefore insured the existence of a measure of provision (*qisma*). God has measured out provision in order to allow this service and obedience, just as a master stands over his servant and bestows upon him what he needs. God has said in revelation, *Command your people to perform the prayer and persevere patiently with it. We do not ask you to provide. We provide for you.*[57]

Finally, consider what you might see if you cast your gaze at the constant eternal wellspring of God's copious sustaining (*qayyūmīya*) that supports every existing thing. Have you not listened to Divine Speech recite, *God—there is no divinity except God, the ever-living, the eternally-sustaining.*[58] God is the everlasting foundation sustaining this world and the next. God is the establisher of this world by divine providence and bestowal, and the establisher of the next world by divine reward and recompense. If you understand the everlasting sustaining of your Lord in regard to yourself and how it keeps you established [in both worlds], then you would pass back the reins to God and hurl yourself down with absolute resignation before God's control. You would throw yourself submissively between the hands of your Lord, expectantly looking forward to what decrees are sent down upon you from God.

BE A SERVANT WITHOUT CLAIMING TO BE A MASTER

Consider the meaning of being a servant. The servant is constantly engrossed in performing the duties and activities of worshipful servanthood. Those duties fill up the whole length of one's life, according to the Divine Speech, *Worshipfully serve your Lord until you reach utter certainty.*[59] When the servants' attention is turned toward safeguarding their duties as sincere servants, they are completely preoccupied from any possibility of looking after their own cares and anxieties. Shaykh al-Shadhili has said, "You must realize that in every moment there is a claim of servanthood upon you from God, a claim demanded from you by command of divine lordship. The servant is held totally accountable for this and is answerable for it and for every moment's breath that has been given to the servant in trust." For those with insight, when is there a spare moment that is free of obligation from the rights God exercises? Where is there a spare moment for you to exercise your own self-concern or look to secure your own personal advantage with respect to profits from your own designs?

The bountiful giving of God reaches people only when they empty themselves of self-concern and restrain their hands from self-preoccupations. Bountiful giving reaches them when they spend their concern in activities beloved by God and devote themselves to what accords with God's desire, tiring themselves out in service and acting out divine will. On account of your being absent from your ego and extinguishing it, God lets you abide in the divine presence. To illustrate this, Shaykh al-Shadhili has said, "You who are arriving along the path of the your salvation, desiring to be present at God's side! You should look to your own external actions if you desire that your insight be opened to the secrets of your Lord's realm of might (*malakūt*)."

Consider how you are the servant of a just Lord.[60] It is the duty of a servant not to be anxious with the Lord, worried about not being supported or given benefits. The very spirit of servanthood is trusting in God and completely resigning oneself toward God. Both of these virtues are negated by care for your own personal concerns and asserting your own choices in competition with God. Rather, it is the duty of a servant to undertake the Lord's service and let the Lord undertake to support the servant with gifts. Servants must establish themselves in the Lord's tasks, while their Lord will support them by apportioning their share. In this light, understand the Divine Speech, *Command your people to perform the prayer and persevere patiently with it. We do not ask you to provide. We provide for you.*[61] It is as if God were saying, 'undertake to serve us and we will undertake to provide you with your apportioned share.'

A PARABLE
ACCEPTING HOSPITALITY WITH GRACE

People's relation to God is analogous to visitors who stay as guests in the house of a generous king. It is the role of the guest to cease worrying about what he will eat or drink. If the guest would entertain any anxiety about that, it would be an insulting allegation of stinginess against the king. It would be harboring a bad opinion of the king's personality! The great Shaykh, Abu Madyan, has presented this analogy before, saying "This world is the house of God, and all people are guests here. God would never command people to stay as guests, as God did through the tongue of the Prophet Muhammad, and then neglect to treat people as guests." Therefore, the person who harbors anxieties over what to eat or drink is hateful in the eyes of the king! If that person didn't prematurely doubt the trustworthiness of God, he would never entertain a care about such matters that are God's responsibility.

REASON ABOUT RISKS

Consider your own lack of certainty about the results of your actions in any situation. Perhaps you planned a certain action while thinking that the outcomes would benefit you, but in the end they harmed you instead. Perhaps benefits have come to you from situations of intense strife. Perhaps toilsome difficulties resulted from situations that appeared at first to be beneficial for you. Harm might come from walking along a routine path, while a more fruitful path might emerge from harm you have suffered. Perhaps secret gifts are concealed in burdensome trials, and trials may come from what appear like gifts. Perhaps you prosper by the actions of your enemies, while you are ruined by your loved ones.

If reality is like this, so far removed from your certainty, how can reasonable and discerning people plot and plan their own futures? How could they exclude consideration of God, as they are ignorant of whether the outcome of what they plan will be beneficial, and so pursue it, or harmful, and so defend against it. To emphasize this point, the Shaykh al-Shadhili has said, "O God! Surely we are incapable of defending ourselves against harm from sources with which we are familiar by means of what we know! How could we ever be able to defend ourselves from harm coming from sources of which we are ignorant by means that we do not know at all?"[62] This single moment of Divine Speech should suffice you. *It may be that you loath something that is beneficial for you, and it may be that you love something that is harmful for you.*[63]

My fellow servant, how many times have you desired something, but once it became actualized for you, you encountered deep sorrow in your heart and discomfort in your self? If the outcome of this desire had been revealed to you before you craved for it, you would have known that God looks after you with apt and wholesome care from sources that you do not perceive and transforms you by means that you do not know. How reprehensible is the person who desires without insightful understanding! How repugnant is the servant who has no tranquil resignation!

> How often did a matter not go my way
> though I ran myself down to secure it
> While you remained with me,
> granting me benevolence and compassion.
> I resolved to not entertain any thought
> in my heart, except what you place before me
> That you never see me engaged
> in what you advised me to avoid
> Since your presence in my heart
> is so crucial and so revered

Listen to this parable that might clarify the matter in your heart. There was once a person who, if something tragic harmed him or trials beset him, would simply say, "Ah, good!" One night, a jackal came along and ate his rooster. He was told about the disaster and simply replied "Ah, good!" Later that night, his dog was beaten and died. When the catastrophe was reported to him, he simply replied "Ah, good!" Later that same night, his donkey brayed once and keeled over dead, and he simply said "Ah, good!" By this time, the man's family was so perturbed by his simple replies that they could bear him no longer. It just so happened that a band of wild desert nomads descended upon the village in a raid and slaughtered everyone in the neighborhood. Nobody survived except this man and his family. The marauding nomads were led to people's homes in the dark by the crowing of their roosters, the barking of their dogs, and the braying of their donkeys. But this man's livestock had all died previously! The loss of all his beneficial animals was the cause of his safety.

Praise be to the One who oversees all affairs with subtle wisdom! Ordinarily, people do not bear witness to the apt and wholesome care of God's arrangement and provision until after the unseen outcomes are revealed to them. However, there are specially selected people who are not like this. The people who understand God from God bear witness to God's wholesome oversight, before the outcomes of any action are revealed to them.

There are differing types and degrees to this power of insight. There are those who bear a good opinion of God, and thus resign themselves before God's decrees, once they grow accustomed to God through the beauty of God's actions toward them and the their subtle grace. There are others who bear a good opinion of God because God allows them to know that their own plans and struggles do not really benefit them, that they do not acquire anything that has not been apportioned for them before time. There are others who improve their good opinion of God by bearing in mind the saying of the Prophet Muhammad, relaying that God has said, "I am as my servant considers me to be (*anā ʿinda ḥusn ẓann ʿabdī bīya*)." Thus these people practice a good opinion of God and divine ways, hoping that God will consider them and their actions likewise in a good light. Because of this, God is with them according to their assessment of God. Indeed, God eases the load for believers by means of secret gifts and subtle aid, since their opinion of God conforms to Divine Speech saying, *God desires for you a lightened burden and does not wish you to be encumbered.*[64] Yet the most noble of these degrees is tranquil resignation toward God and handing over all cares to divine care as just what God deserves rather than for some benefit that might accrue to the person for acting with resignation.

In the first degree, the person has not become free of being a slave to worldly cause-and-effect. The resignation of those who are resigned to God for the sake of the benefits God brings to them is caused by the previous fine outcomes of divine oversight. If there were no previous gifts, there would be no subsequent resignation. In the second degree, people also have not become free of selfish concern, for desisting from plotting and planning in hopes of what good might come to them is not desisting for the sake of God alone. If such people thought that their plotting and planning might get them something for themselves, they might never desist from it. Those who are resigned and maintain a good opinion of God in hopes that God will be as good as their opinion projects still strive to achieve their share of self-directed well-being in the world. They hope to receive bounty from God in fair exchange for their maintaining a good opinion of God. However, those who are resigned and maintain a good opinion of God simply due to awe at the sheer immensity of divinity and the qualities of divine lordship are the real worshipful servants. They alone get it right. It is possible that they are among those described by the Prophet in this way: "God has servants who are so powerful that their one utterance of 'Glory be to God' is like the mountain of Uhud."

God has urged people to desist from selfish calculation through this moment of Divine Speech, *When your Lord took out from the children of Adam their descendents from their loins and made them bear witness concerning themselves, 'Am I not your Lord?' They answered, 'Indeed, we have testified.'*[65] Their testifying in unison that God is their Lord obliges the children of Adam to desist from calculating their own good in competition with the Lord. This agreement was a binding pledge (*mu'āqada*) entered into before each individual soul came into being—the same soul that is so agitated by material existence that it plots and plans for its own benefit in competition with God. True servants remain in their previous spiritual condition [of being a child of Adam who bears witness from before time], with all the veils of alienation lifted, subsiding in the divine presence. Remaining in this condition prevents them arrogating to themselves the power to plot and plan. When the obscuring veil of alienation is swept aside, the propensity to calculate is foreclosed and the agitation it causes is disposed. For this reason, those with intimate experiential knowledge of God do not engage in selfish calculation, for they bear witness to the secrets of celestial realms of divine determination (*malakūt*). Their constant turning to face God precludes

103

that, and dissolves their resolve to determine their actions by themselves. How could a servant who lives constantly in the presence of God, bearing witness to the divine might and loftiness of God, plot and plan in disregard of God?

SECTION THREE: CONSEQUENCES OF SELFISH CALCULATION

You should know that self-concern and self-direction are hugely consequential and terribly dangerous. If we look closely, we find that when Adam endeavored to eat the fruit of the forbidden tree, he was actually reverting to self-concern by presuming to take care of himself. The tempter (*shayṭān*) said to Adam and Eve (*Hawāʾ*) what Divine Speech reports: *He said, your Lord has forbidden you both to eat from this tree so that you would not become angels or take your place among those who live eternally.*[66]

So Adam pondered for himself, and imagined that eternity in intimate proximity to his beloved One was the noblest goal possible. He reasoned that this goal could be achieved by passing from the state of humanity to the state of angelicity, whether it is true that being an angel actually gives one status closer to God and thus is more favored or because Adam simply speculated that angels are more favored in this way. In any case, Adam pondered and planned [how to stay nearer to the divine presence] and thus ate from the forbidden tree. All the consequences of his action are due solely to his planning for himself and being concerned for his own welfare.

In reality, the true One desired Adam to act in this way, in order to cause him to descend to the earth and to make him God's vice-regent in the world.[67] The consequences seem like a disastrous fall in status, but this is in outward appearance only. In its inward meaning, this change was a

The Heights
Qur'an, Surat al-A'raf 7:10-23

It is we (God) who have given you authority and power on earth
And have given you on earth your means of livelihood
But how little you give thanks! (10)
It is we who created you then shaped you then said to the angels 'Prostrate to Adam!'
And they bowed down, except for Iblīs—he's not one who bows. (11)
God said, 'What prevented you from bowing when I commanded you?'
'I am better than he is—you created me from fire and created him from clay.' (12)
God said, 'Then get down from here! It is not for you to act arrogantly here.
So get out, for you are of the lowly ones.' (13)
He said, 'Give me respite until the day when they are resurrected." (14)
God said, 'You are among those who have respite.' (15)
He said, 'For your having misled me, I'll ambush them along your straight path (16)
Then I'll assault them from in front and from behind
From their right and from their left—you will not find many of them grateful!' (17)
God said, 'Get out from here, disgraced and expelled.'
Surely whichever of them follow you—I will fill hell with all of you together.' (18)
O Adam, dwell in the garden, you and your partner
And eat from whatever you desire, but do not approach this tree, neither of you
That you might be one of the transgressors.' (19)
Then whispered the tempter to them both, to make apparent to them both their shame
He said, 'Your Lord only forbids this tree to you both lest you become angels
Or become from among those who live eternally' (20)
And he swore to them that he was one who gives sincere advice. (21)
So he misled them with pride. And when they both tasted of the tree
Their shame became clearly apparent to them.
They sewed together to cover themselves leaves of the garden
And their Lord called them, 'Did I not forbid that tree
And tell you that the tempter is your obvious enemy?' (22)
They both said, 'Our Lord! We have wronged our souls.
If you do not forgive us and have mercy on us
We will surely be among those who are lost!' (23)

great upward development in Adam and increased his status. To illustrate this, Shaykh al-Shadhili has said, "I swear, God did not cause Adam to descend into the world in order to diminish him, but rather caused him to descend in order to complete him. Adam is still progressing and advancing toward wholeness in God, sometimes in an ascension (*mi^crāj*) by means of becoming closer and more specially chosen, and sometimes in an ascension by means of being humbled and abased. The human is made complete through these stages of realizing the truth." In support of this point, every believer must be certain that, as the Prophets and Messengers traverse from one state into another, they always move into a state of fuller completion. In this sense, you should understand Divine Speech, *The next is better for you than the previous.*[68] The commentator, Ibn ^cAṭīya, rephrases the meaning by saying that, "The next state is better for you than what came before."[69]

Once you have understood this, then turn your attention to knowing that God asserts both divine concern and divine will. God asserted will before asserting oversight. God willed that Adam and his human progeny would inexorably inhabit the world and so human beings were brought forth as God willed them to be: some who are righteous and some who clearly oppress their own souls.[70] It is due to the wisdom of divine concern and planning that all of this came to completion and appeared in forms that we witness. To this end, the true One desired that Adam eat of the forbidden tree in order to cause his descent into the world. His descent was to clearly manifest his status as viceregent of God, the status generously bestowed upon Adam. To illustrate this, Shaykh al-Shadhili has said, "How generous it is that God made vice-regency the legacy of disobedience! For through disobedience, God set forth the practice of repentance for everyone after Adam until the day of reckoning."

God had destined and decreed that Adam descend into the world before God had even created the heavens and the earth. Shaykh al-Shadhili has said, "I swear, God caused Adam to descend into the world before even creating him, as God reveals in the Divine Speech, *I am making in the world a vice-regent.*"[71]

Adam's partaking of the forbidden tree and descending into the world was the consequence of God's comprehensive care and concern for his welfare, just as Adam's status of vice-regent to the divine presence (*khalīfa*) and spiritual leader (*imām*) was the result of God's generosity. Let us now finish this description of the actual incident of Adam's descent, and turn our attention to the many benefits and special qualities that were granted to Adam through this incident. We do this in order to understand that the people who specialize in being with God have a condition that nobody else enjoys. God takes care of their sustenance and directs their affairs completely, with a care that is not focused on others apart from them.

Many benefits stem from Adam's eating of the forbidden tree and descending into the world. The first is that Adam and Eve in paradise were mutually acquainted with God, through God's sustaining them, giving to them generously, acting toward them sincerely, and blessing them liberally. However, the true One also desired that they eat from the forbidden tree, through the hidden subtleties of divine concern for them. This was so that Adam and Eve might come to know God through the divine qualities of patient restraint, careful concealment, forgiveness, [acceptance of] repentance, and special selection of them for the highest duties.

The Heifer
Surat al-Baqara 2:30-39

Then your Lord said to the angels
'I am making in the world a vice-regent.'
They said, 'Will you make in the world
 one that will spread corruption in it and spill blood
 while we recite your praise and revere you?'
God said, 'I know that which you do not know.' (30)
And God taught Adam the names and qualities of all things
 Then displayed them to the angels and said,
 'Inform me of the qualities of these beings
 if you are sincere in telling the truth!' (31)
They said, 'Glory be to you! We have no knowledge
 except what you have taught.
Truly you are the wise One, the One who knows all things.' (32)
God said, 'O Adam, inform them of their names and qualities.'
And when Adam told them, God said, 'Didn't I tell you
 I know all that is hidden in the heavens and the earth
 And I know what you reveal and what you conceal?' (33)
Then we said to the angels, 'Bow down to Adam!'
 And they all fell in prostration, except Iblīs—he refused
 And puffed up with arrogance and was one who disavowed. (34)
And we said, 'O Adam, dwell in the garden, you and your partner
 Both of you eat of its abundance as you desire
 But do not either of you approach this tree
 Lest you be among the oppressive trangressors.' (35)
But then the tempter made them both slip from there
And expelled them from where they had previously been.
And we said, 'Get down all of you with enmity between yourselves
 In the world you have a dwelling place and livelihood
 to enjoy for a short time.' (36)
Then Adam received from his Lord words of inspiration
 And turned back to God in repentance
 For God is One ever-returning, a most merciful One. (36)
We said, 'Get down from there, all of you together!
 Then, when you receive guidance from me,
 Whoever follows my guidance will not fear or grieve. (38)
But those who disavow and treat our signs as a lie
 They are the companions of the fire, burning in it beyond time.' (39)

As for patient restraint, you should notice that God did not quickly punish Adam and Eve when they disobeyed. A patient and self-restrained person is one who does not rush to react to others' actions. Rather, such a person gives others respite, whether on the path of pardoning them and blessing them, or on the path of asserting authority over them and taking from them just recompense.

Secondly, God acquainted Adam and Eve with the divine quality of careful concealment. When they ate of the forbidden tree, they became aware of their nudity for the first time. When the noble clothing of paradise [which is intimacy with the divine presence] peeled away from them, God covered them with leaves, as revealed in Divine Speech. *They sewed together leaves from the garden to cover themselves.*[72] That is the first instance of divine concealing.

Thirdly, the true One desired to acquaint Adam with his quality of being specially selected. Two conditions are engendered by this special selection of Adam: his repentance toward God and his guidance from God. The true One desired to acquaint Adam with God's special selection of him [from among all of creation] and with God's careful concern which extends before him. Therefore, God destined Adam to eat of the forbidden tree. Then God did not turn away from Adam and reject him due to his disobedience, and did not cut the lifeline of giving and nurturing extended to him previously. Rather this treatment displayed to Adam the divine loving intimacy that surrounds him and cares for him. One Sufi coined the proverb, "Whoever has been cared for since the beginning will not be harmed by their own disobedience." Look around you! How many common loves have been severed by disobedience or antagonism! But true love flows from a lover who persists and stays with you whether you are in agreement or disagreement.

Listen carefully to this moment of Divine Speech, *Then Adam's Lord chose him specially.*[73] Some might think that the true One chose Adam only after he had eaten of the forbidden tree, but this is a misunderstanding. Rather, Adam was chosen even before he was brought into existence. What happened after Adam's disobedient action was the clear appearance of the effects of God's prior selection of Adam. This clear appearance is indicated in the Divine Speech, *then Adam's Lord chose him specially*, meaning that the effects of Adam's being chosen and cared for by God appeared clearly within his being. The appearance of Adam's selection is evident in the ease with which he turned in repentance toward God and accepted guidance from God.

God made clear Adam's selection, as reflected in this moment of Divine Speech, and thus Adam repented toward God and God granted him guidance. There are three interdependent elements here that you should recognize. The first is the human being's special selection. The second is repentance, which is the result of this divine selection and care. The third is guidance, which is the result of a person turning back to God in repentance. So ponder this sequence!

Thus Adam descended into the world. God allowed him to experience the subtleties of divine wisdom through this event, just as God allowed him to experience the dazzlingly brilliant clarity of divine power while he was in paradise. This is because the world is a place of intermediate means and cause-and-effect appearances [that veil the divine presence]. When Adam descended into this world, he learned the techniques of plowing and planting. He learned all the means of surviving and sustaining life. This was so that God might lead Adam to attain a more complete comprehension of all that he experienced and all he had been taught before he was lowered into the world. As God revealed in

Divine Speech, *The enemy causes you both to go out from paradise so that you bear heavy burdens.*[74] The intended meaning of the expression, *that you bear heavy burdens* (*fa-tashqa*) is the state of being exhausted by the work of this world of intermediate means (*zawāhir*). This is contrary to the fact that these words are commonly read to mean "that you suffer misery," which is the opposite of salvation during the final judgment. The proof of this crucial point is that Divine Speech recites, "that you [singular] bear heavy burdens" and not "that you both [dual] suffer misery." Divine Speech does not address both Adam and Eve in the dual address, but rather addresses Adam in the singular. This is because the daily toil and physical hardship of worldly means lies heavily on men and not on women. Another moment of Divine Speech alludes to this, *Men support and take care of women, by what God has given one more than the other.*[75] If the intent here had been "that you suffer misery," meaning that God severs relation with them or alienates them by an impermeable veil separating them from the divine presence, then God would have revealed, "that you both suffer misery." However, the actual address in the singular voice indicates that the intent is not that God damned both of them in expelling them from paradise and lowering them into the world to keep distance from them in an absolute separation.

But really, even if the Divine Speech addressed Adam and Eve in the dual pronoun, I would still take the expression to mean just what I have claimed. It is crucial to always hold God's intent in the best and most optimistic light. I would still interpret the revealed words to mean that we must bear heavy burdens in the realm of intermediate means, rather than that we are damned in misery.

THE SECRETS OF EDEN

Insight into Adam's situation can provide us with great spiritual benefits. In partaking of the forbidden tree, Adam did not willfully disobey God or contradict divine decrees. Rather, he was forgetful of the divine command and therefore began to eat from what had been forbidden to him. The command had slipped from Adam's remembrance and he was heedless when he ate, as others have pointed out. This is the meaning intended by Divine Speech, *We had contracted a pledge with Adam before, but he has forgotten, and we have not found on his part firm resolve.*[76] If Adam did eat of the tree while consciously remembering [the command of God forbidding him this], then he ate because the tempter misled him by whispering, *Your Lord has forbidden you both to eat from this tree so that you would not become angels or take your place among those who live eternally.* Adam might have eaten due to his love of God, love that filled him with devoted distraction. Adam loved whatever he imagined would lead him to abide in eternal intimacy with God and remain steadfast in the divine presence. He loved what he thought would lead him to become angelic, since Adam speculated on the lofty nature of angels and their close intimacy with God. So he longed to eat of the forbidden tree in order to acquire the status of angels, which is loftier and more intimate to God than the status of humanity. At least that is what Adam thought at the time!

There is a difference of opinion on this point between the scholars of religious texts and the seekers after experiential knowledge of God. Which enjoys a loftier status closer to God, the angels or the prophets? Adam thought that angels must be superior, based on the whispering of the tempter. Adam believed the temptations especially because the tempter said, as reported in Divine Speech, *And he swore to them that he was one who gives sincere advice.*[77] It was as if Adam said, "I never imagined that anyone could willfully contradict God with a deceitful oath!" And it came to pass just as this moment of Divine Speech concludes, *and they were misled and allowed themselves to be deceived.*

Before Adam ate of the forbidden tree, nothing that he had eaten had any negative side effects. Rather, everything he ate nourished him and spread an aroma as pleasant and wholesome as the fragrance of musk. This the case with all the blessed people who enter paradise after death, if they may enter. However, when Adam ate of the forbidden tree, it settled in his gut and weighed heavily there with all its waste. It is as if it were said to him, "O Adam, where will you go now, to a hidden place, or a covered place, or by the shore of a river? Go down into the world, for you can shit there." Just look at what became of the fruit of the forbidden tree! It was simply the instrument by which disobedience was enacted. How much more disgusting will become the one who actually performs an act of disobedience? Ponder this and understand!

A PARABLE
WHY CULTIVATE POISONOUS FRUIT?

Self-concern is like a tree. This particular tree is nourished by the moments when you assume ill of God and ascribe to God narrow motives. The fruits of this tree are separation and alienation from the divine presence. If you consider God's decrees in the best and most generous light possible, then the tree of self-concern that has taken root in your heart will wither away, due to its nourishment being cut off. The fruits of this tree are alienation from God because, whenever you concern yourself with securing your own well-being, you become satisfied with your own rational capacities to plan and manipulate the things of this world. You become content with your own schemes and fraudulently ascribe ownership of your existence to your own powers. This will result in your being transformed from your original nature, preventing you from receiving the subtle sustaining gifts that spring up from within.

A FORTUNATE FALL

Take this as a warning! You should see Adam's tree in each thing that God has forbidden you. You should realize that paradise is nothing but the intimate presence of God. It is said that Adam is your heart, while Eve is your ego.[78] From this perspective, understand this moment of Divine Speech: *Do not either of you approach this tree, or you will both be among the oppressive transgressors.*[79] However, Adam was surrounded and protected by divine care, such that when he ate of the tree, the consequence was that he descended into the world as God's vice-regent. But consider yourself, do you have any such protection? If you eat of the forbidden tree, you will descend into the world of separation and alienation from the divine presence.[80] Consider this deeply and understand.

If you eat of the forbidden tree, you will be expelled from the paradise of concord into a world of alienation. Your heart will be encumbered with burdens and wearied with toils. At the moment of alienation from God's presence, it is the heart that experiences ardor and weariness, not your ego. This is because the ego selfishly takes delight in sensual pleasures and greedily desires during the long sojourn of alienation in the world of separation from the divine presence. The ego is foolishly engrossed in its own heedless passions.

Let's review the sequence of events that led Adam into this world, to clarify their inner significance. First, God disclosed the divine presence to Adam by giving him existence; Adam came to know God through this and called out, "O decreeing One!" Then God gave knowledge of the divine to Adam through the desire that was for him alone; Adam came to know God through this and called out, "O desiring One!" Then God gave knowledge of the divine to Adam through divine commands deciding that approaching the tree was forbidden; Adam came to know God through this and called out, "O deciding One!" Then God gave knowledge of the divine to Adam through pronouncing judgment upon him for the trespass of his eating what was forbidden; Adam came to know God through this and called out, "O overpowering One!" Then God granted him respite instead of rushing to punish him; Adam came to know God through this and called out, "O forbearing One!" Then God refrained from revealing Adam's shame; Adam came to know God through this and called out, "O concealing One!" Then God extended to Adam repentance; Adam called out, "O forgiving One!" At this point, God made clear to Adam that his disobedience did not sever divine love for him; Adam called out, "O loving One!" Then God caused Adam to descend into the world and lightened for him the toilsome means of survival; Adam called out in acknowledgement, "O subtle One!" Then God strengthened Adam to do what was required of him in the world; Adam called out in response, "O supporting One!" Then God revealed to Adam the subtle truth concealed in his eating and forbidding and

115

descending; Adam called out in recognition, "O wise One!" Then God reinforced Adam against the tempting enemy's deceptive snares; Adam called out in relief, "O vanquishing One!" Then God let Adam find felicity in the trials of carrying out his weighty duties; Adam called out, "O helping One!"

Thus God lowered Adam into this world solely to complete for him his experiential knowledge of all the divine names in their comprehensiveness, to make him bear up straight and tall under the burden of his obligations. In Adam, God completed two facets of worshipful humanity: worship in acknowledging the divine presence through intimate knowledge (*ᶜubūdīyat al-taᶜrīf*), and worship in fulfilling obligations and necessary actions (*ᶜubūdīyat al-taklīf*). Through this sequence of events, God greatly enhanced the constant, subtle blessings for Adam and intensified the wholesome divine presence that is with him. Ponder all these facets deeply and understand.

THE STATE OF SERVANTHOOD

The most sublime status that we can aspire to achieve is the status of "humanity worshipfully serving the divine" (*maqām al-ᶜubūdīya*). All other states [that mystics describe as stages on the path] are nothing but service in attaining this absolute state of complete humanity. The proof that clearly shows the nobility of the state of worshipful servitude is this moment of Divine Speech, *Praise be to the One whose servant was taken for a journey by night.*[81] Servants are mentioned again: *What we have sent down to our servant,* and *This is a reminder of the mercy of your Lord to God's servant, Zakariya.*[82] Still further, Divine Speech says, *Yet when the servant of God undertakes to pray to God, they begin to oppress him in a thick crowd.*[83]

116

When the Prophet Muhammad was selected for bearing the message, he faced the choice between being a prophet who is a ruler or being a prophet who is a servant. He chose servanthood to God. That is the most decisive proof that servanthood is the supreme station of spiritual cultivation and the greatest position of intimacy. The Prophet has said, "I am a servant. I don't consume luxuriously. As a servant to God, I eat what servants and slaves eat." At the same time, the Prophet said, "I am the leader (*sayyid*) of the children of Adam—I say this without boasting." My master, Shaykh al-Mursi, explained that the Prophet never boasted of being a leader but rather took pride in being a servant of God. For this very reason, humans were created and given existence, as revealed in Divine Speech: *I created humans and jinn solely that they serve in worship.* Worship (*ʿibāda*) is the outer form of being a true servant (*ʿubūdīya*), while being a servant is the true spirit of worship. If you understand this, then consider that if servanthood is the spirit of worship, then the inner force (*sirr*) that animates its spirit is leaving aside personal choice and desisting from resisting destiny's decrees. Being a servant means avoiding selfish calculation and personal choice despite God's lordship. Since servanthood, the most noble of spiritual states, does not come to completion without desisting from plotting and planning, then the servant must leave planning to God and stay resigned, handing back the reins of control to God. In this way alone does the servant seek to reach that most complete and holistic state, that most excellent model of being.

Ponder this story. Once the Prophet Muhammad walked by Abu Bakr and ʿUmar while they were in worship. He heard Abū Bakr recite the Qurʾan in a hushed voice while nearby ʿUmar was reciting in a strong voice.[84] The Prophet asked Abu Bakr, "Why have you lowered your voice?" He

answered, "I'm reciting for those who have taken refuge
with you for salvation."[85] The Prophet turned to ᶜUmar and
asked, "Why have you raised your voice?" He answered,
"I'm waking up the sleeper and driving off the tempter."
The Prophet said, "Abu Bakr, raise your voice a little…and
ᶜUmar, lower your voice a little." Shaykh al-Mursi explained
that by giving this gentle command, the Prophet sought to
remove each of his companions from his own desire for
himself in deference to the Prophet's stated desire for
them.[86]

If you listen carefully to what the Prophet is saying in
this story, you will learn that being removed from one's
own desire is the highest form of worship. Both Abu Bakr
and ᶜUmar deferred to him when the Prophet asked them
about the intent underlying their behavior in worship. Despite the fact that the Prophet accepted their answers as valid,
he removed them from the mode of worship that they chose
for themselves. Despite the soundness of their intention,
they were asked to adopt what the Prophet chose for them.

WHY WANDER IN THE DESERT?

Ponder another story. When the tribes of Israel were wandering through the Sinai desert, they were given the provision of "mana and salwa."[87] God chose this subtle and refined provision for them and gave it to them freely. God
gave this to the tribes directly, as a gift, without their toil or
labor. However, their coarse lower souls urged them to revert to their accustomed habit. They were overwhelmed and
prevented from bearing witness to God's planning and caring for them. They reverted to desiring the food to which
they were accustomed. They said [to Moses]: *Pray to your
Lord for us, to bring forth what grows from the earth like*

leafy greens, cucumbers, beans, lentils and onions. He said, 'Will you all exchange what is better for what is lesser? Go back down to Egypt! There you will get that for which you ask. They were struck with abjection and poverty and were afflicted with the anger of God. This affliction came over the tribes of Israel because they rejected what God chose for them that suited their condition in favor of what they chose for themselves. Therefore, they were told in a tone of reprimand *will you all exchange what is better for what is lesser? Go back down to Egypt!*

In an outer dimension, this revelation tells of exchanging "mana and salwa" for routine food like beans, lentils and onions. Mana and salwa were types of food that were incomparably delicious and easy to acquire and prepare. In a secret inner dimension, this revelation also tells of exchanging your own personal desires in place of what God desires for you. Will you exchange that which is better for you—that which God desires for you—for what is lesser—that which you desire for yourselves? Go back down to Egypt then! That which you crave for yourselves is suitable only to an agriculturally rich urban metropolis like Egypt. There is a secret inner dimension to the revelation *go back down.* It is as if God were saying, 'Get down from the heaven of resignation to the wholesome care of what we plan, provide and choose for you. Go down to the earth of choosing and planning for yourselves; be lowly and abject since you have chosen for yourselves despite God's caring for you and planning for you.'

The tribes of Israel failed this test, even though they were a community wandering in the desert when they said these words. They were a community humbled and vulnerable, worn transparent so that the light shone through them and their secrets were revealed. See how the tribes of Israel

119

were in the beginning. They caused their exile of wandering in the desert by saying to their Prophet, Moses, *Why don't you and your Lord go ahead and fight together! As for us, here we sit!*[88] See how the tribes of Israel were at the end, when they said to Moses, *Pray to your Lord for us, to bring forth what grows from the earth.* In the beginning they refused to obey the command of God, and in the end they chose for themselves by rejecting what God had chosen for them. There are so many episodes in which they repeat these errors in different ways. This demonstrates their alienation from the true One and their divergence from the sincere path. Remember how they said to Moses, *Show us God for our eyes to see!*[89] And what did they say after that? The moisture had not yet dried from their feet after crossing the parted sea when they began to argue among themselves as they passed through a nation that clung to their idols. The tribes of Israel asked Moses to make for them an idol like the gods that others have. Weren't they just like Moses described them*? He said, 'You are a people who are willfully ignorant'!* Divine Speech relates, *Recall when we shook the mountain over them [the tribes of Israel] as if it were a canopy overhead and they feared it was about to collapse upon them. Take what we [message] have give you and hold it firmly!*[90]

In contrast, consider members of this [Muslim] community. Over their hearts shook the mountains of awe and terror at the might of God. They took firm hold of the message (*kitāb*) with strong faith; for this they became firmly established as a people and received divine aid and confirmation. They were preserved against worshipping the golden calf and other spiritual pitfalls. This is because God selected this community and chose for them what was best for them. God praised them by saying, *You are the best community whom I brought forth for the people* and, *Like this we have made you a community of moderation and balance.* This praise means that the Muslim community consists of people who are just and do good.

Section Four: The Miracle of Desisting from Selfish Calculation

This contrast should make clear to you that selfish calculation and willful choosing are the worst sins and the heaviest burden for which we are held accountable. So if you desire that God's choice be for you, let go of your own presumption to choose. If you desire to be well cared for, never place your own self-concern in competition with God. If you desire to reach the highest goal, you must have no desire other than God's desire for you. When Abū Yazīd al-Bisṭāmī [Bāyazīd] was asked, "What do you want?" he answered, " want not to want!" The only thing he ever requested from God or hoped to receive was that he be able to let go of his power of desire and will in deference to God. He knew that this is the noblest miracle (*karāma*) and the greatest means of achieving intimacy with God.[91]

It is crucial to remember this, because miracles are a tricky matter. It is possible that someone be selected as a conduit for miracles while still retaining the hidden power to selfishly calculate and plot! The two could coexist in a single person. Therefore, the truest and most complete miracle is leaving aside self-concern and calculation in competition with God, while passing back your cares to the care of God's decrees. In explaining this subtle reality, Shaykh al-Shadhili has taught, "Indeed, there are only two comprehensive miracles. There is the miracle of faith for increasing awareness and awe-filled witness. Then there is the miracle of action that emulates the Prophet and follows his example to avoid false claims, pretenses and deceptions. If one is given these two miracles and then proceeds to desire anything else beyond them, that person has fallen into deceitful lying or has erred in true knowledge and right action. Such a person is like one honored by a king in public with a statement that he has earned the king's satisfaction, and then desires to meddle in politics and foments discontent to the point of rebellion. The performer of any miracle that is not accompanied by contentment from God and contentment with God is one misled, lured into temptation, deceived by the ego, still spiritually incomplete or completely defunct and sunk in sin. " From this teaching, learn that a miracle is not really miraculous unless it brings contentment with regard to God. The criterion for such contentment is leaving aside self-concern in competition with God and letting go of self-direction before God.

Some people point out that, when Abū Yazīd [Bistami] wanted only "not to want," he was still wanting! Those who say this have not truly experienced intimate knowledge of the divine. This is because Abū Yazīd, when he wanted not to want, was actually wanting what God chose for him and for all people—that is not asserting their willful wants in contradiction to God. His wanting not to want was actually in concord with God's will for him [rather than an assertion of his own personal volition]. To express this idea, Shaykh al-Shadhili has said, "You have no share of self-will in performing any of the actions and evaluations that constitute the religious law (*shar*ᶜ). In such matters, you just listen and obey. This is understanding the Lord's intent and receiving knowledge directly from God's presence; it is the ground on which descends true knowledge derived from God, for those who are well-balanced and mature."

With this teaching, Shaykh al-Shadhili means that those who willfully choose to enact what is espoused in law and ritual make a choice that does not contradict the state of servanthood that is established on the principle of leaving aside personal choice. This is so that the limited power of reasoning would not be misled from perceiving the truth. Our reason might speculate that reciting litanies, meditation exercises, devotional activities that are established in the Prophet Muhammad's example (*sunna*), and acting according to the sacred law are all acts that take one beyond the clear bounds of servanthood, because one chooses to do them. For this reason, Shaykh al-Shadhili has clarified that "you have no share of self-will" in choosing to follow religious law and the code of behaviors it lays out. You are commanded to leave your concern for yourself and your choice for your own benefit, not to leave aside what God and the Prophet have arranged for your own care. So ponder this matter fully!

Now you can understand that Abū Yazīd wanted not to want only because God wanted that from him; therefore he did not trespass beyond the bounds of worshipful servanthood that was demanded of him. From here, you must understand that the path by which you can arrive in God's presence is truly obliterating all selfish desire and refusing all self-will. So crucial is this that Shaykh al-Shadhili has said, "God's friends (*awliyāʾ*) will never reach God while there remains with them a single self-concern or a single self-will." I heard Shaykh al-Mursi teach that, "The servant will never reach God until he becomes separated from the visceral desire to reach God." By this he intended,

123

and God only knows the truth, that separation from this desire comes from proper humility, rather than from boredom or self-satisfaction. When servants approach closer and closer to God's presence, they witness that they do not deserve such closeness and perceive their own despicable lowiness, and consequently think it impossible to experience the joys that reside in that closeness. So the self-assertive and visceral desire to reach God drops away from them, out of humility rather than out of boredom, self-satisfaction or distraction from God by anything other than God. So if you desire enlightenment and illumination, just drop your self-centered rumination.

A Parable
Don't Hide in the Shadow

People who plan for themselves despite God are like shadows extending across the ground before the sun has reached its zenith. When the sun rises high in the sky, the shadow is obliterated, until there remains of it only the slightest trace that cannot be erased by direct encounter with the sun. By analogy, the sun of mystical intuition acts just like this. When human hearts confront it directly, all trace of selfish plotting is effaced from them, except for the minimal trace of activity that obedient servant must possess in order to carry out their responsibilities.

Set off on the path of those before you, who made the journey toward God. Perceive what they perceived, travel in their footsteps, adopt their methods and imitate their ways. So throw down your staff, for this is the sacred valley and the divine presence is at hand![92]

To encourage you, I present a poem expressing these thoughts that I composed for some of my companions when I was just starting out.

> The caravan's called and is heading off,
>   swiftly moving
> And here we're still sitting?
>   What you do think you're doing?
>
> Are you content to remain stranded behind
>   once they've gone
> With your hopes fallen, infatuated
>   with stubborn resisting?
>
> Listen to the voice of the cosmos
>   announcing clearly
> That all created things are alienated
>   by simply existing
>
> And that none will see the true path
>   other than those
> Who head straight toward the Other
>   undeceived by desiring
>
> Those who have insight in all things
>   see the true One before them
> And fade away, becoming deeds of the One
>   who alone is doing
>
> Who illumines those who head off
>   to travel beyond
> And manifests spiritual secrets
>   in those who are returning

So get up and look at things in the light
　　that gives them reality
For near you today rises the dawn
　　of intimate approaching

So be a true servant, pass back the reins
　　to divine command
Be wary of your self-concern,
　　whom is it really benefiting?

Will you rely on plots and plans
　　while another actually decides?
Dare you struggle against
　　what the divine is decreeing?

Obliterating all desire
　　and all trace of self-will
This is the real legitimate goal,
　　but are you listening?

In this way those before you
　　have taken off, so search
For their traces, making the path easier
　　for those who are following

Let the one who searches for them weep
　　for his own sake
As he sees a glimmer of the luster of those
　　who've lived life loving

Let the one who's been weeping weep
　　for his own sake
For he's wasting time
　　and the moment is swiftly passing!

THE EXAMPLE OF GOD'S FRIENDS

You must know, and may God bring you into accord with divine will, that God has servants from among the people who have passed beyond self-concern. They pass beyond by humble virtues that God has cultivated in them and through teachings that God has brought to their awareness. These illuminations derail all the resolutions of their self-concerned planning. The intimate knowledge they possess and the secrets that are revealed to them demolish the obstinate mountains of their self-direction. They abide in the resting-place of contentment and discover the most blessed repose. They have turned to God alone for succor and called out to God for help, frightened that they might become distracted by the sweet taste of contentment. They fear to let themselves cling to even that spiritual sweetness or to turn to it as a support.

Shaykh al-Shadhili has expressed this in the story of his youth.[93] "When I was still young, I used to be concerned and anxious about what to do in the way of worshipful duties and types of obedience. Sometimes I would say to myself that I need to go out alone into the open countryside and trackless wastes. At other times I would feel the need to return to towns and their populations in order to sit with the learned and the pious. In the midst of these vacillations, one of God's friends was described to me, who lived in Morocco at a particular mountain. I decided to go there to meet him. One night I reached that place, but hesitated to enter his dwelling and disturb him. At that moment, I heard him saying, 'O God, there are people who ask that you subjugate other people to their will—you grant them this request and they are content with you for this. O God, but I ask you to divert other people away from ceding to my will,

127

so that I find no refuge except in you!' Having overheard this prayer, I said to myself, "Into what a sea has this Shaykh plunged so deeply!' I stood there amazed outside his door until morning, and then entered to see him. I greeted him and said, 'Sir, how are you?' He said, 'I am complaining to God of the coolness of contentment and acceptance, just like you complain of the heat of anxious self-concern and self-direction!' So I replied, 'Sir, I know the taste of complaint about the heat of self-concern and direction and know them well, since I'm currently struggling with them. But as for the coolness of contentment and acceptance, I don't understand that at all.' He answered, 'The sweetness of contentment and acceptance distracts one from God.' So I said to him, 'Sir, I overheard you last night saying " O God, there are people who ask you to subjugate other people to their will—you grant them this request and they are content with you for this. O God, but I ask you to divert other people away from ceding to my will, so that I find no refuge except in you!"' He smiled and said, 'My son, repeat what you have just said, but change the wording. Instead of "Make other people submit to me," say "O Lord, be with me." Look, if other people were with you, would they be able to give you what you need? To think that is such cowardice!'"

Why Noah's Son Perished

Take the example of the son of Noah (*Nūḥ*). He was destroyed precisely because he returned to look after his own concerns and was dissatisfied with God's chosen way of caring for Noah and all those who were with him in the arc. Divine Speech relates that Noah said to him, *'My son, embark with us and do not be with the rejecters.' He said, 'I*

128

will take refuge on the mountain that will protect me from the rising water.' Noah said, 'There is no protector today from the command of God, except by divine mercy.[94] In a more lofty spiritual sense, we can see that Noah's son sought refuge in his own power of reason. The mountain that he sought out for protection is the outward form, standing metaphorically for this higher meaning.

It came to pass as Divine Speech describes: *A wave reared up between Noah and his son, and he was one of the drowned.*[95] In outward form, Noah's son sank beneath the raging waves of the storm (*ṭūfān*), while in inward meaning, he sank into alienation and separation (*ḥirmān*). So draw a lesson from this disaster, my fellow servant! When the waves of divine decrees rise in tumult over your head, do not flee to the mountain of your own reason. It will surely collapse and dissolve, leaving you to be *one of the drowned* in the raging sea of alienation. Rather, run toward the arc of seeking protection with God and entrusting to God your affairs. *Whoever turns to God for protection, God guides to a straight and level path.* And also, *Whoever entrusts to God every concern, God is their reward.*[96] If you do this, you will surely find an arc built for you that will deliver you to safety. Then you will disembark, stepping down with intimate closeness granted to you, with blessings arriving upon you and all those who are with you. Those who are with you are the many worlds of your existence, the dimensions within you and the dimensions beyond you. So understand this lesson, and do not be among the heedless ones.

Worship your Lord and do not be from among the willfully ignorant ones.

A PARABLE

THE STRAYING SERVANT

A person who is concerned for himself is like a servant whose master has dispatched him on a mission. The master has sent him to some land that the master owns in order to procure some cloth there for him. When the servant arrives in that place, he begins to say to himself, "Where will I reside? Whom will I marry?" He gets preoccupied with these questions, expending all his energy on anxiety about these concerns, until he is delinquent in executing the commands for which his master had sent him. When his master calls on him, his reward from the master will be that the master cuts him off and separates himself from the servant, since he was totally preoccupied by his own affairs rather than observing the prerogatives and rights of his master.

So it is with you, my fellow believer. The true One has dispatched you to this world and commanded you to serve in it faithfully, and has undertaken to support and sustain your existence contingent on your service. If you become engrossed in worrying about your own concerns for yourself and neglect the rights held over you by your master, then you have turned aside from the path of right guidance and slid down the low road to ruin.

Another Parable
Tale of Two Servants

The contrast between a person who is preoccupied with himself and another who refuses to fall into anxious preoccupation is illustrated by the parable of two servants to the king. The first servant is busy carrying out his master's orders without turning aside to concern himself with what he will wear or what he will eat. Rather, he is completely engaged in the service of his Lord. This makes him heedless of wasting time trying to secure his own wants and needs, which he deems unimportant. The behavior of the second servant is different. No matter what the master requests him to do, he finds the servant busily engaged in washing his own clothes, finding means for his own transportation and adorning his own appearance.

Don't you think that the first servant is more deserving of his master's beneficence and acceptance, when compared to the second servant who is preoccupied with his selfish impulses and acquisitive desires to the point of neglecting the rights of his master? Since when was a servant purchased to serve himself rather than his master?

So it is that you always see an insightful servant busy with carrying out the rightful prerogatives of his master and carefully observing his commands. This distracts him from his selfish impulses and keeps him from giving them any value at all. When a servant is like this, the true One undertakes to support him in every detail and secure for him his every concern and turn to him with generous gifts. This is because the servant sincerely relies on his master. *Whoever totally entrusts God in all affairs has God alone as his recompense.*[97] Can you say the same for the negligent servant? You always find him struggling to collect worldly means to attain his needs and coveting the things through which to satisfy his selfish desires. He stands on the foundation of his own plotting and planning for himself by himself. He fraudulently ascribes to himself ownership of his self and is therefore cut off from beautiful trust in another and sincere reliance upon another.

Desisting from selfish calculation and choosing your own direction is the most crucial thing. Those with certain faith take it upon themselves as a duty, and those who are worshipful servants seek after it. This is the noblest adornment of those with intimate experiential knowledge. I was once at the Ka'ba with a Sufi master. I asked him, "Which way will you take when you return [after the pilgrimage]?" He replied, "It is my custom with God that my own volition does not out-step my footstep." One of the great Sufi masters has said, "When God ushers the saved people into the garden and ushers damned into the fire, if I am left to choose for myself where I would like to reside, I would have no preference of my own."

This is the spiritual condition of the worshipful servants, whose every preference or willful desire is obliterated. There remains in them no desire except what God desires. One of the early followers of the Prophet (*salaf*) has said, "I have been transformed to such an extent that my craving has become reduced to only what is actualized by the decree of God." The Sufi, Abū al-Ḥafṣ al-Ḥadād, once said, "Since forty years I've been in this state: each time God has settled me in a condition, I have never loathed it, and each time God has transported me into a new condition, I have never belittled it."[98] In a similar vein, another Sufi has said, "For forty years, I have desired not to desire, so that I might leave aside all I desire. But I have still not found what I desired all along!"

God has taken charge of protecting and guarding the hearts of people like these. Haven't you heard Divine Speech declare [to the tempter], *Surely you have no authority over my servants.*[99] This is because they have realized in themselves the station of worshipful servanthood, which forbids them self-direction in deference to divine lordship. It arouses in them disgust when they regard willful wrong-doing or proximity to blame-worthy actions. Divine Speech says, *Surely that one (Iblīs, the tempter) has no authority over those who sincerely believe and in their Lord completely trust.*[100] How could selfish calculation's whispering urge affect those hearts over which the tempter, Iblīs, has no authority? How could any gross obscurity cover over the radiance of their hearts?

This moment of Divine Speech makes clear that the tempter exerts no authority over those who keep their faith in God firm and make their trust in God sound. This is because the tempter gets close to people in only two ways: the tempter could raise doubts in your belief or could induce you to lean on other people and rely on them in your need. As for raising doubts in your heart, firm faith negates

133

this vulnerability. As for leaning on others and relying on them, entrusting to God all your concerns deflates this possibility.

A Brush with Stray Thoughts

Not everyone achieves this condition completely, and believers might meet with stray thoughts about plotting and planning for themselves (*khawāṭir al-tadbīr*). You must know that God does not prompt such thoughts. God will never abandon believers to suffer their consequences without aid. Have you not heard Divine Speech assure, *God is the care-taker of those who believe, leading them from obscuring darkness into clarifying light.*[101] The true One draws believers from the obscuring darkness of clinging to self-concern, and leads them into the illuminating light of handing over all concern to a higher authority. The truth of God's veracity is hurled against their vain and baseless anxieties. The foundations of their planning is shaken and the edifices they build come tumbling down—*the truth is hurled against falsehood and falsehood is completely obliterated.*[102]

Therefore if some stray worry or anxiety about self-concern should occur to believers, they should remember that these are just passing events with no foothold through which they might settle in. They vanish with no reality or effect. Because the light of faith abides steadfastly in the hearts of believers, its illumination causes them to be servants. Its brilliance fills their hearts and its luminosity opens wide their chests. The faith abiding in their hearts prevents believers from relying on anything other than God. If stray thoughts do occur, this is just the residue of a habit of the heart, making it vulnerable to receiving the spectral fantasy that one is able to plot and achieve one's own course (*ṭayf*

134

al-tadbīr). When the heart awakens, the dream vision dissolves, for it can only seem real during sleep.

Divine Speech says, *When those who stay warily conscious of God are brushed by a circling lure from the tempter, they recollect—just thus they are aware with insight.*[103] There are many points of spiritual guidance for you to realize in this moment of Divine Speech. It shows us that the first principle of the believers is that God assures them their safety and security. The appearance of circling lures of temptation is only an epiphenomenon that comes and goes. Lures brush the believers from time to time, so that they might come to better know the security of faith with which God has endowed them.

Divine Speech describes the advent of these temptations by saying, W*hen those who stay warily conscious of God are brushed.* It does not say "when they are grabbed" or "when they are seized." Being brushed means being touched lightly, tantalizingly, with a touch that does not exert power or mastery. This expression means that the circling forces of passion and selfish desire exert no firm power over the hearts of believers who stay warily conscious of God. These forces only brush them lightly with an influencing caress, rather than seizing them as they do with those who disavow true belief. The tempter overpowers and takes possession of disbelievers. In contrast, the tempter tries to steal from believers' hearts by stealthy, subtle maneuvers that might lure to sleep their powers of reason and discernment, which keep vigilant watch over their hearts. However, when believers are roused into wakeful awareness, the protecting forces of seeking forgiveness, acting humbly and acknowledging one's utter dependence on God are sent forth from the repository of their hearts. They sally forth and reclaim from the tempter what had been pilfered by stealth, taking back that upon which the tempter had pounced.

Believers *are brushed by a circling lure from the tempter.* The expression *circling* (*ṭāʾif*) reveals that the tempter does not have the ability to directly approach hearts that are awake and aware. The circling forces of heedlessness and selfish desire close in around hearts when they are drowsing in distraction. Those circling lures never close in around hearts that never sleep. Pay close attention to the phrase, *a circling lure from the tempter.* Divine Speech does not say, "When they are brushed by the approach of the tempter" or anything direct like that. This is because these circling lures have no real force or existence to them. They are only images that incite the imagination. They have no true basis in reality. For this reason, God informs us that these circling lures are actually harmless to those who stay constantly aware of the divine presence. What the tempter dispatches to spin around their hearts is like a spectral dream image. You perceive it while sleeping, but when you wake up, it is scattered with no substance to it at all.

Listen again. When they *are brushed by a circling lure from the tempter, they recollect* (*tadhakkarū*). Divine Speech does not say, "They remember (*dhakirū*)." This is to point out that simply remembering [God or God's qualities] is not enough to dispel heedlessness, if the heart is still distracted. Heedlessness is only driven away by active recollection (*tadhakkur*) and contemplative regard (*iʿtibār*). This expression does not refer to recalling the names of God (*dhikr*), because this is the provenance of the tongue. Recollection is the provenance of the heart.[104] When the circling lures of temptation appear, they close around the heart, not the tongue! That which can dispel them is recollection that dwells in the place that they assault—the heart. Only this effaces the effects of their temptation.

When Divine Speech says that *they recollect,* it does not specify what exactly they recollect. It has not said that they recollect "paradise," recollect "hell-fire," recollect "punishments" or anything of that sort. The omission of the object of what *they recollect* conveys a great benefit! We realize that the act of recollection effaces temptation's circling lures from the hearts of those conscious of God. Omission of its object alerts us to the fact that the act of recollection can vary according to the level of certainty and the level of awe-filled consciousness attained by the different Messengers, Prophets, Saints, sincere ones, righteous ones and common Muslims. Each one recollects an object in accord with their spiritual station (*maqām*).[105] Had Divine Speech specified one from the many types of object of recollection, it would have excluded the people who recollect other types of objects! Had it said, "when they are brushed by a circling lure from the tempter, they recollect the punishments of rebellion—just thus they are aware with insight," this would exclude those who recollect the rewards of accord. If it had said, "they recollect the benevolence of God in all that has preceded," this specificity would exclude those who recollect God's generous bestowal in all that will follow. So it is with all the levels of certainty and their appropriate objects of recollection. For this reason, the true One desires to elicit a specific object of recollection, in order to include them each. So ponder this fully!

When they *are brushed by a circling lure from the tempter, they recollect—just thus they are aware with insight.* Divine Speech does not say, 'They recollect, and consequently see with insight' or 'they recollected and then see with insight.' It does not fix the expression with the conjunction "and" since this would not adequately express how insight results from recollection—it would only express coexistence rather than causation. God intended to mean that insight is caused by recollection, so that people might be encouraged to recollect. The expression is not fixed with "then" either, for it, like the conjunction "and," would not expresses causation. "Then" expresses only chronological sequence: that one thing follows another thing after an interval of time. The true One's intent is to show that these people's insight does not come after their recollection. Similarly it does not simply say "thus," since this implies that one follows the other. Rather, the true One expressed the intended meaning with, *they recollect—just thus they are aware with insight,* as if they had never been without such insight. With this precise phrasing, God lauds them and shows the plentitude of subtle gifts granted to their innermost being.

The situation is just as you might say [of a student], 'He recollected the answer to a problem—just thus the answer is true." Your saying this means that the answer has always been true, just as it is true right now when it occurs to his mind. Thus those who stay conscious of God never cease to be aware with insight, even though at times, when circling lures may close in around them, their insight might be obscured. Yet still, its illumination shines within them, and is firmly established. When they awaken, the murky clouds of heedless distraction scatter and the sun of insight spreads its clear illumination.

In this moment of Divine Speech you may detect an expression of reprieve for those who stay warily conscious of God. It expresses a subtle kindness to those who submit to divine will. If Divine Speech had said, 'Those who stay conscious of God are those not brushed by circling lures of

138

the tempter,' this would exclude all except those whom God preserves as faultless (*ahl al-ʿisma*). However, God desired to expand the circumference of divine mercy and thus said, '*When those who stay warily conscious of God are brushed by a circling lure from the tempter*. This is to inform you that the descent of circling lures does not exclude them from the firmness of the effect of being steadfastly conscious of God. Even in this vulnerable condition of being tempted, the term "conscious" is aptly applied to them, if they are as Divine Speech describes: quick to recollect and return to God with clear insight.

This is just like another moment of Divine Speech which also unfurls the high hopes of God's servants and expands the scope of respite given to them. *Surely God loves those who return through penitence and loves those who keep pure*.[106] Notice that it does not say, 'God loves those who do not transgress." If it had said that, only a very few people would come under its power. Therefore, the true One acknowledges how people are engaged in heedless distraction and how weak they are under the demands of their original human nature (*al-nashʾat al-ūlā al-insānīya*) that sprang into existence through gametes of rebelliousness (*amshāj min nawʿ al-mukhālifa*). For Divine Speech has declared that *God desires to lighten your burdens and created the human being weak*.[107] Some scholars hold that *to lighten your burdens* means that God restrains people from engaging in selfish desires (*shahwa*). Likewise, Divine Speech tells us that *God knows you well, since God formed you from the earth and since you were sheltered in the womb*.[108] Since God knows well that human nature preponderates toward erring, God opens for us the door of repentance (*bāb al-tawba*). God points out this door, inviting us to enter through it and promising us acceptance if we repent. God

139

turns to us with intimate regard if we return to God with yearning.

The Prophet Muhammad has said, "Every human being errs, and the best of those who err are those who are repentant." The Prophet teaches you that erring is necessary to your being. Indeed, committing errors is the very essence of your being (*ᶜayn wujūdika*)! Divine Speech reminds us, *Those who, when they act shamefully or wrong themselves, recall God and ask forgiveness for their transgressions—and who forgives transgressions except God?—and do not persist in what they have committed, they are the ones who know.*[109] Notice how Divine Speech does not say, 'Those who do not know shameful acts.' It is like the moment when Divine Speech says, *Those who, when they have become angry, forgive* and doesn't say 'those who do not become angry.'[110] Divine Speech says, *Those who suppress their wrath*, rather than saying 'Those who do not experience wrath.'[111] Understand the reasons for this, may God be compassionate with you! These are secrets made abundantly clear and matters obligatory for those whose lapse would cost them dear.

Let me give you an explication of the levels of recollection actualized by those people who are warily conscious of God. When the circling lures of the tempter brush the people of constant wariness, they are not prevailed upon to persist in rebelliousness against their Lord. This is due to their constant wariness. Rather, their act of recollection returns them to God, the One who protects them. This act of recollection could be of various types. Some concentrate on recollecting divine rewards, others on recollecting divine punishments or standing alone to be called to account. Some concentrate on recollecting all the rewards for desisting from selfish rebellion, while others concentrate on recollecting the wholesome care that has preceded them and thus are ashamed to act rebelliously. Some concentrate on recollecting God's worthy acts of freely giving and thus are ashamed to return the favor with denial and disavowal. Some recollect their intimacy with God, while others recollect the vast scope of the true One surrounding all things. Some recollect the gaze of the true One that always eyes them, while others recollect the covenant with God that always ties them. Some recollect the ephemeral fading away of their sensual delights, while others recollect eternal abiding of God's reclaiming divine rights. Some recollect the evil consequences of opposition and its meanness and thus desist from it, while others recollect the beneficial gains of accord and its worth and thus seek after it. Some recollect the true One's everlasting wellspring providing for them until eternity, while others recollect the true One's elevated might and lofty authority. There are so many levels of recollection! They are in fact innumerable. I have only recounted here a few of them, in order to familiarize you with the varying states of those who keep warily conscious of God. There are so many levels to those who perceive with true insight.

THE FORTRESS OF RECOLLECTION

Divine Speech tells us, *When those who stay warily conscious of God are brushed by a circling lure from the tempter, they recollect—just thus they are aware with insight.* It is possible that the intended meaning of circling lure (*ṭayf*) is a sudden urge or impulse (*ṭāʾif al-ḥājis*). This is like a stray thought that comes to mind unbidden, arising from the natural existence of the self and thrown into motion by the tempter. Such a stray thought, conjured up by the tempter

141

from within the self, is called "a circling lure" because it wanders in circles around the heart. One expert in Qur°anic recitation claims that phrasing should be that they are brushed by a circling force from the tempter [reading *ṭāʾif* instead of *ṭayf*]. Each of these two alternate readings helps to clarify the other. We can understand this lure as a stray thought or spectral image that circles around the heart with a certain force. If it finds an entry through a breach in the walls of the abode of faithful certainty, then it enters the heart. However, if it can find no breach, it dissipates and disappears. The abode of certainty (*maqām al-yaqīn*) and the light that is its foundation can be imagined as the high walls that surround a town and the fortress that protects it. The walls are the illuminating light that surrounds the city of the heart, while upon the walls rise the fortress that defends it, which is the level of certainty.

Some people surround their hearts with walls of light like an impregnable fortress. If they build walls of certainty and keep every level of it sound and fit, then there will be no entry for the tempter to approach them and no resting place for the tempter in their town. Have you not listened to Divine Speech [tell the tempter], *Surely you have no authority over my servants.*[112] It is as if it were saying, 'Because they have actualized the state of servanthood before me and kept it sound, they do not rebel against my commands or oppose my arrangement of their every affair. Rather they entrust me with all their concerns and resign themselves to my care.' Because of this, the true One undertakes to guard them, lending them aid and protection. In turn they channel all their anxieties toward God, and God suffices them from heeding anything or anyone other than God. Once someone said to one who had intimate experiential knowledge, "How is it going with your struggles with the tempter?" He replied, "What tempter? We are a people who have expended all our anxieties and concerns in God, and that spares us from worrying about anything other than God." I heard my master, Shaykh al-Mursi, teach that, "When the true One revealed, *The tempter is an enemy to you, so take him as an enemy*, some people understood this to mean that they should become the enemy of the tempter.[113] So they expended all their efforts and concerns in opposing the tempter, to such an extent that this distracted them from loving the beloved One. However, other people understood this address to them that the tempter is an enemy to them. This implied to them that God is a lover to them. So they were engrossed with the love of God, to such an extent that this spared them from concern about anything other than God." Furthermore, Shaykh al-Mursi told us, "When these people say 'I seek refuge with God from the accursed tempter (*al-shaytān al-rajīm*)", they say it for the sake of God's having ordered them to say it, not because their hearts bear witness that there is any command besides the command of God." How could they bear witness to any who commands in competition with God and be listening to Divine Speech saying, *The power to command is with nobody except God, who ordered that you worship nothing but God* and *The snare of the tempter is feeble*.[114] This resonates with other moments like, *Surely that one (Iblīs, the tempter) has no authority over those who sincerely believe and in their Lord completely trust*. And also, *For those who entrust to God their affairs, God is sufficient*, and also *God is the care-taker of those who believe, leading them from obscuring darkness into clarifying light*.[115] Indeed, the true One has declared, *It is right for us and incumbent upon us to aid the believers*.[116] These moments of Divine Speech, and others like them, offer en-

143

couragement to nourish the hearts of believers. God aids them to vanquish all otherness. If they say, 'I seek refuge with God from the accursed tempter," it is only because God ordered them to do so. If they wrest control from the tempter, it is only because God aids them with the light of certainty to vanquish all otherness. If they are safe from the snares that the tempter lays, it is only because God extended to them support and benevolence. Shaykh al-Shadhili has said, "During my travels, I kept company with a man who gave me some advice. He said, 'There is no saying more helpful in performing any action than *There is no power and no strength except with God.* There is no action more helpful than fleeing toward God and seeking refuge with God. *Whoever seeks protection with God has indeed been led to a straight path.*'[117] Then he said, 'In the name of God, I have fled to God and sought protection with God; there is no power and no strength except with God, and who forgives transgressions except God?' 'In the name of God' is a saying of the tongue. It proceeds from the heart with 'I have fled to God.' Describing the spirit and the innermost secret of the heart (*al-rūḥ waʾl-sirr*) is 'I sought protection with God.' Describing the reason and the self (*al-ʿaql waʾl-nafs*) is 'There is no power and no strength except with God.' Describing divine ownership and command (*al-mulk waʾl-ʾamr*) is 'who forgives transgressions except God?' O Lord, I seek refuge with you from the work of the tempter, for he is an evident enemy who misleads! Then he addressed the tempter, 'This is what God has given us knowledge of concerning you. I believe in God, trust in God, and seek refuge from you in God! If God had not ordered me to seek refuge from you, I would not! Who are you that I should seek refuge from you?'"

SECTION FIVE: PERSISTING DESPITE SELFISH CALCULATION

You must understand, and may God have compassion on you, that such people's hearts consider the tempter so despicably low that they do not ascribe to him any power or attribute to him any volition. The secret of the tempter's creation is that he acts as a manifestation to which we might attribute the causes of our rebelliousness along with our persistent infidelity, negligence and forgetfulness. Have you not heard Divine Speech ask, *Who has caused him to forget but the tempter*?[118] These are the tempter's actions. The secret of his creation is that the filth of attribution be wiped away through him. One endowed with experiential knowledge has said, "The tempter is the dust-rag of my house, with which the dirt of rebelliousness is wiped away, along with every contemptible and despicable quality. Surely if God had willed that there be no rebellion, why would God have created the tempter (Iblīs)?" Shaykh al-Shadhili has taught, "The tempter is like a lusty man while the self is like a lusty woman. The occurrence of transgression between the two is like the birth of a child from their act. Neither of them created the child, but the child appeared through their actions." The meaning of the Shaykh's teaching is this. No reasonable person can assert that a child is created by the father and the mother or given existence by them, even though the child's appearance in this world must be attributed to them. Similarly, the believer knows beyond a doubt that neither the tempter nor the self creates rebelliousness. Rather rebelliousness comes into existence through them, not from them. Its appearance through their actions is attributed to them. The relationship between rebellion, the tempter and the self is a relationship of ascription and attribution, while the description of its real origin

145

and relation to God is one of creation and execution. Just as God is the creator of obedient actions by divine benevolence, so God is the creator of rebellion by divine justice. *Say, 'Everything is from God!' What is wrong with these people that they ponder not a single occurrence?*[119] Divine Speech also says, *God is the creator of all things* and *Is there a creator other than God?* and *Do you think that one who creates is like who does not create? Will you not keep this in mind?*[120] These moments of Divine Speech refute those who make the false claim that God creates obedient acts but does not create rebellious ones. Are you listening? *God has created you all and what all you do.*[121]

Now, some people might object by noting that Divine Speech says, *Surely God does not command shameful actions (al-faḥshāʾ).*[122] But commanding something is not the same as fixing it as destiny. They might continue to protest that Divine Speech says, *What goodness befalls you is from God and what badness befalls you is from your self.*[123] God's intent in making this distinction is to teach people how to comport themselves with proper respect before God. We are ordered to ascribe all good things to God, because they are suitable to the divine being. We are ordered to ascribe all bad things to ourselves, because they are suitable to our being. This is in order to maintain deference and good behavior with respect to God. The wise teacher, al-Khiḍr has said [as reported in Divine Speech], *I wanted to render the boat useless,* just as he said, *Your Lord wanted the boys both to attain their mature age.*[124] Notice that Khidr never says, 'Your Lord desired to render the boat useless' or 'I intended the boys to reach their mature age.' Khidr ascribed his actions of wrecking the boat and rendering it useless to his own self, and ascribed only good actions to his Lord. Likewise, Abraham said, *When I get sick, it is God who heals me.*[125] He never said, 'When God makes me sick, it is God who heals me.' Rather he said, *When I get sick, it is God who heals me.* You see how Abraham attributed his sickness to himself and attributed healing to his Lord, despite the fact that it is God who is the real author of the state of sickness and its sole creator.

What goodness befalls you is from God means that it comes from God, who is the One who creates them and brings them into being. And *what badness befalls you is from your self* means that it comes from you yourself to whom badness must be ascribed and attributed. To explain this, the Prophet Muhammad addressed God in a prayer, "The good is from your hand and the evil cannot be attributed to you." Indeed, the Prophet knew well that God is sole creator of both good and evil, both benefit and harm. However, he took upon himself the proper ethical relationship of respect for the divine in expressing, "The good is from your hand and the evil cannot be attributed to you." So contemplate this.

Now some people might protest by saying, 'Surely the true One is above creating rebellion, since it is horribly reprehensible.' We would answer, 'Yes, rebellion is a horribly reprehensible action (*fiʿl qabīḥ*) on the part of a person, since it is in opposition to divine command [that forbids it]. The repugnance of forbidden acts has no link to the essence of the One who forbade them, except for the sake of the forbidding being dependent upon the One who forbids them. Similarly, that good actions are commendable has no link to the essence of the One who commands them, except for the sake of the commanding being dependent upon that One who commands that they be done. Contemplate these subtleties and understand! The true One requires that you consider the divine essence transcendent beyond any conception of transcendence (*yajibu tanzīhuhu ʿan hadhā al-tanzīh*). Thus, when these objectors assert, 'May God be exalted above having created rebellion,' we reply, 'May God be exalted above having in divine dominion anything that God does not desire to be!' So ponder this, and may God guide you and me to the straight and level path, establishing us in the authentic and firmly-grounded religious way by God's own bounty.

ABRAHAM'S PRINCIPLES REGULATING SELFISH CALCULATION

What is the authentic and firmly-grounded religious way, and how do we stick to it? Divine Speech says, *Those who do not cleave to the religious community of Abraham (Ibrāhīm) make fools of themselves, for indeed we had chosen him as purified in this world and in the next world he is among the righteous. When his Lord said to him, 'Submit!' he replied 'I have submitted to the Lord of all worlds.'*[126] It also reveals that, *The path of religious obligation in the view of God is submission (al-islām)*, and it further specifies that this characterizes, *The religious community of your ancestor, Abraham: he named you 'those who submit' (al-muslimīn) long before.*[127] Divine Speech addresses the Prophet Muhammad, *So if they dispute with you, then say 'I have submitted my self to God, as have those who follow me, and addresses us all with, So submit to God.*[128] It further warns that, *Whoever takes as incumbent a path of religious obligation other than submission (al-islām), it will not be accepted from them and in the next world they will be among the corrupted losers,* and promises that, *Whoever submits their whole self to God and is a doer of good (muḥsin) has gripped the most trustworthy hand-hold.*[129]

Divine Speech also recounts that [the Prophets have said], *Bring me to you at death as one who has submitted (muslim) and keep me close to the righteous, and also I am the first of those who have submitted.*[130] There are so many more moments like these in Divine Speech.

You should know that the repeated mention of submission (*al-islām*) is to emphasize its power and to extol its importance. Submission has both an outer and an inner dimension. The outer dimension of submission is acting in accord with God's will (*al-muwāfiqa*). The inner dimension is the desisting from struggle against God (*al-munāziᶜa*). Thus outer submission is in the dimension of the bodily action, while the inner dimension of ceasing to struggle and reposing in resignation (*istislām*) is in the dimension of heart-felt attitude. Submission is like the form and tranquil resignation is like the spirit that enlivens the form. Submission is the outer appearance, while resignation is the inner beauty of that appearance. The Muslim is one who submits the whole self to God: its outer appearance is carrying out divine commands while its inner beauty is resignation to divine force. The spiritual station of resignation is only achieved after the self struggles with God in coming to grips with divine commands and finally relinquishes control to God without demanding in the slightest appeal or repeal to any commands. Therefore, those who claim for themselves "Islam" as their path of religious obligation (*dīn*) must also take on the responsibility of complete resignation. *Say, 'Bring us your proofs if you are sincere!*[131]

Haven't you observed how Abraham reacted when his Lord demanded of him, *Submit!* He replied, *'I have submitted to the Lord of all worlds.'* When he was bound to the catapult to be hurled into the flames, the angels called out

149

for his aid.[132] They appealed, "O our Lord, this is your intimate chosen friend (*khalīl*) and he is afflicted with that of
which you are best aware!" The true One answered,
"Gabriel, go to him and if he beseeches you for aid, give
him aid. If he does not beseech you, then leave me and my
bosom friend in peace!" So Gabriel came to Abraham when
he was being tortured, hovering on the horizon of his vision
and said, "Are you in need of anything? Abraham replied,
"From you I need nothing, but from God, yes definitely
I'm in need." Gabriel replied, "So ask of God what you
need!" Abraham answered, "Why should I ask when God
already knows my condition?" Abraham did not turn to
anyone other than God for aid. His high-minded resolution
would not take refuge with anyone other than God for shelter. Rather, he was resigned fully to God's decree, contented
with what God apportioned for him from moment to moment. He was freed from the need to look after his own
needs. He was satisfied with the true One's safe-guarding
him, keeping himself aloof from having to protect himself.
He acknowledged that the true One already knew his desperate need, recognizing that the true One is kind and graceful towards him in every changing condition that he may
experience.

For this reason, God praised Abraham highly in Divine
Speech: *It is Abraham who kept faithful.*[133] God liberated
him from the flames, as Divine Speech describes: *So we
said, 'Fires, be cold and Abraham be safe.'*[134] Some scholars have pointed out that if the true One had not said *and
Abraham be safe*, then he would have perished from the
cold! However, those fires served the Lord obediently. Indeed, scholars who are knowledgeable about the lives of
the Prophets have noted that, at this moment in Abraham's
life, not a single flame remained lit on the face of the earth,

from the east to the west; all the fires obeyed this divine command, thinking that they were the fires intended in this address! It is said that the flames roaring around Abraham only burned up the manacles that held him in captivity.

This is an important point. Scrutinize what Abraham said when Gabriel asked him, "Are you in need of anything?" He replied, "From you I need nothing…" He did not say, 'I need nothing' because his status as a messenger and bosom friend of God required that he establish in himself the most straightforward attitude of worshipful servanthood. The spiritual state of worshipful servanthood is conditioned by making apparent one's neediness to God and standing in the divine presence to embody one's utter poverty before God and raise one's high-minded resolution above anything other than God. It is fitting for one in this spiritual state to say, "From you I need nothing," meaning that 'I am in dire need of God, but I need nothing from you.' This reply includes the two criteria of displaying one's neediness to God and raising one's high-minded resolution above anything other than God.

Abraham's attitude is very different from what some Sufis urge, like those who say, "Sufis are not true Sufis until they display no needs before God." This saying is not suitable for people who emulate the noble example of the Prophets and have reached spiritual completion. This saying is attributed to one who intended to mean that the Sufis have fully realized that God has already appointed all of their goods and fulfilled all their needs before creating them. Thus the Sufis have no need before God, for the means to fulfill every need is apportioned and appointed in the eternity before they were created. However, denying a need does not necessitate denying being in need. There is a second interpretation of the saying, "Sufis are not true Sufis until they display no needs before God." It could mean that Sufis ask for God in their high-minded resolution, rather than asking for anything from God. Therefore, "they display no needs before God" means that Sufis have relinquished all their needs and anxieties to God and have resigned themselves totally to God's care. They desire nothing from God except that which God desires for them.

Consider another crucial point. When Gabriel said to Abraham, "Are you in need of anything?" He replied, "From you I need nothing, but from God, yes definitely I'm in need." It is said that Gabriel knew before asking that Abraham would not turn to him for aid and that his heart bears witness to none other than God. So Gabriel quickly replied, "So ask of God what you need!" He meant that, 'You have not turned to me for aid or succor, as incumbent upon you, so that you do not cling to any intermediaries (*tamassuk biʾl-wasāʾiṭ*). So then ask your Lord directly, for God is closer to you than I am.' Then Abraham answered, "Why should I ask when God already knows my condition?" By this he meant, 'I have looked with insight and seen that God is closer to me than my own asking of God. I have perceived that my asking is also from among the realm of intermediaries and I do not want to cling to anything except God. I recognize that God knows everything, so I do not need to remind God with any request. It is impossible that God be negligent or unobservant. So I am content in my knowledge of God that suffices me from needing to ask. I am certain that God never desists from divine kindness and grace in each and every situation.' This is truly the spiritual state of finding God sufficient by observing the rights and duties of *Sufficient for me is God*.[135] What protection comes from finding God sufficient! It is said of Abraham that his provision was preserved from consumption by guests, his son was preserved from consumption by sacrifice, and his body was preserved from consumption by flames. The true One extolled his virtue by saying, *It is Abraham who kept faithful.*[136]

When creating the human being, meaning Adam and all the people descended from Adam, the true One turned to angels and said, *I am making in the world a vice-regent. They said, 'Will you make in the world one that will spread corruption in it and spill blood, while we recite your praise and revere you?' God said, 'I know that which you do not know.'*[137] God refuted the angels' argument when they complained against Adam's creation. God refuted it by having Abraham refuse to turn to Gabriel for aid! It is as if God were saying, *'What do you think of this servant of mine, O you who said, Will you make in the world one that will spread corruption in it and spill blood?'* Abraham's faithful response to Gabriel made manifest the true meaning of God's saying [to the angels], *I know that which you do not know.* To explain how God refutes the angels, the Prophet Muhammad taught, "Angels come among you successively, some angels by day and other angels by night. When the ones that spent the night with you are rising up, God asks them, already knowing well the answer, 'How were my servants when you left them?' The angels reply, 'We came to them while they were praying [at dusk] and we took leave of them while they were praying [at dawn].'" In explaining God's apparent questioning of the angels, Shaykh al-Shadhili has said, "It is as if the true One were saying to the angels, 'O you who said, Will you make in the world one that will spread corruption in it and spill blood? How were my servants when you left them?'"

The intention of the true One in sending the angel Gabriel to Abraham was to openly display to the other an-

153

gels the high status of the bosom friend of God, to extol his power and announce his prestige. How could Abraham seek aid from anything other than God since he did not see anything except God or bear witness to any other than God? Abraham is named *al-Khalīl*, "the bosom friend," because the innermost kernel of his heart is pervaded by the love of God (*yukhalilu sirruhu bi-muḥabbat'illāh*) along with God's greatness and uniqueness. There remains in his heart no room for any other than God, as could be said poetically:

You've allowed the spirit's passage to permeate you to me
    For this, the name "the bosom friend" you win
If ever I speak, you are my speech itself
    And if I'm silent, you are love's fever burning within

THE SECURITY OF RELINQUISHING CONTROL

You should be aware that the true One opened wide the inner heart of Abraham with the light of contentment. The true One granted him the spirit of submission and preserved his heart from looking to other people for relief. Remember how the fire was transformed for him into a cool haven of safety? How could this be unless his heart had relinquished all control to God in absolute submission? He was granted peaceful security because of his submissive serenity (*'an al-istislām kāna 'alayhi al-salām*). His outer status of power and magnitude that appeared to others was based upon his inner spiritual rectitude.

My dear believer, understand this lesson! For those who remain resigned and submissive to God in dire moments of temptation, God turns the thorns of trial into fragrant leaves of basil and transforms the fears of tribulation into security and salvation. When the tempter plucks you up and applies pressure to you, loading you up into the catapult of trial (*manjanīq al-imtiḥān*), then all created things turn to you saying, "Are you in need of anything?" So be like Abraham and say, "From you I need nothing, but from God, yes definitely I'm in need." If objects answer you, "So ask of God what you need," you should answer, "Why should I ask when God already knows my condition?" God will aid you, turning the flames of this lower world into coolness and safety while giving you subtle gifts and virtuous nobility. This is because God has opened the straight road of good guidance by sending Prophets and Messengers. Those with faithful certainty follow in their footsteps and cleave to their example. Divine Speech has clarified: *So we answered him and saved him [Abraham] from anxious worry, and in this way we save the believers.*[138] 'We save the believers' means those who believe and follow the Prophet's traces for orientation, who yearn for the Prophet's radiant illumination, who request things from God with inner humility and self-obliteration, clothing themselves in the outer markers of brokenness and desperation.

Let's conclude our discussion of the story of Abraham, in which there are lessons for those who are morally sensitive and guidance for those with insight. By the wholesome arrangement of the divine plan, God will take charge of those who depart from the urge to take care of themselves by their own wits. Notice how Abraham refused to plot and plan in his desperate situation. He did not pay it any mind at all. Rather he cast his predicament upon God, entrusting it to divine care with resignation. When he did this, the direct result of his resignation was his dramatic preservation, in addition to his honor being raised and his name being praised forever throughout the ages. God has commanded us to cleave to the religious community of Abraham and guard its original name and nature. For Divine Speech says, *The religious community of your ancestor, Abraham: he named you 'those who submit' (muslimīn) long before.*

All who claim to be followers of Abraham are obliged to take on his nature, not just his name. They must desist from selfish calculation for their own good, and refrain from that game. They must never cross-examine God's good will, and keep free from any such claim. *Who turns away from the community of Abraham except those who their own souls defame?*[139] To remain in the community of Abraham requires us to pass back control of our affairs to God and remain steadfastly resigned to divine decrees as they come over us. The goal of this religious community is that you should remain with God such that you have no other goal other than God. I have a poem that expresses this same meaning:

My goal for you is for you to forget all goals
　As long as you persist on the path of guidance,

For you to leave aside existence and not long for it
　And grasp hold only of the cord of firm reliance.

How long will you neglect me while I always
　Watch over you with love and diligence?

How long will you gaze upon what I've created
　Wandering enraptured, entranced with each glance?

And never turn your attention toward my presence?
　You'll pass your life far from the mark in deviance!

My love is timeless—remember "Am I not your Lord"
On that day my uniqueness held you in a trance.

Do you have other than me another sustaining Lord
Who may save you from future disturbance?

You call upon others, the needy to the needy
For the entire cosmos is incapacity and impermanence.

Everything manifest by my will manifests
Through me alone existing things have existence.

In this world that I create, command and possess
Is there anyone to face who claims self-persistence?

Look around with the open eyes of faith and you'll see
Every being's effectiveness depends upon my dominance.

On a journey from nothingness to nothingness
You're headed for obliteration with no hope for permanence.

This is my gift decreed for you—don't reject it,
So from others keep aloof your hope's countenance!

All your plans are suspended at my doorway
So before my presence leave your baggage at a distance.

Accept your inherent quality of lowly humility
See my generosity match your willing compliance.

157

Be a servant to me, like a real servant, content
  Accepting all the master's demands with obedience.

Why hide your lowly qualities with qualities that are mine
  And replace your ignorance with open defiance?

Will you make yourself my partner in ownership
  And compete with me against wisdom's radiance?

If you aim to reach my intimate presence, then beware!
  Your self is raving, so oppose it with stridence.

Plunge into the ocean of obliteration—you might see me,
  Prepare to meet me in the end with confidence.

Continually invoke me for blessings that you encounter
  Apt actions of the master who gives without hindrance,

And spend not a day led by others in dalliance
  For there is nobody else to turn to today for guidance.

Reason between Good and Bad Calculation

Planning is of two fundamental types: some planning is
praiseworthy (*maḥmūd*) while other planning is blameworthy (*madhmūm*). Blameworthy planning is any forethought
or preparation through which you incline to make claim for
yourself rather than to stand in the service of God. Examples
of such blameworthy planning would be making arrangements for actions that rebel against divine directives
(*maʿṣiya*), thinking ahead about securing one's worldly
share while being negligent of one's duties, or setting yourself up to worship with hypocrisy to be admired and gain

fame.[140] There are many such examples. They are all blame-worthy because they result in punishment from God or alien-ation from God. Those who comprehend the blessing of our human power of reason are ashamed to put that reason-ing power to use for any purpose that does not bring them closer to God, into a relationship of intimacy and love.

The power of reason (ʿaql) is the greatest gift that God has bestowed upon us human beings as servants of the di-vine. Don't you see that when God created all existing things, the glorious and transcendent One bestowed upon them two kinds of freely given gifts. First existing things are each brought into being (ījād) and further they are con-tinually supported with sustaining and remaining (imdād). These two blessings are extended to each existing thing without exception. Nothing can exist without these funda-mental divine blessings of being and sustaining. Perhaps you might understand this through Divine Speech: *My com-passionate caring is wide enough to enrich every thing.*[141]

However, while all existing things share in the divine gifts of being and sustaining, the true One desires to distin-guish some of created things above others. This is to make evident the richness of the ramifications of divine desire (irāda) and the profundity of the depth of divine will (mashīʾa). Some created things were distinguished from others by the quality of growth and movement, like plants and animals, including beasts and human beings. In such growing things the divine power (qudra) appears more viv-idly than it does in immobile things. While both plants and animals share in the quality of growth, animals are further distinguished by the quality of being animate (wujūd al-ḥayāt), a quality shared by both beastly and human ani-mals. The true One is more vividly present through divine power in such animate beings than in plants that grow but

159

are not endowed with such individualized life-force. Further, the true One desires to distinguish the human being by the power of discernment, granting the human reason. With the power of reason, human beings were elevated above the other animals.

With reason, God completes divine blessings granted to humanity, drawing us into a unique relationship. Through the discernment of reason, the beneficial structure of this world's relation to the next world is brought to its fullness. The power of reason has a unique ability to expand and fulfill, a capability to be illumined and illuminate, even a potential to become light. Therefore, using the power of reason merely for plotting and planning in this material world, which has no value in itself in God's opinion, is in fact disavowing and denying (*kufr*) the blessing of reason. In contrast, directing the power of reason toward rectifying one's spiritual condition, that will become clear in our inevitable return to the divine, is gratefully acknowledging the wholesome One (*shukr al-muḥsin*) whose goodness benefits us. Only this is giving thanks to the effulgent One (*al-mufayyiḍ*) whose light pours over us and through us. Such use of reason is more worthy, and through it the human being is preferred and distinguished above all creation.

So do not expend your power of reason, which was so generously bestowed upon you, in plotting and planning in this ephemeral world! For this world is as the Prophet Muhammad described it: "The world is a putrefying corpse." Likewise, the Prophet is reported to have asked his companion, Ḍuḥḥāk [ibn Sufyān], "What do you eat?" Ḍuḥḥāk answered, "Meat and milk, O Prophet of God." So he asked, "Then what does it become after you eat it?" His companion answered, "I don't know, O Prophet of God." So the Prophet told him, "God has made what human beings ex-

160

crete an analogy for the nature of this world."[142] Similarly, he said [when he and some of his companions came across the body of a dead sheep], "If this world, in the view of God, had any more weight than the wing of a fly, unbelievers would not be given even a sip of water!"

What to think of a person who expends the power of reason on securing things of this ephemeral world, that has all the disgusting qualities of impermanence, inconsequence and putrescence described above? Such a person is like a man who is the subject of a king. The king gives him a sword that is extraordinarily valuable, endowed with great honor, the likes of which is granted to only a select few of his subjects. The king charges him to take the sword and smite his enemies. So the man struts away, showing off his new beautiful sword for all to see. Then he goes over to a dead body and unsheathes his gleaming sword. He begins hacking at the decaying cadaver over and over again, until the sword's gleaming luminosity is murky, its keen edge is dull, its beauty is dimmed, and its value is lost. Wouldn't the king be right, upon seeing him engaged in such stupidity, to take the sword away from him? Wouldn't it be fitting for the king to pronounce a grievous punishment upon him because of his evil deeds and banish him from the royal presence?

Such is the nature of blameworthy planning in this world. On the other hand, praiseworthy planning consists of any forethought, arrangement and effort you expend to draw closer to God. This would include freeing those under your protection from the rights that others hold over them, either by helping them pay off their debts or taking their obligations upon yourself. Other examples would be rectifying your repentance before the Lord of all worlds, or meditating deeply about how to subdue lust's pernicious agitation and the force of deluding temptation. Planning ahead for such goals is praiseworthy, without a doubt. For this reason, the Prophet Muhammad has taught, "One hour's clear thinking is better than seventy years' ardent worship."

PLANNING IN THIS WORLD FOR THE NEXT WORLD

Consider how planning in the world is of two kinds. There is planning in this world for this world and there is planning in this world for the next world. Planning in this world for this world is exerting your reason and effort on worldly means, making worldly goods your aim, taking pride in their acclaim, and staking in their continuing increase your personal claim. With every little thing that you get of worldly means, you grow in negligence, arrogance and self-importance. This is because success in worldly means preoccupies you from acting in accord with divine directives, leading you to oppose God's will.

In contrast is planning in this world for the next world. This consists of arranging your worldly affairs [so that you have the chance to prepare spiritually for the next world], like engaging in trade, earning money or working in agriculture so that you can eat from things earned lawfully. You can be blessed by giving the fruit of such labor to those who are in need without demanding compensation. Such rightful earning can protect you from having to sully yourself among others by depending on them. The criterion that distinguishes those who plot and plan in this world for the next world is that they do not inordinately grasp after more (*istikthār*) or niggardly hoard what they have in store (*iddikhār*). Rather spend freely for others' aid and give without expecting to be repaid (*is'āf wa īthār*).

There are some who conscientiously minimize their reliance on worldly means (*zāhid*). They have two distinguishing signs: one sign marks them when the world gives them nothing and the other marks them when the world gives them something. When the world gives them something, they are marked by their selflessly giving it away to others. When the world gives them nothing, they are marked by tranquil relaxation. Selfless giving (*īthār*) is their form of gratitude for the blessing of having gotten some worldly good. Resting tranquilly (*rāḥa*) is their form of gratitude for the blessing of being totally impoverished. Such states are the fruits of acute understanding of God from God and intuitive comprehension (*ʿirfān*). Don't you see that, just as the true One blesses you by giving you worldly means, the true One also blesses you by withholding worldly means? In fact, the blessing of having worldly means withheld from you is more complete and more perfect! Sufyān al-Thawrī has said, "The blessings that come upon me through what worldly means God withholds from me are much more perfect than the blessings that come upon me through what worldly means are given to me."[143] Shaykh al-Shadhili has taught, "Once in my dreams I saw al-Ṣiddīq [Abu Bakr]. He said to me, 'Do you know what is the sign that love of this world has left the heart?' I replied, 'I don't know.' So he said, 'The sign that love of this world has left the heart is that one gives things away when one has them and is tranquilly at rest when one does not.'"[144]

A Parable
To Work or Not to Work?

How should we consider the person who works and struggles to earn a living and support a family through intermediate material means (*mutasabbab*)? He is like a servant whose master commands him— "Go out to work and eat by the profit of your labor." In contrast, the person who leaves aside work and lives in isolation (*mutajarrad*) is like a servant whose master commands him—"Stand at attention near me and serve my personal needs alone, and eat what I personally provide for you." Is either one disobedient to the master?

This clarifies that not all people who seek worldly means are blameworthy. The blameworthy ones are those who seek the world for themselves rather than for their Lord. They seek to secure their fortune in this ephemeral world rather than in the enduring world to come. Thus people can be divided into two kinds: those who seek worldly means for the sake of this world, and those who seek worldly means for the sake of the next world. I have heard our master, Shaykh al-Mursi, say, "To those with existential knowledge (*ᶜārif*), this world doesn't really exist for, in their view, this world exists only for the sake of the next world and the next world exists only for the sake of their Lord."

Another Parable
What You Need to Reach the Goal.

People in this world are like servants whose master commands, "Go to a far distant land and prepare yourself to travel from there across a vast stretch of

164

desert. Get ready and prepare yourself for the journey!" When the master gives the servant permission to travel on a mission, it is understood implicitly that the master has allowed the servant to take the necessary funds so that he can quickly and effectively prepare the food and shelter required for the journey. By analogy, you can imagine how God has brought people into being in this world and ordered them to gather from this world whatever provision they need in order to reach the goal. God has said in revelation, *Take your provision, and the best provision is wary consciousness of God (taqwā).*[145] Since God has ordered people to prepare themselves for the journey to the next world, it is understood implicitly that people must gather in this world what they need of provisions, preparations and support, until they meet at the appointed time and reach the goal.

Let the World be in Your Hands Not Your Hearts

From this perspective, we can understand the spiritual states of the companions of the Prophet (*al-ṣaḥāba*) and the righteous early followers (*al-salaf al-ṣāliḥīn*). Everything that came their way of worldly goods and power brought them closer to God. They made of it cause for earning God's contentment. They did not accrue worldly power for the sake of the world, for luxury and its ephemeral enjoyment. Divine Speech describes them this way: *Muhammad, the Prophet of God, and those who are with him keep ardent pressure against those who disavow but treat each other with compassionate care. You see them, bowing and pros-*

165

trating, seeking bounty from God and contentment. Their
mark is on their faces from the traces of prostration.[146]

What do you make of such people whom God chose to
be companions to the Prophet? They were the select audience of the Prophet's discourse that was sent down as revelation. On the neck of every believer, from now until the
day of resurrection, lies the yoke of gratitude to these companions of the Prophet, for the countless blessings they have
given us and the aid they have extended to us. They conveyed to us the wisdom of the Prophet and his command
(*ḥikma wa aḥkām*). They are the ones who clarified for us
what the Prophet permitted and banned (*ḥalāl wa ḥarām*).
They passed on knowledge to us, for those who comprehend profoundly and for what the common man may understand (*khāṣṣ wa ʿāmm*). They opened closed-off regions
and conquered other land; they dominated the rejecters in
other religions and over the idolatrous gained the upper hand.
How true is what the Prophet Muhammad said about them:
"Whichever of my companions you emulate, you will be
rightly guided—they are like the starry band."

In the moment of Divine Speech noted above, they are
described by various qualities, including *seeking bounty*
from God and contentment. The true One, who observes
their secret spiritual states, knowing what is hidden in their
hearts and what they make public, tells us that they did not
desire what the world gave to them. They did not intend the
worldly authority they exercised. They only sought the noble
face of God (*wajh*) and divine bounty (*faḍl*). God describes
them in Divine Speech: *Keep yourself patient with those*
who call upon their Lord mornings and evenings, desiring
God's face.[147] God tells us that the Prophet's companions
wanted nothing from the world except God, and seeking
nothing but this.

In another moment, Divine Speech says, *In houses in which God has permitted the divine name to be elevated and recalled, God is glorified in the mornings and evenings by people not distracted by trading and selling from recalling God, establishing prayer, and giving alms for purification. They fear a day when hearts and eyes will be transformed.*[148] This wording alludes to how God has cleansed their inner hearts and perfected their inner illumination. Therefore, the world does not snatch away what is in their hearts or scar the face of their faith. How could the world snatch away what is in a heart that is filled with God's loving intimacy, which is illumined with the light of divine proximity? God has said [to the tempter], *Surely you have no authority over my servants.*[149] If the world had any authority over their hearts, then the tempter would have authority over their hearts as well. The tempter has no way to reach hearts that are radiant with the light of simplified living through minimizing reliance on the world (*zuhd*). Such hearts are swept clean of the dirt of worldly desire (*raghba*). God's saying, *Surely you have no authority over my servants,* means 'Neither you nor anything existing in the world has authority over their hearts, for the authority of my greatness fills their hearts, preventing them from coming under the domination of anyone or anything else.'

In this moment, the true One affirms that people with such hearts are *not distracted by trading and selling from recalling God.* It does not forbid them from trading and selling! To the contrary, this wording actually confirms the permissibility of trade and commerce; that meaning lies beneath its literal sense, if you ponder it deeply like those with insight. Haven't you listened closely to this moment of Divine Speech specify that such people are *establishing prayer, and giving alms for purification?* If the intent of

167

this address were to forbid the believers from acquiring wealth, it would have forbidden them from engaging in worldly means for their livelihood (*tasabbub*), such as "trading and selling." Don't you notice how God specifies that they are *giving alms for purification*? The fact that Divine Speech makes alms obligatory upon believers to purify their wealth (*zakāt*) is proof that these people might be wealthy yet still have virtuous qualities and pure hearts. Their wealth does not exclude them from this high praise for their spiritual state, since they rise to the duty of observing their Lord's rights over them, despite owning such wealth.

 ᶜAbdullah ibn ᶜUtba has told this story about the wealth of some of the Prophet's companions. "On the day he was killed, ᶜUthman ibn ᶜAffan had in his treasury one-hundred and fifty thousand dinars and one-million dirhams.[150] He left behind land in an estate whose value was two-hundred thousand dinars. Al-Zubayr owned wealth whose value exceeded fifty thousand dinars, and [at his death] left a thousand horses and a thousand slaves. As for ᶜAmr ibn al-ᶜĀs, he died leaving three hundred thousand dinars. The wealth of ᶜAbd al-Rahman ibn ᶜAwf is too famous to be worth mentioning!" The wealth of the world was in their hands, not in their hearts. When the world provided them nothing they patiently endured, and when it provided them wealth they gave copious thanks. The true One tried and tested them with poverty in the beginning of their lives, until their inner illumination was complete and their hearts were pure, then gave them freely of the world's goods. If they were given worldly goods in the beginning, it might have been taken away from them later. But since it was given to them only after they had been made strong and firm in faithful certainty, they behaved with it like the trusted custodian of the treasury. They took to heart the words of Divine Speech:

You should spend from that which has been passed into your care.[151]

From this perspective, you can understand why these early companions, in the first days of the community, were forbidden from fighting (*jihād*). Divine Speech says, *You must forgive and forbear until God comes forth with a command.*[152] If God had allowed them to fight at the initial establishment of the Islamic community, some people who were new Muslims might fight for their own victory, in subtle ways of which they are barely aware. Even ᶜAlī ibn Abī Ṭālib, for example, used to slow down when fighting. He would strike then pull back a little, to let his head cool off a bit, before delivering the next blow, for he was afraid that the next blow might be fueled by his self's anger or pride. This reveals ᶜAli's intimate experiential knowledge of the hidden intrigues of our selfish nature (*dasāʾis al-nufūs*) that lie in wait to ambush us.[153] Therefore, the early companions expended great effort to guard over their hearts and make sure their every action was sincere. They were anxiously concerned that there might be some element in a single action that might turn the face of God away from them.

For this reason, we can say that the world was in their hands, not in their hearts. For proof of this, we can look to how the Prophet's early companions easily gave away worldly goods and gave preference to others before themselves. They are the people whom Divine Speech addresses: *They give priority to others over themselves, even though they are in need.*[154] One day, a companion was given the gift of a prized portion of meat; but he said, "So-and-so is more in need of it than I am." So the meat was given to that person, but he also said the same thing. So the meat was

169

passed as a gift from one to the next, passing through the hands of seven or so companions, until it ended up with the one who had originally given it away! There is sufficient proof for you in the story of ᶜUmar, who brought out half of his treasure [to give away], followed by Abu Bakr, who brought out everything he owned. Or the story of ᶜAbd al-Rahman ibn ᶜAwf, who gave away seven hundred camels loaded down with goods. Or the story of ᶜUthman ibn ᶜAffan, who armed and fed the whole army out of his personal wealth.

There are many more stories of the companion's beautiful acts of generosity that reveal their virtuous spiritual qualities. Divine Speech calls them, *Men who are true to what each has promised to God. Among them are some who have completed their trust, and among them are some still waiting. They do not change their aspiration in what they have promised.*[155] Here, Divine Speech lets us know about their secret sincerity which is hidden from the sight of everyone, but which God clearly sees. This is such high praise—it is the only thing worthy of pride! Normally, in our human perception, our action hides our inner intention and spiritual condition, and we can never really know the inner state of others. But this moment of Divine Speech reveals the purity of the companions' outer actions as well as their inner hearts. It affirms publicly their praiseworthy magnificence and virtuous excellence.

A PARABLE

TASKS AND TOOLS.

God is to people like a master is to his servants. Imagine that a master brings home a servant and instructs the servant to perform specific tasks in the house. The master would not expect the servant to work without the master providing nourishment and hospitality. No, the master is more generous than that! You can think of this world as the house of God and think of yourself as the servant. Your job is obedience to divine commands and the reward for your toil is paradise. In this scenario, God would never order you to perform a task without providing you the tools and support you need to accomplish the task!

THE GUIDANCE OF THE PROPHET'S COMPANIONS

People can be divided into two kinds. There are those who seek worldly means for the sake of this world, like people of alienation who are forgetful and negligent. Then there are those who seek worldly means for the sake of the next world, like the Prophet's noble companions and their righteous followers in the early Islamic community. Take for example when ʿUmar said, "I would get the army prepared for battle even if I were in the middle of prayer." ʿUmar's preparing to achieve goals in this world is totally oriented to God's will and aided by God's decree. It is, in fact, God's planning (*tadbīr ullah*) to achieve certain goals in this world. For this reason, his prayer would not be broken or defective [even if he interrupted it to prepare the army].

Now you might object by saying, "You assert that the early companions did not desire the world for its own sake, and yet the true One revealed Divine Speech about their behavior during the battle of Uhud, *Among you are those who desire this world and among you are those who desire the next world.*[156] In response, some of the companions even said, "We did not think that any one of us desired this world, but then it was revealed that, *Among you are those who desire this world and among you are those who desire the next world.*" Now listen, and may God bring you into accord with perceptive understanding and make you one of those who listen intently to Divine Speech. God has commanded every believer to hold a good opinion (*al-ẓann al-jamīl*) of the companions and to believe in their virtuous excellence above all others. We must draw from their sayings, actions and spiritual states only the most favorable interpretation. We must interpret in this way everything they have done during the time when the Prophet Muhammad was alive with them and also in the time after he passed away. This is because the true One purified their hearts with an absolute purification; it is not limited to a certain time rather than another. Similarly, the Prophet has witnessed to their purification by saying, "My companions are like the stars—whichever of them you emulate, you will be rightly guided."

There are two replies to the objection you might raise by referring to this moment of Divine Speech, *Among you are those who desire this world and among you are those who desire the next world.* It might mean that there are some among them who *desire this world* for the sake of the next world. This would include those who desired worldly gain through the spoils of war to engage God in righteous behavior through what they have taken from the world, such as giving to others or preferring others to themselves. Those among them who were not like this refers to those who did not go to war for the spoils at all. They did not turn to gathering spoils and paid no attention to that aspect of fighting. Among them were those who were virtuous (*fāḍil*) and among them were those who were more virtuous (*afḍal*). Among them were those who were spiritually complete

172

(*kāmil*) and among them were those who were more spiritually complete (*akmal*). The second answer is for you to consider that a master may call his servant anything he pleases, but still we are obliged to respect and honor his servant, due to the close relation (*nisba*) that he has to the master. Whatever the master might call the servant should not be attributed to the servant, and we should certainly not use it to address the servant ourselves! The master, in contrast, can call his servant whatever he wants, in order to incite the servant to serve better. However, we must not transgress the limits of politeness with the servant. When we examine the whole of the Divine Speech, we find many moments when God chastises people. For example, there is a chapter called "He Frowned" (*Surat Abasa*) [in which God chastises the Prophet Muhammad for frowning and turning away from a blind man]. The Prophet was so disheartened by this chastisement that ᶜAᵓisha, his wife, even said, "If the Prophet could hide any part of what came to him in inspired revelation (*waḥī*), he would hide this chapter."

WHY DESPISE THIS WORLD?

This discussion should clarify what kind of desisting from calculation is praiseworthy. It does not consist of refusing to engage in improving worldly matters in order to take refuge only in worship and ascetic devotion to secure a place in the next world. No, the kind of selfish calculation that must be left aside is plotting and planning in worldly matters for worldly ends. The sign that one's plotting and planning is blameworthy is that it leads to rebellion against God's decrees. It leads people to take worldly goods any way they can, whether the means are legal and moral or not.

Think hard about why things are praiseworthy or blame-worthy! They are judged by the consequences they entail. Blameworthy planning is thinking and acting toward any goal that preoccupies you from God and distracts you from rising to serve or prevents you from taking care of God's business. Praiseworthy planning is the exact opposite. It consists of thinking and acting toward any goal that leads you closer to God and brings you into God's contentment. From the same perspective, we don't say that that world is absolutely lowly and despicable in and of itself, nor do we say that it is wonderful. That which is despicable about the world is whatever distracts you from your Lord and pre-vents you from preparing for the next world. One with inti-mate knowledge has said, "Anything that distracts you from God, whether family, wealth, or children, is an evil to be despised." In contrast, anything in the world that assists you to obey God and rouses you to serve is praiseworthy. In general, whatever leads to your being praised is itself praise-worthy, and whatever leads to your being blamed is itself blameworthy.

The Prophet Muhammad has taught that, "The world is a putrefying corpse." He also said, "The world is accursed and accursed is everything in it—except for the remem-brance of God, what leads to it, one who has knowledge and one who teaches others," and also "God has made what human beings excrete an analogy for the nature of this world." These sayings require us to blame the world and feel aversion to it. However, the Prophet also said, "Do not curse the world, for blessed is the believers' conveyance: from the world, good reaches them and through the world they are delivered from evil." From this vantage point you can see that "the world" which the Prophet said is accursed is only that aspect of the world that distracts people from

174

God. For this reason, the Prophet named important exceptions: "except for the remembrance of God, what leads to
it, one who has knowledge and one who teaches others."
He clarifies that these blessed things are not "of this world."
Likewise, when the Prophet says, "Do not curse the world,"
he means the world that leads us to obedient worship of
God. For this reason, he specified, "for blessed is the
believer's conveyance." He praised the world in respect to
its being like a horse that conveys the believer to a better
place, rather than in respect to its being the abode of arrogant delusion and a burden of the conscience's confusion.

If you comprehend this much, then you realize that desisting from selfish calculation does not consist of retreat-
ing from working with worldly means. This would cause a
person to go to waste and become a burden upon others. It
would spread ignorance about the divine wisdom that created the world which works through intermediate means
(*asbāb*) and interconnected networks (*wasāʾiṭ*). Once Jesus
(*ʿĪsā*) was walking along when he came upon an ascetic
devoted only to worship (*mutaʿabbid*). Jesus asked him,
"From where you do get your food?" He replied, "My
brother feeds me." Jesus rebuked him, "Your brother is more
worshipful than you!" The brother is more worshipful even
if he is busy in the marketplace of buying and selling, since
he is the one who assists you to worship and allows you to
free your time for devotions. How can you imagine that
working through worldly means is forbidden once you hear
Divine Speech say, *God has made permissible selling and
has made forbidden taking undue profit*, along with *Take
witnesses when you engage in selling*.[157] Likewise the
Prophet has taught that, "It is permissible for a man to eat
from what his right hand has earned, for David (*Dāwūd*),
the Prophet of God, ate from what he earned." He also said,

"The best earning is what a craftsman earns with the labor of his hands, as long he gives sincere advice to others." He also said, "A merchant who is a trustworthy, truthful Muslim will be with the martyrs on the day of resurrection."

After hearing these teachings, how can anyone claim that engaging in worldly work is blameworthy? Rather, blameworthy is whatever work distracts you from God and prevents you from serving God. If you would leave aside working and become a recluse (*mutajarrrid*), and in that state became distracted from God, then you would be blameworthy yourself! For character weaknesses do not only afflict those who work; rather, they afflict recluses and ascetics as well. *There is no refuge on that day from the command of God, except for those regarded with mercy.*[158]

In fact, character weakness is often more acute among recluses! People who work might be afflicted by character flaws, but they make no claim to be special, so the effect of their flaws might not be severe. Their surface appearance reflects their inner condition, and they freely admit their limitations. They acknowledge that those who devote their time solely to worship are superior to them. The character weaknesses that often afflict recluses are pride, arrogance, hypocrisy and duplicity. Recluses might make their surface appearance beautiful in the eyes of others by being outwardly worshipful and holy, in order to attract the worldly goods that are in the hands of others. Or they might be afflicted with relying too much on other people and acting like parasites upon them. The sign of this weakness is their despising others who give nothing to support them or rebuking others if they don't serve them. Therefore, a person immersed in worldly work to the point of being negligent enjoys a better spiritual state by far! May God keep our intentions wholesome and keep our selves pure from such character weaknesses, through God's bounty and generosity.

SECTION SIX: AVOIDING SELFISH CALCULATION
IN WORK AND WORSHIP

From the previous discussion, you might think that the worker and the recluse are on the same plane. You might think they have the same status. But that is not so. God has not made those recluses who clear their minds for worship and free their time for devotion equal to those workers who enter into worldly work, even if the workers have firm faith. Though workers and recluses might be equal in intimate experiential knowledge of God, still the recluses are superior. Their occupation is loftier and their aspiration more complete. One of the Sufis has said, "The worker and the recluse are like two servants of one master. To one servant the master commands, 'Go out to work and eat from what you earn by your work.' To the other servant he commands, 'Stay close in my presence and serve me and I will personally provide you with whatever you desire.'" Clearly, the second servant has a greater value in the eyes of the master. The tasks he performs for the master earn him the master's kind care.

Very few of those who work remain safe from opposing divine decrees. Very seldom does engaging in worldly work allow you to experience pure moments of worshipful obedience. Working requires you to plunge into contradictions while mixing with people who are negligent or in open opposition to living decrees. The thing that rouses you most intently to worship is seeing other worshippers; the thing that most intently drags you into sin is seeing other sinners.

To this effect, the Prophet has said, "Each person will be gathered [at resurrection] in the religion of his closest friend (*khalīl*)—so let each of you examine whom you take as your bosom friend!"[159] A poet echoes this sentiment:

> Don't ask what a person believes,
>   rather ask who are his friends
> For every person conforms
>   to his friend's virtue or vice
> If his friends are evil,
>   then avoid him with all haste
> And if his friends are good, stay close
>   —follow his advice

It is human nature to imitate and reflect one's surroundings. The self mirrors in appearance the qualities of its environment, especially the people with whom it relates. If you keep the company of negligent people, this makes it easy for your self to become negligent, since negligence permeates the situation in which it is placed. Imagine the danger if, in addition to this, your work causes you to be intimately related to negligent people!

My dear brothers and sisters, may God bring you into accord. You may find your spiritual state when leaving home in the morning is not the same as your spiritual state when you return in the evening. In the morning, you may be full of light, with an open chest, resolved to worship and live simply in this world. But when you return home, you find yourself completely changed, with none of these high aspirations and sweet sensations! This is due to the pollution of mixing with others, of having to immerse your heart in the murky darkness of worldly work. It is the nature of worldly work and rebellion against God that, when they are gone their effects don't go so easily. They cause the heart to delay its return back to God after it had been living in separation and eclipse. The effects of worldly work and rebellion are like fire: perhaps the flames have died down but the black soot remains.

Therefore, people who work require two things to cleanse these effects: knowledge and conscience. Through knowledge (*ʿilm*) one can know what is permissible and forbidden. Through conscience (*taqwā*) one prevents the perpetration of sins. Working people need knowledge of divine commands that regulate affairs of trade and commerce, like the laws applying to selling objects, relinquishing ownership, changing currency and anything to do with market interactions. In addition, they need to know the rulings about religious duties and obligatory acts of worship.

WORKING PEOPLE'S NEEDS

There are several things that working people need to do. Every morning when leaving the home for work, they should make a firm vow with God.[160] They should resolve to forgive anyone who misbehaves with them along the day's route, for the marketplace is the realm of dispute and lawsuit. For this reason, the Prophet has said, "Who among you is unable to act just like Abu Damdam? Every day upon leaving his house he would say, 'Dear God, for my charity I give the offering of turning away from whatever other Muslims do against me.'" Before leaving home, the working person should make ablutions and pray, asking God to keep him or her safe and sound upon leaving. For nobody knows what is going to happen to you when you step outside. Going to the marketplace is like going to the battlefield. The believer should wear the armor of seeking pro-

179

tection with and trusting God that alone can ward off the shots of enemies. *Whoever turns to God for protection, God guides to a straight and level path.* And also, *Whoever entrusts to God every concern, God is their reward.*[161]

As they leave home, working people should place their families, their homes and all their belongings in the care of God. They are not capable of preserving all they leave behind from harm. Let them remember Divine Speech: *For God is the best preserver, and God is the most compassionate of those who care.*[162] Let them remember the Prophet's petition, "O God, you are the companion during travels and the care-taker of the family, children and property left behind." If working people place all this in the care of God, then there is hope that when they return they will find everything in order as they expect and desire. Once a Sufi went on a trip and left his wife when she was pregnant. As he was setting out, he said, 'O God, in your care I place that which is in her womb.' During his absence, his wife died. When he returned, he inquired about his wife, and was told that she died while giving birth. That night, he perceived a light glowing in the graveyard and went outside to follow it. He found that the light was emanating from his wife's grave. In it, he saw her with a little child suckling at her breast. A voice called to him, "You placed the child in her womb in our care, so now you have got it. Had you placed them both in our care, you might have gotten both together!"

Upon leaving their homes in the morning, working people should say: "In the name of God...I trust in God, there is no ability or power except with God." This will deprive the tempter any hope of waylaying them. As they head to their workplaces, they should be ardent in commanding people to do what is right and preventing people from doing what is wrong. They should do this as a form of giving thanks for the twin blessings of power and conscience that the Lord has bestowed upon them. Let them remember Divine Speech: *Those who, when we make them strong in the world, establish prayer and give alms, commanding what is right and forbidding what is wrong. With God is the result of every affair.*[163] If they are given strength in the world, then they should command what is right and forbid what is wrong, as long as this does not entail loss to their selves, their property or their savings. If there is no loss entailed, then they are considered among those made *strong in the world*, and the command is obligatory upon them. However, if they cannot command what is right and forbid what is wrong without entailing such loss before hand, or such loss appears most likely as a consequence, then this obligation is lifted from their shoulders. They can, in such circumstances, let it pass.[164]

On the way to work, they should walk with gentleness and firmness. This is in accord with Divine Speech, *The servants of the compassionate One walk gently over the earth and, if ignorant people address them, they say 'be at peace.'*[165] This is true not only in regard to walking, but also in regard to every single action. Everything you do should be accompanied by the feeling of equipoise and be firmly grounded.

In the workplace, they should recall the names and qualities of God. It is reported that the Prophet said, "The one who recalls to mind God in the midst of negligent people is like a warrior from among those who defend the faith. The one who recalls to mind God in the market-place is like a living one among the dead." Among the Prophet Muhammad's early followers was a man who used to mount his donkey and come to the market-place. There he would engage in recalling God's names and qualities, after which he would return home. He would go to the market only to do this, with no other errand! While working, they should let nothing distract them, neither working nor trading, from rising to prayer at the appointed times in a congregation. If they miss prayer-times out of preoccupation, they incite the wrath of their Lord. In addition, their profits will be empty of blessing (*baraka*). Shouldn't they be ashamed to let the true One see them preoccupied by gaining for themselves while ignoring the rights their Lord holds over them? One of our pious ancestors was carrying out his craft. He had just lifted his hammer over his head when he heard the call to prayer. He let the hammer fall behind him without completing his intended blow, lest he be found working once the call to obey his Lord had resounded.[166] Upon hearing the call to prayer, one should recall the moments of Divine Speech: *O our people! Answer the one who calls you to God*, and *O you who believe, answer God and God's prophet when he calls you to what revives you*, and *Answer your Lord*.[167] ᶜAᵓisha has reported, "The Prophet used to stay in his room, resoling shoes or instructing those who served him. But when the call to prayer rang out, he would rise up as if he didn't recognize any of us."

In the marketplace, people who engage in trade must abstain from swearing oaths or exaggeratedly praising their wares. The Prophet has given the sternest warning about this: "Traders are traitors against righteousness (*al-tujjār hum al-fujjār*), except those who do good and are truthful." Likewise, working people must hold their tongues from backbiting and slander. Divine Speech has addressed this, saying *Do not speak behind each others' backs—would any of you eat his brother's flesh once he's dead? No, that you abhor!*[168] Anyone who listens to gossip and slander is one of the slanderers. So if people engage in backbiting and slander in your presence, you should refute them. If they don't listen and desist, you should get up and leave their company. Never let modesty before other people prevent you from standing up for the rights of the true One, the ruler of all, for God is the only one who really deserves your modesty and shame. Isn't it better for God and the Prophet to be content with your actions than to earn the contentment of other people? It is more worthy for you to be content with God and the Prophet, and ignore the reactions of others. The Prophet has said that one instance of backbiting is worse than thirty-six instances of adultery.

CULTIVATING VIRTUE THROUGH WORK

Shaykh al-Shadhili has said, "There are four points of virtuous conduct that the Sufi who engages in work for a living must cultivate. If they are missing, nothing can shield him even if he is the most knowledgeable of people. These are avoiding the oppressive sinners in this world, preferring those who live for the next world, sharing with the poor out of consolation, and making obligatory the five daily prayers in congregation." How true is this saying of Shaykh al-Shadhili!

By "avoiding oppressive sinners (*zulma*)" one keeps one's moral state (*dīn*) safe and secure. Keeping company with oppressive people eclipses the light of faith, while avoiding them causes one to be delivered from the punishment that awaits them. *Do not rely upon those who oppressively sin, for they will be touched by the fire.*[169] By "showing preference for those who live for the next world," Sufis who work for a living take recourse to the saints, the friends of God (*awliyā' Allah*). They keep company with saints and refer their problems to them, drawing out from them

183

lessons in order to strengthen themselves against the turbidity of working for a living. The sweet breath of the saints wafts over them and the saints' blessings manifest in them. Perhaps the saints' spiritual aid will reach them through their daily work. Perhaps love for and faith in the saints will deflect people from rebellion against God in their labors.[170]

"Sharing with the poor out of consolation" is a way for people to give thanks for the blessings of God granted to them. So if the doors of plenty are opened for you through your work, remember those for whom the doors are shut and locked. Be aware that God has informed the rich about the existence of the poor, just as God has informed the poor about the rich: *We have made some of you a trial for others—will you patiently endure? God is the One who sees all things.*[171] Indeed, the existence of impoverished people is a blessing that God has bestowed on those with wealth. For in the impoverished, the rich have found those who can convey the wealth they carry from this world [transforming it into reward] in the next world. In the impoverished, the rich have found those who, by taking from their wealth, encourage God to remove from them punishment. God is the One who is rich beyond need, deserving of all praise (*al-ghanī al-ḥamīd*). If God had not created poverty, how would those with wealth give away what they have in charity to benefit others? Where would the wealthy find people to take from them, [thereby finding release from their sins]? For this reason, the Prophet taught, "It is as if those who give in charity from wealth earned by rightful labor, for God only accepts what is rightfully earned, have placed that wealth in the hand of the compassionate One directly. Then the compassionate One takes care of them, just as you might take care of a foal or baby camel in your herds. Even the smallest bite of food given away with sincerity has the weight and stature of Mount Uhud." For this reason, one of the signs of the end of time is that a man will not find anyone to accept his charitable offering.

Finally, "making obligatory the five daily prayers in congregation" will renew the light of their faith and through this illumination they will gain insight. The Prophet has said, "Prayer in congregation is preferable to prayer in isolation by twenty-five degrees." This saying is also remembered as, "by seventy-five times the reward." If the rule had been given to people to pray in their homes or shops, then mosques would be abandoned. Indeed, about mosques the true One has said, *In houses in which God has permitted the divine name to be elevated and recalled, God is glorified in the mornings and evenings by people not distracted by trading and selling from recalling God.*[172] Praying in congregation brings hearts into concord, strengthens them through mutual aid, makes their faults clear, and allows the believers to see each other and gather together. The Prophet has said, "The hand of God is with the congregation." This is because a group of people gathered together generates blessings that expand in their hearts, extending to everyone present and illuminating each who bears witness with its light. When people gather for prayer, it is like an army coming into formation: their close ranks and group morale is what gives them victory. This is one interpretation of Divine Speech: *God loves those who fight in God's way, rank upon rank, as if they were a solidly cemented building.*[173]

The Difference Between Sight and Insight

My fellow believer, from the moment you leave home until you return, you must be careful to lower your gaze. Do this in remembrance of Divine Speech: *Tell the believers to lower their gaze and protect their openings, for this is purer for them.*[174] Your eyes are a blessing upon you from God, so do not disavow the blessings. Vision is a trust handed to you by God, so do not betray what is entrusted to you. Divine Speech says, *God knows the deceit of the eyes and what the breasts conceal,* and also, *Do they not know that God sees what they do?*[175] If you want to truly see, then know that God is seeing! If you lower your own sight (*baṣra*), God will open for you insight (*baṣīra*) as a reward. For those who limit the circumference of their vision of themselves in this visible world, God will expand the circumference of their comprehension of the world beyond the visible. A Sufi has said, "When people lower their gaze and refuse to look longingly at what God has forbidden, they find a light glowing within their hearts and taste its sweetness."

From the perspective of those endowed with spiritual insight (*baṣāʾir*), plotting and planning in competition with God is nothing short of wrangling with the absolute lordship of God. If God sends down a situation that you desire to be lifted from you or lifts away a situation in which you desire to remain embedded, it is clear that you are fighting against divine lordship. How could you be anxious in a situation for which you know God is responsible and has set it up for you? You are fleeing from the responsibility of true servanthood.

To address such behavior, we can mention the words of Divine Speech: *Does humanity not see that we have created them each from a speck? Yet each is standing as if an open adversary!*[176] This verse rebukes humankind when we forget our origin and growth as utterly dependent beings. Instead of acknowledging our dependence, we struggle against that which nurtured us and ignore the secret of our lowly beginnings by arguing with our originator! How can it be right for someone who started as a spermazoid (*nuṭfa*), a mere single-celled speck, to argue with God over divine commands or to contradict God by seeking exemptions and appeals? So be constantly wary, my friend who resides in God's mercy, of plotting and planning for yourself.

Such plotting constitutes the gravest kind of alienation that prevents your heart from perceiving the reality beyond what is commonly seen, like a veil before your eyes. Really, your very ability to plot and plan for yourself comes from the creator's loving kindness for you. If you would pass beyond the self and let it fade (*fanā*ʾ) from view and remain subsiding with God (*baqā*ʾ), then you will find yourself beyond the need to plot and plan by yourself for yourself. Is there nothing more awful than a servant ignorant of God's subtle actions, who ignores God's constant care and oversight? Haven't you heard Divine Speech declare: *Say, 'God is sufficient...'*[177] How can it be said that people feel satisfied that God is sufficient if they concern themselves with self-centered strategies despite God? If they would consider God's own decisions truly good enough, this would terminate their urge to decide for themselves in contradiction to God.

SECTION SEVEN: OVERCOMING SELFISH CALCULATION

You should know that plotting and planning in spite of God has especially harmful effects for those who take seriously their spiritual path. This is true especially in their early stages, before they gain profound experience in certainty, strength and mastery. Heedless or evil people have already answered the tempter (*shayṭān*) through their grave sinning, contradicting religious teachings and following their own egoistic urges. So the tempter has no need to beckon them subtly through the urge to plot and plan. If the tempter would beckon them that way, they would surely answer temptation running! However, the tempter has no need for such subtleties. That is not temptation's strongest snare for them.

Rather, temptation penetrates the hearts of people who incline to obey God and their conscience through the urge to plot and plan. This is because the tempter is helpless to get close to them in any more direct way. How many good people who meditate and pray were distracted from their practice (*wird*) because they entertained worry by planning! How many people who are receptive to the presence of God were deflected from that gift because they were constricted by the anxiety of thinking of their own betterment! Even those who receive divine gifts and inspiration are often weakened as the tempter tosses them into intrigues of selfish calculation, soiling the purity of their spiritual moment. The tempter does this out of sheer jealousy! The jealous one (*ḥāsid*) only shudders with increasing paroxysms of envy if you experience a moment of time in spiritual purity. Such moments are unsullied by selfish clutter, so that your soul is whole and wholesome.

The whisperings of the urge to plot and plan resound with each of us differently, according to our distinctive spiritual condition. There are those who plan for how to care for the needs of today or tomorrow. Knowing that God cares for them with divine provision (*rizq*) cures them. Divine Speech tells us that, *There is no creature moving on the earth that does not receive provision undertaken by God.*[178] The details of this divine provision will be revealed and explained a little later in this book, in its own separate chapter, if God wills.[179]

There are those who plot and plan for the sake of deflecting the harm of an enemy who will never obey their command or cooperate with their intention. They are cured by knowing that the one whom they fear dangles from the true One's hand. The enemy can do nothing that is not actually done by the true One by means of the enemy. Such people should remember this moment of Divine Speech: *For whoever trusts completely in God, God is sufficient.*[180] They should remember the question, *Is not God sufficient for God's servant, yet they frighten you with what is other than God?*[181] And they should remember the consolation, *People said to them 'The people have all gathered against you,' to frighten them. But this only increases their faith! They say, 'God will take care of us—God is the best means of protection!' They received grace from God and a bounty they do not deserve. They are untouched by harm. They follow the satisfaction of God and God is characterized by bounteous giving beyond all bounds.*[182] Now listen intently with your heart to Divine Speech [addressing the mother of Moses who feared Pharaoh's order that all male children be killed], *If you are frightened for his sake, then cast him onto the river Nile. Be not afraid and do not grieve.*[183] Isn't God most deserving to receive petition for refuge? So turn to God when you seek protection, in accord with Divine Speech: *Who protects and seeks nothing for protection?*[184] Isn't God most deserving to receive your request for preservation? So preserve yourself in accord with Divine Speech, *God is the best preserver, the most merciful of those who show mercy.*[185]

There are some who plot and plan to pay off debts, debts they cannot faithfully repay in the present and whose creditors refuse to grant them more time. They should realize that the one whose grace made your way easy by having the money given to you is the same one whose grace will make your way easy by [giving the means for] repaying your debts in full. *Is the reward for goodness anything but goodness?*[186] Shame on those people who live for what appears to be in their possession, rather than living for what is provided for them from the true One's hand!

If you plot and plan for the sake of a family, for whose upkeep you are responsible, just remember that the One who will take care of them after your death is the same One who is caring for them while you are still alive, in your presence or your absence. Listen to what the Prophet has said [when embarking on a voyage], "O God, you are the companion during travels and the care-taker of the family, children and property left behind." The one upon whom you pin your hopes while you're alive is the same one who will be hoped for once you are gone! A Sufi once said: "The one to whom I have turned my face is the one whom I have delegated to care for those I've left behind. I don't fear for them since they are under that care, even for a moment, for the bounty of that source is so much wider than anything I might be able to give." God is more compassionate and caring toward your family than you could ever be! So why be anxious about people who are consigned to the attentive oversight of someone greater than yourself?

Maybe you are anxious because of some disease that has overpowered you, and you fear it may be protracted or that you may never recover from it. Just remember that every affliction and each disease has an appointed duration. Just as no living creature dies before the advent of its appointed time, no affliction lasts past its appointed duration. Recall to mind this moment of Divine Speech: *When their appointed time comes, they don't last one moment longer or die one moment too soon.*[187] Once a certain Sufi master had a son. When the Sufi died, his son remained occupying his place. After some time, the son encountered hard times and narrow financial straits in his finances. He decided to turn to one of his father's Sufi companions who had travelled to settle in Iraq [near the capital of the empire, Baghdad]. He gathered up his courage to go and see his father's companion, in hopes that he might have some clout among the people there. When he arrived at the house of his father's friend, the man hosted him generously and honored him warmly. Then he said to the son, "My master and the son of my master, why have you come to see me?" The son said, "I have come upon hard times. I need employment to support myself. I would like you to give me a good reference to the ruler of the country, so that he might grant me a place in his court with a salary that would keep me going all of my days." The old Sufi lowered his head for a while. Then he raised it to look the young man in the eye. He answered, "It is not in my power to make the first hour of the night into morning! I can do nothing for you until he inherits the rule of Iraq!" The son left bewildered and confused. By chance, it happened that the Caliph requested someone to tutor his son, the prince. Some courtier indicated that the Sufi master's son was an accomplished and educated person. The Sufi's son was quickly summoned to court and was appointed as tutor to the Caliph's son. He stayed on, patiently teaching the prince during his student years and after he came of age, the Sufi's son remained to accompany him as an elder advisor. He stayed by the prince's side for forty years. Then the Caliph passed away, and the prince who had been a mere schoolboy with a destitute tutor rose to become the ruler of Iraq!

Maybe you are anxious that your spouse or your house-servant should be in accord with your own state of mind, but they are not cooperating to help you in your affairs. If so, know that the One who made your way easy at the start gives bounty that is never extinguished and performs beautiful acts without ceasing. That One is able to give you divine gifts that are more beautiful and good than what you have now and knows what you currently lack. So don't be headstrong and ignorant!

The various dimensions of plotting and planning due to anxiety are limitless. It is impossible to enumerate each dimension here and thoroughly describe its appropriate cure, because the field of human frailty is so vast and its dimensions are beyond counting! In fact, when God gives you understanding appropriate to your spiritual condition, through your own experience God will let you know exactly what to do to counteract your frailty.

THE TRANQUIL SOUL'S RETURN

We plot and plan for ourselves because of the alienation we feel deep within our souls. However, if the heart can be kept safe from distraction in its environment and protected against whispering temptations that address it, then the heart will not be knocked astray by the blows of anxious planning. I have heard my master, Shaykh al-Mursi, teach that, "When God, the glorified and exalted One, created the earth upon the waters, it was infirm and restless. So God anchored the earth by rooting mountains deep into it. As Divine Speech relates, *God planted the mountains as firm anchors.*[188] In a parallel way, the human soul is restless and infirm. So God has anchored it by fixing in us our power of reason (*ʿaql*) like firm mountains."[189] God sends down the feeling of stillness and equipoise (*sakīna*) to whoever has a strong ability to reason and has an expansive light of in-

The Dawn
Surat al-Fajr 89:15-30

As for human beings, when their Lord tries them
    then honors them with high standing and goods,
    they say 'My Lord has honored me.' (15)
But when their Lord tries them
    then appoints only limited amounts of provision
    they say 'My Lord has humiliated me." (16)
But no, you do not honor generously the orphans (17)
    And do not encourage feeding the needy (18)
    And you consume the inheritance greedily (19)
    And you love wealth with a lust for luxury! (20)
Oh no, when the earth is pulverized dust into dust (21)
    And your Lord comes and the angels rank upon rank (22)
    And the punishing fire that day is brought forth,
    That day the human being calls everything to mind
    but what use will that reminder be? (23)
They say, 'If only I had something to put forward for my life!" (24)
That day God inflicts punishment that none other inflicts (25)
    Binding firmer than any other binds. (26)
O tranquil soul (27)
    Return to your Lord
    well-pleased and well-pleasing. (28)
    Enter in among my servants (29)
    And enter into my garden (30)

sight. That person's soul will be still, unaffected by restless disturbance. Such a person will become a safe deposit for those with worldly means and power. Such a soul is tranquil (*muṭmaʾina*), resting balanced under the commands of its Lord, well-established by the Lord's empowering decrees and receiving help by the Lord's accord and illumination. Such a soul is free of any urge to plot or plan out of selfish calculation. Such a soul does not struggle with the currents of divine decrees. Having become truly Muslim, it is resigned to the will of its Lord, knowing that it will be well looked after. *Or does it not suffice you that your Lord watches over all things?*[190]

Such a soul certainly deserves to be addressed by God: *O you tranquil soul, return to your sustainer, well-pleased and well-pleasing. Enter in among my servants and enter into my garden.*[191]

This moment of Divine Speech is rich in profound qualities. It is laden with special praise for such a tranquil soul. Firstly, you should know that there are three types of souls described by the Qurʾan: the soul that commands harmful acts, the soul that blames, and the tranquil soul (*al-nafs al-muṭmaʾina*). The true One turns to only one kind of soul with a full face of acceptance—to the tranquil soul. To the soul that commands evil, the true One says *Surely the soul is one that commands harmful acts* (*al-nafs al-ʿammāra biʾl-sūʾ*).[192] To the blaming soul, the true One says, *I swear by the day of resurrection and I swear by the soul full of blame* (*al-nafs al-lawwāma*).[193] However, the true One accepts the third kind of soul with a welcoming address, *O tranquil soul, return...*

This moment of Divine Speech gives such a soul a most powerful name, *tranquil*. In Arabic discourse, such naming is a form of magnifying such a soul's might and constitutes

194

the greatest pride for those endowed with insight. This phrase also expresses divine praise for such a soul. It is praised for its tranquility, a result of its resignation (*istislām*) and complete trust in the true One (*tawakkul*). This reveals a paradox! The soul is described by tranquility; that which is tranquil is at rest in the lowest and humblest level of the earth. When the soul rests low in the earth through humility and brokenness, its Lord praises it to reveal its true, lofty value. As the Prophet has said, "Whoever is humbled before God will be raised in value by God."

The address continues, *Return to your sustainer, well-pleased and well-pleasing*. This hints subtly at the fact that God does not permit the soul that commands evil or the soul full of blame to return to God with a fully generous and ennobling return. Only the tranquil soul is invited to such a return, because of its quality of humble tranquility. Only such a soul is addressed by the welcoming invitation, *Return to your Lord, well-pleased and well-pleasing*. It is as if Divine Speech were saying, 'We have permitted your entrance into our presence and allowed you to eternally reside in our garden.' This invitation encourages people to struggle to achieve this spiritual station of tranquility. Yet none can reach it except through utter resignation before God, by abandoning all plotting in self-concern in competition with God.

Listen closely! This moment of Divine Speech says, *Return to your Lord*. It does not say 'Return to the Lord' or 'Return to God.' To those with insight, this shows that the tranquil soul's return is by the gentle, imminent subtlety of God's quality of being the sustaining Lord (*lutf rubūbīya*), rather than by the overpowering, transcendent power of God's quality of being the divinity (*qahr ilāhīya*). For the

195

tranquil soul, this return is an experience of intimacy, characterized by grace, generosity and love.

God calls such a soul *well-pleased*. The soul was pleased with God during its passage through this world, pleased with the divine decrees it faced. The soul is also well-pleased in the next world, pleased with divine beneficence and blessings [in paradise]. In this phrase there is a warning, so take heed! There is no real return to God except through tranquility before God and satisfaction with God. If the soul does not experience these qualities at the deepest level, no real return to God is possible. There is a hint here for you. It's not possible to be well-pleasing to God in the next world without first being well-pleased with God in this world!

You might say that this verse requires us to believe that God's satisfaction with a person is caused by the person's satisfaction with God. Yet there is another moment of Divine Speech that would seem to reverse the priority of this cause and effect relationship: *God is pleased with them and they are pleased with God.*[194] Though each moment of Divine Speech establishes a certain facet of truth, comparing the phrasing of these moments can establish a distinct ranking between cause and effect. In reality, a person's being well-pleased with God is the result of God's being well-pleased with that person. If God were not pleased and satisfied with people initially, people could never [have the tranquility] to be well-pleased with God subsequently. That is established by the first citation. The phrasing, *God is pleased with them and they are pleased with God,* demonstrates that whoever is pleasing to God while living in this world becomes pleased with God in the life to come. That is clear without any ambiguity.

Return to your Lord, well-pleased and well-pleasing.
Focus now on the word *well-pleasing.* This is the highest
praise for the tranquil soul! To be pleasing to God is the
mightiest praise and best description possible. Haven't you
heard Divine Speech extol the blissful blessings enjoyed
by those who dwell in paradise, and then pronounce, *Yet
satisfaction from God is greater!*[195] Their being well-pleasing to God is greater than any blessing they might enjoy in
heaven.

This moment of Divine Speech continues to say, *Enter
in among my servants.* This phrase contains a profound secret meaning for such a tranquil soul. The soul is addressed
directly and invited to take its place among the righteous
servants of God. What servants are these? These are servants who serve with empowerment and special distinction,
rather than servants who serve only through ownership and
coercion. These are the servants whom God has described
by saying, *Over my servants you have no authority,* when
the tempter threatens to waylay all people, *except for your
servants among them who are righteous and sincere.*[196]
These intimate servants are distinguished from the others,
who are also called "servants" in a more general sense, as
indicated by, *Everything in the heavens and the earth approaches the compassionate One as a servant.*[197]

The tranquil soul rejoices at this invitation to *enter in
among my servants* far more than rejoicing at the invitation
to *enter into my garden.* This is because, in the first phrase,
the servants are linked directly to God's presence, while in
the second phrase, they are linked to God only indirectly
through the intermediary form of God's garden. So then
why follow the first phrase with the second, *and enter into
my garden*? In this is a secret allusion to the fact that all
these excellent qualities attributed to the tranquil soul are

what entitle it to be invited to enter into the garden. This means, primarily, the subtle garden of obedience in this world. Only in a secondary sense does it mean the more commonly recognized garden of paradise in the next world. God knows best the true meaning.

In summary, this moment of Divine Speech describes two key virtues, both of which collapse the egoistic foundations of plotting and planning. The true One described this type of soul, with all its special qualities elucidated above, as having tranquility and satisfaction. Both virtues can exist only when one abandons the primal urge to plot and plan in concern for oneself. The soul can be tranquil only after desisting from this urge toward selfish calculation by trusting in the plans of the divine to care for it. If the soul is well-pleased and satisfied with God, it is resigned to God, handing back all power of decision to God and accepting each divine command. This soul is therefore tranquil in the face of God's lordship. The soul settles firmly into reliance upon God's divinity. No restlessness disturbs it, because of the light of reason granted to it. No wayward motion derails it. Such a soul is submissive to divine decrees and abandons all pretense of bargaining or appealing.

The secret of why we are given the power to decide is to reveal the power of God who will override. God desires to reveal to us God's quality of having the power of overpowering (*qahr al-qahhār*). So God created human beings with the ability to freely plan, calculate and chose. Then God drew away from people behind layers of alienation (*ḥajaba*), so that people might gain mastery over their power of choice. Clearly, had people remained in direct sight of God and oriented toward the divine face, they could never exercise the manipulation of plotting and choosing for themselves! The highest angels, for example, have no ability to choose or calculate for themselves.

So when people turned away from God in alienation and began to choose for themselves, God directed the quality of divine overpowering against their flimsy choices. The pillars people erect begin to quaver. The foundations they lay begin to waver. Their buildings of expectation crumble. When God makes divine nature known to us by overpowering our plans, the goal is that we come to know God as the One who overpowers (*al-qāhir*) so that we might seek protection from such might! It is as if God were saying, 'Free will was not created in you so that you should exercise your will without restraint. Rather it was created in you so that divine will could refute your free will and show you that your ego's claims are void!' The goal is for you to acknowledge through your experience that in reality you have no right to choose. Likewise, you have not been made to plot and plan so that you always get what you want. No! Rather you were created to plot and plan in contradiction to what God plans so that you might clearly see that reality follows God's plans, not yours. Your plans amount to sheer illusion. For this reason, when one Sufi was asked, "How do you know God?" the Sufi replied, "Through everything I decide coming to naught!"

Tomb of Abū al-Ḥasan al-Shādhilī (d. 1258)
Humaythira, Upper Egypt

I had promised to dedicate an entire chapter to detail the problem of plotting and planning to secure one's livelihood. This is necessary because selfish calculation penetrates deep into our hearts when we worry about our livelihood. It is the greatest blessing to be granted safety from anxiety about receiving provision to sustain our lives (*rizq*). None are granted such safety except the people of accord (*al-muwaffaqūn*) who sincerely trust God's promises. Their hearts are tranquil in turning to God. They realize in truth how to entrust their needs to God's care.

SECTION ONE: BODILY NEEDS

The issue of how we receive our livelihood is so crucial that one Sufi master has said to his disciples, "All I ask from you is to master this problem of provision, and don't bother with the other spiritual stations!" Another Sufi master has said, "The most intense anxiety is worrying about fulfilling our basic needs." He means that God created humankind very needy. In our neediness, we reach out to grasp with our will and intention, extending our power over objects around us to fulfill our needs. When our instinctual drives (*al-ḥarāra al-gharīzīya*) fire up, their heat animates all the parts of our bodies. The stomach has the quality of driving us to gather food, cook it and consume it. This alone has the power to return each part of the body back to its quiet nature after it had been excited into motion by instinctual drives. If the true One had desired, human existence could have been created free of the need to extend our senses into the wider world and partake of nutrients from

201

the wider world. However, God desired that the animal foundation of our existence be expressed through our need to eat continually to sustain ourselves. God is absolutely free of such need, upon which we animals are so clearly dependent. Divine Speech tells us, *Say 'Do I take other than God as my protector? By the shaper of the heavens and the earth! God it is who provides sustenance and does not partake of sustenance.*[1] God is distinguished by having these two qualities. Firstly, God provides all others with nourishment and sustenance. All living things take nourishment from God's generous bounty and survive by the provision God provides, both nutritional and spiritual. Secondly, God is not sustained by anything other, neither feeding nor partaking. God is holy and wholly other, far beyond the need to eat or consume. Rather, God is the eternally everlasting (*al-ṣamad*), meaning that God alone is self-sustaining without beginning or ending.

God specified that animals must hunt and gather, constantly searching for nutrition in their impoverishment. This quality characterizes animals more than other kinds of created beings, such as plants or material objects. Animals are like this because God has granted to animals more of the divine's own qualities (*ṣifāt*). Animals, and especially humankind, might claim continuity with divinity if God had left them without the need to feed! In divine wisdom and insight, God desired to make humans, like other animals, completely dependent on food and drink for nourishment and on clothing for shelter. God emphasized the human being's innate neediness in order to subdue any urge we might feel to claim divinity ourselves or have divinity claimed for us.

We can say that the true One made us human beings, like all animals, in grave need as a conduit through which

202

we can know God. Don't you see that your need is a gateway to God's presence? It can cause you to arrive closer to God. Haven't you heard Divine Speech announce, *O people! You are in need of God while God is free of need, worthy of praise.*[2] We were created needy and dependent upon God as a means to grow closer to God and remain constantly in the divine presence. In this context, you might better comprehend the Prophet's teaching that, "Those who know themselves know their sustaining Lord (*man ᶜarifa nafsahu ᶜarifa rabbahu*)."[3] Whoever knows the human self in its need, poverty, emptiness and helplessness indeed knows the sustaining One in the fullness of divine ability, authority, overflowing bounty and ceaseless giving that characterize the Lord, from among the other qualities of completeness, perfection and independence which contrast with every human trait.

A PARABLE
FROM WHERE DO YOUR RICHES COME?

Imagine the servant of a master who is famed far and wide for his wealth and goodwill, who is never known to refuse generosity and beneficence. The servant could trust in his master's overflowing generosity and could look to his rich master to insure his wellbeing. This trust removed from the servant any distress from being preoccupied with himself.

This situation is precisely what inspired Shaqīq al-Balkhī to renounce the world, repent and take up spiritual cultivation.[4] He said, "I was traveling abroad in a time of famine. Suddenly I came across a slave boy who was singularly joyful and carefree despite the hard times. He was completely oblivious to the anxieties that plagued other people's

203

thoughts. I said to him, 'Hey, you arrogant boy, don't you realize that other people are suffering?' He replied 'Why should I care when my master owns a whole town for himself and imports each day whatever we need?' So I wondered to myself, 'If his master has a town all to himself, then my master possesses the treasure-house of the whole earth and all the heavens! How much more should I trust my Lord than this arrogant lad trusts his!'" This event was the singular cause of Shaqīq's spiritual awakening.

The true One has intensified the depth of our human need (*ḥāja*) and multiplied the dimensions of our empty void (*fāqa*). This is to insure that we rectify our way of living, aligning it with the inevitability of returning to our creator. In this context, try to understand this moment of Divine Speech: *We have created humankind toiling in suffering.*[5] We suffer the pains of labor to survive in this world and to find our place in the next world. The deeper our need in this world, the higher our potential is in the next world. In order to more generously honor humankind, God multiplied and intensified our neediness, sinking it deep in our human nature. Don't you realize that other kinds of animals are created more independent than we are? They have their claws and fangs. Their pelts and wool replace our need to wear clothes. Their nests and burrows make them free of the need to construct permanent abodes. Human beings are certainly the most needy of animals!

The true One desired to put this human being to the test. So we were made needy in so many ways. This was to see if we would try to depend on our powers of reason and calculation to make our own way, or if we would rather turn to God to receive what is apportioned and appointed for each of us. Seen from a different perspective, the true One wants to enter into a loving relationship with the human servant. So when we find ourselves in need of means to survive and raise those needs to God to provide for us, we taste a kind of spiritual sweetness in the soul and a refreshing restfulness in the heart. This sparks us to renew our love for the One who sustains us. The Prophet has taught, "Love God for what is given to you in blessing to feed you." Each moment we are receiving a blessing of sustenance, there is the potential to rejuvenate our love of God because of the blessing.

From another perspective, the true One wants to be thanked. So God submerged us in need and took on the responsibility for meeting our needs. This is so that we might engage God in thanks for fulfilling our needs and gratefully acknowledge God's generosity and beneficence. Divine Speech pronounces, *Consume then what your sustainer provides for you, and give thanks— A wholesome land and a most forgiving Lord.*[6]

From yet another perspective, we can say that God desired to open for us servants the door of petition and intimate conversation with God (*munājāt*). Every moment that we need food or other blessings to fulfill our needs, we have the opportunity to turn to God with our full attention in order to offer up our anxieties. In this way, we are honored by the chance to petition God and have intimate conversation with the divine about our need. If God had not poured out for us the cup of poverty, the vast majority of people would never trouble their minds to think of God. If people were not submerged in need, only those few people who are overcome by love and longing would ever open the door of petition and conversation with God. We can say that our poverty and need are subtle causes of our engaging in conversation with God. Such prayerful conversation is such an honor for us! It is almost a miraculous gift. It is certainly priceless.

Haven't you heard Divine Speech recount the narrative of Moses (Mūsā)? *So he watered for the two women [their flocks]. Then he turned back to the shade, and said 'My Lord, of whatever you send down for me I am in need!'*[7] This story has been explained by ᶜAli, who said, "Moses requested only a little bread to eat while he was so emaciated that the skin of his belly was translucent." So observe closely, may God have mercy on you, how Moses asked his Lord, even in such dire need, knowing that he owns nothing beyond what God might give. Every believer should be like Moses! Ask for anything, whether great or small, with such etiquette. One Sufi has said, "I don't ask God for anything, even a pinch of salt for the dough of my daily bread!"

My dear believer, do not let the smallness of your need prevent you from asking for what you need! If you don't remember God by asking for the smallest needs, know that you are not worthy to receive even that little bit from anyone other than God. Each request, even if it seems to be of no consequence, becomes an open door to intimate conversation with God, which is of great consequence.[8] Shaykh al-Shadhili has taught, "The point of your petition is not to have your need fulfilled and yet be alienated from your sustaining Lord. Rather the point of your petition is to converse with your Lord in intimacy."

Inherent in this moment of Divine Speech are many subtle insights. Moses said, *My Lord, of whatever you send down for me I am in need!* Firstly, each believer should ask

206

Then he [Musa] turned his face toward the land of Madyan.
He said, 'Perhaps my Lord will guide me to a right path!' (22)
He found there a community of people watering [their flocks]
    and he found excluded two women who were keeping back [their flocks].
He said, 'What is the matter with you two?'
They said, 'We cannot water [our flocks] since the shepherds have pushed ahead
    for our father is an old man.' (23)
So he [Musa] watered for the two women [their flocks].
Then he turned back to the shade and said 'My Lord!
Of whatever good you send down of benefit for me I am in need!' (24)
Later, one of the two women came to him, walking bashfully.
She said, 'My father invites you to come,
    to reward you for having watered for us [our flocks].
When he [Musa] came to him and told his story,
    he [the father] said, 'Do not fear!
It is good that you escaped from an oppressive people [in Egypt].' (25)
One of the daughters said, 'O Father, hire him for wages.
The best of men you could hire [to help us] is one strong and trustworthy.' (26)
He [the father] said, 'I desire to marry one of these, my two daughters, to you
    on the condition that you work for me for eight years.
If you complete ten years [of labor] for me, that would be [a favor] from you.
But I do not want to make you suffer any difficulty.
Rather, you will find me, if God wills, one of the righteous. (27)
He [Musa] said, 'That is [a covenant] between you and me.
Whichever of the two periods I fulfill, let there be no enmity toward me.
God is one to help execute what we have said. (28)
Then when [Musa] had fulfilled the period and was traveling with his family,
    he spied from the direction of Mount Tūr a fire.
He said to his family, 'Wait here, I have seen a fire. Perhaps I can bring you
    some information or a burning coal
    so that you might warm yourselves. (29)
But when he approached [the fire], he was addressed
    by a voice from the right side of the valley
    in a place of hallowed ground, from a tree.
'O Musa! I am God, the Lord of all worlds! (30)
Now cast down your staff!' But when he saw it slither
    as if it were a serpent, he turned his back
    [about] to retreat but did not retrace his steps.
'O Musa! Turn your face here and approach!
Do not be afraid, for you are among those who are secure. (31)
Now move your hand into the folds of your shirt and remove it
    it will be glowing brightly without harm.
Draw in the flight of fear and do not be alarmed.
Those are two signs of proof from your Lord
    to Pharaoh and his powerful chiefs.
In truth they are a community corrupt.' (32)

the Lord for every need, as detailed above. Secondly, notice how Moses called out to God after specifying the name of divine lordship, "My Lord! (*rabbī*)" This address is most fitting in this context, for the Lord it is who sustains you with sincere beneficence (*iḥsān*) and feeds you with generous benevolence (*imtinān*). By initiating the request with "My Lord!" Moses entreated his Lord to look with sympathy upon him, since this is the name of lordship whose conventions are never dispelled and whose benefits are never withheld.

Thirdly, notice how Moses says, *of whatever good you send down for me I am in need!* He does not say, "I am in need of something good." If he had said "I am in need of something good from you" or "I am in need of some good," he would not have included in his request the fact that God sends down his provision, never neglecting his state of affairs. Rather Moses said, *of whatever good you send down for me I am in need,* to show that he trusts in God and knows that God never forgets him. It is as if Moses were saying, "My Lord! I know that you never neglect my need or the need of anything you've created. You've sent down my provision. So pour out for me what you've sent down for me in any manner you will, through any means you will, encompassed by your beneficence and accompanied by your benevolence."

Moses's words contain two kinds of benefit: the benefit of asking in the first place and the benefit of acknowledging that the true One alone sends down his provision. However, this provision is sent down with its timing obscure, its means uncertain and its intermediary ambiguous. This is so that the servant might remain in a state of distressed agitation (*iḍṭirār*). In the asker's agitation is the answer of the petition! This is in accord with Divine Speech:

Or [*is it other than God*] *who answers the distressed when he calls out?*[9] If the timing, means and intermediaries of divine provision were specified for us, we humans would never experience the distressed agitation that comes when these factors remain hidden. So glory be to God, the wise One, the One who is able, the One who knows all!

Fourthly, this moment of Divine Speech shows us that asking from God does not shake the foundation of one's being a true servant. Moses reached completion in the state of servanthood and after that still made requests of God. This demonstrates for us that asking does not invalidate true servanthood. You might object and say, 'If true servanthood is not invalidated by asking God to fulfill our needs, then why did Abraham, the intimate of God, refuse to ask anything of God when he was thrown on the catapult to be hurled into the fire? Gabriel appeared to him, saying, 'Do you need anything?' Abraham answered, 'From you I need nothing but from God, yes, I am in need.' So Gabriel said, 'Then ask of God,' to which Abraham replied, 'What need is there to ask since God knows well my condition?' It was enough for Abraham to acknowledge that God knows his miserable condition and that he never needs to come forth openly with any request. Asking was beneath him." The answer to this objection would be that the Prophets, may God bless and praise them all, act in every situation according to what they comprehend as appropriate to that situation through their intuitive understanding of God.

For example, Abraham understood that his purpose in this particular situation was to not request anything outwardly and remain satisfied inwardly with God's knowledge of his plight. So he remained true to his intuitive understanding of God's purpose for him. This purpose was for God, the glorified and exalted One, to reveal to the highest angels the secret of divine care for humanity. When God told them, *'I am making on the earth a vice-regent,'* [*the angels*] *said, 'Will you make on the earth one who will ruin it and shed blood, while we glorify you with praise and extol your holiness? God said, 'Surely I know what you do not know.'*[10] Because of this prior event, on the day that Abraham was hurled into the torture chamber, God intended to reveal the secret of this statement, *Surely I know what you do not know*. It was as if God were saying, 'O you who asked me, *Will you make on the earth one who will ruin it? What do you think of my intimate friend, Abraham?* Have you observed the difference in behavior between the people of corruption, like Nimrod and those who resemble him, and the people of righteousness and straightforwardness, like Abraham and those loving, kind people who follow his example?" As for Moses, he intuited that God intended for him, in that moment [after watering the flocks of the marginalized women] to exhibit his utter need and to express it verbally in a request. Moses acted exactly as the spiritual moment demanded of him! *To each is a goal they turn to face.*[11] Each Prophet acts upon clear insight and guiding direction in accord with divine intent, safeguarded by divine protection.

Observe closely how Moses requests from God his provision. He does not begin directly with his petition! No, he acknowledges his absolute poverty and need before his sustaining Lord. He bears witness to God's self-sufficiency and transcendent being above need. As Moses acknowledges his own poverty and emptiness, he implicitly acknowledges his Lord's self-sufficiency and overflowing fullness. This is the experience of reclining on the carpet of intimate conversation (*munājāt*). Once it is spread wide for you, its patterns are endless![12] At times, God seats you on the expanse of poverty and you call out to God, "*Ya Ghanī!* O self-sufficient One!" At times, God seats you on the expanse of humility and you call out, "*Ya ʿAzīz!* O mighty One!" At times, you are seated on the expanse of weakness and you call out, "*Ya Qawī!* O powerful One!" There are other patterns on this widespread carpet, each corresponding to one of the divine names (*asmāʾ*). In this way, Moses acknowledged his position of utter poverty and urgent need in respect to God. This introductory gesture itself is an indication of petition. Even if Moses had not explicitly requested anything, he would have implied a request through calling to mind (*bi-dhikr*) the qualities of being a servant, like his poverty and need for God. This is, in effect, calling to mind the qualities of the Lord, like God's all-sustaining being (*wujūd*) and absolute singleness (*aḥadīya*). This is in accord with the Prophet Muhammad's teaching, "The best petitioning prayer of mine and of the Prophets before me is to say, 'There is no god but God, who is One with no partner.'" Muhammad declared this praise of God to be the best prayer and the finest form of petition. Praise of the Lord who owns all by recalling the qualities of completeness is a way to evoke the Lord's bounty and favor with politeness.

> Generous is he whom neither morning
> > Nor evening finds changed in his virtue of giving
> If one day you praise him, once is enough
> > He gives, never forcing you to keep on praising

Divine Speech has told the story of Jonah (*Yūnus* or *Dhū al-Nūn*): *Then he called out in the darkness, crying 'There is no god but you! Glory be to you! Indeed I was one of those who oppressed and did wrong!*[13] To this plea, God spoke, giving information about divine nature, *Then we*

211

answered his request and we rescued him from anxiety. In this way we rescue the believers. Observe closely how Jonah never requested anything directly. Rather, Jonah praised his Lord and submitted himself before the Lord. In this way, he expressed his need to God. The true One takes this as a request.

Now there is another point of insight, and by all rights this one should come before the others. Remember that Moses had an interaction with the daughters of Shuᶜayb [the Prophet sent to the people of Madyan]. He treated the two daughters kindly. He worked for them without demanding any payment or seeking any reward. When he helped them water their flocks, he turned his face to his Lord to ask [for something good to quench his hunger]. He never asked anything from those two women, but rather asked only from his true master who gives to anyone who asks, whenever asked. The Sufi is one who gives fully of the self, not one who gets fully for the self (*al-ṣūfī man yūfī min nafsihi wa la yastawfī li-hā*). To expresses this essential idea more fully, I've composed a poem.

> Why be preoccupied getting
> what you "deserve" from others
> Even for a day, you waste your time
> that is precious and rare
>
> Rather follow the guides
> and remain sincere
> Let the current of destiny
> carry your every affair

People haven't given themselves
 over to God as is right
Expecting satisfaction from people,
 you'll pass away in despair

Admit their rights over you and rise
 to fulfill them
Give of yourself fully
 without restraint, without care

If you do this, you'll surely be
 witnessed by the One
Who knows all hidden things,
 the One ever aware

Moses gave fully of himself rather than expecting to get fully for himself. So with God was his reward—a most complete and perfect reward. God rushed good things to him in this world, in addition to what reward God stored up for him in the next world. One of the daughters married him, forging a connection between Moses and the other Prophet of his era, Shuᶜayb. Through this marriage, Moses was able to keep company with Shuᶜayb and grow intimate with him, until the time when Moses' own prophetic mission began and he was sent with the message. So learn from his example, my dear believer, and don't entrust your affairs to anyone in competition with God. In this way, you might receive profit and God might honor you with generous gifts given to those servants who stay warily conscious of God (*al-muttaqīn*).

DRINKING COOL WATER AFTER HARD WORK

Look carefully now at the phrase of Divine Speech, *So he watered for the two women [their flocks]. Then he turned back to the shade.* There is proof in this moment of revelation that the believer is allowed to take shelter in the shade from the scorching noonday sun, to drink cooling water in the heat of work, and to take the easier of two paths rather than the more arduous. Taking advantage of this ease does not nullify the believer's basic ascetic virtue. Haven't you noted how God recounts for us that Moses finished his work *and then he turned back to the shade*, meaning that he turned toward the shade and went over to it.

Now someone might object, saying, "Some people interpret this phase to mean that Moses went to the shade and found that the sunshine had moved along the ground to shine directly on the jug of water from which he would drink. He realized this and said [to himself], 'When I placed the jug there, the sun wasn't shining there [making the cool water hot]. But now, I am too humble to go there and move it for my own sake.'" Now, my dear believer, you should know, and may God be merciful with you, that this would be the spiritual state of servants who are in the process of demanding from themselves absolute sincerity (*ṣidq*). By denying the self its every wish, such servants hope to keep the self occupied and aloof from the temptation of growing neglectful of the Lord. If such servants persevere at this stage and their spiritual state grows complete, then they would, in contrast, go over and lift the jug of water from its place in the sun, in order to uphold their own rights that God has ordered them to uphold. They do not do this to procure some selfish benefit to which they are not entitled, but rather to uphold the rights granted by their Lord. For God has declared in Divine Speech, *God desires for you ease and does not desire for you hardship* and also, *God desires to lighten your burden, for the human being is created weak.*[14] For this reason, jurists warn us against the practice of walking barefoot to Mecca for the pilgrimage. The jurists permit wearing shoes and do not oblige us to go barefoot, for the goal of religious law and custom (*shar*ᶜ) is not to tire people with exhausting demands. Nor did the systems of religious law come to forbid us from pleasurable activities. How could this be when religious law and custom were created for the sake of people themselves?

A story about ᶜAli illustrates this point. Once al-Rabīᶜ ibn Ziyād al-Ḥārithī said to ᶜAli, "Help me deal with my brother, ᶜĀṣim!" ᶜAli asked, "What about him is bothering you?" Al-Rabiᶜ said, "He's taken to wearing the [woolen] cloak, intending to increase his piety through ascetic denial (*nask*)." So ᶜAli suggested, "Bring him to me." Al-Rabiᶜ went and brought his brother, ᶜAṣim, who was wrapped up in his rough woolen cloak, his hair in shambles and his beard all tangled. ᶜAli looked him sternly in the face and said, "Woe be unto you! Have you no shame in front of your family? Have you no compassion for your children? Don't you see that God has made permissible for you enjoyment of the good things of this world? But you, man, you hate to get anything good from the world. No, rather, you insult God! Haven't you heard Divine Speech say, *And the earth, [God] set it in place for humankind. In it are fruit and date palms with clusters like sleeves. And grain with shocks and straw, and fragrant herbs. Then which of your Lord's favors will you deny? God created humankind from clay like pottery, and created jinn from smokeless fire. Then which of your Lord's favors will you deny? Lord of the two Easts and Lord of the two Wests. Then which of your Lord's favors will you deny? God released the two seas that meet,*

215

between them is a barrier they do not transgress. Then which of your Lord's favors will you deny? From them come forth pearls and precious coral. Then which of your Lord's favors will you deny?[15] Do you think God has made all this permissible for people only for us to act as if it were all base and degraded, or rather so that people might praise God for each good thing that God might reward them? Your despising the blessings of God in deed is better than despising it in word." To this exhortation, ᶜAṣim replied, "How then do you justify the roughness of the clothes you wear and the simplicity of food you eat?" ᶜAli responded, "How wrong you are! God has made it compulsory on the true leaders of the community (*al-aʾimma*) to take upon themselves the weakness and humble means of the lowliest of the people they lead."

It is clear from ᶜAli's example that the true One never demands that people abstain from pleasurable activities. God only asks us to be truly thankful for the pleasures we enjoy. Consider Divine Speech, *Eat from the provision of your Lord and give God thanks,* and also, *O you who believe! Eat of good things that we have provided you and give thanks to God.*[16] It also commands, *O Prophets! Eat good things and perform good deeds.*[17] God never said, 'Don't eat' but rather said, 'Eat and act.' Now you might protest that "the good things" (*al-ṭayyibāt*) in these examples were intended to mean "lawful things" (*al-ḥalāl*), since only lawful things are good in respect to religious law. It may be the intent of Divine Speech that "good things" means "lawful things" because a lawful thing is good in respect to its not being related to sin or blameworthiness and not causing alienation from God. However, it is equally possible that "good things" is intended to mean delicious and enjoyable things.

216

In that case, the secret of God's making these delights permissible and ordering us to eat of them is to convey that those who eat and enjoy will have their spiritual aspiration energized to give thanks. In giving thanks, they will rise to serve others, guard the rights of others, and respect their sacred boundaries.

A PARABLE

YOU ARE HOW YOU EAT

Imagine that a man has an orchard, and that he orders his servant to tend it, planting trees and cultivating them to secure their wellbeing. If the servant rises to the occasion and endeavors to obey his master's orders expeditiously, then why would the master criticize him for eating of the produce of the orchard? How could the master prevent the servant from nourishing himself from it? If he works hard, the servant will only make use of what is in the orchard for the purpose of rendering service in the orchard. He would not eat of the orchard for his own pleasure and indulgence.

In regard to God's making enjoyments permissible, Shaykh al-Shadhili has taught that "My Shaykh [Ibn Mashīsh] said to me, 'O my son, consider the importance of cool water! For if a person drinks hot water, he would say *Praise be to God* without full enthusiasm. But if a person drinks cool, refreshing water, he would say *Praise be to God* with such enthusiasm that he would, in every fiber of his body, affirm *Yes, praise be to God!*" Then Shaykh al-Shadhili returned to the moment of Divine Speech under consideration [about Moses and the shade]. He said, "Consider the person who finds that the sunshine has moved to shine on his water-jug, and when it is suggested to him, 'Why don't you move the jug [to the shade]?' He answers, 'When I set it down there was no sunshine there, and I'm now too shamed to go and move it for my own sake.' Such a person is possessed of a spiritual state (*ṣāḥib al-ḥāl*) particular to him. Others are not obliged to follow his example!"[18]

YOU ARE CREATED TO SERVE

Earlier, I had revealed to you the secret of why God made all animals in need of constant nourishment through food, especially this human being. Now, let me speak about how the true One takes responsibility for providing such nourishing food and establishes the means for conveying it into our grasp.

Consider carefully how the true One made animals in need of food through which they preserve their existence in this world. In the case of two species of sentient beings, humans and jinn, such need was coupled with the command to worship God and the request to obey by living in accord with God's will.[19] Divine Speech intones, *I have created humankind and jinn only to worship me. I do not desire from them any provision and I do not want from them any sustenance. God it is who is the provider, possessor of steadfast power.*[20] God makes clear in this Speech that these two species of sentient beings were created solely to worship and serve God. The reason they were created was to be commanded to worship. It is just as you might say to your slave, "Hey, slave, I purchased you only to serve me—I command you to do what I need from you in any moment, so rise to the occasion!" It could be that your slave might contradict you and refuse! Still, that does not change the fact that you did not purchase the slave to rebel and refuse, but rather to perform acts that are important for you and to take care of your needs.

When interpreting this moment of Divine Speech, the rationalist theologians (*mu^ctazila*) treat it literally. They think that the true One created humans and jinn to obey; therefore they conclude that infidelity (*kufr*) and rebellion (*ma^cṣīya*) proceed from people's own volition. I have shown earlier how such rationalist views are null and void.[21] However, some clarification is necessary here as to the real secret behind the creation of humans and jinn, so that you and others might understand why you were brought into existence and don't remain ignorant of what God truly desires of you. If people remain ignorant of this secret, they will veer from the path of guidance and be lost, neglecting the ever-present watchfulness that guards over them.

It is said that each day, four angels answer each other in harmony. One of them starts by saying, "If only these [sentient] creatures had never been created!" Another angel answers, "Since they have been created, if only they knew why there were created!" to which a third responds, "If they realized why they were created, if only they would act on that knowledge!" Another sings out, "Having failed to act on what they know, if only they would beg forgiveness for what they have done!" The true One has made clear that human beings are not created for their own sake. Rather they were created only to worship God and make God One (*yuwaḥḥidūhu*). You don't purchase a slave to look after himself and his own needs! No, you purchase a slave to act as a servant for you. Divine Speech offers a decisive proof of the falsehood of people who are preoccupied with themselves, allowing concern for their own good to overshadow their awareness of their Lord. Such people allow their vain desires to divert them from obedience to their true master.

219

Once Ibrahim ibn Adham, went out hunting.[22] During this venture, he had an encounter that led him to repent of his former life and sparked his spiritual journey. While riding along, he heard a voice call out to him from the horn of his saddle! "O Ibrahim, for this purpose you were created? To do this you were commanded?" Then he heard the voice a second time, "O Ibrahim, not for this purpose were you created! No, not to do this were you commanded!" Intelligent and rational people are those who understand deeply the secret of their creation and act aptly upon that knowledge. This is real understanding (*al-fiqh al-ḥaqīqī*) [to which literal or legal understanding of religion is incomparable]. Whoever is given real understanding is given the greatest gift. About such understanding the great jurist, Mālik ibn Anas, has said, "Understanding does not come from knowing a lot of traditions [about the Prophet]. Rather understanding is an illumination that God lights in the heart."[23] Similarly, my master, Shaykh al-Mursi, has taught that, "Educated people are those who have pierced the veil that covered the eyes of their hearts (*al-faqīh man infaqaʾa al-ḥijāb ʿan ʿaynay qalbihi*)."[24]

Those given such understanding by God are aware of the secret of their being called into existence, namely that God brought them into existence that they might obey and created them so that they might serve. Such understanding drives them to live in the world with ascetic simplicity and to direct their full attention to preparing for the next world. It causes them to desist from grabbing what is good for them; rather, it causes them to become engrossed with maintaining the rights that their master claims over them. They ponder their inevitable meeting with their Lord, constantly preparing themselves to face their master. So assiduously do they serve that one Sufi has said, "If I were told that tomorrow I would die, I would find nothing more to do in preparation!"

A Parable
The Lion and the Fly

The person who pays too much attention to the life of this world while neglecting to prepare for the life to come is like a man being attacked by a lion. Imagine that the lion is poised to pounce upon him when a fly suddenly lands on his nose. If the man stopped to swat the fly instead of fending off the lion, wouldn't he be an idiot? He must have lost his sense of reason! If he had a grain of reasoning power, he would certainly pay attention to the imminent onslaught of the lion with its deadly pounce while ignoring the disturbance of a mere fly. If people grow preoccupied with their lives in this world and neglect to prepare for the life to come, it proves that they, too, are idiots. If they had any understanding, insight and reasoning power, they would get ready for the upcoming life after death. That is their ultimate responsibility. For this they will each be held accountable. They should hardly be preoccupied with matters of material provision. Concern for material goods in comparison to concern for spiritual health is like the taking care of the annoying fly instead of the impending pounce of the deadly lion. Idiot!

Worthwhile Distractions

Once there was a Sufi whose mother said to him, "My son, why don't you finish eating your bread?" He answered,

221

"With each mouthful of bread, between eating each individual crumb, I recite fifty verses of the Qurᵓan." The Sufi community consists of people whose faculties of reason are distracted from concern for this world. Their powers of reason attentively observe the horror of the dawn [of the final day]. They direct their thoughts in expectation of the terrors of the day of resurrection (*al-qiyāma*), the moment of meeting the compelling One who dominates the heavens and the earth (*jabbār al-samawāt waᵓl-arḍ*). Such consciousness absents them from awaking to the pleasurable experiences of this world and its vain diversions.

To illustrate the extremes of this virtue, one Sufi has told this story. "I once visited a Sufi master in Morocco. After a while, I rose to fill a bucket at the well to make ablutions. The Sufi master rose as well to get the water for me, but out of respect I refused to let him. He protested, and in the end he insisted on filling the bucket from the well himself. So he grabbed the rope and began letting it down, hand over hand. In the courtyard of his home, just beside the well, there grew an olive tree, spreading wide like an arbor over the house. Observing this, I suggested, "O master, why don't you sling the rope over a branch of this tree to ease pulling up the bucket from the well?" He replied, "Is there a tree here? I've lived in this house for sixty years and never knew that there was a tree in the courtyard of this house!" May God open your powers of hearing with this story and its example, my friend, and may God be merciful to you! Know that God has servants among the people who are distracted by God's presence from even the simplest things. God's greatness preoccupies their faculties of reason and calculation. God's awesomeness perplexes their sense of self. God's love and intimacy resides in the innermost secret core of their hearts. May God make you and me be from among those servants and never let us depart from them!

Listen to a similar story. Once a man was in the company of a saint in the highlands of upper Egypt. They were at a mosque. One of those who served the master requested that he be allowed to take a palm fiber from one of the master's sandals [that were made of woven palm leaves] that were placed by the door of the mosque.[25] The master gave him permission to do so. As he went over to remove a little palm fiber, he asked "O master, from which of your sandals should I take the fiber—from the yellow sandal or from the reddish one?" The master replied, "My son, I've been at this mosque for forty years now, and never knew there was a red sandal different from a yellow one!"

Once a Sufi master was in his dwelling place when his children were passing by. They decided to stop and visit him. He asked, "Whose children are these?" He was told, "These are your own children!" But he never recognized them, let alone acknowledged them as his. He was engrossed to such an extent in God's presence. One Sufi used to say of his children whenever he saw them, "These are orphans, even if their father is still alive!" To reflect freely on this point of light will take us far beyond the humble goal of this book.

SECTION TWO: UNDERSTANDING PROVISION'S GUARANTEE

When Divine Speech says, *I have created humankind and the jinn only to worship me*, God knows that they are created with frail human nature (*basharīya*). Their nature makes many demands on them, disturbing the orientation of their sincerity (*ṣidq al-tawajjuh*) toward worship and servanthood. In recognition of this difficulty, God has guaranteed them their provision. This would free their minds from worry and allow them to face serving God, so that they would not let searching for provision distract them from worship.[26] For this reason, Divine Speech continues, *I do not desire from them any provision.* It is as if it were saying, 'I don't desire that they provide for themselves. No, I spare them from that through my own apt capability and my guarantee. I don't want from them any sustenance, for I alone am the powerful One (*al-qawī*), the eternally everlasting One (*al-ṣamad*) who is not fed, who needs no feeding.' To express this idea, Divine Speech continues, *God it is who is the provider, possessor of steadfast power.* The meaning is as if God were saying, 'I do not desire people to provide for themselves because I alone am the provider (*al-rāziq*) for them. Nor do not want them to feed me. I alone am the possessor of steadfast power and whoever has the power in its essence is the self-sufficient (*al-ghanī*), without need to be fed or to feed.'

This moment of Divine Speech guarantees to all people that their provision exists for them. It tells us, *God it is who is the provider.* This guarantee obliges the believers to assert that God is the only One who grants provision (*yuwaḥḥidūhu fī rizqihi*). They must refrain from attributing any single thing from their provision to God's created world. They must refuse to compound their own provision onto the intermediate means by which it arrives (*asbāb*) and must not rely on their own powers of acquisition to receive it. A story is recounted about the Prophet Muhammad that teaches about provision. "The Prophet spoke to us in the morning, after an astronomical event that occurred that night [that corresponded to a much-needed rainfall]. The Prophet said to us, 'Do you know what your Lord has said?' We answered, 'No, O Prophet of God.' He replied, 'Your Lord has said that some of my people have woken up this morning as believers who have faith in me while some have woken up as infidels who deny me. Those who say, "It rained down on us by the occurrence of such a tempest or by the influence of such an astronomical body" deny me and believe in the stars.'"

For believers, there is a great lesson in this reported event; for those with certainty it provides deep insight. It teaches us how to trust the Lord of all worlds with proper respect (*adab*). It is as if the Prophet were forbidding you, my dear believer, from turning your attention to knowledge of the stars (*ᶜilm al-kawākib*) and attributing worldly events to their influence. It is as if he were forbidding you from praying to the stars, conjuring up their influence or invoking their astrological constellations. Rather, you must realize that with God there is an eternal decree (*qaḍāʾ*) destined for you which must necessarily, inevitably and inescapably come to effect. God has pronounced a command (*ḥukm*) that will become manifest. So what use is it to try spying into signs of the unseen world beyond our knowledge? Remember how God has explicitly forbidden us from spying on other people's private affairs (*tajassus*), saying *Do not spy on others.*[27] In the same way, you should not spy into God's unseen order with the intention of manipulating it for your own advantage.

> The astrologer read my nature, saying
> 'You deny your fate that the stars decree,'
> For I know that what will be and what is destined
> by the Overseer necessarily comes to be

This moment of Divine Speech employs a rhetorical flourish through Arabic grammar in saying, *God it is who is the provider.* By declaring *the provider* in the form of "*razzāq*,"

225

there is rhetorical intensity connoting that God is the ever-providing and all-providing One. This is in contrast to using the routine active participle, "*rāziq*," which would convey the meaning of one who provides once in a particular act. This intensification could be to emphasize the vast number of beings who are given provision by this providing One, as if it were saying, "the provider for everyone." Or it could be to emphasize the constant frequency of acts of provision by this providing One, as if it were saying, "the provider in every moment." Or the intent could be both types of intensification at once!

There is another insight to be gleaned from the discipline of grammar as it applies to rhetorical eloquence (*ᶜilm al-bayān*). To prove a point using an adjective to describe someone's quality is more forceful than using a verb to describe someone's action. This is especially true when the intent is to express praise for a person. For example, to say "he is good" is much more forceful that to say "he is doing good" or "he has done good." This is because an adjective (*ṣifa*) denotes a well-established quality that persists in a person or thing, while verbs (*afᶜāl*) express actions that, by principle, arise then terminate then have to be renewed. For this reason, saying *God it is who is the provider* is more forcefully eloquent than saying, for example, 'God it is who provides.' If the Qurʾan were saying, 'God it is who provides,' it would only denote that the provision has come from God by God's act. In contrast, the Qurʾan says, *God it is who is the provider*, restricting all acts of provision to God's agency, to the One who encompasses all possible provision in all circumstances at any time. *God it is who is the provider* uses the adjectival quality of that name, is like saying, 'There is no provider except God (*lā rāziq ilā Allah*).'

226

A Parable
Parent and Child

God is to humanity as a father is to his child. With the father nearby, the child does not worry a bit about provision and fears no want. The child knows that the father is undertaking to meet all his basic needs. The child lives well when completely trusting the father, but suffers anxiety and grief when that reliance is withdrawn. Likewise, believing people who trust God are not distressed by anxieties. No grief overcomes the open expanse of their hearts due to worry about material sustenance. Such believers know that they are never neglected by the true One, whose bounty has no end and who never cuts people off from generosity and goodwill.

Now let's turn to another moment of Divine Speech that explains the issue of provision. *God it is who created you all, then provided for you all, then makes you all to die, and then brings you all back to life.*[28] There are two important points to note here. The first is that creation is integrally connected to provision. Observe how easily you submit to the fact that God is the One who creates, without claiming any pretension that you possess ability to create yourself in cooperation or competition with God. Just as easily, you should admit that God is the One who provides, without claiming for yourself any such power. You could express this in a pithy aphorism: just as you admit that God is unique in creating and bringing into existence, God is also unique in providing and extending subsistence.[29]

To convey this insight, Divine Speech integrally connects these two things, creation and provision. This obliges us and prepares us to bear the evident paradox that God's

227

provision seems to come from what is other than God. Indeed, God's goodness appears to us to come through God's created beings. However, the reality is this: just as God creates without mediation and without means, so God provides without making provision conditional on any mediation (*wāsiṭa*) or dependent on the existence of any intermediate means (*sabab*).

The second points is that, by saying, *God it is who created you all, then provided for you all,* Divine Speech reveals that the giving of provision is a matter already decided. It is something decided before time, beyond any change or appeal. In destined decrees, there are no topics to be newly decided in coming moments and no subjects to be postponed for a later time. Destined matters manifest at a particular time, but the existence of the decree was established before time. Provision can be thought of in two ways. There is provision that has been destined before time in pre-eternity (*al-azal*), and there is the provision that begins to appear manifest after a person comes into this world. This moment of Divine Speech could be addressing provision in both senses. If the intention is to address provision destined before time, then the discourse aims to inform us of this unseen reality. If it intends to address provision as it appears for us within time as experienced by us, then the discourse aims to caution us to evaluate provision properly.

The secret of this moment of Divine Speech, the whole point of its being pronounced, is to establish the singular divinity of God (*ithbāt al-ilāhīya li*'*llah*). It is as if it were saying, 'You who worship anything other than God! It is God who created you, then gave you provision, then causes you to die, then brings you back to life. Do you find these qualities in any one else? Can they inhere in any created being? So acknowledge the divinity of the One who is unique in possessing these qualities, and declare that being's lordship to be absolutely singular!' For this reason, Divine Speech immediately follows this address by saying, *Are there any from those whom you claim as associates in divinity who do for you anything similar to these acts? Glory be to the transcendent One, beyond anything they ascribe as partners.*[30]

A Parable
There is No Good That's Lacking

God treats humankind like a master treats servants. While servants toil in one place, the master builds for them a large home in a distant place, furnishing it well and decorating it in grand style. That home contains gardens well tended and provides within its walls all manner of good and wholesome things, everything that could be desired. The master does all this in the hopes that the distant servants will move in and enjoy its comfort. Imagine that this is the ultimate intent of the master for each servant: keeping riches in store for them in a new place for them enjoy after a long journey. Would such a master refuse the servants adequate gifts and provisions along the way, after having prepared for them at their destination such an astounding endowment of treasures? Hardly!

So it is between God and humanity. God has placed us in this world of scarcity, having prepared for us the destination of paradise in the next world. God refuses to give without restraint in this world only so that we prepare our existence in the next world. For this reason alone God says in revelation,

Eat and drink from the provision of God, and, *Eat
from the provision of your Lord and give thanks.*[31]
For this reason alone God says, *O you Prophets, eat
of wholesome things and perform good works,* and,
*O you who believe, eat of the wholesome things that
we have provided for you.*[32]

If God has given some things to you and held the rest in
reserve for you, why do you count it as a loss? Why do you
think about things that are absent as if they were lacking? If
God withholds goods from you, what is withheld has not
been measured out for you in the first place. What has not
been measured out for you is not yours to have or to miss in
not having. That act of withholding is actually an act of
giving! Consider it closely and you will know that the withholding is for your own good, to keep your affairs in order.
A gardener tending an orchard stops the flow of water to
his trees when they have had just enough. The trees would
be ruined with continual watering!

PROVISION IS CONDITIONAL UPON SERVICE

Another moment on the topic of provision demands our
attention. *Command your people to perform the prayer and
persevere patiently with it. We do not ask you to provide.
We provide for you. The good outcome is with wary consciousness of God.*[33]

Inherent in this moment of Divine Speech are many beneficial lessons. The first is that, despite the fact that it is
explicitly addressed to the Prophet Muhammad, its command and its promise applies to all members of the Islamic
community. To every person, this address says "Command
your people to pray, be patient with them, and do not worry
about your provision for we provide for you—and the re-

230

Therefore bear patiently whatever they say
    and glorify your Lord with praise
    before the rising of the sun and before its setting
    and for part of the hours of the night.
Glorify also during the extremes of the day
    that you might reach contentment. (130)
And do not strain your sight longing
    for what we have given to others for worldly enjoyment
    of the splendor of the life of this world
    through which they are put to trial and temptation.
Rather, the provision of your Lord is better and more lasting. (131)
Command your people to perform the prayer
    and persevere patiently with it.
We do not ask you to provide. We provide for you.
The good outcome is with wary consciousness of God. (132)

sults depend on your wary consciousness of God." If you comprehend this, then know that God commands you not only to pray yourself, but to enjoin your family members to pray. It is your responsibility to take care of your family and relatives with worldly means of livelihood through self-less giving (*īthār*); similarly it is your responsibility to care for them spiritually, by guiding them toward obedience to God and helping them avoid rebellion against divine commands. If your family deserves your wholehearted goodness in matters related this ephemeral world, how much more do they deserve your care in matters related to the eternal world to come? You are like a shepherd and your family is like your flock, so watch over them. The Prophet Muhammad has taught that, "All of you are watchful protectors and each of you are responsible for taking care of your flock." In another moment, Divine Speech directs, *And warn your immediate family, the closest to you of your tribe,* reaffirming the commandment in the moment quoted earlier.[34]

Observe closely how God ordered the Prophet through this Divine Speech to command his people to persist patiently in prayer, before commanding him to do the same. This is so that you might understand that the discourse is worded in a specific form: to command one's family to pray. Conclusions beyond this come by way of consequence, not by explicit wording. Of course the intent is for the Prophet also to persist patiently in prayer. Every believer knows without a doubt that she or he is commanded to pray, as an individual. Yet the true One warns people about this in a way that reminds them of what they might otherwise neglect, that is encouraging others to pray as well! So the Prophet was commanded in this specific form, addressing his family and relatives, so that all the believers might hear it and follow it. The goal is for each to make haste to pray, encourage others to pray, and to persist zealously in a wide network of prayer.

It is clear that you should command your family members to pray. This would include your wife, your maid, your daughters—everyone in your household. You should also punish them for neglecting to pray. If they don't listen, you don't need decisive proof from God, like saying "I was commanded to do this." All they need to know is that it bothers you if the people of your household fail to pray, just as it bothers you if they ruin a meal or fail to do some important task around the house. Don't let them leave prayer! No, they are accustomed to your demanding that they help care for your worldly needs while you neglect to demand that they observe the rights that God claims over them (*ḥuqūq Allah*). For this reason, don't allow the people of your household to ignore the prayer. Whoever preserves the sanctity of prayer times for himself and lets his family ignore them without commanding them to join in the prayer will be raised on judgment day in the group of people who wasted the prayer times.

You might rightly protest, "I commanded them, but they did not act upon my command. I advised them, but they did not accept my advice. I punished them for this with a beating, but still they did not take to it willingly. So what should I do?" The answer to such a protest is that you should part company with those whom you can leave. Sell off servants or divorce spouses. You should shun those whom you cannot legally leave. You should turn away from them and flee to God. Abandoning loved ones for God's sake makes God care for you like a loved one.

The words of this discourse, *and persevere patiently with it,* indicate that prayer is a burden that weighs heavily on the human soul. It appears onerous to the soul because prayer comes at times when people are either relaxing or working. In either case, prayer demands that people leave what they are doing to stand alone before God, empty of everything other than God. Haven't you observed how the dawn prayer comes at the time when people are asleep, just at the moment when sleep is most delightful? The true One demands that people stop claiming their rights to their portion of worldly good and their own desires, in order to do what is desired of them. For this reason, the call to prayer at dawn repeats twice the special phrase, "Prayer is better than sleep!" As for the noon prayer, it comes at the moment when people return home to rest a little from working to secure their worldly sustenance. The afternoon prayer comes just when people are engaged in trade and engrossed in business, turning their attention to their worldly livelihood. The sunset prayer comes just when people sit down to eat a meal, to build up their bodily constitution. The night prayer comes when they are tired out by the worldly activity of the day. For this reason, God says, *Persevere patiently with it.* Similarly, Divine Speech says in other moments, *Preserve the prayer times and the prayer in between*, and, *Prayer is obligatory for the believers at appointed times.* And also, *Establish the prayer regularly.*[35] Other moments clarify for us that prayer is an obligation that contradicts what human nature urges us to do: *Call for help in practicing perseverance and prayer, for indeed it is a difficult practice except for those who fear [God].*[36] Divine Speech integrally connects prayer and perseverance to show that people need great patience in order to perform the prayer: patience in observing their exact timings and living up to all its requirements and ritual processes. Patience prevents the human heart from neglecting prayer. For this reason, after mentioning patience,

234

Divine Speech says, *For indeed it is a difficult practice except for those who fear [God]*.

Notice that this phrase singles out "prayer" as a difficult practice, rather than "perseverance." This demonstrates what I have said above. It also could be said that "a difficult practice" actually describes "prayer" as its direct antecedent, and also "perseverance" that comes before it, for prayer and perseverance are integrally connected. Each is enjoined in tandem with the other, as if one were the essence of the other. There are many such essential pairs mentioned in the Qur'an: *It is more fitting that they satisfy God and God's Prophet*, and *Those who hoard in treasuries gold and silver do not spend of it in the way of God*, and *If they see profitable business or diversionary pleasure, they shake off their laziness*.[37] You can gain so much insight from understanding such essential pairs and why they are linked!

So prayer is gravely important and in God's regard it is weightily significant. For this reason, Divine Speech pronounces that, *Indeed prayer snuffs out pernicious behaviors and reprehensible acts*.[38] When asked what is the best action possible, the Prophet Muhammad said, "Prayer at its appropriate times." He also said, "Those who pray take their Lord into their confidence," and, "The closest that people come to the Lord is when they are prostrating [during prayer]." I think that ritual prayer, in the form practiced by Muhammad and his community (*salāt*), includes a whole range of worshipful practices that are not so comprehensively gathered together in any other practice. It includes purification [of the body and of intention], silent awareness, turning to face the ritual orientation, initiating prayer by invoking God's greatness beyond all comparison, recitation of Divine Speech, standing before God, bowing and prostrating with one's face to the floor, glorifying God during bowing and prostration, and imploring God with requests during prostration. This process of ritual prayer draws together numerous kinds of worship. Meditation by recalling to mind God's qualities (*dhikr*) in itself is worship. Recitation of the Qurʾan in itself is worship. Glorifying God or petitioning God are in themselves worship, as is bowing or prostrating or standing at attention. Each in itself is an act of worship. However, ritual prayer encompasses them all! I fear this discourse might go on too long if I expand on the secrets of each act of worship and disclose how each radiates a certain kind of light. This small ray illuminating the subject will suffice us for now. To God be all praise!

DIVINE SUPPORT SERVICES

There is another benefit to be gleaned from the moment of Divine Speech under consideration. *Command your people to perform the prayer and persevere patiently with it. We do not ask you to provide.* It is as if God were saying, 'We don't ask you to provide for yourself, your family and your dependents. How could we order you to do that and make you responsible to provide for yourself and others when you are unable to do so? How could we demand your worship and service then not undertake to support you?' It is as if God knew that thinking about provision would disturb people. This would distract them from constant obedience and alienate them from keeping their time free for action that is in accord with divine demands. For this reason, God addresses the Prophet Muhammad, such that all people might hear, saying, *Command your people to perform the prayer and persevere patiently with it. We do not ask you to provide. We provide for you.* This means 'Rise up in service (*khidma*) while we undertake to sustain you with what we apportion for you (*qisma*).'

236

Service and support are two different things, but are closely related. Support is guaranteed for you, so don't pursue it. Service is demanded from you, so don't neglect it. How woefully ignorant are those who are obsessed with getting what has been guaranteed for them, to the point of neglecting what has been requested from them! They are headstrong without measure and heedless without limit. How little they pay attention to one who warns them to wake up. Rather, it is more deserving for people to be obsessed with what is demanded of them like true servants, to the point of neglecting what has been guaranteed for them. Since God has provided sustenance for even stubborn people who ignore the divine, how could God not provide for wary people who witness to the divine? If divine providence flows to the people of deceitful infidelity, how could it not flow to the people of faithful sincerity? O fellow servant, know that worldly existence is guaranteed for you. Guaranteed is everything you need from the world to support you, so that you might work with this world to prepare for the next world! This is in accord with Divine Speech saying, *Get prepared now, for indeed the best preparation is wary consciousness of God.*[39]

How could you, who are endowed with reason (*ᶜaql*) and insight (*baṣīra*), be concerned with what has already been guaranteed for you and cease to be concerned with what is demanded from you? One Sufi has said, "God has guaranteed for us this world and demanded from us the next world—how much simpler it would be if only God had guaranteed for us the next world and demanded that we work for sustenance in this world." So Divine Speech says, *We provide for you,* with the verb in the present continuous tense, to demonstrate to us God's constancy and endurance in providing. Consider what you might say to other people.

237

Saying, "I have provided generously for you," is different from saying, "I provide generously for you." The second saying, "I provide generously for you," implies that you provide for the other constantly, time after time. In contrast, saying, "I have provided generously for you," means that you provided once and the action is completed in the past without implying that it will be repeated in the future or that its effects will endure. So pay attention to how Divine Speech says, *We provide for you.* It means, 'We provide sustenance after sustenance, without our giving ever being disrupted or our blessings ever being interrupted. Just as we showed preference to humanity by bringing you into existence, we also extend to you in every moment your subsistence.'

After this, Divine Speech specifies, *The good outcome is with wary consciousness of God.* It is as if God were telling us, 'I know that you have devoted your life to my service and turned your whole being to my obedience, looking away from material means in the world, desisting from preoccupation with them. So your provision in the world will not be the provision of those who live in sumptuous luxury and your livelihood will not be like those whose needs are limitless. But endure this with patience, knowing that the outcome depends on wary consciousness of God.' This is just like another moment of Divine Speech: *Do not extend your gaze to what we have bestowed upon others of the splendor of the life of this world, by which they are tried with temptation. The provision of your Lord is better and more lasting.*[40]

You might object by asking, "Why is consciousness of God specifically tied to the outcome [the next world] when those who are conscious of God are given not just eternal blessings in the next life but also a wholesome existence in this life, according to Divine Speech: *To those who do good,*

238

whether man or woman, and are believers, we surely give a wholesome life."[41] You must realize how God addresses people according to their own power of reason. It is as if God were saying, 'Listen up, people! Just as you see that the people of spiritual neglect and enmity have the upper hand in the beginning, know that the people of consciousness and faith will have the upper hand in the end. Therefore, *the good outcome is with wary consciousness of God.*' In this way, God addresses people through expressions that their powers of reason can follow and their capacity of understanding can comprehend. For instance, we say, "*Allah Akbar*! God is greater!" In reality, nothing else shares in divine greatness with which we could actually make a valid comparison. However, our human psyche can witness the greatness of the effects of God's actions, as Divine Speech says, *Surely the creation of the heavens and the earth is greater than the creation of human beings!*[42] It is as if God were saying, 'If you have witnessed greatness in anything, and how could you not see greatness in the created cosmos, then know that God is greater than that thing—greater than any greatness!'

The same metaphoric strategy can be seen in the dawn call to prayer, which announces, "Prayer is better than sleep!" If it called out "Sleep is no good," then the human psyche would say, 'I am aware of the delightfulness of sleep and the comfort it brings. That of which I'm aware is more trustworthy [than that which the call to prayer is saying].' Therefore the call to prayer says to the human psyche, 'What we have called you to do is better than what you consider good for yourself. Prayer is better than sleep! The good you desire through sleep is an ephemeral phenomenon. What we're calling you to do is an action whose reward lasts eternally and never fades away.' *And what is with God is better and more lasting.*[43]

This moment of Divine Speech teaches people, those endowed with understanding of God, how to request their provision. If the intermediate means (*asbāb*) that act as the conduit by which their livelihood comes to them should falter and stop, they increase their worship and devoted service in accordance with divine will. Divine Speech shows them the way. Don't you see that God says, *Command your people to perform the prayer and persevere patiently with it. We do not ask you to provide. We provide for you.* The promise to provide for you comes after two orders: to command your people to pray and to persevere in prayer. Only after that does Divine Speech promise, *We provide for you.* So those with intuitive understanding of God comprehend that if their means of livelihood should be interrupted or stop, they must knock on the door of provision by dealing directly with the providing One (*al-razzāq*). This contrasts with those who are negligent and blind. If their means of livelihood should stop, they only intensify their toil, with hearts heedless and minds absent of God's remembrance.

How could those with an understanding of God do otherwise? They have heard Divine Speech advise, *Come into homes through their proper doors.*[44] They acknowledge that the proper door opening onto provision is obedience to the providing One. How could they request their promised provision through rebellion against God or expect God to continue divine bounty while they contradict divine will? The Prophet Muhammad has taught, "Nobody earns what God has stored for them with discontent or displeasure." This means that the only way to request one's provision is by behaving in accordance with divine will. To clarify this, Divine Speech says, *Whoever remains warily conscious of*

*God, God will make for him a way out [from difficulties],
and provide for him in ways he cannot calculate.* And also,
*If they persist in walking upright on the path, surely we
bestow on them water in abundance.*[45] These and other
moments illustrate that wary consciousness of God is the
key to both kinds of provision: provision for natural existence in this world and provision of blessed persistence in
the next world. To this effect, listen to Divine Speech say, *If
the people who have received the message [previously]
would believe and stay warily conscious of God, surely we
shield them from their wrong deeds and induct them into
blessed gardens. If only they would establish the Torah and
the Gospel and what revelation has been sent to them from
their Lord, they would eat from what is above them and
what is beneath their feet.*[46] Here, God enjoins people to
establish the truth as revealed to them in the Torah and the
Gospel, meaning that they practice what is conveyed by
these two scriptural messages. If they would do that, they
would partake of what is above their heads and beneath
their feet, meaning that God would increase their provision
and enrich it with even more bounty. However, the tone of
Divine Speech is full of rebuke, as if it were saying, 'But
they don't do what I love for them to do, and for that reason
I don't do for them what they desire!"

WHAT IS GUARANTEED IS APPORTIONED

The next moment of Divine Speech that addresses the topic
of provision is this. *There is no creature on earth except
that God takes responsibility for its provision. God knows
its place of remaining and space of deposit. Everything is
recorded clearly.*[47] These words clarify how the true One
guarantees to each creature its provision. These words cur-
tail the assault of stray thoughts and anxiety-provoking

241

misgivings that bombard believers' hearts. If waves of such temptations rise over their hearts, the forces of faith and trust in God rear up and drive them off. These words of Divine Speech rout such anxieties and put them to flight. *No indeed, the truth is hurled against falsehood and falsehood is completely obliterated.*[48]

Now when Divine Speech says, *There is no creature on earth except that God takes responsibility for its provision,* this constitutes a firm guarantee. Through the guarantee, God takes responsibility for people's provision so that they might know God's love for them. Such an act is not incumbent upon God. No, God willingly takes it up as necessary through the divine qualities of noble generosity and undeserved bounty. Further, God extends this guarantee to everything in creation. It is as if God were saying, 'O my servant, I take responsibility for providing not just for you, but rather for all creatures on the earth. I alone take responsibility for giving them provision and assigning the means by which provision will reach them as nourishment. Having witnessed this act, why don't you acknowledge the abundant capacity of my stewardship and the total sufficiency of my lordship? Nothing is beyond my all-embracing comprehension. So trust me to care for your management, and appoint me as your sole agent. You see how well I plan to provide sustenance for the animals. I watch over them and meet their every need. Yet you are the neediest of animals! Isn't it more fitting that you, more than other animals, trust in my care and look expectantly to my bountiful giving?' Don't you see how Divine Speech has told us, *We have ennobled the children of Adam with honor.*[49] Human beings are honored above all other kinds of living beings. This is because God called humankind to serve and worship, promising us entrance into the garden of paradise as a consequence. With this, God invites us to enter the loving embrace of divine presence.

You may need some clarification about how human beings have been ennobled above all other created things. All things have been created for humanity's sake, just as humanity is created for the sake of basking in the divine presence. I've heard Shaykh al-Mursi teach that, "God has said, 'O children of Adam, I have created all things for your sake—and I created you for my sake.'"[50] So don't let what is created for you distract you from that for which you are created! Divine Speech informs us that, *The earth, [God] set it in place for humankind,* and further that, *God has made subject to you everything in the heavens and the earth.*[51] Shaykh al-Mursi has taught us, "All created things are made subject as servants to you, while you are servants of the divine presence (*al-ḥaḍra*). Divine Speech says, *God, who has created the seven heavens and the earth like them [in seven levels], sends down the command between them, that you may acknowledge that God has power over all things. And that God encompasses all things in knowledge.*"[52] Now you realize, O child of Adam, that the heavens and the earth are created for your sake, so that you might gain knowledge. Understand that the heavens and the earth are created for your sake, either for you to use or for you to learn from, which is also a form of use. Having grasped this, ask yourself if God provides sustenance for all that is created only for you, then how could God not provide for you? Haven't you heard Divine Speech say, *Fruits and fodder [we cause to grow], for the use and enjoyment of you and your herds.*[53] The moment of Divine Speech, *There is no creature on earth except that God takes responsibility for its provision* continues to assert that *God knows its place of remaining and space of deposit,* assures you that God

243

takes care of the animals. Neither are their places of refuge hidden from God nor is any aspect of their lives. Rather, God knows their places of dwelling and storage, and causes whatever sustenance is apportioned for them to inevitably reach them.

Consider this moment of Divine Speech about the issue of provision. *And in the heavens is your provision that you have been promised. By the Lord of the heavens and the earth, indeed this is the truth, just as you can speak.*[54] These words rinse all doubt from the believers' hearts and set the lights of faithful knowledge gleaming within them. These words descend upon them, guaranteeing much more than just the munificence promised to them. These words also mention the place where provision is stored and how it is apportioned. It further likens God's nature to a metaphor that is clear and reliable. Let us discuss these beneficial points one by one.

First, consider how God comprehends that the anxieties we suffer by living in this world multiply densely in the human soul. God mentions repeatedly in revelation each person's apportioned provision, knowing that opposition and confusion cloud our hearts in growing profusion. God restates the proof as we revisit the problem, for other people will wrangle with you and force you to revisit the problem, as uncertainties abound in matters of knowing what is yet unseen. This is comparable to how God repeats the issue of our inevitable resurrection after death, aiming to prove it to us over and over. [In the time of the Prophet Muhammad] unbelievers kept raising doubts and anxieties about the truth of resurrection. Admittedly, it was hard for them to conceive of a person returning to life after the body had died and its outer form had decayed and reverted to dust. They could barely imagine that a person, whose remains had been

The Winds That Scatter
Surat al-Dhariyat 51: 7-23

By the skies, intricate and interwoven (7)
    You are all saying contradictory assertions (8)
Deluded are those who are open to delusions (9)
May those perish who foment confusions (10)
    Those who flounder in the flood, heedless. (11)
They ask 'The day of judgment hasn't yet come?' (12)
That day they will be tried over fire (13)
    Taste your trial—this is what you sought to hasten!(14)
Indeed those conscious of God are in gardens with springs (15)
    Taking what their Lord gives them,
        for they lived wholesomely before (16)
    Sleeping only lightly for part of the nights (17)
    And in the dawns were praying for forgiveness (18)
    And in their wealth setting a portion for the rights of the needy,
    Those who ask and those who are prevented. (19)
In the earth are signs for those of certain faith (20)
    And in themselves—will you not ponder with insight? (21)
And in the heavens is your provision that you have been promised. (22)
By the Lord of the heavens and the earth,
Indeed this is the truth, just as you can speak. (23)

eaten by lions or jackals, might be resurrected back to life. For this reason, God presents to us many different proofs and metaphors in the powerful language of revelation, repeating them many times. Among them are these words: *God coins for us this metaphor for one who is heedless of God's power to create and says, 'Who revives dry bones that have turned to dust?' Say, 'The One who revives them is the One who has created them in the beginning.*[55] This idea is repeated in so many different ways in Divine Speech such as, *It is such an easy thing for God,* or *Indeed the One who has revived them is the reviver of what has passed into death.*[56]

The true One knows the intensity of the doubt and uncertainty that afflicts our souls when we face the issue of securing our livelihood in this world. Because of this, God has affirmed in multiple moments the proof that our provision is already guaranteed for us. From among the many instances are the moments in Divine Speech mentioned above, and there are many others to mention. Because God knows our difficulty in accepting what we cannot see, Divine Speech repeats for us statements like, *Indeed God is the only providing One (razzāq)* and, *God is the One who created you and has provided for you* and, *The One who has apportioned for you provision and has safeguarded for you receiving your due portion.*[57]

In the moment of Divine Speech under consideration, God clarifies the location of each person's apportioned provision, saying, *And in the heavens is your provision that you have been promised.* Our hearts can rest content, knowing the exact location of what has been promised and apportioned. Isn't it true that a valuable object held for us in a known place is far more reassuring than a valuable object held for us in an unknown place? It is as if God were addressing us, 'We are not obliged to specify for you the location of what we have apportioned for you. It is enough that we have set portions and make them arrive to you when the right moment comes without clarifying from what place or through what means it will arrive." However, due to compassion, grace, generosity and unconditional giving, God has actually specified for us the place where our provision is stored, in order that our souls should rest in divine care with absolute trust, resolutely resisting any creeping doubts.

There is another purpose to this specification of the location of our provision. It removes the focus of our anxiety away from other people. It forces us to seek our provision only from the true One, the One who owns (*al-mālik al-haqq*). If you find your heart greedy for something or needy for some material good and you look to other people for means to secure it, then God addresses you directly, *And in the heavens is your provision that you have been promised.* It is as if God were saying, 'Listen, you who seek material security and wellbeing from other people created in this world who are as weak and unable as you! Your provision is not in their hands. It is with me alone, for I am the One who rules, the powerful One.'

There is a story of how this powerful message moved an Arab in the time of the Prophet Muhammad. Upon hearing this particular moment of Divine Speech, he slaughtered his camel and fled from worldly possessions into the care of God alone. He said, "Glory be to God! How do I seek wellbeing from the world when my provision is with God?" So consider this point carefully, may God have mercy on you! The bedouin Arab understood the point of this Divine Speech, through which God intended to remove all anxiety from us servants and focus our attention on God alone. We should only desire things from what is in God's control. It is just as another moment of Divine Speech makes clear: *Indeed there is nothing except that it comes from us to its storehouses. Nothing comes down into the world except in already-apportioned amounts.*[58] These words shift the focus of our anxieties over material gain to the real origin of all material goods—God's portal. They urge our hearts to take shelter in the shadow of that threshold. My dear, be an elevated being whose origin and livelihood is from on high! Don't be a lowly earthbound being tied to this dusty world! To urge us on to great heights, some Sufi master has sung this poetry:

> If you desire to saddle your mean and base nature
>> Let contentment with what you have
>> Rein in every boastful and hypocritical urge

> Be a real man whose body is of dust
>> But whose head crowned with aspiration
>> Rises into the heavens

> For the spring that pours forth the water of life
>> Lies beneath the wellspring
>> Of the One who gives life after death

LIVING UP TO THE PLEDGE

I have heard my master, Shaykh al-Mursi, say, "By God, our only nobility consists of raising our anxieties away from other people in this world!" My dear brothers and sisters, may God grant you compassion, recall in this context the words of Divine Speech, *With God is the nobility, and with the Prophet and with the believers.*[59] This nobility with which God has empowered the believers consists of a single act: removing all anxiety and care from a focus on the world

248

and redirecting it to God. This is done by trusting God and not projecting trustworthiness onto anything except God. Aren't you ashamed before God to do anything less? After you have been clothed with the vestments of faithfulness and adorned with the jewels of insightfulness, will you allow yourself to be governed by heedlessness and overshadowed by forgetfulness? Will you incline toward the material world and search anywhere other than God for a trace of wellbeing or helpfulness? To try to raise your aspiration to these heights, listen to this poem of a Sufi master.

> How far I've ventured
> Into spiritual knowledge
> After delighting in the gifts
> Given by my creator
>
> From the heights of nobility
> I look down on the cosmic realms
> A portion spread for me keeps me from looking
> To any but my provider

If your soul, which is negligent and makes you forget your Lord, charges you with fulfilling your needs from other people in this created world, then offer up that soul to the One on whom the entire created world depends to fulfill its every need. Beware, for it is easy for your soul to disgrace you, sullying your faith in exchange for fulfilling its desires. It is easy for your soul to demean you, searching for ways to satisfy its constantly fluctuating whims. A Sufi poet [Yaḥyā ibn Aktham] has wrapped this meaning in verse:

> I undertook to humble my soul, in order to respect her
> So easy it is for her to ruin my nobility
> and virtue's beauty

She says, Yaḥya ibn Aktham, have fun,
  neglect your duty
So I say, Yaḥya, consign her to the Lord and neglect her[60]

How contemptible it is for believers to look to anything lower than God in order to fulfill their needs, despite their knowledge of God's absolute singularity and lordship over all that exists. How despicable it is to look to others after hearing the words of Divine Speech declaim, *Is not God enough for God's servant?*[61] Such behavior is distasteful for anyone. So how much more lowly is it for a believer who should always remember God's Speech, *O you who believe, live up to the pledges.*[62]

Human souls have entered into many pledges with God. From among them is the pledge not to look to any other than God to solve their needs or depend on any other. For this reason, your soul was obliged to confirm that God is Lord on the "Day of Destinies." That was the day [when God removed from the loins of Adam all the future souls and asked them] *Am I not your Lord? And they said, You are indeed.*[63] How could you have acknowledged God and witnessed God's singularity in lordship on that day, and then proceed to act in ignorance of the pledge into which you entered? Yet all the while God constantly multiplies goodwill to you and lets the copious flood of graciousness wash over you, giving to you without your asking? Ask yourself this as you listen to the verses of a Sufi poet:

You have a dwelling-place deep in my heart
  Where no other beauties, no Suᶜda or Lubna, stay
I knew you when I was but the minutest of specks
  How disgraceful to deny you now that my beard's
    flecked gray

250

The test of all renunciants and the criterion of all saints is simply this: to not see others as the source of your provision and to resist asking anything of them.

Just as essences will be weighed in the balance [on the day of judgment], so also spiritual states and personal qualities will be weighed. *Settle the weight in the balance with equity.*[64] In the balance of trial, the sincere person shows forth sincerity and the hypocrite shows only adulterated trickery. *It is not God's way to leave the believers alone in each endeavor until the rotten is distinguished from the ripe.*[65] God afflicts those Sufis who are not truly sincere. Through God's wisdom and subtle gifts, the desires they conceal and the selfishness that holds them captive becomes apparent. They get themselves in trouble with the worldly people. They put on a welcome face for them and lower themselves to suit their desires, agreeing with their opinions in order to be pleasing in their sight. In this way, insincere Sufis push their way to the doors of worldly people, begging. You can see them preening like brides dressed up in gaudy tinsel, obsessed with fixing their outward appearance while neglecting to improve their inward conscience. Indeed God makes them handsome with an allure that reveals their inner faults and exposes them for who they really are.

One such insincere Sufi was especially famous. He was known as ʿAbd al-Kabīr, Servant of the Great, if he was ever sincere in his relation to God, the great One. With his evident hypocrisy he lost this name and became known by all as Shaykh al-Amīr, Sufi of the Prince. Such fakes lie before God and divert people away from the company of the true Friends of God (*awliyāʾ*). What the common people see of their hypocrisy, they consider the character of everyone claiming a special relationship to God, without consid-

251

ering whether they are sincere or fraudulent. In this way, insincere Sufis obscure the realized saints and cloud over the rays of those that divine accord has made glow like the sun. They beat the saints' drum, wave their standard, and wear their crest and armor. However, when battle draws close they turn tail, tripping over themselves in retreat. Their tongues are full of conceit and platitude while their hearts are empty of righteousness and rectitude. Have you heard this moment of God's Speech: *Surely the sincere ones will be questioned about their sincerity.*[66] If even the sincere saints are questioned, can't you see that God will never leave the insincere hypocrites without inquiry and trial? Consider another moment of Divine Speech: *Say to them, 'Act out your deeds and God will see how you act, along with God's messenger and the believers.' You will be referred back to the world of what is seen and what is unseen, and you will be informed of each moment of what you have been doing.*[67] In outward guise, hypocrites appear like sincere ones. However, their actions are like the deeds of rebels and those who reject the truth.

> The tent appears like their tents
> But I see that the neighborhood women
> Are not like the women who dwell there

> No, by the God to whose house
> The Quraysh make their pilgrimage
> Turning their faces toward the pillar
> in its open square

> I never lay eyes on a tent of that tribe
> Without overflowing with tears
> For my love who has disappeared[68]

252

Now you see, may God grant you mercy, that the most beautiful quality of those on the Sufi path is refusing to ask others in this created world to fulfill their needs. This is the characteristic that distinguishes those favored by God. I have composed a poem to drive this point home:

Do you rail against fate with such cupidity
    As if averting your eyes from destiny gives
        you security?

Why rebuke your fate when you can never
    Demand from its vicissitudes faithfulness
        or clarity?

What does it matter if the world leaves me anonymous?
    The full moon is full whether shining openly
        or in obscurity.

God knows that I have set my aspiration higher
    Than to scorn the world absolutely
        or accept it in totality.

Why should I hide my status from people's eyes?
    Let them witness one loftier than kings in nobility!

I show them only that I am a *faqīr*,
        poor and belongingless
    Whom none of them can order or control
        with impunity.

A weak man complains to the weak,
        as if a sick man
    Thinks his stretcher-bearer can heal him—
        that's stupidity.

So consider God your sole provider whose goodwill
Nourishes all beings with grace and magnanimity.

Take shelter in God, who is more
    than you can hope for,
Never stray from that threshold in greed
    or in perplexity.

WHAT IS APPORTIONED IS DELIVERED

Let us consider this moment of Divine Speech from another angle. *And in the heavens is your provision.* It is possible that God's intent in these words is to convey that each person's provision is already established. Its exact amount in every detail is already determined and is inscribed on the "preserved tablet" (*al-lawḥ al-maḥfūẓ*). If this is Allah's intent behind the words, it is to comfort God's servants, conveying that, 'I have inscribed your provision, each thing that nourishes and sustains you, indelibly from myself, establishing it in my record. I have destined it in my signs even before you were brought into being. I specified its amount and time of allocation before your appearance in existence. So why should you grow troubled and anxious? Why aren't you tranquil and why don't you trust what I've promised to you?'

The intent of the Divine Speech, *in the heavens is your provision,* might be to point out the material means by which provision is delivered. From this point of view, it would imply that the means through which provision comes to you is in the heavens. This clearly indicates that the means is water. God has said at a different moment, *We made everything living from water, and yet you do not believe.*[69] In this vein, the early Qurᵓanic commentator, Ibn ᶜAbbas, has said that "provision" refers to the rains. Therefore, the words

254

in the heavens is your provision could refer to the fact that the essential element of water, from which is derived all provision and support of life, comes from the skies above. Indeed, water in itself is provision for life in its most essential form.

From yet another angle, it could be that the true One, in revealing these signs, intended something deeper: to prevent human beings from foolishly claiming the power to secure provision through their own devices. Imagine the rain that falls from the heavens. If God were to cut off from the earth the flow of rain, what profit or provision would come from anyone's work or effort? Not just reaping and sowing would grind to a halt, but everything depending on growing things would also fail. Traders, tailors, and writers would be helpless to help themselves. It is as if God were saying, "It is not your effort and work which provides for you directly. No, it is I who am the only One who provides for you. From my power, your efforts are facilitated and bear fruit. It is I who cause to descend into the world everything with which you work. None but I cause it to yield profits for you."

Look again at this moment of Divine Speech, *And in the heavens is your provision that you have been promised.* It forges a crucial connection between "provision" and "promise." When believers apprehend that their provision has been promised to them prior to their being, they know that there is no doubting its existence. They know that nothing they do can delay or preempt its arrival. No strategy can divert it from its destination. With this understanding, you can hear these words as if God were saying, "Just as you know without a doubt that whatever I promise you will come to be, likewise have no doubt that I have apportioned what will provide for you. Just as you are unable to speed up the fulfillment of my promise, likewise you cannot hope to pre-empt the provision, the amount of which my lordship has apportioned and the timing of which my divinity has appointed."[70]

There is a subtle but crucial point hidden in Divine Speech, *And in the heavens is your provision that you have been promised. By the Lord of the heavens and the earth, this is the truth, just as you can speak.* God swears by divine lordship in order to offer us human beings an irrefutable proof that the Lord is faithful in fulfilling all that is promised without breaking any appointment. By God's very nature, God measures out for all people what has been assured for them, and swears to this by saying "By the Lord." This oath is in accord with divine knowledge that every soul harbors doubts and anxieties deep inside. Some angels cried out when they heard these words, "The Children of Adam are ruined! They have angered their Lord so that God has sworn by God's own lordship!" But other angels said, "Glory be to God! Those who take refuge with the generous One by this oath while their trust in you is infirm, what need do they have of an oath? And if you know their anxieties and doubts in regard to what you've promised, you have sworn for them by this oath." So these powerful words made some angels joyful so that they raised their voices in warning and made other angels bow their heads in humility.

Those who reacted with joy are at a more advanced stage of understanding. These words increased their faith and established certainty in their deepest conscience. These words aided them in conquering the whisperings of tempting forces and the doubts gnawing at their souls. Those who grew ashamed realized that the true One knew of their lack of trust and wracking anxiety. They realized that God, with these words, put them in their place: the station of doubts. For that reason, God swore this oath and rendered them ashamed with their heads bowed. This humiliation benefited them greatly with more penetrating understanding of God. *By the Lord* is an oath that makes some people jump with joy and others sink into sorrow, each according to their own level of understanding, insight and intensity of inspiration's light. The story of Abu Bakr illustrates this point; so consider it carefully.

At the end of the Prophet's lifetime, these words of Divine Speech were revealed through him: *This day I have brought to completion your religious way and brought to fullness my blessings for you and I am satisfied with your way of being at peace (islām).*[71] At hearing these words, the Prophet's companions celebrated with joy, except for his closest friend, Abu Bakr. These words plunged him into the deepest sorrow. He understood that these revealed words signaled the impending end of Muhammad's life, and so he began to weep alone. He understood that if something arrives at its completion and fulfillment, then there is the fearful possibility of its corruption, decay and loss. The same idea is encapsulated in this poem:

> As anything reaches completion
> Only decline and loss lie ahead
>
> Look forward to its disappearance
> If you say, 'Now it is complete!'
>
> If you enjoy blessings and prosperity
> Safeguard them carefully at their source
>
> For the tide of negligence
> Will wash away any blessing

257

Abu Bakr realized that this newly completed religious way [called Islam] would not begin to fade and degrade as long as the Prophet remained alive. While the other companions were joyful at the appearance of the good news of these revealed words, their insight did not penetrate to the further meaning hidden within it. Only Abu Bakr penetrated to this level, and he began to weep. This incident disclosed the secret of the Prophet's earlier comment about Abu Bakr, when he said to his companions, "Abu Bakr does not surpass you all in fasting or praying, but rather in a secret that is entrusted to his breast." That secret by which Abu Bakr surpassed all the other companions was his perceptive insight that compelled him to understand what the others did not.

In this way, everyone hears the same Divine Speech but understands it differently, according to the level of insight and understanding that each has attained. Consider, for instance, the story of Shaykh Abū Muḥammad al-Marjānī when he heard the following moment of Divine Speech: *Surely God buys from the believers their souls and their belongings so that they might have paradise. They fight for the sake of God. They kill and are killed.*[72] Shaykh al-Marjani said, "Some companions of the Prophet heard this Speech and rushed forward to sell their souls, their faces glowing with joy, for they perceived that God pronounced them worthy to have their souls purchased. They saw their own capability praised, since God was pleased to purchase their souls. They were overjoyed with the amazing value at which their souls were assessed and with the wondrous recompense that they were to receive in exchange. However, other companions of the Prophet were ashamed when they heard these words of Divine Speech. Their faces paled yellow at

258

the idea that God might buy from them what God already owned: their souls and their belongings. They understood that God would say, *God buys from the believers their souls,* because God knows of the arrogance hidden in their souls. God knows their secret claims to own things and be masters over things, especially over their own souls. To those whose faces lit up with joy, God gives gardens of paradise with vessels of silver from which to drink. But to those whose faces yellowed with shame, God gives gardens of paradise with vessels of purest gold, as if the gardens themselves were forged from gold."

If believers come to real accord with the truth and surrender any remaining traces of self-aggrandizement, they would not find themselves in a situation of wrangling with God to buy and sell for a price. Notice that God says, *God buys from the believers,* without saying that God buys from the Prophets or the Messengers. This is because the Prophets and the Messengers have already given up any sense of ownership over themselves. Shaykh al-Shadhili has commented, "There are three kinds of souls, ranked according to their value. There are souls that are not purchased because they are flimsy and worthless. There are souls that are purchased because they retained their noble nature. Finally, there are souls that are not purchased because nobody claims to own them!" Worthless souls belong to people who disavow God and make a lie of the Prophets' mission. Souls that are purchased for a price belong to the believers who ennoble their souls through their actions in this life. The souls of the Prophets and Messengers are free. They are not purchased because Prophets and Messengers have already released their souls from any claim of ownership or propriety.

There is another dimension to this moment of Divine Speech, *And in the heavens is your provision that you have been promised. By the Lord of the heavens and the earth, this is the truth, just as you can speak.*[73] Notice that God has sworn an oath by the lordship that sustains the heavens and the earth. Why did God swear by this particular aspect of divine nature rather than by any other of the divine names and qualities (*asmāʾ*)? This is to focus your attention on the lordship that takes responsibility for supporting everything in the skies and on the earth. The purpose is to urge you to entrust your own support and provision to that lordship alone. That lordship is responsible for upholding the cosmos in its vastness, of which you are the smallest part. Yet, if you relate yourself directly to that lordship, you become unique and precious like nothing else in the entire cosmos! For this reason, Divine Speech aims to arouse your absolute trust in that particular divine quality. Therefore, God swears by the lordship of the heavens and the earth, rather than by other names and qualities, such as "by the One who hears," "by the One who knows" or "by the compassionate One." Dwell on this insight for a while.

In this moment of Divine Speech there is a profound reference to "truth." God says *By the Lord of the heavens and the earth, this is the truth, just as you can speak.* The truth (*al-ḥaqq*) is the opposite of the false (*al-bāṭil*). When contradicted by the truth, the false is voided (*maʿdūm*), revealed as something with no basis and no firm establishment in reality. So provision is a truth in reality, just as the One who provides, God, is a truth in reality. Any doubt about the reality of your provision is a doubt about the reality of your provider. Once there was a man who made a living by robbing graves [in Egypt]. Eventually, he repented and renounced his greed. He joined the company of a Sufi master.

He told his master, "I have robbed over a thousand graves of their treasures, but was amazed to find all the bodies in all those graves facing away from Mecca."[74] The Sufi master responded, "In that ancient era, people did not trust God to provide for them [in life or after death]. Therefore, even their bodies are left facing away from the source of all provision!"

The moment of Divine Speech we have been considering ends with the words, *This is the truth, just as you can speak*. These words give final emphasis to the issue of provision and firmly resolve its reality for each of us. Believers should harbor no doubts that their portion is measured out and apportioned before time; believers should never be hampered by uncertainty that their portion will be delivered at the destined time. The heart's insight witnesses the reality of this spiritual dimension of the world, just like the eye's sight witnesses the logic of the observable dimension of the world. This Divine Speech translates a subtle and invisible spiritual meaning into visible and tangible form. It creates an analogy or likeness (*mithl*) between what is unseen and what is seen, so that any doubt about provision will be terminated at its root cause. Consider how you think with logic to understand the outward movements of the universe and have no doubts that you understand what you see with your eyes. Just like that, you should have no doubt about how your provision and sustenance comes to you [directly from God through intermediate material means]. The means of your receiving provision are grasped in the light of certain faith with the perception of the heart.

So look carefully, may God be compassionate with you, at how thoroughly God addresses this matter of provision. Understand the importance that God gives to it in the revelation of Divine Speech. Ponder how the teaching about provision is repeated from different angles and in different ways. Observe how the spiritual reality of provision is clarified and likened to sensible and material conditions, so that our powers of observation, reason and logic can arrive at the truth. Then we can trust this understanding of the heart just as we trust what we witness with our own eyes.

To this reality, God swears an oath of truthfulness by the lordship that encompasses everything in the earth, skies and cosmos. The Prophet Muhammad has affirmed this point in his oral teachings. He is reported to have said, "The Holy Spirit (*rūḥ al-quds*) has breathed into my inner conscience (*rūʿ*) an inspired knowledge that no soul will pass away through death before completely receiving the whole provision appointed for it. So stay warily conscious of God and beautify the way you beseech and request." The Prophet also said, "If you rely on God alone for your provision, as you should, then God provides for you as God provides for the birds. They wake up hungry in the morning and rest well-fed in the evening without a care." Likewise, the Prophet has said, "God takes responsibility for providing sustenance to the one who seeks after knowledge." Besides these few examples, there are many other instances when the Prophet has offered teachings about how to trust in God alone for sustenance.

SECTION THREE: SEEKING PROVISION

It is crucial for us to understand that trusting in God's provision for us should never prevent us from working to earn a living. The Prophet himself implied this when he said, "So stay warily conscious of God and beautify the way you beseech and request." He implied that it is acceptable to request material support and to seek to earn a living in the world. If relying on God negated the need to request, search and earn, then the Prophet would never have declared it acceptable and admonished us to beautify the way we go about it. The Prophet never said, "Don't request," but rather said, "Beautify the way you beseech and request." It is as if he were telling us, "When you seek provision and request it, beautify the way that you seek it. Be polite, courteous and humble in presenting your needs, always turning over final say in every matter to God alone." With this advice, the Prophet has allowed us to request provision through intermediate means (*al-ṭalab min al-asbāb*). Intermediate means could be supplicating God or working in the world. The Prophet had previously pronounced, "It is allowable for people to live off their rightful earning (*kasb al-yamīn*)." This is just one instance among many when the Prophet showed that working and earning money is allowable as an intermediate means by which we receive our provision. Indeed the Prophet encouraged us to work and struggle to earn and improve our lot.

There are many benefits to engaging the world through hard work. The true One knows the weakness of human hearts, acknowledges our inability to clearly see what is apportioned for us, and compensates for our frailty by guaranteeing that we will receive our provision. In divine wisdom, God has allowed us the option of working and relying on intermediate means for earning, as a way of receiving this provision. Through divine benevolence, God has granted this to us as a support for our feeble hearts and repose for our forgetful souls.

Working for your living protects you from lowering your dignity by having to beg for support from others. It preserves the luster of your faith from the tarnish of having to ask from other people. Whatever God gives to you by means of your work does not come as a gift from others, necessitating some subsequent obligations upon you. If someone hires you for a job or pays you for some service rendered, your boss cannot count it as a gift or charity, for your work helps to further the boss' own goals. You take your livelihood as earnings from the boss, not as charity. You take it as a right and not as a request.

As you work to earn a living, you are distracted from sinful pursuits. You are saved from the curse of idle time, which gives you the opportunity to act against God's commands. Just observe how negligent people, when they have vacation from work or periods of unemployment, dispose of their time in sinful pursuits! For such people, working for a living is a form of compassion from God; it keeps them from temptation, trouble and inevitable negative consequences. Further, earning a living allows you to be compassionate with those who do not work. The profits you earn are a means of providing the gift of livelihood to those who dedicate themselves to worship or keep their time unencumbered for meditation. If not for those who work and give of their earnings, how could anyone spend time in isolated prayer or dedicated service to God? Indeed God has made earnings a form of service for others who dedicate their lives entirely to God.

From another perspective, God desires believers to grow close to each other in relationships of mutual interdependence. This is reflected in Divine Speech, *Surely the believers are siblings (ihwa).*[75] Earning a living through work causes people of different backgrounds to come together, to get acquainted, to cooperate, and to learn to love each other. For this reason, only a stubbornly ignorant or foolishly heedless person would deny the efficacy of working to earn a livelihood. We have no report of the Prophet Muhammad commanding people to stop working and earning as he called them to live in accord with God. Rather, in calling his followers to divine guidance, he urged them to engage in the kinds of work that are pleasing in the sight of God. The Qurʾan and the Prophet's teachings are full of exhortations to work. The poet excelled who exclaimed:

God commanded Mary, in her starvation
  "Shake the palm tree in your desperation
    And gather the dates that fall as it leans!"

The dates could have fallen, if God had willed,
  And without a shake her needs could be filled
    But nothing occurs without intermediate means.

How clearly the poet points out the meaning of Divine Speech [as it tells the story of Mary when she was pregnant with Jesus and living in isolation]: *Shake the trunk of the date palm so that the dates fall into your gathering arms.*[76] Once the Prophet stopped at someone's house and was offered a meal of cucumbers and fresh dates. He pronounced, "This offsets the damage of that," meaning that the cucumbers require hard labor to cultivate while dates come almost freely. However, this is an exaggeration [since cultivating dates, too, takes labor].

When the Prophet said to be like birds and "wake up hungry in the morning and take rest well-fed in the evening," he was teaching that working for a livelihood was the established norm in this religious community. The birds, as they wake then rest, are analogous to us in our work.[77] We wake in the morning to earn and acquire; in the evening we return home to rest and enjoy what we earn. There is a maxim that explains this point: working with intermediate means is necessary for rectifying your material being, just

265

as withdrawing from intermediate means is necessary for clarifying your spiritual seeing. God established intermediate means through divine wisdom's subtlety, but do not rely on them fully to acknowledge God's absolute singularity.[78]

MAKING WORK BEAUTIFUL

You may ask what "beautify the way you request" actually means in the Prophet's advice, "Stay warily conscious of God and beautify the way you beseech and request." In reality, beautifying the way you ask has many dimensions. I will describe for you here what God has disclosed to me of these dimensions through divine generosity.

My dear, you should know, and may God be merciful to you, that people who search for sustenance are of two basic types. Firstly, there are people who search for means of livelihood with obsessive preoccupation, to the point that their attention is diverted from God. Aspiration and attention, if focused obsessively on any one thing, divert a person from everything else. Shaykh Abu Madyan once described this effect, "The heart can face in only one direction—the direction it faces seals the heart off from any other focus of attention." Indeed, this saying comments succinctly on a moment of Divine Speech: *God has not made two hearts in one chest.*[79] By these revealed words, we understand that God does not give a person's heart the ability to face in two directions at any one moment. This is because human beings are too weak to face two ways at once.

If a person tries to focus attention in two directions simultaneously, surely one of these will be warped and spoiled. This ability to be directed in many ways at once and focus full attention in various directions in a single moment without any disturbance or interference is a characteristic of divinity alone. For this reason, God has revealed that, *God is in the heavens divinity and on the earth divinity*, meaning that God turns attention to the denizens of heaven and to the denizens of earth at the same time.[80] Turning to face the heavens and its inhabitants does not distract God from turning to face the earth and its inhabitants. Neither does caring for the earth distract God from caring for the heavens. Nothing distracts God's simultaneous attention from any other direction or dimension of being. For that reason, God repeats in this moment of revelation the word *divinity* in relation to many dimensions or directions at once. If the word *divinity* had not been repeated in this way, we would not benefit from this insight and would not comprehend what it makes obligatory upon us. This repetition makes clear to you that people who seek livelihood and sustenance in an obsessive way that alienates them from God are not beautifying the way they seek.

A PARABLE

THE FOOL AND THE SPIGOT

Imagine two men, one who is clever and reasonable and one who is a foolish idiot. Both of them enter the public bathhouse. In the midst of their bathing, the water suddenly stops flowing from the spigot. The clever man knows that there is a channel behind the wall that brings the water from its source to the spigot, as well as a caretaker who oversees its flow. He walks out of the bath to check out what might be obstructing the flow of water in the channel beyond the wall, and to tell the caretaker to look after the problem.

Meanwhile, the idiot kneels down in the bath-house and yells at the spigot, "Hey, Mr. Pipe! Pour out some water for us! What's wrong with you that you've cut off your water?" If you were there, wouldn't you say to him, "You are an absolute idiot! Can the spigot hear a word you say? Can the spigot do anything to help you?" The spigot, you would tell him, is only a particular thing with a specific function that lets flow from it what flows through it. The spigot is neither the actual source nor origi-nator of anything.

Another dimension to beautifying your way of seeking is to ask God for sustenance without specifying the amount, the time, or the means by which it might come. Isn't it bet-ter to leave it to God to give sustenance in whatever way, at whatever time and by whatever means that God wills? This is the way to request politely with proper comportment (*adab*). Those who request sustenance and specify the amount, the means, or the time by which it should arrive have set themselves up as lords over the Lord. Clearly neg-ligence and forgetfulness have clouded their hearts. One Sufi has said, "Once I yearned to leave aside making a liv-ing by intermediate means. I beseeched to be given instead two pancakes each day that would suffice me and give me respite from the daily weariness of working. Then one day I was thrown into prison. In the dungeon, I was given only two pancakes each day to keep me alive. This wretched condition persisted for a long time, until my spirit was bro-ken. One day I was considering my sorry state when I heard a voice tell me, "You asked me specifically for two pan-cakes each day but you did not ask me to give you wellbeing. I've given you what you begged for, so why complain now?"

So I beseeched God for forgiveness and turned to God for help. Suddenly, I found the door to my prison cell broken. I was able to slip out and be free."

O believers, take this lesson to heart! Don't give in to dissatisfaction by asking to be removed from one condition and placed into a different one when you are in a condition that accords with the state of your heart and mind. That is rude and impudent towards God! Instead, be patient so that you avoid receiving just what you have asked by your own designs and efforts while being frustrated from enjoying it in peace, comfort and tranquility. How many people have left one kind of work to engage in another kind only to find weariness and difficulty as a result of choosing for themselves. In another book, I have written a wisdom saying that encapsulates this teaching. "Asking for isolation when God has set you up working with others is a manifestation of hidden selfishness, while asking to work for a living when God has set you in isolation is a decline in your lofty aspiration."[81]

So think hard about the wiles of your enemy! The whispers of temptation come to you in whatever condition in which God has established you. They make you despise that condition so that you ask for something different from what God has established for you.[82] By this clever scheme, your heart becomes uncertain and your being in the moment becomes murky and muddled. The tempter creeps up on people who work, whispering, "If you quit this job and free up your time for meditation, then illumination would shine upon you, your heart would be pure and your conscience would be light. Just look at all the people who have done this with such great effect!" These working people are not destined for a life of isolated meditation and are unable to follow its discipline. They are made whole by their work in the world. If they listen to temptation and leave their work, their faith would be shaken and they would fall to pieces while their certainty drifts away. They would turn about in desperation, begging for food and money from others. They would get obsessed with searching for daily bread and be thrown headlong into the depths of alienation. Alienating us is the goal of the tempting enemy who comes to us in the guise of giving good advice. If the tempter came without this clever guise, who would listen? The tempter came to Adam and Eve disguised as an advisor and said, *Your Lord has forbidden you both from eating of this tree only so that you do not become angels or eternal beings.* The tempter swore to them, *that he was one who gives sincere advice.*[83]

Recluses are assaulted by temptation just as workers are. The tempter whispers to recluses, "Why have you left constructive work in the world? Don't you know that leaving labor makes your heart covet what other people possess and opens the gate of envy? Not owning anything prevents you getting the blessings of giving charity to others, being generous to those in need, and helping others to secure their rights. It has made you expect to receive what is in the hands of others—how pitiful you are!" The recluse had previously felt each moment to be ripe, wide open and illumined; the recluse had found comfort and tranquility in isolation from other people and social demands. Yet if the recluse listens to temptation and returns to work with others, the compromises he has to make leave him miserable and he is overcome by the darkness of their demands.

Such a lapsed recluse is far worse than the simple man who works for a living and persists in working. The latter has not taken on a spiritual discipline and then reneged; he has not aspired to a high goal and then given up! So consider well where you are and take refuge in God from temptation. *Whoever takes refuge in God is guided to a straight path.* The tempter aims to divert people from being content with God in whatever condition they find themselves. Temptation makes people long to escape what God has chosen for them in favor of what they imagine to be better. In whatever situation God has placed you, know that this is for your own good and your protection. If you persist in creating a new situation for yourself, God will let that situation control your affairs. *Say, 'O Lord, make me enter each situation sincerely and make me exit each situation sincerely, and let an enabling authority from yourself watch over me.'*[84] A sincere entrance is that you enter each new situation free from your own devices. A sincere exit is to leave each situation, likewise, not by your own choice. Ponder this carefully! The true One demands from you that you abide with the situation that confronts you until the true One alone oversees your leaving it and moving on to something new, just as the true One alone brought you to that situation in the first place. It is not for you to renounce work and worldly means. Rather, work and worldly means will leave you if you are meant for a meditative life detached from others and dependent upon their work. A Sufi master once said, "How many times I renounced work and left aside toil to lead a meditative life. But each time I eventually returned to work. Then finally, at a certain point, intermediate means abandoned me and I was unable to work. Since that moment, I have never turned back to my former mode of living!"

I myself have had a similar experience. When I was younger, I determined for myself to lead a life of utter dependence on God by refusing to work. So I went to visit Shaykh al-Mursi, after making this decision. I said to myself, "It is better to arrive at God's presence through a re-

271

clusive life than through a life busied with studying religious tradition and law, teaching it to others, and getting all
mixed up with people and their problems." Without my revealing any of these thoughts, Shaykh al-Mursi said to the
assembly, "Once a man used to keep company with me. He
was always busy studying and teaching the outer religious
disciplines of knowledge. In fact, he was a leading religious
authority in our town. Then he experienced a little spirituality on this Sufi path—just a taste. He immediately came
to me and said, 'O master, I'm leaving the life I had been
leading and I'm devoting all my time to sitting with you.' I
told him, 'Mind your own business! Abide with the condition in which you find yourself, for whatever God has appointed for you [of spiritual insight] that comes to you
through my agency will come to you—your work is no obstacle to that!'" Having relayed this story, Shaykh al-Mursi
looked directly at me and said, "The sincere ones are like
that. They leave nothing by their own devices and choices
until the true One governs their leaving one situation and
moving on to the next." Upon leaving the Shaykh's gathering, I found that God had washed my heart clean of all those
misleading thoughts.[85] I found an amazing spiritual repose
in relegating all control to God alone. Of course, Sufi masters are such people who can convey such rest and repose
to others. The Prophet Muhammad himself described them
by saying, "they are such people that the one who sits with
them never suffers."

There is another way to beautify your way of seeking.
You might ask things of God without the goal being the
actual things for which you ask; the real goal might be the
intimate conversation with God that takes place while asking (munājāt).[86] The things requested would be just a means
to achieve a line of communication. Shaykh al-Shadhili

described this phenomenon by saying, "While praying, don't be concerned with success in getting what you need and what you ask for. Those things will alienate you and separate you from your Lord. Rather, let your intention focus on conversing intimately with your Lord." It is said that Moses used to circulate through the tribes of Israel saying, "Is there anyone who needs me to convey a message to the Lord?" He took up requesting the needs of others only to prolong his intimate conversation with God, rather than to actually receive what he was requesting.

It is possible to beautify your way of seeking in another way. You could seek things from God while seeing that those things that are apportioned for you are in reality seeking you! You could invert the routine way of seeing, knowing that you have already been appointed to receive things, rather than you receiving things as a result of asking and beseeching. In this way, you can ask for something while sinking deeply into the sea of humbleness, submerged by your own poverty and neediness. You could beautify your seeking by asking for things to show the depth of your noble servanthood rather than to crave your rightful share. A story about the early Sufi, Sumnūn the Lover, illustrates this point. He used to say, "I have no share in anything apart from you—go ahead and try me any way you like!" Sumnun was subsequently afflicted with a terrible disease that blocked his urinary tract. He bore patiently this agonizing pain without any complaint. Then he was condemned to be lashed. He bore this patiently without any show of pain or discomfort, even though the lashing lasted a long time. Even as he was being lashed, one of his followers approached him and said, "My master, I heard you yesterday beseeching God for release from these afflictions and for wellbeing," even though he had not beseeched God for anything. As the lashing continued, a second follower came up repeating the same thing—then a third and a fourth. At this point, Sumnun realized that the true One wanted him to exhibit his own neediness and poverty. So he called out, beseeching God to grant him release. After he was freed, he took to frequenting the Qurʾan schools and telling the children there "Pray for your poor Uncle, the Liar!"[87]

Another way to beautify your seeking is to ask God for just what suffices for your simple needs, rather than for more which will be a burden for you. Don't look for anything beyond the minimum that you need. Don't let your gaze be inflated by selfish desire. The Prophet Muhammad taught us this virtue when he said, "Dear God, make the nourishment for Muhammad's people to be just enough." One who asks for more than is barely sufficient is blameworthy, but there is no blame in asking for just what suffices. The Prophet is reported to have said, "There is no blame in sufficiency." The story of how the Prophet dealt with his persistent follower, Thalᶜaba ibn Ḥāṭib, clarifies this point. Thalᶜaba came to the Prophet saying, "O Messenger of God, pray that God provide me with wealth!" The Prophet answered him, "Thalᶜaba, having a little that leads you to give thanks is better than having much that doesn't lead you to give thanks." He repeated his request. The Prophet repeated his answer. Thalᶜaba didn't get it and insisted that the Prophet pray for his wealth. In the end, the Prophet gave in and prayed to God, asking for Thalᶜaba to be provided wealth.

What resulted from Thalᶜaba's insisting on what he chose for himself and ignoring what the Prophet chose for his own good? His wealth began to increase and kept increasing, until it distracted him from making his ritual prayers on time behind the leadership of the Prophet as he had previously done. Then his wealth increased to the point that he missed praying with the Prophet except during Friday's communal prayer. Soon his wealth increased in livestock and servants until he was totally distracted from even Friday prayers. The time of year came when the trusted servant of the Prophet came to Thal^caba's house to assess his property for obligatory alms (*zakāt*). The assessor surveyed Thal^caba's wealth and said to him, "In my opinion, you owe only the poll-tax assessed against unbelievers (*jizya*)," and would not allow Thal^caba to pay anything more as the alms of Muslims to purify his ownership of belongings. The incident is famous in the early days of the Muslim community, and served as the occasion for God to reveal Speech in the Qur°an. *Some from among them insisted that 'God bring us goods from God's bounty, that we might give charity and be from among the righteous ones'. Then when God provided them from divine bounty, they became miserly, turned their backs and joined the ranks of the rejecters. The consequence is hypocrisy in their hearts until the day when they confront that which they pledged to God and that which they had reneged and that which they had been denying.*[88]

What are other ways to beautify your seeking? You can ask for your share of the world while remembering the consequences of the next world. As Divine Speech reveals, *From among the people are some who say, 'Our Lord, provide for us in this world,' and they have nothing created for them in the next world. And from among the people there are others who say, 'Our Lord, provide for us what is good in this world and what is good in the next world and keep us from the burning punishment.'*[89] Alternatively, you could ask for something without doubting that what you will get has already been apportioned for you. In this way, you do

275

not stray from respectful humility before God. Or you could ask for something without expecting a quick response, for it is certainly not beautiful to ask for a favor and then goad the benefactor into a hurried response! The Prophet Muhammad has forbidden such indecencies when he said, "God will respond to each of you if you do not rush your expectations by saying, 'I prayed and you have not yet responded to me!'" Consider how Moses and Aaron prayed to God to punish the Pharaoh, as their story is narrated in Divine Speech. *Our Lord, scatter their wealth and put pressure on their hearts, for they will not believe until they experience a painful punishment.* God responded to them, *I have answered your petition, so stand straight and do not follow the path of those who have no knowledge.*[90] Never forget that forty years passed between the moment when God said to Moses and Aaron, *I have answered your petition*, and the time when Pharaoh came to ruin! Shaykh al-Shadhili has taught that *stand straight* means to stand firm without rushing to expect a quick response for what you ask and pray. Correspondingly, the words *do not follow the path of those who have no knowledge* refers to the behavior of those who ignorantly rush to expect a quick reply.

Beautifying your way of seeking could consist of your asking for something and consequently thanking God if it comes, yet keeping clear sight of the Lord's good judgment and fine choice if it does not come. How many people ask and don't give thanks when a good thing comes. Even more people ask and don't see the Lord's wise choice if what they wanted doesn't come. Those who ask for something must trust that it will be given only if it is in their best interest! How could stubbornly ignorant people imagine they know better than God's knowledge of what is good for them? Can we claim to know the unseen and the not-yet-occurred as God knows? It is ignorance enough for you to choose for yourself to ask for things—so why take a second step into utter heedlessness? If you ask for something, then ask while simultaneously turning over all control in the matter to God without plotting, planning or craving in contradiction to God's actions. *Your Lord creates by divine will and chooses what is best for them.*[91]

The words *and chooses what is best for them* are gravely profound and deeply ambiguous. I will try to clarify for you what it means that things are *best* for us. All things fall into three categories. Firstly, there are things that are absolutely good for us; we should ask God for such things without exception or condition. These are things like faith, any kind of worship, or an obedient act in response to divine commands. Secondly, there are things that are absolutely bad for us; we should ask God to keep us safe from them without exception or condition. These are things like denying the truth of the Prophets or rebelling openly against divine commands. Thirdly, there are ambiguous things like wealth, power or high social standing. If we ask for these things from God, we should ask conditionally, while saying, "If you know this to be good for me." I heard my own master, Shaykh al-Mursi, petition God in this way.

Finally, you can beautify your seeking by asking for whatever you please while acknowledging that even the power to ask has been apportioned for you by God before the time of your existence. This way, you don't rely on your own authority even in asking. It is beautiful to ask while bearing witness that you don't deserve to ask by your own power or right. People who ask with such humility deserve the free gifts bestowed by the Lord of all worlds. Shaykh al-Shadhili has said, "I never ask God for anything without first bringing before my mind's eye all my bad qualities and weaknesses." With this teaching, he strives to avoid asking anything of God as if he deserved to be given what he seeks. Rather, he only asks for God's bountiful giving due to the prior bountiful giving of God. Out of compassion for us, we have been given the illusion that we have the power to ask.

These are ten different perspectives on beautifying the way you seek. I specified ten only, but these do not exhaust the issue in the least. The issue at hand is vaster than that! I have only described ten perspectives through which one can apprehend a bit of the unseen through the blessing of the Lord, glory and majesty be to God. This is discourse inspired by One of all-encompassing illumination. You can absorb and understand of this brilliant speech according to the capacity of your own inner light. You can pluck pearls of understanding from the vast sea of its meaning according to your stamina in diving to the bottom. You can understand according to your own place in the spiritual stations of life (*maqāmāt*), in which God has placed you and through which God transports you. *We pour for each the same water and give some precedence over others in food.*[92] However much you understand is so much less than the vast expanses that remain to be understood! Listen to what the Prophet Muhammad says when he admits, "I was given the all-inclusive discourse and even this was abbreviated for me to comprehend."

If those who know of God with intimate spiritual understanding would discourse on a single word of this Divine Speech forever, they could not reach the horizon of the knowledge that a single word conveys or understand it to its deepest core. A Sufi master once said, "Consider the saying of the Prophet: 'To leave aside what does not concern you is what makes wholesome a person's *islām.*' I prac-

278

ticed this advice for seventy years and still never reached the furthest extent of its wisdom!" That Sufi spoke truly—may God be content with him. If one's life in this world lasted forever, one could neither fulfill the obligations that this advice of the Prophet makes incumbent on us nor completely comprehend the amazing insights that it can convey or the secrets that it can display. After this important digression, let's return to the main discussion.

FLYING WITH TRUST LIKE THE BIRDS

Examine again the Prophet's words, "If you rely on God alone for your provision, as you should, then God provides for you as God provides for the birds. They wake up hungry in the morning and rest well-fed in the evening without a care." Consider these words carefully, and you will see that they urge us to trust in God and rely upon God without denying the value of working for a living. Rather, they affirm the need to work, as the Prophet says "wake up hungry in the morning and rest well-fed in the evening." He affirms that the birds wake up and take off, then come home and rest. That is their mode of work. It involves labor. However, while the birds work, they do not hoard, save or feel anxious about tomorrow. It is as if the Prophet were saying to you, "If you trust in God as God deserves to be trusted, you would not hoard wealth against an uncertain future. Trust in God would make you rise above the need to hoard in denial of God's constant provision. Instead, God would provide for your welfare and leave you free as a bird. The birds get what they need each day without having to worry about saving up for tomorrow. They trust that God will not let them go to waste. And you who believe, now much more do you deserve divine care than simple birds!" The Prophet has taught, by implication, that the impulse to hoard wealth

279

out of anxiety comes from weakness of faith and ignorance of God's true nature.

The person who doesn't hoard the goods that come to him is like a servant in the fields of his master, who knows that the master will not forget him or neglect to care for his needs. Rather, the servant trusts that the master will exert every effort to secure his welfare and send good things his way. Such a servant has no need of hoarding what comes to him and considers himself above such desperate subterfuge, since he shares in the wealth of his master and can rely on that to the exclusion of all else. Such a servant seeks only the acceptance of the master, and is dependent only on that single source for sustenance.

You may pause here to ask if all saving should be considered detestable. You might inquire if perhaps there might be various kinds of saving that would be considered less offensive. In reality, there are three kinds of people who save, each one different in nature. First, there are the oppressors who hoard up wealth out of miserliness, stinginess and greed. They amass goods by grabbing them and clinging to them to aggrandize their egos or dominate over others. Their hearts are overpowered by heedlessness and their souls are ruled by evil. On this world alone is their concentration and beyond it they have no aspiration, which confirms their intellectual poverty and abased spiritual station. If they appear wealthy by worldly criteria, this only reveals their inner nature as even more lowly. They may appear powerful and mighty, but their cravings in this world will never be sated and their pursuit of worldly goods is exhausting without respite. They misunderstand the value of working with intermediate means in this world; it plays with their minds, tricking them into foolish destruction and diverting them from spiritual guides. *Those people are like dumb cattle—no, they are more misled. Those are the heedless and forgetful ones.*[93] There remains no space in their hearts for the inner voice of inspired wisdom to speak and no capacity for them to hear its advice. When you confront them just say, "Let me be above their actions and stay pure of their spiritual conditions."

A PARABLE

THE INSULT OF HOARDING

The person who hoards what goods come to him is like a servant whose master assigns him to care for his orchards and fields. The servant has the right to eat from the fruit and grain of that agricultural land. He can eat whatever makes him strong enough to keep planting and harvesting there. He has no need to hoard and save for the future, since the fruits of that orchard and the grain of that land are always replenished. His master is wealthy and always able to provide. If the servant were to hoard the harvest, he would be claiming for himself what actually belongs to his master. That is an insult to his master and a clear betrayal of his master's trust!

The fear of poverty has possessed the hearts of such people. The Prophet has addressed them by saying, "Nothing people do will count for good if their hearts are possessed by the fear of poverty." Believers should steer clear of such obsessive mind-sets and wasteful actions in order to maintain their vitality and wellbeing. Confronted by such hoarders, believers must praise God and give thanks for what God has granted of benefits, bounties and blessings. Whenever you see such people, you could offer the following prayer: "Praise be to God who keeps me healthy and safe from what

281

afflicts these people, who preferred me over so much of creation with a special preference." Offer this prayer of thanks just as you would if you saw someone who was physically sick and you praised God for keeping you healthy, bearing witness to the blessings granted to you by your Lord. Be thankful that God has kept your body healthy just as you give thanks that God has kept your soul healthy from being overcome by worldly goals and suffocated by intermediate means.

Observe how others are afflicted with this disease, but do not condemn them! Rather, in place of condemning them, be compassionate toward them. Instead of asking God to curse them, pray for God to favor them. Emulate the actions of the Sufi who knows God's true nature, Maʿrūf al-Karkhī, for his actions are a gold-mine of virtue.[94] One day Maʿrūf and his companions were crossing the Tigris river. There they saw a group of Samarians frolicking in the water of the river; many of them were involved in frivolous games, dancing and licentiousness. On seeing them, Maʿrūf's companions called out, "O teacher, pray for God to come down against these people!" Maʿrūf raised his hands in petition and said, "Dear God, just as you make them joyful in this world, make them joyful in the next world." His companions reproved him, saying, "O teacher, we had asked you to pray against these people!" Maʿrūf answered them, "If God makes them joyful in the next world, it means that God has forgiven them, so how does this harm you in any way?" At that very moment, the Samarians headed for the shore, the men to one side and the women to the other. They stood on the shore, washing themselves, and then went their way, repenting to God of their former lives. Many of them became ascetics and devoted worshipers, all by the blessing of Maʿrūf's petition in their favor.

So if you meet people enmeshed in worldly pursuits and evil habits, don't be fooled! Know that they are living under a divine ruling that governs them, which is known before time in God's all-encompassing knowledge and willed by God's all-powerful will. If you don't keep this in mind and don't bless them accordingly, you will be in danger of being afflicted with trials such as theirs and suffer the same alienation. Listen to what Shaykh al-Shadhili has taught: "Be generous and noble to the believers, even if they are rebellious sinners and given to licentiousness. Order them to do good and deny them the means to do evil. If need be, exile them. But do all this with compassion for them rather than as a display of your own power over them." He also said, "If you could see the light of a believer's heart, even if he were an obdurate sinner, you would find this light stretching from the distance between the highest heavens and the lowest earth. Since this is the case, what do you imagine you would see emanating from the heart of a believer who does good?" It is sufficient for you to praise believers and think well of them, even if they are negligent and forgetful of God's words: *Then we make those from our servants whom we have chosen to inherit the message (kitāb). From among them are some who oppress their own souls, some who follow their own goals, and some who, by God's permission, have been previously granted good.*[95] Consider these words closely. See how God has affirmed that these people are chosen to receive the message despite the fact that they oppress their own souls with foul deeds. God did not allow their oppressive deeds to exclude them from being chosen and from inheriting God's message. God has chosen them by granting them faith, even if they are oppressors engaging in stubborn and willful sin. Glory be to God, whose compassion is so vast and whose magnanimity is so great!

You should realize that in God's creation, there must be some people whose role is to be governed by the divine quality of forbearance (*hilm*) and whose lives are the stage for the manifestation of divine compassion and forgiveness. Through their lives, intercession might occur. In this light, you can understand what the Prophet Muhammad has said, "By the One who holds my soul! If you don't sin, God would erase you and create a people who sin and then ask for forgiveness, so that God could shower forgiveness upon them." In a similar way, he has said, "I will intercede for those of my community who commit grave sins."

Once a man approached Shaykh al-Shadhili and said, "My master, yesterday I committed a certain sin with a slavegirl of mine." He was a man known for piety and upstanding behavior, such that everyone was surprised and amazed to hear this confession. The Shaykh turned to them and said, "You want him not to sin against God in the world? You think it better for him not to sin against God in the world? Then you prefer that God's forgiveness not manifest in the world and for the message of God's own intercession to not take effect in the world!" How many sinners there are whose evil deeds increase and whose opposition hardens, but whose lives turn into a channel for the Lord's compassion! So with sinners be compassionate, according to your level of faith, even if the sinner should be a religious scholar or a Sufi.

The second kind of people who save are self-serving. There are people who save and hoard because they feel in the souls a deep anxiety about their wants and needs, but not because of obsessive craving, egoistic aggrandizement or competitive boasting. They know that if they do not save, anxiety about the future will disturb their faith and shake their certainty. They save out of respect for their own weakness, acknowledging that their faith is not strong enough to fully rely on God with absolute trust. The Prophet Muhammad has told us, "A strong believer is good in God's estimation, better than a weak believer, even if both are good." Strong believers are those whose hearts are illumined by the light of certainty. Such people know that God sends them provision whether they save or don't save. They know that if they desist from saving, God will save for them. They know that those who save place trust in their savings, while those who rely on God place trust in God and nothing else. Strong believers never rely on intermediate means, whether they work with them or live isolated from them. In contrast, weak believers engage in working with intermediate means and end up relying on them. If they leave aside intermediate means, they still look longingly at what is in the hands of others.

The third kind of people who save are those who rush forward (*al-sābiqūn*). They rush forward toward God in order to rid their hearts of anything except God. They let no obstacle stand in their way and are not distracted by relationships in worldly affairs. Since there is nothing holding them back, they rush forward toward God. What holds people back from God is the pull of their own relationships to things in the world or anything other than God. Whenever their hearts aspire to venture toward God, their relationship with whatever has a hook in their hearts drags them back and returns them to that thing; it turns their faces toward it and away from God. Whoever is stuck in such elastic relations with worldly things is prevented from being present before God. A Sufi master has said, "How do you expect to enter into God's presence when something behind you is dragging you back?" From this perspective, you might comprehend Divine Speech: *On that day, no wealth will be of use to anyone and no offspring will benefit anyone, except for the one who comes to God with a whole heart.*[96] The whole heart is one that is not attached to anything except God and is therefore not pulled back, diverted and scattered.

Listen again to Divine Speech. *You come to us each as individuals, distinct just as we had created you in the first instance.*[97] Your coming to God and arriving in the divine presence is impossible unless you come alone, distinctly individual with no attachment to anything other than God. *Were you not found as a relationless orphan and given refuge?*[98] God will give you refuge in the divine presence when you are as relationless as an orphan child, depending on nobody and nothing except God. The Prophet has said, "Surely God is single and loves what is one of a kind." He means that God loves the human heart that allows no obstruction from among the traces of worldly events to come between it and the divine presence. Such hearts belong to God and stay with God. People with such hearts let God arrange all their affairs for them. They never set themselves up as dependable deputies nor allow themselves to plot and plan for what seems best for them. No, these hearts belong to the people of divine presence, for whom the spring of free-flowing gifts is opened wide. The ephemeral beauty that dances before their eyes does not cut them off from God's presence. The dazzling splendor of beauty unveiled does not distract them from God. One of my poems tries to express this idea:

O dazzling beauty inspiring rapture
   Whose likeness has never been cast
      into the realms of cosmic vastness

The secret of my intrinsic inner relation to you
  is revealed through the closed lids of my two eyes
    reuniting duality and extending only singleness

A Sufi master once said, "If I were forced to see anything other than God I could not, since nothing other than God truly exists that I should see it instead!" Such is the spiritual state of the people over whom God guards and for whom God cares. How could they plot and plan for themselves or devise schemes to save for the future when they live in the presence of the Lord of all worlds?

If such people do save material goods, they do not save like those who rely on their savings or who selfishly hoard. How could they rely on anything else when they constantly witness divine singularity? Shaykh al-Shadhili has taught, "I was once empowered to see God's presence directly and I asked for this vision to be veiled from me. A voice said to me, even if you asked God as Moses, who conversed with God, or asked as Jesus, who breathed the spirit of God, or asked as Muhammad, who was purified by God, asked, then God would not grant you that for which you are asking. Rather, ask God to give you the strength to bear this vision. So I asked God for this alone, and God gave me the strength." How could a person of such spiritual stamina be in need of saving things? How could he ever rely on others?

A PARABLE
FREE TO BE A TRUSTEE

People may store up goods that accrue to them as a holding in trust. Such people are like servants of a master who don't claim to own anything independently of the master and don't rely on saving up goods in their own control to spend on themselves.

287

Rather, servants choose nothing for themselves except what the master chooses for them. If servants understand that the master desires them to store goods, they store goods—not for themselves but only for their master. Servants will enact the will of the master even in spending of what they save. They will spend of what they have when they understand clearly that their master desires them to spend it in certain ways. Saving up goods in this way is not blameworthy, since the servants save for the sake of the master, not for their own sake.

Those who have intuitive knowledge of God are just like such servants. If they spend, they do it for the sake of God. If they save, they do it for the sake of God. They desire only what will satisfy God and nothing else, whether spending or saving. For this reason, such people are the most trustworthy treasurers, the greatest servants, the most liberal and generous nobility. The true One has liberated them from the slightest trace of being affected by worldly gain. They do not incline toward it out of desire to acquire and they do not acknowledge it by recoiling from toiling. They are kept free of this by the love and passion for God that dwell in their hearts and by the majesty and exaltation of God that fill their breasts.

The one who saves for God spends for God. The one who spends for God saves for God. In the hands of such guardians of the trust, worldly objects flow as if directly from the divine treasuries. Even before goods arrive to them from others, they know that God is the owner and controller of others and everything that others possess. The one who does not save goods for the sake of God cannot spend goods for the sake of God. So consider the subtleties of these truths deeply!

It is enough for a believer to store up faith, trust in God and rely on God. Those people who understand God's true nature rely on God with absolute trust. Then God stores up bounties for them. They protect their relationship and in turn God protects them from all concerns and anxieties. They exist for and with God, and in response God extends support to them in each exigency, relieving them of whatever burdens them and deflecting from them whatever worries them. They stay busy with what God has ordered them, rather than worrying busily over the provision already guaranteed from them. They know that God has not delegated their wellbeing to others and never cuts them off from divine bounty.

Therefore, they are serene, relaxed and composed. They live in the paradise of resignation (*jannat al-taslīm*). They delight in passing all concerns to a higher authority. For this reason, God has raised their standing high and completed their inward illumination. God has made them deserve a clear account [without weighing their good deeds against their bad deeds], by divine grace. The Prophet once said, "Seventy thousand people of my community are entering paradise without accounting." Those who were present asked him, "And who are they, O Messenger of God?" The Prophet answered, "They are those who are not possessed and who take nothing as their possessions, who do not fluctuate and always rely on God." It is clear that being called to account after death is only for those pretenders who aren't true. Weighing and measuring on the scales of justice is for the forgetful ones who think that they own things and act on their own will despite the power of God. Those who refuse to save due to trust and reliance upon God, their provision is poured out like water, refreshing their being with serenity and enlivening their hearts with being above need.

These concepts can be illustrated with a story. A Sufi master once ran out of money and was unable to buy grain to feed his family. He said to his wife, "Take everything we have out of the house and give it away to others!" She did as he suggested. She gave away everything except for their millstone, since she was fearful that they might need to use it later to grind grain. The Sufi reprimanded her, "If you had given away the millstone too, we might have been given grain that is already ground into flour. But you kept the millstone, so we will receive only grain that you must grind through your exhausting labor."

When those who rush toward God do save, they do not save material goods as if they own them. Rather they save as if material goods were placed in trust with them (*amāna*). They are the faithful keepers of the storehouse of treasures. They are servants of the highest trust. If they take hold of the world, they take hold of it only as it should be held, respecting the rights of the One who truly owns. If they spend of it, they spend rightfully. They hold things of the world rightly only to spend of things rightly. They do not grasp material wealth or objects as if they owned them in competition with the rightful ownership of God over all creation. Rather they see what is in their hands as deposits entrusted to them temporarily by God. They spend and save from these deposits only as deputies, to whom God has delegated conditional authority. They have heard the words of Divine Speech, *Spend from that over which you have been given authority.*[99] From this they understand that they do not claim to own anything in competition with God. Rather, they consider "ownership" to be relative and conditional, a relationship between themselves and the object established by God. Such a relationship is established as a blessing for you, in order to see how you will behave with these objects entrusted to you. For God is the One who knows, the One ever-aware, who realizes whether you regard only the outer form of objects or penetrate into their deeper secrets.

For this reason, the Prophets were never required to give obligatory alms from their belongings (*zakāt*), because they never actually kept anything in their possession in competition with God that would require them to purify their belongings for their own use. In contrast, you are obliged to give alms each year on what you claim to own. The Prophets see their possessions as deposits entrusted to them by God for a short time, from which they must spend at the apt time and withhold at other inopportune moments. The wealth that the Prophet Muhammad collected as alms from the believers was obligatory for him to collect, so that others might have their possessions purified. He was commanded, *Take from their wealth a portion for charity that they might be purified and made clean through giving it up.*[100]

All the Prophets are free of moral impurity since they are protected from sin (*ʿiṣma*). Like the Prophets, children are not required to pay alms from what they may own, according to the ruling of Abū Ḥanīfa, because they do not bear responsibility for acting contradictory to the law (*mukhālifa*). People bear this responsibility for sin only once they reach the age of legal majority (*taklīf*) after passing through adolescence. From this perspective, you can understand the Prophet's saying, "We Prophets do not leave belongings to be inherited by others. That which we leave after death is considered charitable gifts." This he said to clarify the subtle points we have elaborated above. If the saints, who truly know God's nature and bear witness to God's absolute singularity, do not see themselves as owning anything in competition with God, then you can imagine how far the Prophets and the Messengers are above these pretenses! May God's blessings and salutations be upon them, each and every one without distinction. The saints only channel small amounts from the vast seas of the Prophets. They only reflect the brilliant light of the Messengers.

Jurists and saints may not think alike about the matter of ownership, as revealed by the following story. Once the famed jurists, Muḥammad ibn Idrīs al-Shāfiᶜī and Aḥmad ibn Ḥanbal, were sitting together when along came the Sufi, Shaybān the Shepherd.[101] Ibn Ḥanbal turned to al-Shāfiᶜī and said, "I feel like asking this Sufi a tough question." Al-Shāfiᶜī replied, "Don't bother him." Ibn Ḥanbal insisted, "No, I must test him with a question." As Shaybān approached, Ibn Ḥanbal hailed him, "What is your legal opinion about a man who performed a ritual prayer of four cycles but forgot to prostrate four times?" The Sufi answered, "Dear Aḥmad, such a heart that is negligently forgetful of God must be disciplined so that it never returns to such an imperfect act." Upon hearing this answer [that did not declare the faulty prayer invalid] Aḥmad ibn Ḥanbal was shocked and dumbfounded. When he recovered, he asked the Sufi, "What is your opinion about a man who owns forty sheep— how many sheep must he give in obligatory alms (*zakāt*)?" Shaybān responded, "Do you want an opinion according to your method of deciding (*madhhab*) or according to mine?" Ibn Ḥanbal was astounded, "You mean that your method of deciding would diverge from mine in this simple matter?" "Of course," the Sufi asserted. "According to your method of deciding, a man who owns forty sheep for a full year must give one sheep as alms. According to my method of deciding, servants cannot own anything in competition with their master!"

A legally minded listener might protest that the Prophet Muhammad has said, "Save enough food for a year." How can this be reconciled with all we have said above, that the saving of the Prophets is only holding objects in trust in order to decide the appropriate time to spend them for wholesome ends? There are several possible answers. The Prophet Muhammad's saving material goods could have been for the benefit of his family of dependents. Or it could have been to demonstrate to his community of followers that saving is allowable, even if it is not the ideal, as long as one does not save for further than one year, as that would constitute transgression against trust in God. There is proof that the Prophet saved only to demonstrate the permissibility of saving to his general community. Most of the time, the Prophet was known to save nothing for his own future. The few times when he did save was only to ease the burdens of his followers, to make his religious way one of compassion for them, and out of pity for those who were weak. If the Prophet were to have never saved or spoken positively of saving, then no believer after him would have had recourse to saving! He saved only to establish the legal rulings that govern saving and owning while clarifying the wisdom inherent in refusing to save. Didn't the Prophet say, "I am not negligent, and I do not neglect the negligent!" In this way, he makes clear to you that negligence is not in his nature and that none of his actions can be described as negligent. No, the Prophet entered into the ambiguous zone of saving in order to show us the rules that govern it, the wisdom that inheres in it, and the conditions that regulate it for his community. You should think the best of him and understand for yourself!

A Parable

Carrying Out the Struggle

Imagine a servant whose king orders him to set up camp in a certain place in order to fight against his enemy who is nearby. He orders the servant to expend every effort in the struggle against the enemy. If the struggle grows prolonged, then it is understood that the soldier servant is allowed to eat from the produce of that land and the treasures entrusted to him in order to keep himself fit to fight the enemy, as ordered by the king.

In this way, you should understand that God has ordered people to fight against the forces of temptation (*shayṭān*). God has said in revelation: *Struggle for God's sake in the true struggle* and, *Indeed the tempter is an enemy for you, so take him as your enemy.* When God commanded people to struggle against temptation, God also naturally gave them permission to partake of divinely appointed provision, whatever they need to carry out the fight. If you forgo eating and drinking, you could never endeavor to carry out God's commands. You could never stand firmly in service. The order of the king to fight includes in it permission to eat from what belongs to the king which is appointed for you. You must partake of this as it is entrusted to you. You deserve it on the condition that you preserve the trust.[102]

294

PROVISION FOR THOSE WHO SEEK KNOWLEDGE

Consider the Prophet's teaching, "God takes care of the provision of those who seek knowledge." You should know that "knowledge" has a specific meaning in the Qurʾan and in the teaching of the Prophet: it means knowledge that is beneficial and is accompanied by humble fear. Divine Speech says, *Those of God's servants who have knowledge are those who fear God.*[103] This clarifies that fear is inseparably fused with real knowledge. Therefore, those who have real knowledge (ʿ*ulamāʾ*) are those who cultivate the awe-filled fear of God. The Divine Speech repeatedly stresses the importance of knowledge: *Thus said those who were given knowledge* and, *Those who plunge deeply into knowledge and say 'my Lord, increase for me knowledge.'*[104] Likewise, the Prophet Muhammad taught, "The angels place their wings over those who quest for knowledge." He even declared that, "Those who have knowledge claim the inheritance of the Prophets."

All of this makes evident that, when the Prophet taught, "God takes care of the provision of those who seek knowledge," he meant those who seek a special kind of knowledge. We should seek knowledge that is spiritually beneficial and overwhelms our base instincts that demean us. This specification is absolutely essential, since the words of Divine Speech and the words of prophetic discourse are loftier than what can be applied to any kind of knowledge other than this. We have argued this conclusively in writings other than this book.

Beneficial knowledge is that which helps the one who knows to obey the directives of God. Beneficial knowledge makes you cleave to the fear of God. It awakens in you caution, warning you to desist from trespassing against the limits ordained by God. In short, beneficial knowledge is the intuitive knowledge of God's nature (ma°rifa bi°llah). Beneficial knowledge includes the direct knowledge of God and also the indirect knowledge of what God has commanded us to understand, as long as such indirect knowledge is pursued for God's sake alone. In this sense, "God takes care of the provision of those who seek knowledge" means that God causes the provision of those who seek beneficial knowledge to arrive to them in ways that give them tranquility, authority and safety from being alienated from God through intermediate means. It is for an important reason that I offer this specific interpretation of the words, "God takes care of the provision," pointing out that it means this special way of caring. Clearly, the true One undertakes to care for the provision of all people without exception in a general way, whether they search for knowledge or not. The fact that the Prophet singled out for specific mention this kind of "undertaking care of provision" proves that God takes special responsibility for those who pursue knowledge.

This special responsibility is what Shaykh al-Mursi invoked in his litany [known as The Litany of Light (ḥizb al-nūr)]. In it, he beseeches God to give him a long list of things. Among these requests, he asks for "Provision that is wholesome with no alienation in this world and no inquisition or accountability or punishment in the next world—provision spread on the wide expanse of knowledge, knowledge of God's oneness and knowledge of the law—provision of those kept safe from selfish fancy, greedy desire, and abject craving."[105] Shaykh al-Mursi beseeched God for wholesome provision; that is the provision that God undertakes to specially care for those who quest after knowledge. He explained that wholesome provision is provision unaccompanied by alienation from God in this world or in the next world. Clearly, any provision that comes along with alienation is not quite wholesome. Any kind of alienation fragments and scatters people's inner being (*sirr*), sealing them off from the divine presence and closing them off from spiritual insight.

This is contrary to what worldly people habitually understand about wholesome provision. Normally people think that the best provision is getting nourishment or profit without exhausting labor. Negligent people conceive of wholesomeness in terms of their bodies only. In contrast, insightful people conceive of wholesomeness in terms of the qualities of their hearts. Alienation might creep into how you receive your provision in one of two ways. You might grow forgetful and observe only the outer means by which your provision arrives, thereby allowing them to distract you from God's presence. Or you might consume your provision without the intent of being fully conscious of obeying God in all you do. The first is alienation in receiving provision while the second is alienation in consuming provision.

Shaykh al-Mursi asked God not just for wholesome provision without alienation, but also for provision that causes "no inquisition or accountability or punishment in the next world." By inquisition, he means inquiring about the rights of the giver and the gift (*ḥuqūq al-niᶜam*), as revealed in Divine Speech, *You will be asked what you've done with what you've been given.*[106] One day, the Prophet Muhammad and his companions had consumed a meal, when the Prophet said, "By God, *On that day you will be asked what you've done with what you've been given.*" Shaykh al-Mursi has explained that being asked about what you've done is of two types: inquisition to ennoble and inquisition to rebuke. God inquires of the people who live in divine accord and care about what they have received in order to ennoble them by forcing them to answer. But God inquires of the people who live in opposition against the divine in order to rebuke them by forcing them to answer about what they have received.

Try to understand this inquisition, my dear, and may God be merciful with you. The true One inquires of sincere people about the gifts they have been given in order to openly display their degree of sincerity to others and to spread news of their virtuous qualities. Surely God already knows their condition and every secret they might conceal. God has no need to inquire! In this way, a master might inquire of his servant, "What did you do today?" even though the master had given the servant exact orders and told him what to do. The master desired only to show others present how much he cares for the servant, how closely he follows his activities, and how pleased he is with the work. Ponder this!

Shaykh al-Mursi asked for provision without accountability. Accountability is the consequence of inquisition. If people submit to inquisition about their affairs, they must subsequently submit to accountability for their answers. If they submit to inquisition and accountability, they must further submit to punishment or reward for their deeds. The Shaykh has mentioned all three stages of reckoning individually, even though they follow logically one from the next, in order to show how these subtle blessings follow as consequences of receiving provision. If any one stage were independent from the others, the Shaykh would have been free to beseech God for one without the others.

Shaykh al-Mursi continued to beseech God to make this provision be "spread on the wide expanse of knowledge, knowledge of God's oneness..." It is as if he were saying, "I bear witness that you alone are the One who provides for me in every moment of my provision. I see that you are the One who feeds me and I acknowledge no other source of provision or nourishment. I attribute these qualities to nothing else in your creation in addition to you." In this way, the people of God eat off the expansively spread table of God, no matter who apparently feeds them in this phenomenal world. This is because they know that nobody owns anything in competition with God. With this intuitive knowledge, the vision of their hearts desists from looking to people as the source of provision. They do not dispense their love (*hubb*) to other people but only to God. They turn to no one other than God with their desire (*wadd*). This is because they see clearly that it is God alone who feeds them, provides for them from divine bounty, and ennobles them with divine generosity.

About this singleness of love, Shaykh al-Shadhili has taught, "I do not love anyone or anything except God. This means that the love in me never turns to created things or people for fulfillment." Somebody present in the Shaykh's circle rejected this teaching and protested, "Sir, your ancestor [the Prophet Muhammad] disavowed this idea when he said, 'Hearts are shaped by love for whomever treats them virtuously.'" Shaykh al-Shadhili responded, "You are quite right! We are a Sufi community who see no good thing except that it comes from God, the virtuous One (*al-muhsin*). For this reason, our hearts are shaped by our love for God alone."

People who see God as the sole provider of their food will have their love for God renewed and increased each time they sit down to eat what has been given to them. This is in accord with the Prophet's teaching, "Love God to the extent that God nourishes you with food freely given." Acknowledging God as the provider of food gives people an aloofness that protects them from being abased or despised by others. It protects their hearts from inclining with love toward any but the One who truly possesses. Haven't you heard the oath of Abraham, as revealed in Divine Speech: *By the One who gives me food and drink!*[107] Abraham swore an oath to God by God's singularity in providing him food and drink, acknowledging God's absolute uniqueness as provider.

Shaykh al-Mursi has asked provision "spread on the wide expanse of knowledge, knowledge of God's oneness and knowledge of the law." He mentioned knowledge of the law after knowledge of divine unity. This is because people might learn the arts of making the divine utterly singular by witnessing that all ownership is God's and there is no possessor beside God in competition with God, yet fail to limit their behavior by the outward norms of Islamic law. Such a failure would throw them headlong into the raging sea of hypocrisy (*zandaqa*), and their spiritual condition would revert to sinful contamination. The real goal is to be empowered from within by spiritual truth while being restrained from without by religious law and custom.

Those who achieve spiritual realization follow this formula: no running beyond all bounds with spiritual truth and no stopping short with the literal or legal truth. *It is established firmly between extremes.*[108] Stopping at the literal meaning of religious teachings is idolatry, ascribing partnership of created things with God (*shirk*). Taking spiritual insights as absolute and unbounded by religious law and custom is audacity, stripping insight of its necessary form thereby ruining it (*taʿṭīl*). People of good guidance stand between these two destructive extremes. *Between bile and blood is a milk, pure and easily digested for those who would drink of it.*[109]

SECTION FOUR: RECEIVING PROVISION

There are many pitfalls and obstacles in this matter of receiving and using provision. Shaykh al-Mursi has listed many of them during the invocation of his litany. He beseeched God to "make this issue of provision easy for me. Keep me from greed and exhaustion in searching for it. Protect me from having my heart preoccupied by it and being weighed down by anxiety over it. Rescue me from being lowered to the level of worldly people because of it. Reprieve me from worrying and plotting to secure it. Restrain me from being avaricious and stingy after receiving it." The obstacles arising in our path when we search for, receive, and consume provision cannot be enumerated in any comprehensive way. Let's limit our discussion here to the few basic points revealed by the words of Shaykh al-Mursi. In regard to their provision, people must be in one of three spiritual states. Initially, there is the state before getting provision, during which people struggle and strive. After this comes the state of receiving provision. And after this comes that state of having consumed or used the provision.

In the initial state, there are obstacles that confront us, like "from greed and exhaustion in searching for it, preoccupation and anxiety over it, being lowered to the level of worldly people because of it, and worry over plotting to secure it." Greed is a desire arising in the soul to grasp and hold provision, strengthened by the willful determination to get it. Greed grows strong in the absence of trust in God due to weakness of faith. These two conditions come to the fore due to loss of illumination in the heart, which is caused by the dark veiling of alienation. If the heart were suffused with the light of bearing witness and infused with gifts of spiritual fitness, then the blows of greed would never buffet

301

it. If the light of faith would spread over the heart, it would clearly reveal destiny's prior apportioning of provision and give greed no way to grow strong. The heart would know that prior apportioning had measured out provision and that there is no doubt in receiving what has been apportioned.

As for exhaustion in searching for provision, it might be of various types. It could be physical exhaustion from struggle. You should pray to God to protect you from physical exhaustion. If exhaustion in searching for provision rules over your material and bodily being, you will be easily preoccupied and distracted from obeying divine commands. Conversely, provision that comes with physical ease and comfort makes it easier for you to rise to the occasion of obeying divine commands in worship and other kinds of service. Searching for provision could lead to exhaustion of the heart rather than of the body. This is even more dangerous, and you should pray to God for deliverance! It is the very responsibility of searching for provision that exhausts the heart, while it is simply the search that exhausts the body. It is constantly thinking about it and the burdens that come with it that exhausts the heart. There is no respite from this mental exhaustion except in relying on God, rather than on yourself. The one who trusts God to provide drops all these burdens and allows God to bear them. According to Divine Speech, *God suffices for whoever entrusts God*.[110]

After greed and exhaustion, Shaykh al-Mursi mentions other obstacles, such as "preoccupation and anxiety." Preoccupation of the heart over the issue of provision is a grave pitfall. Shaykh al-Shadhili alerted us to this by saying, "There are two things that most severely alienate people from God: preoccupation with provision and fear of other people." Of these two deadly alienations, preoccupation with securing provision is more intense. Most people can overcome their fear of others, but how many overcome their preoccupation with material livelihood? Very few indeed! This is especially because your very existence bears constant witness to your utter poverty. It renders you totally dependent upon your own willful intent and personal power. Shaykh al-Mursi also singled out anxiety that follows upon preoccupation with getting what you need. Anxiety erupts when you give your full attention to your need for provision and become engrossed in it, to the extent that your heart has no room for anything else. This leads you into a spiritual state of being cut off, extinguishing the illumination of intimacy with others and God. The one who suffers this state lives with a heart in ruins, emptied of the light of faithful certainty and bankrupt of spiritual ability.

Shaykh al-Mursi further highlights the obstacle of being lowered to the level of worldly people because of the need to find intermediate means for provision. People whose faith is weak and who have been granted only a small allotment of reasoning power (*'aql*) feel greed and covetousness in regard to what others have. This leads them to try to get what they perceive others to possess, this behavior that lowers their dignity and demeans them, since they lack trust in the real One who owns. They lack trust because they have not witnessed how God has previously measured out provision for all; they have not given a sincere response to God's promise. Therefore they look with longing at other people and what they have received, taking refuge in others for their needs. This is the consequence of forgetting the presence of God. It is their punishment during their lives. This is bad, but the consequences are surely more intense and awful after death on their inevitable day of reckoning!

If people's faith were sound and their trust in God were strong, they would not be demeaned and lowered, but rather raised up and empowered. *To God belongs the elevated*

303

THE BOOK OF ILLUMINATION

power and to God's messenger and to the believers.[111]
Through this moment of Divine Speech, you can see that
the elevated status of believers depends on their relationship to their Lord. They do not gain power or might through
any other because they know that all elevated power belongs to God. One of God's names is the empowered One
(*al-ᶜazīz*) that reflects God's quality of loftiness and power.
God is the empowered One and there is none with raised
status except God. In turn, God is the empowering One (*al-
muᶜizz*), and there is no other to give power or raise status
except God. Believers get elevated status from trust in God;
believers get empowered by entrusting to God all affairs.
They are never demeaned as long as the sincerity of the
trust in their Lord's apportioning stays firm. They never
grieve as long as they rely on their Lord's subtle gifts to
bring their existence to its appointed term.

Believers have heard the voice of Divine Speech declare, *You are not demeaned nor do you grieve—You are of
elevated status if you remain firm believers.*[112] It is clear
that the raised status of believers is dependent upon their
desisting from coveting what others have and trusting that
God is the only One who truly possesses. Their faith restrains them from feeling the need to look to any other than
their Lord to fulfill their needs. It contains their impulse to
direct the desires of their hearts toward any other source.

Forbidden to those who make the One hallow
    Is seeking help from any other in straits narrow

Let me stay fine-tuned, my friend, to the true One
    On a frequency I die by today and revive
        by tomorrow

So declare to worldly rulers, 'Try as you might
    You can't claim that treasure you can neither
    buy nor borrow

There are people whom God has liberated from the bond-
age of covetousness and has elevated with the quality of
wary consciousness. God lets flow to them copious bene-
faction and brings to completion their lofty aspiration.

A PARABLE
STICK TO YOUR SOURCE

How can you imagine the person who has broken
through self-preoccupation to be connected to God
while still earning a living in the world? That person is like a man sitting directly under a roof-gutter's
drain pipe. [After a long dry spell] it begins to rain.
He doesn't think of running from the spot where he
sits, in vain hopes of catching twice as much water
to store up for the future. No, he gives thanks to
God from the spot where he is. Such a man knows
that, even if he were sitting somewhere else, he
would never have such a steady stream of water for
his use!

In this way, intermediate means of getting material benefit in this world are like drain pipes that
channel God's gifts of provision right to you. If you
engage these means of earning while keeping your
spiritual aspiration focused upon God alone, this
engagement will not harm you and there is no fear
that what comes to you through it will ever run dry.
But people who engage intermediate means shal-
lowly, neglecting what is beyond them and thinking

305

them to be primary causes of wellbeing, are like dumb cattle. Consider how cattle stand there as their owner passes right before their noses. They pay no attention and just keep chewing! The one who passes before them is their owner; he is the one who gives their caretaker all the means to provide for them without exhausting his supplies. Despite this, the cattle don't recognize him. However, if the mere caretaker walks by, the cattle cast loving glances his way and look expectantly at him, for they are used to sensing him as the one who gives them food and water.

People are no different from cattle! If some good things come to them by means of others, they perceive that the good actually comes from others and they fall entangled into this snare. Such people are no better than cattle. No! The cattle are in a better state, aren't they? Just listen to Divine Speech as it describes them: *Those people are like dumb cattle—no, they are more misled. Those are the heedless and forgetful ones.*[113]

Now listen clearly, you true believer. God has given you sandals to wear on your journey: one sandal of faith and one sandal of intuitive knowledge, one of obedience and one of example. Do not get these sandals dirty with the grime of greed for what is in the hands of others or with the murk of depending on any other than the Lord of all worlds. Shaykh al-Shadhili has said, "I once saw the Prophet Muhammad in a dream vision. He said to me, 'O ᶜAli, cleanse your raiment of defilement and you will obtain the help of God with every breath!' I asked, 'What is my raiment, O Prophet of God?' He replied, 'God has clothed you with the vestments of intuitive knowledge, then with the vestment of love, then with the vestment of belief in divine oneness, and then with the vestment of faith, and then with the vestment of submission.' In that very moment, I understood fully Divine Speech when it says *And your clothing keep pure.*"[114]

Whoever really knows God considers everything else entirely insignificant. Whoever loves God considers all else despicable. Whoever makes divinity absolutely One considers nothing else equivalent or in partnership. Whoever believes wholeheartedly in God is kept safe from everything else. Whoever submits totally to God will not rebel against divine will—and with any instance of rebellion will immediately seek pardon while God embraces the offer of apology. Realize, my dear sisters and brothers, that those sojourning on the path to the next world need aspiration high above desiring anything from others in the world. Such an aspiration is more beautiful for them than a groom's wedding jewels. It is more valuable to them than the water of life. Those who remove from their feet the shoes of possession are protected and preserved in their journey. They are worthy of abiding in the divine presence. They can never be robbed on the way. Their achievement cannot be stolen from them. But the one who has soiled the sandals of divine gracious gifts does not deserve to be left free to abide in that presence.

So dear brothers and sisters, keep your faith clean of the grime of greed for created things and created beings! Lean on nothing other than the Lord of all worlds! If you draw intimate to God, you are raised to heights of power. You will abide there without fear of falling, as long as you abide in God's intimacy. But should you incline to anything else and hope to be empowered by anything else, your worth will pass away. That from which you seek power and support is itself passing away. Some Sufi sang for me this poem:

> As long as you're empowered
> by your Lord's intimacy
> Your status will remain
> firm without lapse

> But if you draw power from
> what fades in contingency
> Then your status is nothing
> but that of a corpse

Once a man entered the company of a saint, weeping profusely. The saint asked, "What's wrong with you?" He said, "My guide (*ustādh*) has died!" The saint asked, "Why did you chose as a guide one who dies? Haven't you heard that if you draw power from anyone other than God or rely on anything except God then you have missed God!" *So look to your god under whose shadow you crowd so zealously! I have burned it and scattered its ashes in the Nile! No, you have no god but God, in competition with whom there is no other divinity, who encompasses all in knowledge.*[115]

KNOW YOUR ENEMY LIKE ABRAHAM

My dear brothers and sisters, be like Abraham! Your ancestor Abraham has said, *'I do not love that which wanes and vanishes.'*[116] Doesn't everything other than God wane? Either its existence passes or its power fades. Divine Speech has praised *the community loyal to your father, Abraham.*[117] So follow the religious practice of your ancestor, Abraham, and cleave to his community. All believers are obliged to follow Abraham's example. He gave us the example of setting high the sights of his aspiration, far above relying on things and people. When he was thrown onto the catapult to be hurled into the fiery furnace, Gabriel appeared to him and asked if he was in need of anything. Abraham replied, "From you I need nothing, but from God, yes definitely I'm in need." Gabriel replied, "So ask of God what you need!" Abraham replied, "Why should I ask when God already knows my condition?" Examine closely how Abraham raised his sights from created things and focused his concentration upon the One who truly possesses all things. He never beseeched Gabriel for aid or succor. He did not even take recourse to asking from God. Rather, he considered the true One closer to him than Gabriel who appeared to him in tangible form and more dear to him than requests addressed to the unseen. For this reason, he was delivered from Nimrod and his tortures. He was blessed with generosity and selected for precedence with magnanimity.

Belonging to the community of Abraham means making anything that distracts you from God to be your enemy. It means expending your fullest effort to turn from created things and return to the presence of God. This is emulating Abraham's declaration, *Indeed they are all enemies to me except for the Lord of all worlds.*[118] If you want demonstration of what it means to be an enemy to such things, you can look at the common feeling of despair at the hands of others. Shaykh al-Shadhili has said, "I have despaired of any hope of benefiting myself through myself, so why not despair of benefiting myself through others? I ask that God help others achieve what they need, so why not ask God to help me achieve what I need?" This insight is the alchemic elixir that turns base materials to gold. Whoever achieves this achieves total sufficiency in which there is no need, the absolute loftiness in which there is no debasement, and the constant flow of all that sustains which never vanishes and never wanes.

Such is the alchemy practiced by those who understand God with intuitive insight. Shaykh al-Shadhili has told this story. "Once a young man came into my company and turned out to be a real burden. So I tried to liven him up and make him laugh. Slowly, his mood lightened. So I asked him, 'My boy, what do you need and why have you come to me?' He confessed, 'Sir, I've heard that you know about alchemy. I keep coming to you to see if I can learn alchemy from you.' I replied, 'You have spoken the truth and those who have informed you have spoken the truth. However, I think that you won't be able to accept what I have to teach!' 'O no,' he answered eagerly, 'I will certainly accept it!' So the Shaykh told him, 'I looked at people and saw they were of two kinds: those for whom I felt enmity and those for whom I felt love. So I turned to my enemies and I learned that they were unable to jab me with thorns that could turn me to God. So I desisted from looking to them at all. Then I grew dependent on my friends and I learned that they were unable to give me anything beneficial that could turn me to God. So I desisted from despairing at not receiving anything from them. Then I attached myself to God alone and a voice called out to me saying, 'You will not arrive at the truth of this matter until you desist from complaining about me and despair of anyone else giving anything other than what I have apportioned for you!'" Another time, someone asked Shaykh al-Shadhili about alchemy. He answered, "Rid your heart of greed! Have no hope that your Lord will give you anything except what has already been apportioned for you! That is the real alchemy."[119]

It is not your outward actions that show your status. It is not your constancy in praying or meditating that displays your piety. The only thing that shows your inner light is being satisfied with your Lord and restraining your heart from reaching out to others, being liberated from the shackles of greed, and adorning yourself only with the jewels of wary conscientiousness. Only with these interior virtues are your exterior actions made whole, sound and beautiful. Only with these virtues are your inner spiritual states made pure. Divine Speech teaches us that, *We have made the surface of the world attractively beautiful in order to test them—who will act most wholesomely, soundly and beautifully?*[120]

Beautiful actions come only with intuitive understanding of God. Real understanding is taking God as sufficient for you in disregard of everything else, as I have described above. Those who understand that God is enough rely on nothing but God and offer all needs and cares up to God in order to stand constantly in the divine presence. These virtues are the fruits of intuitive understanding. If you lack wary consciousness of God in your soul, it is more debilitating than lacking anything else! So purify your heart of greed for what others have. But this is not easy. If the person who feels greed washes the heart in the waters of seven seas, it will not be cleansed if there are not the essential factors of despair at the prospect of benefiting from others and raising one's sights from them entirely.

Once ᶜAli came to the city of Basra. He went to the communal mosque there and found many storytellers preaching to the people. ᶜAli grabbed them one by one and had them thrown out of the mosque, until he came to al-Ḥasan al-Baṣri who was a young man preaching to the people.[121] ᶜAli saw some sign of virtue and guidance in this youth and therefore warned him, "My boy, I'm going to ask you about something and if you answer correctly, you may stay here in the mosque. If not, I'm going to throw you

311

out like the rest of your companions." Al-Ḥasan answered, "Ask what you like." So ᶜAli asked him, "What is it that enriches a person's religious life?" He answered, "Wary consciousness in regard to God (al-warᶜ)." Then ᶜAli asked, "And what is it that bankrupts a person's religious life?" He answered, "Greed in regard to others (al-ṭamᶜ)." ᶜAli responded, "Stay here in the mosque, for only those like you are fit to preach to the people."

Indeed, I have heard my Shaykh al-Mursi reflect on the exemplary teaching of al-Ḥasan al-Baṣri. He has told us, "In my early years, while I was spending time in isolation in the caves near Alexandria, I needed a little something. I went to someone I knew and gave him half a dirham to go and buy something for me. I felt a moment of fear that he might take the money without getting me what I need. Suddenly I heard a voice declare to me, "Your religious way is only secure if you are released from the grip of greed in regard to others. The greedy person is never sated. Each of the letters that make up the word 'greed' is hollow, like a bottomless pit." O you who seek God, don't look to what others have! Raise your vision from them and don't debase yourself before them. Your provision has been apportioned for you before your existence. The way it comes to you has been established before your appearance.'" A great Sufi master has said, "Every bit of food that you chew has been apportioned for you before time. So chew each morsel conscientiously! Chew it in a way that ennobles and empowers you, not in a way that demeans and debases you." People who know God intimately trust God's guarantee and guardianship. God does not bring people into maturity until they are more sure of what is in the hands of God than they are of what is in their own hands. Until they trust their contract with the One real being more than they trust their contacts with created beings. If you cannot manage this, you deserve to be called ignorant.

Once a man noticed something strange in the communal mosque. There was a saintly man who lived there, who never worked or left the mosque. The man was amazed and wondered at how he lived like that. He kept thinking to himself, "How does this guy eat?" One day, his curiosity moved him to ask, "How to you get food to eat?" The saint replied, "I have a Jewish friend who has pleaded to come each day and bring me two pancakes." The man said triumphantly, "So that's how you do it!" The saint scolded him, "You poor fool, you think I would trust the pledge of a Jewish friend rather than trust the promise of God, the glorious and transcendent One, whose is ever sincere in what is promised and never breaks any pledge? Haven't you heard God say, *There is no living creature on the face of the earth whose provision does not come from God, who alone knows where it is established and how it is deposited.*" [122] The meddler scurried away in shame.

Once a Sufi was living in isolation in the mosque. He was praying behind the Imam of that mosque. The Imam grew curious about how he managed to live in the mosque all the time without leaving and without spending any money. If he does not work, how does he eat? At this point, the Sufi cried out, "Stop! I have to repeat my prayers from the beginning, because I cannot pray behind the leadership of someone who harbors doubts about God!" There are many stories illustrating these points. Someone once asked ᶜAli, "If a man entered a building and the building collapsed upon him trapping him there, how would the provision appointed to him get to him?" ᶜAli answered, "His provision arrives to him the same way his life arrives to him—in a measure fixed and immutable!"

Let's return to the litany of Shaykh al-Mursi. He beseeched God, "Reprieve me from worrying and plotting to
secure provision." Worrying is a play of thoughts that fills
your soul stressing the urgent necessity of food for tomorrow and calling you to build an intention to get it. Plotting
is the next step of the cycle, as you say to yourself, "I will
get it from here or there, no, rather from there and not here."
Such thoughts multiply and spin the heart this way and that,
to the point that as you pray you don't know what you are
praying and as you recite scripture you aren't aware of what
you are reciting. With such worrying and plotting, your acts
of worship are sullied and spoiled; you do not receive illumination or insight from your worship. If such a structure
of worry builds up in your heart, demolish it quickly with
the sturdy spade of trust. Level it until you uncover the firm
bedrock of faith.

You should know, may God have compassion on you,
that God has undertaken to plan for your welfare long before you existed. So if you want the best for yourself do not
bother looking after yourself. Your plotting and planning
for your benefit is actually harmful to you. This will cause
your welfare to be transferred to your own feeble care and
cut you off from receiving the subtle gifts of divine support
that are extended to you. God does not abandon the believers to their own plots and plans. God does not leave them
free to wrangle and wrestle with divine decree. If you feel
that you are abandoned and left alone with your worrying
and your mind conceives this to be the extent of reality, you
are not living in the real world. The light of faith and certain knowledge would dispel such illusory shadows. Divine Speech reveals that, *It is our real nature to support the
believers.*[123] Even further, it proclaims, *the truth is hurled
against falsehood and falsehood is completely obliterated.*[124]

FREE YOURSELF FROM MISERLY ANXIETY

In his litany, Shaykh al-Mursi concludes by beseeching God for restraint from "being avaricious and stingy after receiving provision." Avarice and stinginess are obstacles that arise in our hearts after we have already received the blessing of provision. These obstacles grow in a heart that is weak of faith and lacking in trust. God has criticized avarice and stinginess in us through Divine Speech, *Those who shield their souls from avarice are spiritually prosperous.*[125] This means that those who harbor avarice in the soul will reap no spiritual success and prosperity. They will experience no illumination, since spiritual prosperity is the cultivation of light. Divine Speech has described the hypocrites: *Avaricious when others receive goods! No, those people do not believe, so God makes their actions fall into nothing.*[126] Further they are criticized, *There are some of them who try to coerce God into a contract, saying 'If God gives us of divine bounty and then we will be sincere believers and act righteously.' But when they are given plenty by the bounty of God, they are stingy and turn their backs.*[127] The furthest extent of this critique is that, *Those who are stingy with others are really only stingily denying good to themselves.*[128]

Avarice and stinginess describe three types of actions. Firstly, you might resist spending of what you have to fulfill the duties you have toward God in worship. Secondly, you might resist spending and giving of what you have in dealing with others beyond necessary obligations. Thirdly, beyond material possessions you might resist giving up your very self to God.

In the first instance, you might resist giving up part of your wealth as alms (*zakāt*) even though it is obligatory upon you by the command of Divine Speech. Or you might

315

resist paying someone who has rights over you, even though this has been clearly specified for you to do, such as supporting your parents, your children and their dependents or your spouses. In short, if you are miserly in giving and spending for any obligation that God has specified for you, you deserve to be called despicable and incur inevitable punishment for your actions. This is reflected in the Divine Speech, *As for those who store up treasure of gold and silver without spending of what they have in the way of God, alert them to their painful punishment.*[129] Scholars have clarified that *treasure* means wealth and possessions upon which alms is obligatory and in arrears; if one has given alms from what one possesses, that possession is not considered to be *treasure* as pronounced in Divine Speech. Wealth that is purified through alms is not the focus of this threat of punishment and does not deserve censure.

In the second instance comes a wider variety of miserliness. You may give alms from what you own and but then fail to spend anything else in ways that benefit others. Even though you have met your apparent obligations that God has commanded, you are still miserly if you think this minimal step is enough. Spending only to fulfill your minimum obligations and repudiating every opportunity to perform additional acts of goodness and charity is the mark of those who are weak in faith. Believers who take care to keep their relationship with God sound and wholesome should never consider their work finished just when they fulfill their minimum obligations under the law. The person who does this with wealth is like the person who offers the five obligatory prayers each day but neglects other acts of worshipful service.

For proof of this, it should suffice you to hear the words of God as reported by the Prophet Muhammad [in this *hadīth qudsī*]: "Those intimate to me draw close by performing what I have made obligatory upon them. My servants keep drawing closer to me with other acts of worship (*nawāfil*) until I love them. And if I love them, I become their hearing and their sight, their tongue and their heart, their thinking and their doing and their strength."[130] God declared in this moment of inspired Speech that continuous acts of worship beyond what is obligatory make a person deserving of God's love. Such acts of worship include everything beyond the minimum of what Divine Speech has specified for us: beyond ritual prayer, alms, pilgrimage and such things.

Let us contrast these two personalities. One person offers obligatory prayers but no other form of worship or gives alms but avoids other opportunities to give and the other who offers prayers in addition to other acts of worship and gives alms while also finding other opportunities to spend for other people. We can think of them in a parable. There are two servants to one master. The master entrusts to each servant two dirhams a day. The first servant takes the two dirhams, then goes about his business. At the end of the day, he returns the two dirhams to his master safe and sound. The master does not find fault with him, but he does give the master anything or provide the master reason to regard him with love. The second servant takes the two dirhams and invests it wisely so that he can not only return the two dirhams entrusted to him but also give sweets and fruit to his master. Surely the second servant is more esteemed in the eyes of the master, who will love him more and consider him with greater acceptance and generosity. The servant who simply returns exactly what is entrusted to him shows no love for the master; he returns what is entrusted to him only out of fear of punishment. However, the second servant who not only returns the trust but also gives more

317

in addition behaves in a way that shows his love for the master and evokes love from the master. He is more deserving of winning the master's intimacy and fondness.[131]

God has made certain acts of worship obligatory for a reason: to test people to show whether there are weaknesses in their spiritual state or laziness in their souls. So God has made obligatory that which is obligatory. If God had made these acts voluntary, very few people would find in themselves the strength and motivation to live up to them. How very few indeed! So God set the parameters of obligatory actions and demanded obedience within these from all. God has made fulfillment of these obligations to be a condition of entering paradise. It is as if God drives people on toward paradise by binding them in chains of obligation. Your Lord is amazed at people who are urged toward paradise only in chains.

. Here is something for you to ponder, may God be kind to you. I have examined all the religious obligations and have found that the true One has established each obligation upon a certain kind of obedience that is wider than the specific act of obligatory worship. This is so that any instance of obedience of that sort might restore a person's weakened motivation to fulfill the specific act of obligatory worship. The Prophet Muhammad has taught that God will first examine a person's acts of obligatory worship; if there is any lack, God will make up for it by drawing upon a person's acts of obedience outside of these specific acts of obligatory worship. Ponder this and understand! Don't be self-satisfied with fulfilling only the acts of worship that God has made obligatory for you. Rather, evoke love by committing yourself to interacting with God in everything you do beyond obligatory acts of worship. If you die and find in the scales of your balance only the bare minimum of fulfilling obligatory acts and avoiding forbidden acts, you will have missed goodness and subtle gifts that are valuable beyond assessment. Glory be to the One who opens for us the gates of continual interaction in everything we do and who clarifies for us that there are endlessly diverse means of reaching intimacy with God.

Surely God knows that some people are weak while others are strong. Therefore God has delimited the obligatory acts of worship. Those who are weak scrape by with the minimum of offering what is commanded and avoiding what is forbidden. Their hearts are not ruled by the power of love (*sulṭān al-ḥubb*). They do not feel passion burning their guts that would enable them to interact with God beyond the economy of obligation. Recall the parable of the servant. The master did not specify two dirhams to entrust to the servant because he wanted two dirhams back. He specified two dirhams so that the servant would have some way of investing to return much more!

In this way, you should understand the specificity with which God has delimited obligatory acts of worship. God has appointed times and manners for acts of obedient worshipful service. Ritual prayer is delimited through the times of the day: sunrise, sunset, noontime, evening and night. Alms are obligatory at the passing of a year throughout which wealth has been keep in one's possession, if the wealth is in coinage, storable agricultural goods or livestock. However alms are obligatory immediately at the time of harvest for agricultural goods that are perishable and cannot be stored, according to the Divine Speech, *Give what is due on the day it is harvested.*[132] For fasting, certain times are delimited by the lunar months, like the ten days of ᶜĀshūrā in the month of Dhū al-Ḥijja and the whole month of Ramaḍān. In this way, God has appointed times and lim-

319

its for obligatory acts of worship, leaving other times for working with intermediate means and enjoying the fruits of one's labor.

However, the people who belong to God and truly understand God experience time differently. They see all time as hallowed for worship, unifying their times rather than differentiating them. For them, each moment is filled with seeking a way toward God. They conceive that each moment belongs to God and they ascribe no time to anyone other than God. For this reason, Shaykh al-Shadhili has taught us, "You are to undertake only one method of meditative worship (*wird*) at all times: leaving your own desire and fully loving your true master (*isqāṭ al-hawā wa muḥabbat al-mawlā*)." True love prevents the lover from doing anything that is not in accord with the will of the beloved.

Those who understand God know that their every breath is a trust (*amāna*) that the true One lends to them as a deposit secured with them. They are entrusted to safeguard each breath in each moment. They focus their intense concentration on this task. Just as God's lordship is absolute without lapse, so you must guard the rights that lordship has over you in every moment without gaps. God's lordship over you is not limited to a certain time or duration. Likewise, you must guard the rights that this lordship holds over you in every moment of time without routine differentiation. For this reason, Shaykh al-Shadhili has taught, "Every moment manifests a dimension of your servanthood made necessary by the command of the true One's lordship." Let me draw in the reins of this discourse now, in order not to spill beyond the immediate goal of this small book!

Let us return to our discussion of miserliness and generosity. The third kind of avarice is the refusal to give up your very self (*al-ithār bi⁰l-nafs*). This is the most valuable kind of giving or spending possible, for one gives one's whole self to another only for the sake of the other. This is far superior to the practice of giving of your possessions what God has demanded but nothing more, or the practice of giving what God has demanded and then giving something more. In neither of these practices do you give yourself to God in an act of total generosity through self-sacrifice. Such generosity in giving up the self is the virtue of sincere believers and the action that distinguishes people of true faith. They deeply understand God's nature and therefore readily offer up not just their belongings but their souls for God's sake, knowing that a sincere servant claims to own nothing in competition with the master. Just as giving up one's soul to God is the best dimension of giving, clinging to the soul is the ugliest dimension of stinginess. For this very reason, Shaykh al-Mursi has asked God for restraint from "avarice and stinginess after receiving it [provision]." He offered a glimpse of this meaning but did not pour it forth openly. In this book this topic cannot be pursued fully.[133]

THE CHALLENGES OF REGRET AND LOSS

I have explained that spiritual obstacles arise with regard to our pursuit of provision in three different states. There are obstacles that arise prior to receiving provision and obstacles that arise while we receive provision. These obstacles I have illustrated through the words of Shaykh al-Mursi's litany, the details of which I've explained in my own words. This leaves the third state: the state after receiving provision as we use it and it is consumed. Obstacles that arise in this state include regret, sorrow at its passing away and looking forward expectantly for more in the future. Now listen closely to Divine Speech: *So that you do not regret what you lose and do not take joy in what you gain.*[134] This is clarified by the words of the Prophet, when one of his daughters' children died and she grieved that God had taken her child away. He said, "Tell her that God does not take away what belongs to us— rather everything that is given to us truly belongs to God." Those who regret the loss of anything other than God have openly declared themselves ignorant of God and are living in a state of spiritual alienation. If God were found to them, what else could be lost? Those who are present with God allow nothing else to be present with them except God. How could they experience the lack of anything?

Sincere servants know that whatever it is they seemingly do not have is not of their provision. What they don't get is not intended for them as their provision in the first place! If it were their provision, how could it be lost and acquired by someone else? Rather, that thing was lent to them to hold for a brief time until the true owner could come and reclaim the loan. In this way, the thing has simply been returned to its rightful holder from your hand into which it was temporarily deposited—nothing is lost. Consider a boy who has a girl cousin. He is promised to marry her from his boyhood. As he grows up, there occur some events that make a marriage between them impossible, and the girl cousin is married to some other young man. He might be filled with covetous regret, thinking that he has lost the bride he assumed was his. Wise people would advise him, "It is best for you to go and beg the pardon of your cousin's new husband. You were expecting her to be your bride, but she was actually destined to be his bride from the time before time. What's wrong is your attitude and not her husband's action!"

For a warning about the dangers of regret over what you perceive to have been lost, it suffices a believer to listen to Divine Speech. *There are some people who worship God conditionally. If good befalls them they are tranquil while if crisis befalls them they instantly change and are overturned upon their faces. They are hopeless losers in this world and the next world; their loss is most evident.*[135] Here the true One criticizes those who are content with things during the time that they are at hand. Haven't you heard how God says, *If good befalls them, they are tranquil* and content with their good things? But if they truly understand God with insight, they would not be content with anything less than God. Those who are saddened by the loss of something other than God are addressed by, *if crisis befalls them.* The crisis is losing that special something for which you lust, upon which your contentment depends. How quickly such people *instantly change and are overturned upon their faces.* Being "overturned" means that their powers of reason are astonished, their souls are bewildered, and their hearts grow forgetful. This is all due to lack of intuitive knowledge of God (*maᶜrifa*). If they knew God at all, they would realize that God is sufficient for sustaining their being without their needing any other existing thing. They would feel enriched with God and ignore anything they had lost.

Whoever has lost God can gain nothing. Whoever has found God can lose nothing. How could anything be lacking with someone who has found the One in whose hands is command over everything that is? How could anything be lacking with someone who has found the One who gives being to everything that is? How could anything be lacking with someone who has found the One who appears in everything that is? In the view of those with intuitive knowledge, things other than God do not merit the description of "being bad" or "being lacking." In reality, there is nothing that exists other than God. That is a consequence of affirming God's absolute singularity. Therefore, nothing other than God can be lacking, since something without real being can not be said to be lacking. If the veils of self-delusion (*ḥijāb al-wahm*) would be pulled back, one could clearly see that everything in material appearance is, in fact, existentially lacking. When the light of faithful certainty radiates, it eclipses the [relative] being of existing things.

If you understand this, my fellow servant, then you should never despair over the loss of anything and never place your reliance on the existence of things. Those who get something and begin to rely upon it, or lose something and grieve over it, affirm that their servanthood is to that thing. Having it gives them joy and losing it bring them sorrow. If you were satisfied with God alone, my dear fellow believer, then nothing could hold command over your heart except the love of God alone.[136] Surely your nature is nobler than to be a servant worshipping anything except God! God has made you a noble servant with a generous nature, so do not become a despised and miserly servant. Indeed, God has forbidden those who intimately understand God to exist for anything other than God.

Listen to this saying of Shaykh al-Shadhili in his prayer, called the Great Litany (*al-ḥizb al-kabīr*): "Make us worshipful servants to you in each and every circumstance."[137] This means, 'Please do not let our servanthood be conditional to changing circumstance.' Shaykh al-Mursi has clarified this concept by saying, "Those who remain unruffled and content in any circumstance are of two different kinds.

One is the person who is in the circumstance for its sake. The other is the person who is in the circumstance for the sake of the One who transforms any circumstance at any moment (*al-muḥawwil*). The first kind of person, who is content with circumstance for its own sake in what it gives him or her, is a servant who worships the circumstance. The second type of person, who is content with circumstance for the sake of the One who transformed the circumstance to be such as it is, is a servant who worships the One who transforms." The Shaykh means that people who worship their circumstance are those who anticipate it anxiously before it arrives, then are overjoyed by its existence while it exists, then are wracked by sorrow when it slips away. These are people who worship circumstance. Such people belong to the ephemeral circumstance, while the ephemeral circumstance in no way belongs to them! If one were a true worshipful servant of God, one would not anticipate anything other than God, feel joy due to anything other, or grieve at the loss of anything other. Do not let joy at what is given distract you from the real One who gives!

EVERYTHING PASSES AWAY

If you want to be a true follower of Abraham, then do as he did: *I do not love that which wanes and vanishes.*[138] Every circumstance wanes and vanishes. It is ephemeral and will pass away. One poet has said,

> Coming from nothing
> Going to nothing
> It's called circumstance
> Because it circles.
> Everything that appears
> By necessity disappears.
> Look at the shadow as you stand
> To what end does it come?

325

No matter how long it is,
It inevitably grows less and less

As I said, whatever circumstance you find yourself in, whether you enjoy it or despise it, will without a doubt pass away. If you desire that the true One keep you in a particular state permanently, you desire to be kept in a state of incomplete imperfection! It is as if the true One were saying to you, 'Do not ask me to keep you permanently in one circumstance, for I do not treat you in this way. Do you not want the effects of my lordship to permeate you thoroughly? Rather, ask me to let you feel my gracious kindness in whatever way I desire in whatever circumstance I establish you, that you might be with me and for me, not with the circumstance and for the circumstance.' Divine Speech tells us, *Everyone in the heavens and earth asks the One who is every day in [a new] activity.*[139] This means that God is, in each moment, engaged in different activities with regard to created beings: giving and withdrawing, laying low and rising up, constricting in straits or expanding in joy, empowering or enfeebling. This list of divine effects (*athār*) that leave traces in the circumstances of created beings could go on infinately. It is as if God were saying to you, 'O my servant, do not despair over your lack of anything, as long as I remain with you. Do not take joy in having anything, if I am not with you. For I am so valuable as to compensate for the loss of whatever is other than me, whereas nothing other than me can be sufficient to fulfill your need. Do not be one of those people who worship me weakly (*bi-l'ʿilal*), diverted by their surroundings, for those are the servants of changing conditions (*ʿabīd al-ḥurūf*) who worship conditionally. Rather, worship me directly through me! For I alone am characterized by perfect needlessness. I alone am known by the permanence of my actions.'

Consider again the moment of Divine Speech, *There are some people who worship God conditionally. If good befalls them they are tranquil while if crisis befalls them they instantly change and are overturned upon their faces. They are hopeless losers in this world and the next world; their loss is most evident.* This refers to people who worship God to ask for having some need fulfilled or have some obstacle removed. When this need or obstacle vanishes, the value of their worship also vanishes. As the circumstance that impelled them to worship contracts and shrinks away, so their being in accord with God also contracts and shrivels. They are hopeless losers in this world and the next world. It is as if God were saying, 'They are losers, because we have removed from them that for which they asked, yet they remain fixated on that thing. In contrast, they must necessarily remain with what we ask from them [worship] until we alone remain with them.' Whoever worships God for the purpose of acquiring what is other than God is actually worshipping something other than God. Whoever worships God for the sake of God's generosity (*jūd*) or blessing (*ni'mā*) is not worshipping God but only worshipping the generosity or blessing.

We are the servants of whatever we love. The Prophet Muhammad said, "May the servant of a dinar wither! May the servant of a dirham wither! May the servant of coins wither! May their hands wither, their heads hang low, and their feet stumble! If they should step on a thorn may there be nobody to remove it for them!" So be a servant of God with every object and in every situation, whether you are given to or prevented from receiving, whether you are debased or ennobled, whether you are raised to power or stripped of power, whether you are enriched or impoverished, whether you are expanded with joy or contracted with pain, whether you have what you need or need what you

327

don't have, whether you are in a hopeful condition or a desperate condition, whether you are passing away or remaining. These states are all the changing traces of divine activity. They are circumstances other than God that necessarily change and, in changing, transport you.

Now it is clear to you that people who are with their circumstances exist only for circumstances, while circumstances exist for those who are with the One who transforms their circumstances. Shaykh al-Mursi has said, "Those who love to appear before others are servants of appearing. Those who love to be hidden from others are servants of hiding. But servants of God do not care whether God makes them appear before others or become hidden in anonymity." Realize that the eternal One places you in a circumstance in order that you take something from the circumstance rather than having the circumstance taking something from you. Circumstance comes upon you bearing a gift for you: the potential for you to gain new knowledge about God. So turn to face each new circumstance uttering the name of the One who initiates (*al-mubdī*). Enter each changing circumstance and remain in it as you have received the gifts that it bears for you. Stay respectfully attentive and cultivate proper comportment while it faces you, turning your whole attention toward it. Recognize when it is beginning to pass away and, uttering the name of the One who calls to return (*al-muʿīd*), return it to where it came from and let it expire. Did the Prophet of God demand to stay around once his duty of conveying the message of Divine Speech was complete? He was entrusted with a duty, so why should he stay around after that trust is fulfilled? Hypocrites are plainly evident when their circumstances change and they are removed from higher levels to lower ones. Then the screens of deception are rent asunder and their defects are brought naked to the light.

This is the meaning of, *There are some people who worship God conditionally.* Some people worship God on condition of one state. If that states passes away, so does their ability to adequately worship, and their accord with God is shattered and scattered. If we truly understand God, we worship and serve in each circumstance in a new way as demanded by that changing circumstance, just as God is your Lord in every circumstance and not just in one or the other.

So be a sincere servant to the Lord in each and every circumstance. Divine Speech continues, *If good befalls them they are tranquil.* Here, *good* means that a circumstance manifests that which you consider to accord with your desires and therefore, in your own view, this is "good." But in reality, there is no absolute good. The same thing you might consider "bad" in a different context. *If crisis befalls them they instantly change and are overturned upon their faces.* When the thing or circumstance that you considered "good" and that made you tranquil inevitably passes away, you call this *crisis.* It is a crisis because the believer's faith is tested by losing something. With apparent loss, the actual spiritual state of people becomes apparent. How few people think that they are saved from need by God's presence with them! Most people think they are safe from need by the intermediate means of work and the compounding of their earnings. How few people consider their intimacy to be with their Lord, for most people are intimate only with their circumstances. The proof of this is that changing circumstances, which replace a "good" time in which they feel secure with a "bad" time, can alienate them from their former way of drawing intimate to God. If their intimacy was to their Lord directly, it would not change but remain constant as their Lord is constant. *They are hopeless losers in this world and the next world; their loss is most evident.* They are losers in this world because they have lost what they desired from this world. They are losers in the next world because they have not worked to prepare for it. They have lost the chance to do what is required. For we are required only to belong to God alone. Think through this deeply!

CONCLUSION: INTIMATE CONVERSATION WITH GOD (*munājāt*)

The effect of these subtle spiritual realities well up from within the human being, as if they formed a voice speaking from the heart. It is as if this were the voice of God, conversing intimately with God's servant in a dialogue about planning and provision. It is as it God speaks to you like this:

O my servant, listen intently as you bear witness, so that your benefit from me may increase with fullness. Pay close attention with your heart's ear, for I am not far away but rather so near.

O my servant, I was with you caring for you even before you were with yourself caring for yourself. So be with yourself now without a care for yourself. I guard you tenderly, from before you were born and as you emerge, and even now I am watching over your every need and urge.

O my servant, I alone can create with form and span; I am singular in forging my command and my plan. So don't ascribe partners to me in my shaping of creation; don't compete with me in your direction and volition. I alone arrange the affairs of my dominion, with no equal; I alone ordain and decree with no minister or consul.

O my servant, I'm the one who fulfilled your needs before you ever suspired, so do not wrangle with me in something you've now desired. The One who has accustomed you to watchful dedication, don't oppose now with obstinate obfuscation.

O my servant, I have routinely controlled for you your affairs; now leave aside your concerns and selfish cares. O my servant, why do you doubt me after your own experience of me? What is this perplexity after I've made myself clear? How do you go astray after I've given you guidance? Doesn't it affect you to know that there is none beside me who directs your affairs? Doesn't it deter you from quarrelling to acknowledge all you've received from me to relieve your cares?

O my servant, examine carefully the relationship between your being and all the dimensions of my cosmic creation. Don't you see that you are an inextricable part of its evanescence that is destined to dissipation? Can't you see the relation of every created thing, including you, to what will never dissipate, never fade and never decay? You have come to peace with me as the establisher of my vast creation, so quit contesting my mastery. Desist from opposing, through your competing with me in arranging your own affairs, my essential divinity.

O my servant, is it not enough for you that I am providing for you? Doesn't recalling my aid to you, before you could help yourself, motivate you to accept with tranquility what I now provide for you?

O my servant, whenever I have made you seem necessary to yourself, it is to test your mettle. Whatever you take from my cosmos as a sufficient means to the exclusion of me will consume you and corrode you.

O my servant, I have prepared for you my boundless generosity even before I gave you bounded form. I give from my being's immensity. Through each phenomenon I shine forth my power's luminosity. So how can you persist in your obstinate lack of reciprocity?

O my servant, consider this! When has anyone who relies on me to fulfill needs ever been frustrated? When has anyone who looks to me for support ever been devastated? O my servant, busy yourself with serving me. Let your service to me distract you from requesting what I've already measured out for you. Free yourself by thinking well of me. Let your good opinion of my intentionality prevent you from suspecting any fault in my mastery's totality.

O my servant, how can you falsely accuse One of negligence, whose attribute-revealing name is benevolent (*muhsin*)? How can you wrangle with One who is omnipotent (*muqtadir*) or oppose One who overcomes all obstacles (*qahhār*)? How can you contravene the judgment of One who is incisively wise (*hakīm*)? How could you harbor anxieties with One whose grace is infinitely subtle (*latīf*)?

O my servant, whoever desists from self-will in deference to me achieves success, while whoever persists in guile against me is beguiled and outwitted by the simplest of problems. Whoever is sincere in turning to me for every need has obtained the treasure of boundless riches. Whoever perceives every movement to be moving by my will deserves my aid. Whoever intuits that I am the means to all gain cleaves to the most powerful means to attain. Indeed, I have promised to repay the people who look after their own cares with turgid and turbulent lives. I upend the foundations of whatever they strive to build and loosen the knots that they tie, letting their plans crumble into decay while allowing their desires to lead them astray. Such people will never feel the refreshing spirit of contentment or taste the bliss of freedom from cares. If they had the least glimmer of insight into my nature, they would joyfully be satisfied with my care for them and leave aside anxiety about themselves. They would trust me to guard them rather than seeking to guard their own security.

It would be so easy for me to send them down the path of contentment and security, to train them through guidance without obscurity and lead them along the pathways of purity! I would make my care for them a shield protecting them against everything that they fear, and a means of realizing everything for which they hope. This would not be hard for me in the least, but the key lies in their hands.

O my servant, all I desire of you is that you desire me, rather than desire things from me. I prefer for you to prefer me to any of your personal preferences. I will only be content with you when you are content with me and discontent with anything other than me.

O my servant, if I include in your destiny what seems to go for you, it is only to show you my unbounded generosity. If I include in your destiny what seems to go against you, it is only an occurrence of the inscrutable subtlety of my graciousness toward you.

O my servant, do not repay me with ceaseless wrangling over the blessings I bestow upon you. Do not remunerate me for the priceless favor of my granting you the power of reason by contesting me. For it is the gift of reason that makes you unique in the universe, able to distinguish right from wrong, essential from trivial, and eternal from ephemeral.

O my servant, you are at peace with me as the One who orchestrates my celestial skies and maintains my terrestrial lands, and you admit that I alone dictate their motions and their fate. With such ease why don't you also submit your every existence to me in peace? For you belong to me. Why struggle to plot and plan for your own wellbeing when you are with me? Just as you have taken me as your guardian, now trust in me as your provider, who gives generously to prepare you for a glorious and enviable final portion.

O my servant, I have decreed before time that my servants' hearts cannot harbor two contradictory forces: the illumination of being at peace with me and the obscuring darkness of dissatisfied wrangling with me. With me, it is one or the other. You choose for yourself which one it will be. You choose, knowing that I have made your willpower strong enough that you may grow preoccupied with yourself. So don't underestimate the power of your will, you whom I have raised up to the heights of power and prestige! Don't abase yourself by relying on anyone other than me, you whom I've ennobled! It may help you to know that I've made you mightier than to grow preoccupied with anything other than me. I created you to stand in my presence. I have spoken to you, summoning you to my presence. I have drawn you to me with the attractive force of my care for you. If you stay preoccupied with yourself, I conceal myself from you. If you follow your selfish desires, I spurn you. If you pass beyond yourself, then I draw closer to you. If you confirm your intimacy with me by turning away from everything other than me, then I love you.

O my servant, aren't you satisfied that I've fulfilled your needs? Whom will you follow now that I've undertaken to give you guidance? For I alone have created and stand above all creation. I have given you the trust and empowered you to return it one day. Isn't that enough to prevent you from disputing with me about what I've decreed and preclude you from opposing me in what I send your way?

O my servant, those who plan for themselves don't attest to my incomparable unity. Those who complain to others about what I've sent down for them don't satisfy me.

Those who choose for themselves despite me do not choose me. Those who aren't at peace with my overpowering destiny do not conform to my order. Those who don't turn control of their affairs over to me don't know me. Those who don't entrust to me their wellbeing are ignorant of me.

O my servant, in reality unfaithful ignorance (*jahl*) is abiding with what you pretend is in your control rather than abiding with what is in my control. If it has been chosen for you to choose me, then the choice is mine, not yours. Consider carefully! Sincere servanthood and personal choice cannot coexist. You cannot turn your attention to me and turn toward temporary traces and phenomenal effects in the world at the same time. Either I am looking out for you, or you are looking out for yourself. The choice is clear. Do not exchange good guidance for a formula of failure.

O my servant, if you ask me to let you plot and plan for yourself and you remain steeped in headstrong stubbornness and irrational anxiety, just imagine what your life would be like if you simply let me direct your affairs for you. If you persist in asserting your will and never getting what you think you deserve, just stop to imagine what your life would be like if you asserted that only I could choose for you according to my will.

O my servant, even though I have allowed you the freedom to care for yourself, you should be humble enough to refuse this offer and desist from taking care of yourself. How could you, when I've ordered you not to, become anxious for your own welfare? O you who are fraught with anxieties over your selfish concerns, if you passed them on to me, you could relax. You fool! Selfish calculation is such a heavy burden that can only be borne by mastery, a burden which fragile humanity is not capable of bearing. Shame on you! Your nature is to be carried, not to carry. Your nature is to be borne along, not to bear. I desire only your ease, so don't let a selfish calculation exhaust you. The one who took care of you in the womb's darkness and carried you into existence with everything you could possibly desire doesn't want that you wrangle now, disgruntled with what is willed for you.

O my servant, I ordered you to serve me. I guaranteed you a share of life from me. But you have neglected my order and doubted my guarantee. I was not content to guarantee your livelihood to you until I appointed for you a measured amount that is limited but immutable. I was not content to measure out shares for you until I gave you metaphors through which to comprehend me. I called you "my servant" so that you might understand. I said, *And in the heavens is your provision that you have been promised. By the Lord of the heavens and the earth, indeed this is the truth, just as you can speak.*[140] Beyond how I've described myself, I'm content with how the sages have described me and how those who have realized certain truth have ascribed to me honor and graciousness. Even if I had not given explicit promises in Divine Speech, they would know that I would never interrupt my support. Even if I had not pronounced a guarantee, they would still trust in my beneficence. I have apportioned life even to those who ignore me or rebel against me, so how could I not apportion life to those who obey me and respect me?

You fool, consider the gardener who plants a tree and undertakes to water it. He knows all about the inner disposition of the tree and endeavors to support and cultivate it. Isn't it enough for the tree that the gardener is caring for it and fulfilling its needs? All existence is from me and all sustenance is through me alone forever. All creation is from me and is given provision by me alone forever. You fool—

do you invite someone to your home without intending to feed your guest? Would you cultivate a relationship with someone without wanting to be generous with your relation?

O my servant, place your anxiety about provision in its proper place. Whatever burden you release I will bear, and it will never weigh you down. But if you bear those burdens yourself, I leave you to yourself and your own incapability. Would I bring you into my home and refuse to give you nourishment? Would I cause you to appear in existence and refuse to aid you with support and subsistence? Would I pour you into being without continuous giving? Would I charge you with guarding rights for me and refuse provision for you? Would I oblige you with duties and not apportion for you supplies?

You fool! So many gifts of infinite variety I have for you. Through you I've caused my mercy to show forth. Not content to give you this world, I've stored up even more for you in a future paradise. As if gardens were not enough, I have promised to present you with the chance to see me directly. If my actions are like this in the world you experience, how can you doubt that I would exceed it in my boundless munificence?

O my servant, whoever takes from me receives blessings without a doubt and whoever turns to me will be granted favor. Surely I have no need to benefit from anyone's benefiting from me, and here is proof of this beyond questioning. If you asked me to refuse you your provision that I had previously measured out for you, I would not answer your request. If you beseeched me to prevent you from receiving my favor, I would never carry out your request. So consider how you are always asking things of me and requesting so much from me. What do you expect? Be ashamed now about what you were previously so impudent in demanding! Through this modesty, come to understand and appreciate me. For the one who is given to understand me has been given the consummate gift beyond which nothing more is needed.

O my servant, consider me good enough and do not consider anything other than me better. Orient your heart toward me with simple sincerity. If you do just this, I will show you the extraordinary grace of my subtlety and the amazing devices of my generosity. Your inner conscience will delight in bearing witness to my presence. I have made clear the path of spiritual progress to people of understanding and keenness, and I have shown the signposts of guidance to those granted concord and success. Those with certain knowledge have come to accord with me through true faith, while those who believe trust in me though clear understanding. They know that I am better for them than are their own limited selves. They know that I care for them better than they could ever care for themselves. Thus they willingly submit themselves to my lordship with easy resignation and throw themselves into my hands, releasing all cares and relinquishing all controlling urges. For this, I recompense them with comfort in their souls, illumination in their reasoning faculties, intuitive knowledge in their hearts, and the immediate experience of my intimate presence in the innermost kernels of their conscience. That is what I give them in this ephemeral world. And when they draw near to the next world after death, I give them a mighty status, a lofty abode, and expand the riches of splendor over them. And if, beyond all this, I bring them into my immediate presence, then they have what no eye has ever seen, no ear has ever heard, and no human heart has ever conceived!

O my servant, you will face a time in the future beyond death when I will not ask you to struggle and serve. So why do you worry now in seeking provision for yourself? If I've made you responsible for serving me now, I surely provide you means with which to serve! If I charge you with important work, I surely provide you with nourishment and upkeep. Know that I never forget you, even when you forget me. Know that I remember you long before you may remember me. Know that my provision is measured out for you always, even if you rebel against me. If this is my behavior when you come out in open opposition against me, just imagine how I will be if you turn to me with an open and accepting heart. You don't assess my true value or respect my right if you don't confess my power and submit to my might. You don't protect the rights of my beneficence if you don't respect my commands with obedience.

Don't turn away from facing me, for you will find none better for replacing me. Are you confident of being enriched by possessing anything other than me? Nothing over which you're obsessing can make you independent of me. I created you by my power. I spread the world out before you through my undeserved giving. Just as there is no creator other than me, there is no provider other than me. Do I create just to turn over provision of my creation to others, when I am infinitely giving to my servants and there is none more generous than I?

So trust in me, my servant, for I am a worthy Lord to those who serve me. Leave aside all your desires that conflict with me, and I will bring you to the wellspring of desire fulfilled. Call to mind my past graces and gifts to you and don't ignore the reality of my love for you.

339

CONCLUDING PRAYER (*du ͨā*)

O God, we know that your command cannot be resisted and your decree cannot be contradicted. We are incapable of rebuffing what you have decreed or repealing what you have decided. So we ask only for your grace in what you decree. We ask only your support in bearing what you decide. In all this, we ask that you include us among those whom you guard and protect, O Lord of the universe.

O God, you have already measured out for us our provision and you alone bring each portion to us. So let us come to it with wellbeing. Let us be secure from all distress and preserved from all uncertainty and alienation, encompassed in receiving it by the illumination of arriving near you. Let us bear witness that our provision is from you. Let us be thankful toward you and ascribe it to you alone and to nobody else in all worlds.

O God, from your hand comes all provision, in this world and in the world to come. So provide for us in both worlds, and give us only as much as you know to be good for us and only as much as will benefit us. O God, make us to be from among those who choose you, not from those who prefer anything else to you. Make us to be from among those who pass control back to you, not those who stand in opposition to you. O God, we stand in absolute dependence upon you, so give to us. We stand weak and unable to obey you thoroughly, so empower us. Give us the ability to carry out your will and turn us from rebellion against your will. Make us stand in peace, at peace with your lordship over us, patiently enduring the commands of your divinity, standing ennobled by our relationship to you, with repose in our hearts from our reposing complete trust in you. Make us to be among those who enter the courtyards of contentment. Let us wash our feet in the heavenly river of being at peace, plucking the ripe fruits of knowing you directly, wearing the sandals of being specially selected, rapt with the inscrutably delightful gift of intimacy with you, held open to presence of divine love. There, let us eternally serve you. Let us fully realize our knowledge of you. Let us faithfully live up to the example of your Prophet, Muhammad. For we have striven to inherit his virtues and take allegiance to him. We come to realization through him, standing in for him with full responsibility. Seal for us a good fate, O Lord of all worlds.

May God bless the Prophet, our leader, Muhammad.

May God bless the people of Muhammad and give them peace.

Amen.

The shrine of Abu al-ᶜAbbas al-Mursi (d. 1288) Alexandira, Egypt.

Shortly before he died in 1258 CE, Shaykh al-Shadhili delegated both his spiritual and communal authority to Shaykh al-Mursi, who was recognized as the second axial saint (*quṭb*) of the Shadhili lineage. Authority was delegated in an outward dimension. However, in an inward dimension, al-Mursi had so assimilated his Shaykh's personality that no distinction was made between them. According to Ibn ᶜAtaᵓ Allah, "Shaykh al-Shadhili said, 'Abu al-ᶜAbbas, I only took you as my companion in order for you to be me, and me, you.'"

TRANSLATOR'S INTRODUCTION

This appendix translates a short composition of Ibn ᶜAtaᵓ Allah, a complement to the longer composition translated above. If Ibn ᶜAtaᵓ Allah's *The Book of Illumination* introduces beginners to the Sufi path, then this short pamphlet is an incitement for beginners to begin. Ibn ᶜAtaᵓ Allah wrote this pamphlet, entitled *The Sign of Success on the Spiritual Path*, as a commentary on a famous Sufi poem of Shaykh Abu Madyan (1115-1198 CE). This is a poem still respected by Sufis in Morocco; I learned it from a friend from Marrakesh, Azeddine Chergui, who heard it in the form of a song, sung by Sufi beggars on the streets in his childhood. Later, I read it in a wonderful English translation by Vincent Cornell, who also provided a facing edition of the Arabic text.[1] This poem is one of the pithiest statements of the how and why of Sufi spiritual cultivation. It is no surprise that Ibn ᶜAtaᵓ Allah turned to it to urge beginners to find the courage to begin.

The Sign of Success is an apt partner for *The Book of Illumination* in this translation. As we have seen, *The Book of Illumination* addresses the inward dimension of Sufi life: it aims at changing the outlook, belief and motivation of the reader. In contrast, *The Sign of Success* addresses the outward dimension: it aims at changing the behavior and comportment of the reader. It urges us to change our habits through companionship with a shaykh or spiritual guide, and to cultivate loyalty with a spiritual community. It fo-

343

cuses upon the outward virtues of generosity, forbearance, forgiveness, and mutual respect that are not just the reasons to follow a shaykh but are the very means to follow a shaykh. In *The Book of Illumination*, Ibn ᶜAtaᵓ Allah extols human greatness, urging us to raise our aspiration and fulfill our human nature as the potential manifestation of God's qualities. However, in *The Sign of Success*, Ibn ᶜAtaᵓ Allah urges us to take refuge in extreme humility, always acknowledging our brokenness and incapacity, so that we might not fall into the illusion that we can raise our aspiration by ourselves. Rather, our sight is raised only by relying on others: relying on the company of our fellow "impoverished ones" (*fuqarāᵓ*), on our spiritual masters, on the Prophet whose authority they have inherited, and ultimately on the power of God.

It is no coincidence that Ibn ᶜAtaᵓ Allah chose a poem of Abu Madyan as the vehicle through which to discuss the outward aspect of Sufi behavior. Abu Madyan was the exemplary Sufi guide in North Africa, the greatest founder of a particularly North African Sufi community, with outer rules of conduct and inner methods of meditation and illumination. Born in intellectual Andalusia and educated in aristocratic Fes, he met and learned from many Sufi masters and Muslim scholars. However, he eventually followed most lovingly the rugged, rigorous and rustic spiritual guide named Abu Yaᶜza Yalanūr, the "Bearer of Light" (d. 1177). Abu Yaᶜza was an illiterate but wise and charismatic Berber from the Middle Atlas region, who was stern with himself (through intense asceticism and strict vegetarianism) but gentle with others (through graceful advice and physical healing). Abu Madyan became the main spokesman for Abu Yaᶜza, and was called upon to defend him from jurists and literalists who denounced him.

Abu Madyan entered into intellectual debates, legal discussions and literary composition. Yet throughout these arguments, he maintained that humility demands absolute sincerity and simplicity; in this way, he sought to remain answerable to the Sufi training of his guide, Abu Ya°za, who taught that sincerity is a sharpened sword that cuts through all egocentric hypocrisy and a brilliant light which dispels all darkness of alienation from the heart: "Were the light of certainty to dawn, the existence of the universe would surely be concealed!"[2] Abu Madyan championed the ideals of pursuing mystical knowledge (*ma°rifa*) within the framework of establishing a brother-and-sisterhood of social justice (*futuwwa*). It is the outer dimension of maintaining human relations in balance, respect and equity that comes across so clearly in his poem, the *Qaṣīda in Rā᾽* (Ode Rhyming With R).

By writing a commentary on his poem, Ibn °Ata᾽ Allah was not just extolling Abu Madyan's ideals and personality. He was also creating a textual link between the relatively new Sufi community of Abū al-Ḥasan al-Shādhilī in North Africa and the widely acknowledged figure of Abu Madyan (whose fame had spread from Andalusia and Morocco to Egypt and Yemen then across the sea-lanes to Western India).[3] In fact, Abu Madyan was praised as "the Sufi Master of the West" in ways that parallel how °Abd al-Qādir al-Jīlānī (d. 1166 in Baghdad) was praised as "the Sufi Master of the East." Ibn °Ata᾽ Allah cements this equivalency in this commentary, by quoting °Abd al-Qādir to explain the inner meaning of Abu Madyan's words. To understand the deep impact of these choices, we must remember that Ibn °Ata᾽ Allah was the first member of the Shadhili community to write books. His compositions were crucial in explicating not just the subtle spiritual ideals of his community but also its powerful political ideology.

In the world-view ᶜAtaᵓ Allah lays out in writing, ᶜAbd al-Qādir was the first great spiritual master to bring Sufi training to the public by building an outward community of followers. Abu Madyan was the next great spiritual master, who emulated ᶜAbd al-Qādir's example by building a public Sufi community rooted in North African culture and mores. Finally, Abu al-Hasan al-Shadhili was the culmination of this tradition and the most contemporary expression of these ideals; he was the "Axial Saint of the Age" who represented the Prophet Muhammad's authority and personality in the later days and whose Sufi community would revive Islamic life within the constraints of the times. Ibn ᶜAtaᵓ Allah did not write as a neutral observer, but rather as the authoritative follower of al-Shadhili, the third Axial Saint in his lineage. As he writes in *The Sign of Success*, "Only one individual achieves the supreme triumph via this path [becoming the axial saint], one unique individual after another."

Explicating his ideals indirectly through the words of Abu Madyan was a brilliant way for Ibn ᶜAtaᵓ Allah to make a strong case for the salvific role of his own community leadership while still upholding the bounds of humility that are so central to his teachings. With this strategy, he called to himself all those who were searching for a spiritual guide, and his commentary on this poem seeks to explain in simple language the value, dynamics and even the dangers of taking on a spiritual guide. As Abu Madyan has said, "The shaykh is one to whom your essence bears witness by entrusting itself [to his care], and [to whom] your innermost self [bears witness] by respecting him and magnifying him. The shaykh is one who instructs you with his morals, re-

346

fines you with his skills, and illuminates your inner being with his radiance. The shaykh is one who makes you whole in his presence [with God] and preserves you when you are far from the effects of luminosity."[4]

At the very end of this commentary, Ibn ᶜAtaᵓ Allah explains its purpose. "This composition is for those who thirst at night for the inner meaning of these couplets [of Abu Mayan], and yet I acknowledge my inability and incapability on expressing their deepest meaning. But surely all acts are judged by the intentions that motivate them! And God alone knows best." On the surface, Ibn ᶜAtaᵓ Allah expresses his humility as a commentator and inability to truly plumb the depths of Abu Madyan's poem. Yet on a deeper level, Ibn ᶜAtaᵓ Allah says "God knows best" to acknowledge that he is not the first to write a commentary on this poem. Rather, the great Sufi, Ibn ᶜArabī, composed a commentary on it probably a half-century earlier.

Ibn ᶜArabī composed his commentary on Abu Madyan's poem in the form of another poem, in a style called *takhmīs* or "penta-metering." This is a fascinating poetic style of taking a two-line couplet of a *qaṣīda* by someone else and embedding it in a five-line stanza of your own, such that the line of the couplet forms the fourth and fifth lines of each stanza (with the rhyme of the first three new lines determined by the last word of the first line of the original couplet, and the last line of the stanza echoing the rhyme of the original *qaṣīda*). The effect is to clothe each couplet of the original poem in a new garment of poetic lines that unfold from the rhyme and meaning of the original couplet. In this way, Ibn ᶜArabī composed a commentary on Abu Madyan's poem without stepping outside the poetry itself.

Ibn ᶜAtaᵓ Allah's approach to composing a commentary was more conventional and also more exact. He relied on prose to explain the inner meaning of Abu Madyan's poem, and embroidered his prose studded with comparative quotations from other poems, both piously Sufi poems and more secular love poems. His style may be less artistically subtle than Ibn ᶜArabi's style, but it is more explicit and more accessible to a wide popular audience. Surely making ideals accessible to nonspecialists is no less inspired a spiritual project than is making such ideals rarified in a beautiful or challenging form for specialists.

As translator, I have followed the same stylistic and intellectual guidelines here as in the preceding text, *The Book of Illumination*. The English translation of Abu Madyan's poem here embedded in Ibn ᶜAtaᵓ Allah's commentary reproduces Vincent Cornell's very precise English translation.[5] The translation of Ibn ᶜAtaᵓ Allah's commentary does not include the intricate invocation in rhyming prose (*dībāja*) that gives praise to God (*ḥamd*). This is because it is a verbatim replica of the invocation of *The Book of Illumination*, which later editors must have added to the commentary as a conventional introduction. Readers are urged to return to that invocation at the beginning of the translation of "The Book of Illumination" before beginning with the actual commentary below, in order to get a feel for the original Arabic composition.

TRANSLATION: THE SIGN OF SUCCESS ON THE SPIRITUAL PATH

In the name of God, the compassionate One, the One who cares. Praise belongs to God who alone deserves praise. The Prophet Muhammad has said, "Each person will be gathered [at resurrection] in the religion of his closest friend (*khalīl*)—so let each of you examine whom you take as your bosom friend!" Since you know this, my dear brothers and sisters, take as your close friend only one whose spiritual state (*ḥāl*) uplifts you, whose conversation (*maqāl*) guides you toward God. The only person like this is a spiritual seeker who embraces poverty (*faqīr*) and has relinquished everything with the single-minded pursuit of facing the Lord in full sincerity. There is no delight in life except taking such a seeker as friend (*mukhālila*). There is no bliss except serving such a friend (*khidma*) and keeping his or her company (*muṣāḥiba*).

For this reason, the great Shaykh Abu Madyan, the one who knows God intimately and grants others mastery, has said [in his famous poem, the *Qaṣīda in Rā'*]:

> What delight is there in life other than
> companionship with the *fuqara*?
> They are the sultans, lords, and princes.

The meaning of this question is, 'What delight is there in the life of the spiritual seeker (*sālik*) on the path of returning to the Lord other than companionship with the poor (*fuqarā'*)?'

The poor indicates the collective plural, a gathering of those like one who embraces poverty (*faqīr*). Such people stay aloof from relying on others for worldly success (*mutajarrad ʿan al-khalā'iq*), and avoid any encumbrance that hinders their passage (*muʿarraḍ ʿan al-ʿawā'iq*). Such a person turns to face no direction (*qibla*) except toward God, and has no goal except reaching God. Therefore, the one who embraces poverty refuses everything that is other than God. In this way, such a person realizes the true reality of the words, 'There is no god but God and Muhammad is the messenger of God.'

Keeping the company of one such as this allows you to taste the delight of the spiritual path (*ṭarīq*), and causes to flow through your whole heart the liquor of this [Sufi] community, the sweetest of pure wine (*raḥīq*). Through such companionship, you learn about the spiritual path, cease deserving reproach, and make all obstacles fade from your heart. Such a companion has a spiritual aspiration through which you are uplifted and raised to the loftiest degree. Someone like this is a ruler (*sulṭān*) in the deepest reality, an authoritative lord (*sayyid*) over those committed to the spiritual path, and prince (*amīr*) for those endowed with acute insight. So, my dear seeker, never contradict their way!

Struggle to your utmost, my diligent seeker, to acquire such companions, and keep their company. Cultivate respect in their company so that the blessing that comes through their presence might wipe away your every fault and clear away your every obstacle. As the Shaykh [Abu Madyan] has said:

So befriend them and learn the ways of their assemblies,
And keep your obligations, even if they ignore you.

So befriend those who embrace poverty and restrain yourself with them through respect in their assemblies. For surely companionship is the form (*al-ṣuḥba shibh*) and respect is its spirit (*al-adab rūḥuhā*). If the form and the spirit become joined for you, you gain the living heart of companionship; but if they are not joined together, your apparent companionship is like a dead corpse.

One of the most important aspects of respect in companionship is that you leave behind your demands to get what you think you deserve (*ḥuẓūẓ*), paying attention to nothing other than conforming to their demands so that your efforts might earn their gratitude. If you can internalize this virtue, then proceed directly [to their assemblies] and profit from the presence. Maintain pure sincerity in this endeavor until your spiritual rank is raised and your aspiration becomes lofty. In short, it is just as the master has said:

Profit from [your] time and participate
  always with them,
And know that [Divine] satisfaction distinguishes
  one who is present.

Yes, profit from the moment of your companionship with the Sufis (*fuqarāʾ*), and participate always with them by means of your inner heart (*qalb*) and your outer body (*qālib*). In this way, their excellent qualities will come through to you and their bounties will accrue to you.

Admonish your outer being (*ẓāhir*) to adopt their respectful comportment. Polish your inner being (*bāṭin*) to reflect the manifestation of their radiant enlightenment. For surely, you resemble the one with whom you sit (*man jālasa jānasa*). If you sit with those sunk in sorrow, you get depressed; yet if you sit with those who expand with joy, you get happy. If you sit with those preoccupied with forgetfulness, you grow negligent as well; yet if you sit with those engaged in remembrance (*dhākirīn*), you grow wary of your own negligence and are overcome by wakeful awareness.

Indeed, they [Sufis] are such people that the one who sits with them never suffers. If this is true for one who simply sits with them, how could the one who serves them suffer? Or the one who loves them? Or the one who becomes intimate with them? How beautifully did one poet [other than Abu Madyan] express this:

I have masters full of power and might—
  my forehead is at their feet

351

Though I'm not of them, let me love them—
I might good fortune meet

You must know that this satisfaction and the spiritual station associated with it only distinguishes one who is
present—one present before them with attentive respect and
absent from one's self with humility and brokenness. So
leave yourself when you are present before them. Throw
yourself forward and lay broken in humility when you grace
their assembly. Only in this condition will you taste the delight of true presence (*ḥuḍūr*).

To help you achieve this, take recourse to self-imposed
silence (*mulāzimat al-ṣamt*). Keeping quiet will kindle the
light of joy in your heart and immerse you in happy tranquility, just as Abu Madyan points out.

Make silence obligatory
unless you are questioned, then say:
'No knowledge have I'
and conceal yourself with ignorance.

Sufis who take to the spiritual way consider that there are
great benefits to be gained by those who make silence obligatory upon themselves. Doing so raises their foundations high
and plants firmly their roots. Silence is of two types. There
is silence of the tongue (*ṣamt biʾl-lisān*) and then there is
silence of the heart (*ṣamt biʾl-janān*). Both of these are necessary on the path. Whoever is silent in the heart yet speaks
with the tongue speaks with wisdom. Whoever is silent with
the tongue and silent in the heart perceives the manifestation (*tajallī*) of the inner conscience (*sirr*) and is addressed
by the Lord.

This is the ultimate goal of silence, as made compre-
hensible through the discourse of the Shaykh [Abu Madyan].

So make silence obligatory upon yourself, my dear seeker, unless you are questioned. If you are questioned, return to your roots and reach your goal and answer simply, 'No knowledge have I.' Conceal yourself with ignorance, so that you might be enlightened by the rays of intimate knowledge that comes directly from the divine source (*cilm laduni*). Whenever you acknowledge your ignorance and return to your roots [weakness and incapacity], the glimmers of intimate knowledge of your true self dawn to your sight. And if you know your true self you know your Lord, as it is recorded in a saying of the Prophet [*hadith*]: "He who knows himself self knows his Lord" (*man carifa nafsahu carifa rabba-hu*).

All of this knowledge is the fruit of silence and observing its proper bounds with respect. So keep silent, bear yourself respectfully and stand humbly at the doorway so that you might be recognized as a beloved friend of the master of the house. How beautifully this has been said by a poet:

> I won't leave the doorway
>   till they set right my deficiency
> Lest they greet me while I'm bent
>   with my shameful incapacity

> If you are satisfied with me
>   imagine my honor and my nobility!
> Yet if you reject me, is there any hope
>   for my impertinent rigidity?

So stand up straight with humility at the doorway of your master, my sisters and brothers! Stand at attention as a lofty aspirant and realize your highest self in being a lowly servant, that the master may illumine you with the splendor of divine light. To this state, the Shaykh [Abu Madyan] hints when he says,

> Regard not any fault,
>   but that acknowledged within yourself
> As a manifest, clearly apparent fault,
>   though it be concealed.

This means that you should come to realize your own inherent qualities: your poverty, your weakness, your inability and your lowliness. If you realize these qualities of yours and bear witness to faults inherent in your self, even if they are concealed from others, then you are able to receive the manifestation within yourself of your master's qualities. It is said, Glory be to the One who concealed in the human appearance the secret chosenness [of the Prophet], and who makes apparent lordship's magnification through servanthood's manifestation.

With this saying, you can understand the secret meaning of Divine Speech: *Glory be to the One who set forth on a night journey the servant.*[6] Note that Divine Speech does not say that God sent forth on a night journey 'the prophet' or 'the messenger.' Rather, Divine Speech indicates the lofty and subtle meaning of this journey that can only be achieved through embracing one's existential humility as "the servant." As one poet said [about his beloved],

> Address me only as "her servant" when you call me
> For this is the noblest name that you might call me[7]

O my sisters and brothers, let yourselves be broken with humility and hurl yourselves onto the path of this journey! Only by not claiming for yourself any spiritual state or authoritative statement can you be released from all obstacles and hindrance.

Seek forgiveness from every errant thought that comes into your heart that imperils your constancy in servanthood. Stand at the feet of justice (*ʿalā qadam al-iʿtirāf*) and admit your faults in fairness. In this way, you may reach the highest degree of sublimity and pass beyond your mere humanity, as the Shaykh [Abu Madyan] says.

> Lower your head and seek forgiveness
>   without [apparent] cause,
> And stand at the feet of Justice,
>   making excuses [in your own behalf].

This couplet instructs you to be humble and lay yourself low. Take that which is highest of yourself, your head, and place it on that which is lowest around you, the ground. In this way, you might gain the station of intimacy (*maqām al-qurb*), as hinted at in this saying of the Prophet. "The closest possible that people can come to God is when they are prostrating." This is because people draw close to God only in embodying their humility (*tawāḍuʿ*), embracing their brokenness (*inkisār*) in order to leave behind their own qualities of human frailty (*basharīya*). So bear witness constantly that you are in error, even if the cause of your error is not openly apparent unto you, for the human being is never free of shortcomings.

Stand at the feet of justice (*inṣāf*) because of your errors, with head bowed in shame in light of your bad deeds and internal faults. Whoever behaves like this in the company of other people (*makhlūq*) will become beloved to them, even if they perceive his or her faults. If this is true with other people, then how much more true is it if one

355

behaves thus in the presence of the true companion (*ṣāḥib ḥaqīqī*), under whose divine intimacy one realizes one is free from being owned by anything or anyone else. Such a profound meaning is conveyed in a hadith, in which the Prophet is reported [to have left control and companion-ship only to God] as saying, "O God, you are the companion during travels and the caretaker of the family, children and property left behind."

So dedicate yourselves, my sisters and brothers, to re-spectful behavior in the company of your family, the *fuqarāʾ*. Treat them in this way, that you might travel by means of their earthly company in a spiritual ascension (*miʿrāj*). By means of this inner cultivation of virtue, you might arrive at the station of dealing so respectfully directly with the Lord of the heavens. In this way, you might gain approval by both human beings (*khalq*) and the One who creates them (*khāliq*). Your way of dealing with the world will become pure. The light of spiritual realities (*ḥaqāʾiq*) will illumine your being. To convey this meaning, [Abu Madyan] con-tinues:

If a fault appears in you, acknowledge it, and direct
    Your face toward that within you which comes from you.

Say, 'Your slaves are more worthy [than ourselves]
        of your forgiveness,
    So excuse us and be kind to us, oh *fuqarāʾ*!'

By giving preference to others they are exalted,
        for it is their nature,
    So do not fear that they will punish or harm you.

These couplets mean that your state should always be humility and brokenness, in which you seek excuse and forgiveness, regardless of whether any fault appears in you or not. If a fault appears in you, acknowledge it and seek forgiveness for it. For indeed, one who repents from an error is like one who has never erred.[8]

It is not the point here that you never err! Rather, the point is to never become habituated to erring. The regretful wailing of one who sins is better in God's regard than the pious murmuring of one who prostrates with conceit and pride, don't you think? For this reason, I have said in the *Sufi Aphorisms* (*al-Ḥikam*): "Sometimes He opens the door of obedience for you but not the door of acceptance; or sometimes He condemns you to sin, and it turns out to be a cause of arriving to Him."[9] Disobedient rebellion that gives you low status with humbleness is far better than pious obedience that leads to high status with self-righteousness.

Then as you admit your fault and seek forgiveness, direct the face of your acknowledgment toward that which comes from you. This is a means to wipe away the fault from you. In this way, enter into acceptance by being lowly, acting humbly and admitting your brokenness. And say, 'Your slaves are more worthy of your forgiveness' because humble slaves have nothing but what comes to them from their master. It has been said no better than this:

Upon your doorstep my burden's dropped
    I don't dwell on anxieties that once weighed me down
My straits have faded, my joy's expanded
    It's all changed to hope what once made me frown

So forgive and pardon your slaves, oh *fuqarāʾ*! Adopt a kind regard (*rifq*), and treat me gently! For I am a poor servant (*ᶜabd faqīr*), who is suitable for only forbearing pardon and undeserved kindness. I can rely on nothing but undeserved kindness, rather than my own means or power. My religion is weakness! Be at peace, nothing more can be said.

Then he [Abu Madyan] says that they [the Sufis] are exalted by this [giving preference to others]—it is their nature. They never cease to give preference to others without their deserving it, for this is the way they treat their companions—it is their characteristic. How can this not be their inherent characteristic, for they have taken as their own the virtues of the One who is their master (*takhallaqū bi-akhlāq mawlāhum*). Just as it is related [in a hadith attributed to the Prophet Muhammad], "Internalize as your own the virtues of Allah." So do not fear that they will harm you, my dear seeker, as you keep their company! Rather, cling to the hem of their robes, for they are such people that the one who sits with them never suffers.

If you understand this, dear seeker, then internalize their noble virtues and realize yourself through them. Expend every effort in magnanimity toward your brothers (*ikhwān*) and avert your gaze from their stumbling or failing. Assess them in all their characteristics by assuming only the best. To this end, [Abu Madyan] says:

> And in magnanimity toward the brothers
> be forever limitless,
> Out of feeling or understanding,
> avert your gaze if one of them stumbles.

So treat your brothers and sisters nobly, and be generous toward them always. You may be generous through things that you feel with your senses (*fī'l-ḥiss*), like giving to them of your wealth and property. Or it may be through things that you understand through ideas (*fī'l-ma'nā*), like focusing on them your spiritual aspiration. Never hold back in stinginess from giving them whatever you can. For allowing others to benefit is the spiritual path's pinnacle, and those who realize this virtue have removed from their hearts every obstacle.

To this end, Shaykh ᶜAbd al-Qādir al-Jīlānī has said, "My brothers and sisters, I did not arrive in union with Allah by staying awake all night in worship, by staying aware all day fasting, or by staying engrossed learning knowledge (*ᶜilm*)! Rather, I arrived at union with Allah by generosity and humility and letting my breast be at peace." This teaching of the Shaykh shows that generosity is the foundation, while humility completes for the spiritual seeker a firm rooting upon the foundation; if these two things are complete, the seeker's breast rests at peace, unfettered by any obstacle and unencumbered by any shackle. A hadith refers to just this state: "In the heavenly garden there are rooms whose outside is visible from within and whose inside is visible from without—God has prepared them for those who speak patiently to others, feed the hungry, follow one fast with another, and pray all night while others are sleeping." Ponder this saying, my dear brothers and sisters! Notice that the Prophet begins by praising those who speak gently to others, for this is the virtue of humility. Then he praises those who feed others, for this is the virtue of generosity. Only after this does he mention praying and fasting, confirming just what Shaykh ᶜAbd al-Qādir said.

My dear, rouse yourself to strive after such glorious exploits! Strive without swerving! Combine with such character becoming beautiful with the most noble of virtues (*makārim al-akhlāq*)! Avert your gaze from any wrongdoing of your fellows (*masāwī al-ikhwān*) if you come to know of one of them stumbling. Only see what is best and most

359

beautiful in them, just as the Shaykh [Abu Madyan] has suggested. He has also said in his own Wisdom Sayings of Spiritual Opening (*Hikam Futūhīya*): "Seeing other's wholesome qualities and concealing their wrongs is evidence of one's making God completely One."[10]

If you see God as the true actor in everything
You see everything in existence as beautiful

If you realize in yourself these noble qualities, my brothers and sisters, you will come to deserve the approval of a shaykh, a spiritual guide. So stand at the threshold of the shaykh's doorway and observe him with all your sublime aspiration, just as the Shaykh [Abu Madyan] has pointed out:

Observe the shaykh attentively in his states, for perhaps
A trace of his approval will be seen upon you.

When you have cultivated the refined behavior detailed before, and you have arrived in the presence of the shaykh, aware of your own poverty and full of your own frailty, and you have clung tightly to that threshold, then just observe the shaykh. Observe the shaykh attentively in his spiritual states (*ahwāl*) and strive to earn his satisfaction. Be pliant before him. Yield to his demands in every circumstance, for the shaykh is the elixir and the cure. The hearts of spiritual guides are the curing balm and those who are happy with them achieve whatever they desire and glide through every mire.

So strive, my dear, to bear witness to this subtle reality so that, perhaps, a trace of the shaykh's approval will be seen upon your own spiritual state. One Sufi has said, "The worst kind of alienation is that you manage to keep the company of God's friends (*awliyā* *allah*) but fail to be nourished by their approval!" Such a failure would be due only to your own disrespectful behavior, rather than to any stinginess from them or lack on their part. It is just as I have said in the *Sufi Aphorisms* (*Hikam*): "The point at issue is not the existence of searching (*wujūd al-talab*). The point at issue is only that you be provisioned with virtuous conduct (*husn al-adab*)."[11]

Once there was a worldly ruler who visited the tomb of Abū Yazīd [Bāyazīd Bistāmī]. There he asked, "Is there anyone here who was a companion of Abū Yazīd?" People pointed out an old man who was present there at the tomb. The ruler said to him, "Have you heard anything of Abū Yazīd's teachings?" The old man answered, "Yes. He said, 'Whoever visits my tomb will not be burned by the fire.'" This saying shocked the ruler, who exclaimed, "How could Abū Yazīd have said such a thing when Abu Jahl saw the Prophet yet still he was burned by the fire?"[12] The old man said to the ruler, "Abu Jahl did not see the Prophet! Rather, he saw a penniless orphan under the care of Abū Tālib. If Abu Jahl had seen him as the Prophet, he would never had been burned by the fire!" Hearing this, the ruler understood his teaching, and stood amazed at the old man's answer.

Abu Jahl had never seen the Prophet in a way that admitted his greatness, extolled his nobility and fostered belief that he was God's messenger. If he had seen the Prophet as a Prophet, he would never have been consigned to the fire of hell. But alas, Abu Jahl saw him with the eye of denigration and believed that he was nothing but an orphan under the care of his uncle, Abū Tālib. Therefore, seeing him was of absolutely no use to Abu Jahl. What about you, my dear sisters and brothers? If you were in the presence of the saint who is the axis of the age (*quṭb al-waqt*), and you did not behave with respect and humility, seeing him would not benefit you at all. In fact, that experience would be more damaging to you than beneficial!

Now if you understand this, my dear seeker, then cultivate respectful humility in the presence of the shaykh. Struggle to take on the most wholesome way of behaving. Seize whatever you come to know with serious exertion and sincere effort (*jadd wa ijtihād*). Rise to serve the shaykh and do so with selflessly pure intention, so that you rise to preeminence with one who is a master. To this end, [Abu Madyan] has said:

> Display earnestness
>   and be eager in his service;
> Perhaps he will be pleased,
>   but beware lest you see annoyance.

> For in his satisfaction is that of the Creator
>   and obedience toward Him;
> He has granted you His good pleasure,
>   so beware lest you forsake it.

Stand at attention to serve the shaykh with earnestness, so that perhaps you will earn his pleasure. If so, then you rise to power under the care of one who is a master. But beware to not cause any annoyance (*ḍajr*), for in your annoying him is your own corruption (*fasād*). Stay constantly at the shaykh's threshold, morning and evening, so that you might earn his love (*wadūd*). How beautiful it has been said:

Patiently endure the difficulty of setting out before dawn and
    the ardor of your vows to worship in the early morn.
Say to those who strive earnestly to achieve their hopes:
    when patience sets out, triumph is her constant companion.

Now if you, my dear seeker, achieve triumph by winning the satisfaction of the shaykh, then God also is satisfied with you. You have won more than you could have possibly hoped for. So wear yourself out, my sisters and brothers, in earning the contentment of your shaykh by obeying, so that you might triumph by obeying the One who is your real master and earning the ultimate contentment.[13] You might gain success through the superabundance of the shaykh's spiritual gifts (*karamāt*). My sisters and brothers, grit your teeth and persist despite all difficulty to diligently serve your shaykh. If triumph should come to you because you have come to the shaykh, know that salvation encompasses you from every side, for God has let you know this and has allowed you to comprehend it.

Such triumph is priceless. It is more valuable than the elixir of happiness (*al-kibrīt al-aḥmar*) [literally the red sulfur], especially in times such as these. For the Sufi path is now decadent (*darāsa*) and the state of one who preaches it today is as you see. However, if divine grace (*ᶜināya*) comes to your aid, you may still achieve success. You may still catch a whiff of the fragrant breeze, sweeter than the pungent aroma of musk. With this in mind, the Shaykh [Abu Madyan] has said:

[Know] that the Way of the Folk is [now] decadent,
  And that the state of one who preaches it today is as
    you see.

When shall I see [the true Folk of God], and how am I to
    have sight of them,
  Or my ear hear news of them?

How can I or one like me dispute with them
  Over spiritual experiences about which
    I am not familiar?

363

I love them, am courteous to them, and follow them
With my innermost soul–especially one person
among them.

The Shaykh began by stirring up in novice seekers the longing to join the Sufi path. Yet he also informed them that the
path today is decadent and the spiritual state of those who
preach it is as you can see. It is so decadent that people
might even despair of raising their aspirations to join it any-
more!

This is the nature of the spiritual path due to its priceless value and lofty status (*ᶜizza*). It is as if, in every age, it
appears to be absent from sight. Only one individual
achieves the supreme triumph via this path, one unique individual after another (*al-fard baᶜd al-fard*). This is just the
way it is. It is its well-known pattern (*sunna maᶜhūda*). Isn't
it true that a priceless jewel is always rare, to the point that
its value almost requires it to be almost beyond routine existence? In this way, the masters of the Sufi path are hidden
in this world. They are unknown like the night of destiny
(*laylat al-qadr*), whose precise date is unknown at the end
of the month of fasting (*ramaḍān*).[14] They are unknown
like the hour of congregational prayer, whose precise moment on Fridays around noon is obscure, so that those who
seek to know it must strive hard to determine its truth, to
the extent of their capabilities.

However, whoever seeks, finds, and whoever knocks,
gains entrance. Now after having mentioned that it is necessary to have a shaykh on the spiritual path, there may be
questions that he [a shaykh] might venture to answer. So if
someone asks, "How can we be told to have a shaykh on
the path, even when it is said that such a shaykh is like the
red sulfur or the mythic phoenix, or other rare things through

which alone one can gain the ultimate triumph? How can you order me to find someone who is like this?" The Shaykh would answer, "If you are sincere in your search, you must behave while searching [for a shaykh] like a lost child and a person perishing from thirst, who are completely restless and unsettled by anxiety until they reach their goal in triumph." In this answer, he indicates that the shaykh undoubtedly exists. How can he not exist, when the structure of the universe is built around his likeness? Indeed, the universe is in the form of a person (*shakhṣ*) and the saints are like the person's spirit (*rūḥ*). The universe exists only as long as its form is animated by the saints' existence within it. However, because of the intensity of their obscurity and their invisibility, people judge that they are not present.

Therefore struggle, my sisters and brothers, and remain sincere in your constant search until you find the goal. In your search, seek aid from the One who knows all things unseen (*ᶜallām al-ghayb*), for triumph in this search comes only with undeserved bounty from the One. If God leads you to find a shaykh, in fact God has led you to find God, just as I have said in the *Sufi Aphorisms* (*Ḥikam*): "Glory be to Him who has not made any sign leading to His saints save as a sign leading to Himself, and who has joined no one to them except him whom God wants to join to Himself."[15]

Then, when the Shaykh [Abu Madyan] mentions the priceless value of the Sufi path and the apparent absence of its [axial] saint, he expresses regret over the difficulty keeping his company and longs to do so. He makes it seem like achieving this is far from him. He declares what an honor it would be to meet him [the axial saint], out of humility before him, lowliness at the thought of him, and amazement at his own long-suffering trial and his own impoverishment.

For this reason, he says, "How can I or one like me dispute with them over spiritual experiences about which I am not familiar?" This is the nature of those who know themselves through themselves (*li-nafsihi bi-nafsihi*), who are filled with intuitive knowledge from their Lord (*ma'rifa min rabbihi*), who manifest to others through disclosures of divine holiness. Such people do not see themselves as possessing any state or any speech. Rather, they see themselves as the least and the lowest. Such vision is the most complete vision, as a poet has expressed:

> As one's knowledge increases,
>> one's humility gains weight
> As one's ignorance increases
>> one's arrogance will inflate
>
> A branch laden with fruit
>> hangs low for harvesters' perusal
> But stripped bare of any fruit
>> The branch rises high in refusal

In this light, regard Shaykh Abu Madyan and his lofty station on the spiritual path! Even though he has trained over twelve-thousand disciples who have arrived at spiritual completion under his direction, see how low to the ground he bends. How heavy have become the branches of the tree of his intuitive insight, such that they hang low to the earth of modesty and humility, even to the extent that he doesn't see himself to deserve keeping the company of the Sufis! Such lowliness only increases him in loftiness. Doesn't a tree's uppermost branches grow higher and higher as its roots sink lower and lower.

So sink deep into humility on the spiritual path, my sisters and brothers. Grasp firmly this root principle, learned from this empowering poem, so that all obstacles might be removed from your path. After this, he [Abu Madyan] says, "I love them, am courteous to them, and follow them with my innermost soul." By this, he means to say, "Though I may not be from among them, I do love them." Yet whomever one loves, one can be counted among them. This is conveyed in a hadith, "People are with whomever they love" (*al-mar³ maᶜa man aḥabba*), and also in these couplets [by another poet]:

> Though I'm not of them, the righteous I love
> that I might earn from them intercession
> Those who trade in disobedience I detest
> even if I'm equally burdened with rebellion

This, too, comes from his [Abu Madyan's] complete self-effacement in humility, to complete and bring to perfection what he had expressed before. Because of his exemplary humility, whose generous nobility none in this field can follow, he lets us cling to the hem of his trailing robe. For such is the character of the Sufi masters and such is their purity. Because of this character, their spiritual station is raised high and their gifts overflow, just as he describes them:

> They are a folk noble in character; wherever they sit,
> That place remains fragrant from their traces.

> Sufism guides one quickly by means of their conduct;
> A fitting harmony is theirs, delightful to my sight.

They are my loved ones, my family, who
   Are among those who proudly hold up
      the Hems of Glory.

I am united with them still, brought together in God,
   And through Him our transgressions are pardoned
      and forgiven.

So [may] blessings [be] upon the Chosen One,
   our Lord Muhammad, the best of those
      who fulfill their vows.

They are a folk whose character is noble and whose spiritual aspiration is great. Because of this, the place where they sit remains fragrant from their traces. Their aroma remains after they are gone. And wherever they turn to face is brightly lit by the sunbeams of their intuitive knowledge. They enlighten hearts and their presence sets right both this world and the world to come. Sufism guides the ardent seeker by means of their excellent conduct which shows the way of the spiritual path, through which one can journey through a praiseworthy life

For this reason, they have gathered in the best of conduct, that those who observe them become delighted with realization. They have perfected the most subtle symbolic meanings such that the eye of intuitive insight is beatified with the dark eyeliner (*kohl*) of their antimony. For this reason, the Shaykh [Abu Madyan] then says, "They are my loved ones, my family, who are among those who proudly hold up the Hems of Glory." For in reality, people love those who are like them, and love only those with whom they share intimacy. These couplets point out that he [Abu Madyan] is really one of the Sufis, formed from the same clay. The humility and lowliness that he expressed earlier is proof that he has realized this majestic status and excellent station, as has been pointed out earlier. So we ask God to lead us along the best and noblest of paths.

Then he [Abu Madyan] petitions God and asks that he be always united with them, that they be brought together in God. Then he requests that his errors be forgiven. Finally, he asks also that the most complete blessings and peace be upon our master, Muhammad, the chosen Prophet, the most faithful of those keep their vows, who warn their community and who give generously to their neighbors. And we ask for peace and blessings upon his family and righteous companions, as well as his followers and their followers who act with goodness, until the day of judgement. This composition is for those who thirst at night for the inner meaning of these couplets [of Abu Mayan], and yet I acknowledge my inability and incapability of expressing their deepest meaning. But surely all acts are judged by the intentions that motivate them![16] And God alone knows best.

APPENDIX TWO: THE CHALLENGE OF GENDER
IN TRANSLATING FROM ARABIC

As noted in the Translator's Introduction at the outset of this work, Ibn ᶜAtaᵓ Allah most likely assumed his audience to consist of male persons, and his texts in Arabic reflects this. When he addresses his audience directly, he calls them his "brothers" (*ikhwān*). This translation renders his texts not only into another language but also for another wider audience, and its contemporary English readers consist of women and men on equal footing. Therefore, this translation renders his address as "my sisters and brothers" to preserve the sense of intimacy, mutual care and respect of calling distant people one's own siblings, while widening the audience to reflect contemporary reality. The Translator's Introduction provides readers with a guide as to how and why this was done.

The issue of gender in the human audience is complex enough. However, the issue of gender is complicated when we raise our gaze from human beings to God. Readers may have noticed that this translation also avoids using masculine pronouns (as well as feminine ones) to stand in for God. This appendix will illustrate in more depth the linguistic and theological arguments behind this simple but potentially controversial decision. It is generally acknowledged that God has no gender, even if the languages through which we speak about God (or through which God speaks) are highly gendered. God has no gender in any way comparable to human gender. Although the proper name, God or *Allah* ("the God"), is rendered into the pronoun *huwa* (he/

it) in Qurᵓanic Arabic, as any masculine being is, this does not mean that God can be said to have a gender.

That the proper noun "God" is conventionally replaced by the pronoun *huwa* (he/it) only means that Arabic is a binary-gendered language. In Arabic, every noun (whether referring to an animate being, an inanimate object, or an abstract concept) is rendered in pronoun as either "he" or "she," for there is no neuter pronoun in Arabic like the English "it." Thus, the noun sun (*shams*) is grammatically feminine, while the noun moon (*qamar*) is grammatically masculine. Despite this strict binary gender differentiation of pronouns in the language, the Qurᵓan does not anthropomorphize these objects in any systematic way: the moon is not a man and is not compared to a being with human masculine qualities just as the sun is not a woman and is not compared to a being with feminine qualities. The great Sufi scholar, ᶜAbd al-Raḥmān al-Sulamī, noted this insight long ago when, after writing the biographies of famous Sufi women, he wrote the following couplets.[17]

> If all women were like the ones I've mentioned
>   Before women all men would pale
> For there's no blame for the sun to be called feminine
>   And no pride for the moon to be called male

Al-Sulami observed that masculine and feminine genders in Arabic grammar are simply conventions of the language. They should be clearly differentiated from the social hierarchies that separated actual men from women in his day. In fact, it has taken us many centuries of struggle to change social hierarchies and inequalities until we can realize politically the full depth of al-Sulami's insight from the medieval period!

371

Gender among human beings is a condition of duality that is specific to humanity; gender is a social role constructed around biological function and anatomical difference. The Qur°an cautions us against projecting onto God qualities that are human, like anatomical features, biological functions, or social fictions. The adept translator from Arabic and Islamic literature, Michael Sells, has addressed this point most clearly.

> To translate that which is the creator of the male and female, and therefore necessarily transcendent to the male and the female, as "him" is to risk the loss of the transcendence of gender that is part of the Qur°anic oath.... The loss of the Qur°anic gender dynamic in translations reinforces one of the most misleading stereotypes about Islam and the Qur°an—that the Qur°an is based on rigid, male-centered language. Yet this stereotype of a language of "he-God and he-man" is at odds not only with Islamic theology (which denies that God is male or female) but also with the intricate and beautiful gender dynamic that is a fundamental part of the Qur°anic language.[18]

In this discussion, Michael Sells refers to a specific moment in the Qur°an (Surat al-Layl 92:3, The Night) when the association of God with the masculine pronoun most clearly reveals itself to be just grammatical convention devoid of deeper significance. I feel that the insight gleaned from his attentive reading to this one moment should give us reservations about rendering God in the masculine gender in every moment of Qur°anic discourse, as well as the Islamic theological and Sufi mystical writings based upon it. In the Qur°an, God is not a father or a mother, and has no relationship to people through metaphors of reproductive biology: *Say, God is a singular One, the eternal One, never begetting and never begotten, to whom no other bears comparison.*[19] God may have qualities that we humans, through the filter of our patriarchal cultures, commonly associate with men (such as strength, authority and might) as well as qualities that we associate with women (such as care, nurture, and gentleness). However, these qualities do not make God a gendered being in any way comparable to male or female human beings.

It is not a human body, among sensory phenomena, that can be most closely compared to God; rather it is light. "The One who is light" (*al-nūr*) is one of the ninety-nine names of God in Islamic theology. The Qurʾan states, *God is the light of the heavens and the earth*, and then proceeds to coin metaphors for describing the nature of that light in ways that our limited human imagination can grasp.[20] The Prophet Muhammad, too, came close to "seeing God" during his ascension experience (*miʿrāj*); when his followers quite naturally asked him "what God looked like," he answered that God is light.[21] In Arabic grammar, light (*nūr*) is a masculine noun replaced by the pronoun he, or *huwa*, just as is the noun God (*Allah*). Nobody would assert that light has a gender, despite the fact that it occupies a grammatically gendered position in language. God "has gender" in the same way that light "has gender"—only in the binary construction of language.

If we accept that the assignment of gender is merely conventional, one might reasonably ask why God is assigned a masculine grammatical gender rather than a feminine grammatical gender. I might venture a speculative guess. Beyond the strong association between God and light, which both have masculine grammatical gender, there is also an oppositional tension between God and the human soul or self (*nafs*). In Arabic, "soul" has a feminine grammatical gender, regardless whether the body animated by the soul is male-or-female with regard to reproductive anatomy or masculine-or-feminine with regard to social roles. This feminine gender assignment reflects the soul's close association with the mineral body made of clay and earth (*arḍ*) which is also of feminine gender. Body and soul are joined by the spirit (*rūḥ*) which bridges the vast distance between divine nature and human nature, for in the Qurʾan God says, *I shaped and breathed into [the human being] some of my spirit.*[22] "Spirit" is one of the only Arabic nouns that can be either masculine or feminine in gender, just as its ambiguous nature partakes of both lofty divinity and corporeal humanity by infusing the body with life and the soul with awareness.

In Arabic, the conventions of grammar reinforce a series of mythic images that, with a little rational ordering, make up the basics of Islamic theology. The grammatical gender that language assigns to these spiritual forces takes on meaning in the mutual relationship of these forces, rather than in any reification of God as a masculine being. It must be admitted, however, that Ibn ʿAtaʾ Allah offers metaphors for God's nature that explicitly compare God to a masculine person: a man, the head of a patriarchal household who owns slaves, or a king. These may stand out to contemporary English readers who are no longer accustomed to living with kings and slaves.[23] However, to Ibn ʿAtaʾ Allah, like most Muslim theologians and Sufis of the medieval period, these images were drawn from social reality; they provided immediate and forceful (if not unavoidable) ways of talking about the power and authority of God.

Arabic is a language-world in which there is no neuter "it" to refer to a thing or idea. Rather, in Arabic all objects must be either masculine or feminine in a pattern quite unlike that of English. As Michael Sells noted, an English translation of Arabic that simply renders "God" into a pronoun "he" is quite problematic. Yet it is a problem from which there is no easy escape. Capitalizing "He" to refer to God does not solve the problem, but only exaggerates it. Using "He" simply makes God into an enormous man of superhuman proportions, rather than constituting a strategy to avoid projecting human dualities of gender onto the incomparably transcendent divinity. A translator cannot use the pronoun "it" in English, for that applies to an inanimate object or abstract concept, whereas in Islamic theology (and other Abrahamic traditions), God is the very font of life and the essential source of being, rather than being a simple abstraction. Therefore, I have taken recourse to simple strategies to avoid reducing the divine being to the limited conceptual shape of a human being. In my humble opinion, there are only two acceptable strategies: to use "God" wherever possible to refer to God, or to use "One" as a pronoun to stand in for the name God. This is the only way I have found to translate with one eye on linguistic accuracy and the other eye on the ethics of gender justice. I have done this even if it means contradicting established translations of the Qur²an that have become standard reference works in English.[24]

Readers of a conservative mind-set might remain skeptical of this apparent innovation, while readers not accustomed to Arabic might be perplexed at the binary gender constructions which are so different from English. To assuage both kinds of doubt and to more fully illuminate the choices made in this translation, this appendix ends by pre-

375

senting a short passage of Ibn ᶜAtaᵓ Allah's Invocation and Opening Address that provides a more literal rendering of masculine and feminine gender. Readers may compare this passage, below, to the full translation offered above of the opening pages of *The Book of Illumination* to gain a deeper understanding of the subtleties and challenges faced by any translator who struggles to find the text's truth in an altogether new environment. Ibn ᶜAtaᵓ Allah's commentary, *The Sign of Success on the Spiritual Path* begins with the same Invocation. Those who translate God as He are faced with two choices. First, they could admit that God is "he" while other abstract concepts and objects are also "he" because there is no "it" in Arabic, and consistently translate all pronouns as either "she" or "he" while avoiding "it." This might be called a "universal literalism" and has the benefit of being internally consistent even as it breaks with the logic of the English language. Or second, they could translate objects and abstract concepts as "it" as is customary in English, while making an exception by retaining "He" as the pronoun for God, even as the pronoun is capitalized to distinguish Him from male human beings. In this case, they might be accused of a "selective literalism" that anthropomorphizes God as a being who is, in some way, male rather than female.

The consequences of both choices are clearly unsatisfactory. Most translators of Sufi literature choose the second option. The alternate translation, appended below, exercises the first option. Readers should be aware that "he" refers to the single male human being, who is the person addressed in the original Arabic. The capitalized pronouns "He" and "His" and "Him" refer to God. The plural pronouns "they" and "their" and "them" refer to a collective group of men (though in Arabic this pronoun retains the possibility of some women being subsumed within the group of predominantly male people). The feminine pronouns "she" and "her" and "hers" refer to the plural of inanimate objects or abstract concepts, like "voices" or "creation" or "souls," for there is no neuter pronoun in Arabic. The masculine singular "he" could also refer in some instances to a singular inanimate object or concept, like "book."

All translations are betrayals of the original. The real question for us is which style of betrayal effectively communitcates the essential meaning to the perceived audience. As audiences change, the essential meaning of the texts they read also changes to reflect their shifting experience. With this challenge, I hope the reading audience can make their own judgment and forgive my shortcomings. As Ibn ᶜAtaᵓ Allah would say, "And God alone knows best."

ALTERNATE TRANSLATION: THE BOOK OF ILLUMINATION

In the name of God, the Compassionate, the Caring.

Praise belongs to God alone, the Unique in the act of creation, the uniquely Concerned for each being's direction. He is the Singular in the power of decision and execution, the Sovereign for *there is nothing similar to Him, the Hearer, the Seer*. He has no mediator to oversee His dominion. He is the Ruler, and from His jurisdiction nothing escapes at all, whether great or small. He is the Hallowed, and His perfect qualities allow no comparison or competition. He is the Transcendent, and His perfect essence is beyond likeness or depiction. *Do they not know Him who created them, He who is the Subtle, the Aware?* He is the Knower, who encompasses with His knowledge each thing's beginning and her ending. He is the Hearer, who admits no difference in His hearing between voices' whispering and her resounding. He is the Provider, and He blesses creation by leading her to her sources of nourishing. He is the Establisher, and He steadfastly supports her in her changing states of flourishing. He is the Bestower, and He freely gives each soul the existence of her life. He is the Decider, and He calls each soul to return after the completion of her passing. He is the Recounter, and He repays her [each soul] on that fateful day when she presents her good acts and her wayward errors.

Praise be to Him above any god, for He freely bestows upon all people benevolence, even before their worldly existence. He undertakes to sustain them, whether they act toward Him with compliance or resistance. He extends support to every thing living through the prior existence of His giving. His Being safeguards the being of all creation with His self-sustaining effusion. He appears in His world through traces of His wisdom's subtlety, and He manifests in His heavens by evidence His power's potency.

I witness that there is no god but God, alone by Himself, who shares no partnership in His oneness. These words of witness come from a servant who has handed over all his concerns and cares to His deciding, who has peacefully submitted to the current of His decreeing and His executing. I witness that Muhammad is His worshipful servant and messenger, that Muhammad is preferred over all the rest of His many prophets who preceded him, and that he is especially selected by His bounty and His bestowal. Muhammad is both the opener and the closer, which are qualities that none of the other prophets share with him. Muhammad is the intercessor to whom each soul will turn when the Truth gathers her [the souls] to divide her in His judgment. May God bless him and preserve him, with all His other prophets. May He bless his family and his companions who adhere to his benevolent presence and follow him. May He multiply blessings upon them all.

My brother, God made you to experience His love. He has granted you the rare gift of nearness to Him. He has offered you a taste of the liquor sipped by the people of His intimacy. He has safeguarded your continual intimate connection to Him from any chance of His opposition or His termination. He has made you the followers His servants who are chosen to bear His messages. Their hearts break with longing when they realize that He can never be perceived by their vision—then He strengthens their broken hearts through insight as He manifests in their lives, bestowing upon them light. He has opened for them the gardens of nearness to Him. He has stirred up from her [these gardens] the fragrance of His indwelling presence, wafted her inspirations over their hearts, and showed them the depth of His prior concern for their well-being. Then He revealed the subtlest of His artful actions through which He sustains lives, and they desisted from resistance and obstinate self-will.

In response, they quieted themselves before Him and entrusted their concerns tranquilly under His care, for they know that nobody reaches the goal of satisfying God except through being completely satisfied with Him. They acknowledge that nobody arrives at purest sincerity except by the fullest inner submission to His dictates and His decrees. Thus their disposition is never sullied by the murk of distraction, as one from among them has said poetically:

Fluctuations in time never beguile them in vain
In the most intense trial, they keep hold of the rein

His decrees flow over them, and they act aptly, with respect for His might and allow themselves to be led by its powerful currents.

> His acts flow over your anxious self
> And bows down the head of your concern

He who seeks an intimate connection with God must realize for himself that this matter is actualized by Him. The connection to Him comes by means of His devising. In traveling this path, beware of being concerned for your own interests and rebelling against the conditions the divine has decreed for you! This is the most important obstacle to be avoided, from which you should abstain and keep pure. I have composed this book in order to clarify this single crucial point, and to make explicit all the subtleties therein. I have entitled him [the book], *The Book of Illumination*, so that his title would perfectly reflect his [the book's] contents, so that his words would communicate the intended meaning.

I beseech God, the Generous, that He make him [this book] sincere for His sake alone, and that He accept him [this book] by virtue of His all-embracing comprehensiveness, and to allow him [this book] to benefit the specialist, he who has chosen the path of becoming a Sufi, as well as the common seeker. I ask all this for the sake of the Prophet Muhammad, may he be blessed and preserved. Surely He is the Executer of whatever He may will, and He is the Fullfiller of whatever need there is to fill.

1. The Urdu original is: *Ultī ho gayīn sab tadbīren, kuchh na davā ne kām kiyā / dekhā is bīmārī-yi dil ne ākhir kām tamām kiyā.*

2. Muhammad Asad, *The Road to Makkah* (Delhi: Adam Publishers, 1992), 308-9. New edition by Fons Vitae.

3. Surat al-Takaththur 102 as translated by Muhammad Asad. Hereafter, English versions of Qur°anic verses are the work of this translator, rendered in ways that reflect the reading of Ibn °Ata° Allah, as revealed in the prose context of their citation. Otherwise I have based the translation largely on that of Abdullah Yusuf Ali (though without his use of archaic rhetoric that hearkens back to the King James version of the Bible or his patriarchal rendering of gender neutral terms as masculine).

4. From his work as a journalist in the Middle East before his conversion, Muhammad Asad became an author, translator of Islamic literature, and international diplomat. Having befriended the philosopher-poet Muhammad Iqbal of Pakistan, Asad became the UN representative for the newly created nation and deeply insightful theorist of ways in which Islam and modernity might be reconciled. His written works include his famed English translation of the Qur°an, translations of the Prophet's oral teachings, and his literary autobiography, *The Road to Makkah.*

5. Asad, *The Road to Makkah*, 309-310.

6. It is high time that we get rid of the facile distinction between "East and West" that has so little descriptive validity. However, we can realistically talk about "the Economic North," a network of nations in the Northern Hemisphere (whether in Europe, North America, or Asia) that have developed through industrialization and dominate an international system that keeps their neighbors to "the South" in poverty. Exceptions to this general picture are the southern outposts of settler colonialism, like Australia, New Zealand and South Africa.

7. See Vincent J. Cornell, "Fruit of the Tree of Knowledge: The Relationship Between Faith and Practice in Islam" in John L Esposito (ed.), *The Oxford History of Islam* (New York: Oxford University Press, 1999), 63-106 for the epistemological basis, ethical scope and historical precedent for this project.

8. David J. Wellman, *Sustainable Diplomacy: Ecology, Religion, and Ethics in Muslim-Christian Relations* (New York: Palgrave/St. Martin's Press, 2004).

9. Farha Ghannam examines how "spaces are actively used and reconstructed by social actors who are not the original makers of those spaces" in new neighborhoods of Cairo built by people of limited economic means; see *Remaking the Modern: Relocation, Space and the Politics of Identity in a Global Cairo* (Berkeley: University of California Press, 2002), 22.

10. Julio de Santa Ana, *Sustainability and Globalization* (Geneva: World Council of Churches Publications, 1998), 14, as discussed in Wellman, *Sustainable Diplomacy*. From a more secular ethical perspective informed by economics, see Joseph E. Stiglitz, *Globalization and its Discontents* (New York: W.W. Norton, 2002) or Daniel Little, *The Paradox of Wealth and Poverty: mapping the ethical dilemmas of global development* (Boulder: Westview Press, 2003).

11. Jonathan Sacks, *The Dignity of Difference: How to Avoid the Clash of Civilizations* (London: Continuum, 2002), 13.

12. Maxime Rodinson, *Islam and Capitalism* (London: Penguin Books, 1974).

13. Surat al-Maʾida 4:82.

14. Surat Yunus 10:3.

15. Surat al-Raᶜd, 13:2, see also Surat Yunus 10:31.

16. Surat al-Sajda 32:4.

17. Surat al-Maᶜarij 70:16-26.

18. Victor Danner (trans.), *Ibn Ata'illah's Sufi Aphorisms* (Leiden: E.J. Brill, 1994), 23 note 5.

19. Aphorism number 93; see Victor Danner, *Sufi Aphosisms*, 37.

20. Surat Sad 38:75.

21. Lenn Even Goodman (trans.), *Ibn Tufayl's Hayy ibn Yaqzan* (Los Angeles: Gee Tee Bee, 1996), 17.

22. Max Weber, *The Protestant Ethic and the Spirit of Capitalism* (New York: Charles Scribnerr's Sons, 1958), 180.

23. Weber, *The Protestant Ethic*, 181.

24. Victor Danner, *Sufi Aphorisms*, 1-11 provides an excellent biographical introduction Ibn ᶜAtaʾ Allah's life. Those who aspire to read fuller accounts should avail themselves of the excellent scholarship of Victor and Mary-Ann Koury Danner.

25. Zakia Zouanat, *Ibn Mashish, maitre d'al-Shddhili* (Casablanca: Imprimerie Najah al-Jadida, 1998). Ibn Mashish's tomb is located near

his spiritual retreat on top of Jabal ^cAlam, the highest mountain in the region. After the Shadhili community subsequently became popular in Morocco, his tomb became an important pilgrimage point and devotional center. It is the only tomb of an early Shadhili master located in Morocco.

26. Nancy Roberts (trans.), *The Subtle Blessings in the Saintly Lives of Abul-Abbas al-Mursi and His Master Abul-Hasan, the Founders of the Shadhili Order* (Louisville: Fons Vitae Press, forthcoming, Fall 2005), chapter 1.

27. Roberts, *The Subtle Blessing,* chapter 3.

28. Roberts, *The Subtle Blessing,* chapter 2.

29. His full name is Abū Faḍl Aḥmad ibn Muḥammad ibn ^cAbd al-Karīm Ibn ^cAṭāʾ Allah; his name is often preceded by the honorific title Tāj al-Dīn (Crown of the Faith), and followed by the nickname al-Iskandarī (from Alexandria). He was born into an elite family, the clan of Ibn ^cAtaʾ Allah, that had produced generations of Maliki jurists and judges in Alexandria.

30. Roberts, *The Subtle Blessing,* chapter three; and Ibn ^cAtaʾ Allah, *Laṭāʾif al-Minan* (Cairo: Maktabat ^cAlam al-Fikr, 1993 second printing), 114-115.

31. Roberts, *The Subtle Blessing,* chapter 3.

32. Roberts, *The Subtle Blessing,* chapter 3.

33. Roberts, *The Subtle Blessing,* chapter 3.

34. Roberts, *The Subtle Blessing,* chapter 3.

35. Roberts, *The Subtle Blessing,* chapter 3.

36. From this translation, 272 and also Roberts, *The Subtle Blessing,* chapter 3.

37. Roberts, *The Subtle Blessing,* chapter 3.

38. Scott Kugle, *Rebel Between Spirit and Law* (Bloomington: Indiana University Press, forthcoming) describes this tradition of Sufi-Jurists in the Maliki school of law.

39. From this translation, 318-19.

40. Muḥayy al-Dīn Muḥammad al-Ḥātimī ibn ^cArabī (d. 1240 in Damascus) was one of the most profound and prolific Sufi thinkers during the crucial thirteenth century CE that witnessed the growth of institutional Sufi communities. Born in Andalusia, (in Murcia), he traveled widely in Morocco, Tunisia, Arabia, Syria and Iraq. A poet, philosopher, theologian and spiritual iconoclast, Ibn ^cArabi is known as "the Great Master" (al-shaykh al-akbar). There is some debate about how Ibn ^cArabi's thought affected the Shadhili Sufi community in its

early formation. Ibn ʿAtaʾ Allah's thought contains many ideas that are analogous to those of Ibn ʿArabi, as revealed by Victor Danner, *Sufi Aphorisms*, 18 and note 1. Yet being a professional jurist made Ibn ʿAtaʾ Allah more circumspect in pushing these concepts to their more speculative horizons the way that Ibn ʿArabi did. Richard McGreggor argues that Ibn ʿAtaʾ Allah's writing do not reflect the systematic use of Ibn ʿArabi's concepts; Richard McGregor, "The Akbarian Legacy of the Wafaʾiya," presentation at *Colloque International: La voie soufie des Shadhilis* (April 18-21 2003, Alexandria, Egypt) and also McGregor, *Sanctity and Mysticism in Medieval Egypt: the Wafa' sufi order and the legacy of Ibn 'Arabi* (Albany: SUNY press, 2004), 39-47.

41. ʿAlī Wafāʾ (d. 1405) is a Shadhili master and Arab poet, who is buried near Ibn ʿAtaʾ Allah in the Qarafa cemetery of Cairo. For his life and teachings, see the copious biographical entry on him and his immediate family in Shaʿranī, *al-Ṭabaqāt al-Kubrā* (Cairo: 1355 AH), 2:21-65. For information on other famous followers of Ibn ʿAtaʾ Allah, see Victor Danner, *Sufi Aphorisms*, 11-12.

42. Ibn ʿAbbād, Muḥammad ibn Ibrāhīm al-Rundī (d. 1390), *Sharḥ ʿalā Matn al-Ḥikam* (Cairo, al-Maṭbaʿa al-Khayrīya, 1886) by the alternate title, *Ghayth al-Mawāhib al-ʿĀliya* (Cairo: Maṭbaʿat al-Saʿada, 1970). Zarrūq, Aḥmad ibn Aḥmad (d. 1493), *Sharḥ al-Ḥikam al-ʿAṭāʾīya*, ed. ʿAṭiya, Aḥmad Zakī (Benghazi: Kulliyat al-Ādab, 1971) and *Ḥikam Ibn ʿAṭāʾ Allah: sharḥ Zarrūq*, ed. Maḥmūd, ʿAbd al-Ḥalīm and Maḥmūd Ibn al-Sharīf (Cairo: Dār al-Shaʿb, 1969).

43. Victor Danner, *Sufi Aphorisms*, 23.

44. Victor Danner, *Sufi Aphorisms*, 17.

45. ʿAlī Muttaqī, *al-Manhaj al-Atamm fī Tabwīb al-Ḥikam* (Damascus: Dar al-Qadiri, 1998), 70-71 notes that these aphorisms include numbers 2, 3, 4, 5, 18, 19, 114, and 171 and groups them under the topical heading, "Submission to God's Decree and Desisting from Your Own Choosing." ʿAli Muttaqi (d. 1567-8) took an initiation into the Shadhili community in the sixteenth century, which was a very unusual and productive connection between Indian and North African Sufis. See Kugle, *Rebel Between Spirit and Law*, on the connections between Shaykh Ahmad Zarruq and his South Asian followers.

46. John Renard (trans.), *Ibn Abbad ar-Rondi: Letters on the Sufi Path* (New York: Paulist Press, 1986), 174-5. In his translation, Renard followed Victor Danner in citing the title of *Illumination* as "Light on the Elimination of Self-Direction."

47. Zarruq, *Tuḥfat al-Murīd wa Rawḍat al-Farīd wa Fawāʾid li-Ahl al-Fahm al-Sadīd wa al-Naẓr al-Madīd*, (manuscript Rabat: al-

Khizāna al-ᶜAmma, D 2587). See Scott Kugle, *Rebel Between Spirit and Law*, chapter 3.

48. Zarruq, *Qawāᶜid al-Taṣawwuf* (Beirut: Dar al-Jil, 1992), 166.

49. Juan José González (trans.), *Sobre el Abandono de Sí Mismo* (Madrid: Hiperión, 1994) and Abdellah Penaud (trans.), *Sur l'abandon de la propre volonté* (private publication).

50. ᶜAlī Muttaqī, *Kitāb al-Tawaṣṣul fiᵓl-Yaqīn waᵓl-Tawakkul* (manuscript at Aligarh, India: Maulana Azad Library, Subhanullah Collection shamil 297.7/51 taṣawwuf farsi; and Lahore, Pakistan: Punjab University Library 3923/871 folios 173-179).

51. Ibn ᶜAṭāᵓ Allah, *Kitāb al-Tanwīr fi Isqāṭ al-Tadbīr* (Cairo: Maṭbaᶜ Abbās ᶜAbd al-Salām Shaqrāwī, undated) is a reliable printing but has many typographical errors.

52. Ibn ᶜAṭāᵓ Allah, *Kitāb al-Tanwīr* (Cairo: ᶜAlam al-Fikr, 1998).

53. The catalogue of manuscripts for the Bibliotheque de l'Université Quaraouyine in Fes lists these four hand-written manuscripts: numbers 1353 part 3, 1356, 1364 part 1, 1833. In correcting the published versions of the Arabic text, the first listed manuscript was used primarily, with secondary reliance upon the three subsequently listed manuscripts.

54. The powerful woman saint, Sayyida ᶜAᵓisha bint ᶜImrān al-Mannūbīya, is revered in Tunis as one of the companions of Shaykh al-Shadhili. There is some dispute about her relationship to Shaykh al-Shadhili, and she seems to have incurred the wrath of several contemporary male jurists for her very forceful assertion of female sainthood. See *Encyclopedia of Islam*, 1:308-9 and the scholarship of the Tunisian social historian, Nelli ᶜAmri.

55. Asma Barlas, *Believing Women in Islam: Unreading Patriarchal Interpretations of the Qurᵓan* (Austin: University of Texas Press, 2002) provides an insightful effort to recover gender equality and specificity in reading and interpreting the Qurᵓan.

56. John Renard, *Seven Doors to Islam: spirituality and the religious life of Muslims* (Berkeley: University of California Press, 1996), 54 initiated the use of "One" to translate the names of God (*asmāᵓ*).

57. In addition to grammatical considerations, there is a theological reason to avoid the kind of rampant capitalization that marks many translations of Sufi texts. Capitalization tends to mark certain names or qualities of God as transcendent. By being capitalized we are forced to imagine that they belong to God alone, far above the same quality that might exist in a human being if left in lower case. Such a visual emphasis on transcendence tends to downplay the fact that God's attributes

have both transcendent and immanent qualities. Qualities like God's mercy, wrath, beauty and hearing are both similar to human qualities but also utterly different from human qualities. It is the tension inherent in this play between transcendent and immanent qualities that gives these attributes their power to move us and inspire us. In my opinion, rampant use of capitalization tends to sever this creative tension and over-determine the reference of the name or quality cited.

NOTES TO THE INVOCATION, OPENING ADDRESS, AND CHAPTER ONE

1. Surat al-Shura 42:11. The verse in its fuller context reveals how Ibn ᶜAtaᵓ Allah's choice of this phrase alludes to the essential subject of this work: *The decision over whatever thing about which you differ and conflict lies with God. Say 'God is my Lord, to God I entrust my affairs with complete trust, and to God I turn with repentance to act on my behalf.' For God is the One who creates the heavens and the earth, and has created for you pairs from among yourselves and created pairs from among cattle [on which you depend] by means of which you multiply. There is nothing similar to God, the most acute of hearing, the most penetrating of vision. To God belong the keys of the heavens and the earth. God enlarges and restricts the means of sustenance for whomever God wills, for God is the One who knows all things.*

2. Surat al-Mulk 67:14.

3. Muhammad is the "opener" since he was created as light before all things, and is the "closer" because his human mission came last in the historical series of Prophets. There is a hadith in which the Prophet Muhammad is reported to have said "Verily I was the first among the Prophets to be created and the last to be deputed."

4. Shaykh al-Shadhili also directly addresses the paradox of intention, in which people who strive to become purely sincere cannot achieve it because of the egoism involved in choosing to strive; see Ibn Sabbagh, *Durrat al-Asrār wa Tuḥfat al-Abrār*, published as Elmer Douglas (trans.), *The Mystical Teachings of al-Shadhili* (Albany: SUNY Press, 1993), 141.

5. Surat al-Qasas 28:68. This saying of Shaykh al-Shadhili is also relayed by Ibn Sabbagh; see Douglas, *The Mystical Teachings of al-Shadhili*, 146.

6. Surat an-Nisaᵓ 4:65.

7. Surat al-Najm 53:4.

386

8. Surat al-Fath 68:10.

9. Surah Maryam 19:2.

10. This style of exposition, unfolding the meaning of a single saying in a chain of equivalent sayings, was practiced with piercing accuracy by Shaykh al-Mursi; it dazzled the young Ibn ᶜAtaʾ Allah during his first meeting with the Shaykh, as he reported in *Lataʾif al-Minan*, 114-115 (corresponding to Roberts, *The Subtle Blessings*, chapter 3).

11. Surat al-Tur 52:48.

12. Surat al-Talaq 65:3.

13. Surat al-Zumar 39:36.

14. Surat Al ᶜImran 3:165. This moment of Divine Speech censures the early Muslims who grew despondent after their near-defeat in the battle of Uhud, after they had previously won the battle of Badr against all odds.

15. Other Shadhili Sufis picked up this topic for further discussion, and Ibn ᶜAbbad praises those who not only endure pain and suffering, but even see agony as a special gift of the divine beloved; he discusses these same narratives in Renard, *Letter on the Sufi Path*, 124.

16. Surat al-Ahzab 33:43.

17. Surat al-Zumar 39:10.

18. Surat al-Baqara 2:216.

19. This is aphorism 105 from Ibn ᶜAtaʾ Allah, *Kitab al-Hikam*; See Victor Danner, *Sufi Aphorisms*, 39 who translates this aphorism as, "To soften for you the suffering of affliction, He has taught you that He is the One who causes trials to come upon you. For the one who confronts you with His decrees of Fate is the same who has accustomed you to His good choice."

20. Surat al-Tur 52:48.

21. Surat Yusuf 12:31. This single verse conjures up the well-loved tale of Yusuf, the Biblical Joseph, who was the epitome of masculine beauty. According to the Qurᶜanic account, the wife of the owner of Joseph, who was a household slave in Egypt, fell in love with Joseph. When she heard other women's malicious talk criticizing her for being in love with her servant, she prepared a banquet for them, giving each of them a knife. When they were about the cut their fruit for desert, she called Joseph to come into the room. When the women saw him, they were so astonished that, staring at him they cut their hands rather than the fruit.

22. This is one of the boldest theological claims that Ibn ᶜAtaʾ Allah makes as a Sufi master. He asserts that descriptions of paradise

387

are not really real in themselves, but are only manifestations of divine self-disclosure that depend upon the divine presence but also veil the divine presence behind a curtain of what is other-than-God. This phrasing is comparable to the boldness of the early Sufi, al-Niffarī (d. 965 in Iraq), whose poem *Mawqif al-Maḥḍar waʾl-Ḥarf* sifts the scriptural images of paradise into the qualities of God, which all depend on the very presence of God. See Reynolds Nicholson (trans.), *The Mawaqif and Mukhatibat of al-Niffari* (London: Gibb Memorial Series No. 9, 1935), 111-116 and Michael Sells, *Early Islamic Mysticism* (Mahwah: Paulist Press, 1996), 291-301.

23. There is some ambiguity in different manuscript texts of *The Book of Illumination* over whether the term is *taʿrīf*, God's giving intimate knowledge or *taṣrīf*, God dispensing of decrees. These terms look very similar in manuscript writing, differing in the shape of only one letter. However, this visual nearness evokes a conceptual nearness as well, for the meaning of the two terms is also closely linked in Ibn ʿAtaʾ Allah's discourse. God's dispensing of decrees in assigning to each person a destiny is God's way of giving each person intimate experiential knowledge of God's nature; in English we can observe the same conceptual pairing in the saying, "Calamity is opportunity." The inevitable collision of what you desire with the vicissitudes of reality (the ripples of the actions of God) leads to the opening of windows of knowledge, leading to certitude after insight. Or if you like, you could say, "Suffering disappointment is opening insight."

24. Ibn ʿAtaʾ Allah recorded Shaykh al-Mursi's original exposition of these four possible conditions in *Lataʾif al-Minan*, 115 and 191 (corresponding to Roberts, *The Subtle Blessings*, chapters 3 and 8).

25. Surat Ibrahim 14:7.

26. Surat al-Baqara 2:216.

27. Surah Al ʿImran 3:123.

28. Ibn ʿAtaʾ Allah's style of exposition raises hypothetical objections that might arise in the listeners' minds, especially those listeners with a literalistic reading of scripture or a legalistic understanding of religion. Anecdotes about Shaykh al-Shadhili reveal that jurists and scholars did attend his gatherings and object to some of his interpretations; he welcomed their interjections but often scolded them in his answers. His response to an objection of the chief jurist of Alexandria, for instance, warned of the imminent demise of his worldly career; see Douglas, *The Mystical Teachings of al-Shadhili*, 151.

29. Surat al-Qasas 28:68.

30. Surat al-Nahl 16:17.

31. This passage offers commentary on the aphorism 171; see Victor Danner, *Sufi Aphorisms*,48 "Everything depends on the Divine Will, but It Itself depends on nothing at all."

32. Surat al-Najm 53:24.

33. Surat al-Maʾida 5:122.

34. The heart is more than an anatomical organ in Islamic theology in general, and Sufi thought in particular. It is also a faculty of spiritual perception, analogous to the five commonly-noted faculties of perception. For a discussion of the heart in Sufi ritual, see Scott Kugle, "The Heart of Ritual is the Body: anatomy of an Islamic devotional manual of the nineteenth century," *Journal of Ritual Studies* 17/1 (2003): 42-60.

35. Surat Al ᶜImran 3:19 and 85.

36. Surat al-Baqara 2:132.

37. The role of discursive theologians (*mutakallimūn*) in Islamic society is to offer clear proofs for God's existence, actions, and oneness and to defend the authenticity of the Qurʾan and the Prophet Muhammad's other teachings as a religious guide. Many early Sufis were theologians in this sense, though not all theologians were Sufis. Mysticism (*taṣawwuf*) shares these goals, and adds to them the active cultivation of virtue and circumscription of selfishness. Sufis sometimes came into conflict with rationalist theologians because Sufis did not trust reasoned discourse as an adequate means to realize the nature of God, for reason tends to reify divine transcendence without addressing the fact that cultivation of virtue relies upon divine immanence.

38. One edition reads *shirk bi-rubūbīyatihi*, "infidelity toward God's lordship" and another reads *tark rubūbīyatihi*, "leaving aside God's lordship."

39. Abū al-Qāsim Muḥammad al-Junayd (d. 910 in Baghdad) was an early Sufi who brought intellectual clarity and abstract precision to the discipline. His Sufi colleague, al-Haddad, said: "If intellect and reason were a man, he would have the form of Junayd." Junayd is the paragon of the "sober" tradition of scrupulously pious Sufism, built upon the foundation of al-Muhasibi's writings. In general, the Shadhili community took its ideals of mysticism from this tradition.

40. Ibn ᶜAtaʾ Allah stresses the importance of reason in mysticism, continuing a long tradition in "sober" Sufi thought. The early Sufi who most clearly articulated the necessity of reason in mystical cultivation was al-Muḥāsibī (d. 857 in Baghdad), who asserted that reason was the necessary means to achieving wariness of God (*taqwā*). Al-Muhasibi was a bridge between the rationalist theologians and Sufi

mystics. He was attacked by the traditionalist, Ahmad ibn Hanbal, for using reasoned discourse to argue about the nature of God.

41. This passage offers commentary on Ibn ᶜAtaᵓ Allah's aphorism number 3: see Victor Danner, *Sufi Aphorisms*, 23 who translates it as, "Antecedent intentions cannot pierce the walls of predestined decrees."

42. Al-Husayn ibn Mansur al-Hallaj (d. 922 in Baghdad) was an early Sufi radical and martyr. He proclaimed the primacy of love over all things, even the ordinances of religious law and custom. This teaching brought him into close relationship with an extremist Shiᶜi political and religious movement, the Qaramatians, who held that Islamic religious customs and law were distracting from Muslims' realizing the presence of God. Such alliances, whether real or only perceived, brought al-Hallaj into conflict with the ruling Sunni authorities, who had him executed. Al-Hallaj held that ephemeral human qualities could be extinguished, allowing the mystic to "return" to God's presence as he was before time, in a relationship of total identity and absolute loving ecstasy.

43. Things exist as archetypal potentialities (*aᶜyān thābita*) that are established by God's knowledge of them before they exist as actualized being in their material manifestations. The concept of the archetypal potentialities is developed more fully in Ibn ᶜArabi's fusion of Sufi thought and existential philosophy; see William Chittick, *The Sufi Path of Knowledge: Ibn al-ᶜArabi's Metaphysics of Imagination* (SUNY Press, 1989), 83-4.

44. The Day of Destinies (*yawm al-maqādīr*) is the moment of primordial covenant, when God questioned the souls of all humans before their creation, evoking from them the testimony that they bore witness that God alone was divinity.

45. Surat al-Qamar 54:55

46. Surat al-Nahl 16:53.

47. Surat al-Muᶜminun 23:12-16.

48. Surat al-Talaq 65:3.

49. Surat al-Baqara 2:189.

50. Surat al-Anᶜam 6:91.

51. Surat Maryam 19:40.

52. Surat Ghafir (Muᵓmin) 40:57.

53. Surat al-Tawba 9:111

54. Ibrahim ibn Adham (d. 777) was an early Sufi exemplar from Central Asia. He advocated asceticism and voluntary poverty. He claimed to have left this world to those who seek this world and left reward in the next world to those who seek the next world; in this world

he wanted only the remembrance of God and in the next world he wanted only the vision of God.

55. This tradition is retold in a letter of Ibn Abbad al-Rundi (Letter 9 from the smaller collection). The verses are translated by John Renard, *Letters on the Sufi Path*, 162 in the following way:

All is forgiven you, for it is little consequence to Us

What We have left up to you is passing

What goes forth from Us endures

56. Surat al-Hajj 22:47. Abu Madyan Shuʿayb al-Anṣārī (d. 1197 in Tlemcen, Algeria) was one of the most important figures to establish institutional Sufi communities in North Africa. He was born in Andalusia near Seville, migrated to Fas (Fez) for education and Sufi training, and established himself as the leader of a broad Sufi community in Bijaya (Bougie). See Vincent Cornell, *The Way of Abu Madyan* (Cambridge: Islamic Texts Society, 1996). His personality was paradigmatic for the leaders of the early Shadhili community, such that Shaykh al-Mursi once related that, "Once I was led up on a journey through God's celestial realms, when I saw Shaykh Abu Madyan clinging to a pillar of the divine throne. He had light reddish hair and bluish eyes"; see *Lataʾif al-Minan*, 76 (corresponding to Nancy Roberts, *The Subtle Blessings*, chapter 1).

57. Surat Ya Sin 20:132.

58. Surat Al ʿImran 3:2.

59. Surat al-Hijr 15:99. "Until you reach *yaqīn*, utter certainty," is commonly interpreted as meaning until you die.

60. Ibn ʿAtaʾ Allah cites the phrase "servant of a just Lord (ʿabd marbūb)" from al-Muhasibi, *al-Riʿāya fī Ḥuqūq Allah* (Beirut: Dār al-Kutub al-ʿIlmīya, 1985), 44 where it is discussed in detail. In one phrase, he evokes a profound concept developed over a long period of prior Sufi practice and writing.

61. Surat Ya Sin 20:132. This verse will be interpreted in depth later, in the section "Provision is Conditional upon Service" on pages 230-241.

62. This phrase is from Shaykh al-Shadhili's prayer, "The Noble Litany and the Mighty Veil"; see Douglas, *The Mystical Teachings of al-Shadhili*, 68.

63. Surat al-Baqara 2:216.

64. Surat al-Baqara 2:185.

65. Surat al-Aʿraf 7:172. This is the Day of Destinies, as cited earlier in note 44.

66. Surat al-Aᶜraf 7:20.

67. The human being alone accepted the trust (*amāna*) to become God's vice-regent on earth, after the heavens, the earth and the mountains refused to accept it, as detailed in Surat al-Ahzab 33:72.

68. Surat al-Duha 93:4.

69. This rephrasing gives the verse a broader, more general meaning applicable to the traversal of any state, rather than the more common, limited reading of the meaning as "life in the next world is better for you than life in this world." Ibn ᶜAtiya is the author of the Qurʾan commentary, *al-Muharrir al-Wajiz*, (The Concise Liberator). Tradition relates that this was the single commentary preferred by Shaykh al-Shadhili: see *Lataʾif al-Minan*, 117 (corresponding to Roberts, *The Subtle Blessings*, chapter 4).

70. This is a fine example of *iqtibās al-qurʾan*, a literary technique that seamlessly weaves reference to a Qurʾanic verse into a text's prose. In this case, the reference is to Surat al-Safat 37:113. "And we blessed him (Abraham) and Isḥāq (Isaac), and from among his progeny are some who are righteous and some who clearly oppress their own souls."

71. Surat al-Baqara 2:30. For this teaching of Shaykh al-Shadhili, see *Lataʾif al-Minan*, 85 (corresponding to Roberts, *The Subtle Blessings*, chapter 1).

72. Surat al-Aᶜraf 7:22. The same expression appears in another Qurʾanic narrative of the same incident, in Surat Ta Ha 20:116-128. Surat Ta Ha emphasizes the condition of Adam and Eve after their descent into the world and the beginning of revelation and guidance.

73. Surat Ta Ha 20:122.

74. Surah Ta Ha 20:117.

75. Surat al-Nisaʾ 4:34.

76. Surat Ta Ha 20:115.

77. Surat al-Aᶜraf 7:22.

78. This analogy is facilitated by Arabic grammatical genders: the heart, *qalb*, is a masculine noun, aligning it metaphorically with Adam, while the ego-self, *nafs*, is a feminine noun, aligning it with Eve. This is in accord with the gendered analogies in Mawlana Rumi's famous Persian Sufi epic, the *Mathnawi*, despite the fact that Persian language does not have gendered nouns. In the opening allegory of the *Mathnawi*, the ego is a (female) slave-girl, and the spirit that dwells in the heart is a (male) king who falls in love with her. She, however, is herself sick with love for a goldsmith, who represents the material world, and cannot be cured by the king's doctors, who represent reason's power to

calculate and arrange affairs (*tadbīr*). See Ḥājjī Imdādullah Muhājir Makkī, *Sharḥ-i Masnavī-yi Mawlavī-yi Ma'navī* (lithographic printing Kanpur, India: Matba'-yi Nāmī, 1321 AH), 7. It is fascinating to compare these two Sufi masters who were both artful authors, Ibn 'Ata' Allah and Mawlana Rumi; they were not just contemporaries but are both credited with writing works that, in Arabic and Persian respectively, are so profound that they bear comparison to the Qur'an. Of Ibn 'Ata' Allah's *Hikam*, it is commonly said among Shadhili Sufis that, "If any other words were allowed to be recited during prayer other than the Qur'an, they would be the words of the *Hikam*." Comparably, Rumi's *Mathnawi* is known, among Sufis from Persian-speaking lands, as "the Qur'an in the Pahlawi (Persian) tongue."

79. Surat al-Baqara 2:34.

80. Ibn 'Ata' Allah paraphrases an oral teaching of Shaykh al-Mursi; see *Lata'if al-Minan*, 216 (corresponding to Roberts, *The Subtle Blessings*, chapter 8).

81. Surat Bani Isra'il (or al-Isra') 17:1. The servant "taken on a journey by night" refers to the Prophet Muhammad. His "night journey" from Mecca to Jerusalem initiated his ascension through the heavens into the intimate presence of God. The humility of being "a servant" thus precedes Muhammad's "being raised" to a lofty status. See Frederick S. Colby (trans.), *Subtleties of the Ascension: Early Mystical sayings on Muhammad's Heavenly Journey as compiled by Abu 'Abd al-Rahman Sulami* (Louisville: Fons Vitae, forthcoming, 2005).

82. Surat al-Anfal, 8:41, and Surat Maryam 19:1-2.

83. Surat al-Jinn 72:19.

84. Abu Bakr was the Prophet Muhammad's best friend and closest follower from outside his immediate family. He became the first leader of the Muslim community (*khalīfa*) after the Prophet's death. 'Umar ibn al-Khattab had initially opposed the Prophet violently, but then experienced a change of heart and become his staunchest supporter; 'Umar became the second leader of the Muslim community after the death of Abu Bakr.

85. Abu Bakr here makes a subtle pun, for the verb "to save by giving refuge" (*najā*) is very similar to the verb for "to have an intimate whispered conversation" (*najwa*).

86. See *Lata'if al-Minan*, 181 (corresponding to Roberts, *The Subtle Blessings*, chapter 6).

87. Some commentators believe that "manna" is a kind of cotton-like seed that floats on the breeze and is as nourishing as bread, but can

be eaten raw without toil, while "salwa" refers to wild quails that live in the desert and are easy to catch without much labor.

88. Surat al-Maʾida 5:24.

89. Surat al-Nisaʾ 4:153.

90. Surat al-Aʿraf 7:138 and 171.

91. Abū Yāzid (Bayazid) Bisṭāmī (d. 820) was an early Sufi from North-Western Iran. This early Sufi embraced rigorous austerities in order to strip himself of frail human qualities and encounter God face-to-face. He championed the idea of identification with God through self-nullification.

92. This is another fine example of *iqtibās al-qurʾān*, subtly incorporating Qurʾanic phrasing in a prose sentence, this time from two incidents in the narrative of Moses and his confrontation with God's presence at Mount Sinai in Surat al-Naml 27:10, and Surat Ta Ha 20:12.

93. *Lataʾif al-Minan*, 87 and 210 (corresponding to Roberts, *The Subtle Blessings*, chapters 1 and 10) recounts the same story of how Shaykh al-Shadhili in his youth met his master. His master was ʿAbd al-Salām ibn Mashīsh (d. 1227), a Sharif and Sufi from Morocco, who gave spiritual training to Shaykh al-Shadhili, his only known disciple. When asked, "Who is your master?" Shaykh al-Shadhili said, "I took an oath of discipleship with Shaykh ʿAbd al-Salam ibn Mashish. However, now I do not have a relation of dependence and discipleship with anyone. Rather, I dive deep in the ten seas. Five are human seas: the Prophet Muhammad, Abu Bakr, ʿUmar, ʿUthman and ʿAli. And five are spiritual seas: Gabriel, Michael, Asrafael, Azrael, and the greatest Spirit (*al-rūḥ al-akbar*)." See *Lataʾif al-Minan*, 77 (corresponding to Roberts, *The Subtle Blessings*, chapter 1) and Douglas, *The Mystical Teachings of al-Shadhili*, 157.

94. Surat Hud 11:42.

95. Surat Hud 11:43.

96. Surat Al ʿImran 3:101, and Surat al-Talaq 65:3.

97. Surat al-Talaq 65:3.

98. Abū al-Ḥafs al-Ḥaddād (d. circa 885 in Baghdad) was an early Sufi in the circle of Junayd and worked as a blacksmith. In addition to this story of him dropping his hammer, there is another famous story of his being so immersed in listening to someone recite the Qurʾan that he grew distracted while working, reached into the furnace and with his bare hand drew out a piece of white-hot metal. See Ibn ʿAtaʾ Allah's aphorism number 19 describing this issue; Danner, *Sufi Aphorisms*, 26 translates it as, "Do not request Him to get you out of a state to make

use of you in a different one, for, were He to desire so, He could make use of you as you are, without taking you out!"

99. Surat al-Hijr 15:42.

100. Surat al-Nahl 16:99.

101. Surat al-Baqara 2:257.

102. Surat al-Anbiya� 21:18.

103. Surat al-Aᶜraf 7:201.

104. For a detailed exposition of Ibn ᶜAtaᵓ Allah's conception of *dhikr* or ritual recollection of God's qualities, see his text *Miftāḥ al-Falāḥ fī Miṣbāḥ al-Arwāḥ* which is one of the earliest and most detailed Sufi explanations of the theory and practice of *dhikr*; see Mary-Ann Koury Danner (trans.), *The Key to Salvation* (Cambridge: Islamic Texts Society, 1996).

105. Ibn ᶜAtaᵓ Allah provides a detailed description of how saints inherit the authority of the Prophets and Messengers through internalizing their qualities and radiating their light; see *Lataᵓif al-Minan*, introduction.

106. Surat al-Baqara 2:222.

107. Surat al-Nisaᵓ 4:28.

108. Surat al-Najm 53:32.

109. Surat Al ᶜImran 3:135.

110. Surat al-Shura 42:37

111. Surat Al ᶜImran 3:134.

112. Surat al-Hijr 15:42.

113. Surat Fatir 35:6.

114. Surat Yusuf 12:40, and Surat al-Nisaᵓ 4:72.

115. Surat al-Baqara 2:257, Surat al-Talaq 65:3, and Surat al-Nahl 16:99.

116. Surat al-Rum 30:47.

117. Surat al-Kahf 18:39, and Surat Al ᶜImran 3:101.

118. Surat al-Kahf 18:63.

119. Surat al-Nisaᵓ 4:78.

120. Surat al-Zumar 39:62, Surat Fatir 35:3, and Surat al-Nahl 16:17.

121. Surat al-Saffat 37:96. "Those who make false claims" refers to the Muᶜtazila, rationalist theologians who argued that God is not the creator and originator of acts that are unjust, like disobedience, oppression and ingratitude. In reaction, Sunni theologians from the Ashᶜari school of thought rejected this formulation as limiting the omnipotence of God and, at the risk of diluting human agency, stressed that God is the originator of all actions though human beings acquire accountabil-

ity for unjust actions. Sufis like Ibn ᶜAtaᵓ Allah inherited and upheld the Ashᶜari position.

122. Surat al-Aᶜraf 7:28.

123. Surat al-Nisaᵓ 4:79.

124. Surat al-Kahf 18:79 and 82. This refers to the story of Moses and his wise companion, Khidr. Moses asked to keep company with him, but keeps attributing bad motives to Khidr's actions, which seem to hurt others. This harm is only on the surface, since it is revealed that each action is actually in accord with divine wisdom. Khidr breaks a hole in the boat of poor sailors, and it turns out that if it had not been rendered temporarily useless it would have been commandeered by an unjust ruler's army. Khidr rebuilds a wall in the town of evil people, and it turns out that beneath is was hidden a treasure that belonged to two orphan boys who would have been deprived of their inheritance had it been found before they reached maturity. Finally, Khidr kills a youth, and it turns out that he would have grown up to plague his righteous parents. The narrative is told in Surat al-Kahf 18:65-82.

125. Surat al-Shuᶜaraᵓ 26:80.

126. Surat al-Baqara 2:130-131.

127. Surat Al ᶜImran 3:19, and Surat al-Hajj 22:78.

128. Surat Al ᶜImran 3:20, and Surat al-Hajj 22:34.

129. Surat Al ᶜImran 3:85, and Surat Luqman 31:22.

130. Surat Yusuf 12:101, and Surat al-Anᶜam 6:163.

131. Surat al-Naml 27:64.

132. Abraham's story is narrated in different moments of the Qurᵓan. At one stage he rejects the worship of the stars and heavenly bodies. In another, he confronts his father and community by refusing to worship idols and breaking those they worshiped. In another, he is persecuted for this defiance by being hurled into a furnace to be burned alive. This popular tradition associates this episode with the Assyrian king, Nimrod, as in the Biblical narrative. However, Nimrod is not named as such in the Qurᵓan, which could be read to imply that Abraham's own people load him into a catapult and propel him into a raging fire. The story of Gabriel appearing to Abraham while he was strapped in the catapult appears not in the Qurᵓan but rather in the popular genre of "Stories of the Prophets" (qiṣaṣ al-anbiyāᵓ); see Muhammad Gameiah (trans.), *Stories of the Prophets by Ibn Kathir* (New Delhi: Islamic Book Service, 2000), 82.

133. Surat al-Najm 53:37.

134. Surat al-Anbiyaᵓ 21:69.

135. Surat al-Tawba 9:129.

136. Surat al-Najm 53:37.

137. Surat al-Baqara 2:30.

138. Surat al-Anbiyaᵓ 21:88. "Him" refers specifically to the Prophet Dhū al-Nūn (Jonah) but stands for the Prophets in general.

139. Surat al-Baqara 2:130.

140. The text here offers a commentary on aphorism number 18; see Victor Danner, *Sufi Aphorisms*, 24 "Your postponement of deeds till the time when you are free is one of the frivolities of the ego."

141. Surat al-Aᶜraf 7:156.

142. See *Laṭāᵓif al-Minan*, 177 (corresponding to Roberts, *The Subtle Blessings*, chapter 6).

143. Ṣufyan al-Thawrī (d. 778) was an early scholar of the Qurᵓan and Prophetic traditions, and founded an early school of Islamic law in Kufa, Iraq. He was known for his creative thinking, critical piety, and independent thinking. Sufis claim him as an early authority in their movement, along with al-Hasan al-Basri, with whom he is buried in Basra.

144. Abu Bakr was famous in the time of the Prophet for selflessly giving away his great wealth for the benefit of the early Islamic community.

145. Surat al-Baqara 2:197.

146. Surat al-Fath 48:29.

147. Surat al-Kahf 18:28.

148. Surat al-Nur 24:32.

149. Surat al-Hijr 15:42.

150. ᶜUthman ibn ᶜAffan was a close friend and follower of the Prophet Muhammad, and became the third leader (*khalīfa*) of the Muslim community upon the death of ᶜUmar. He came from the aristocratic and wealthy tribe of the Banu Umayya. The others mentioned in this anecdote are all famous companions of the Prophet who helped spread the early Islamic empire, thereby amassing great wealth.

151. Surat al-Hadid 57:7.

152. Surat al-Baqara 2:109.

153. ᶜAlī ibn Abī Ṭālib (d. 660 near Kufa, now known as Najaf) was the closest follower of the Prophet Muhammad, being his cousin and son-in-law after having been raised from adolescence in the Prophet's own household. Sunni Muslims consider him the fourth leader of the Muslim community (*khalīfa*) after the death of the Prophet, while Shiᶜa Muslims consider him the first and only legitimate leader after

the Prophet. However, his life was cut short by civil war. He is considered by Sufis to have been the one to receive spiritual teachings, meditative techniques and inner illumination from the Prophet, and to have handed these on to others, thus becoming the first axial saint (*quṭb*). For the interpretation of this role in the Shadhili Sufi community, see *Laṭaʾif al-Minan,* 91 (corresponding to Roberts, *The Subtle Blessings,* chapter 1) where Ibn ʿAtaʾ Allah explains: "The formal spiritual method (*ṭarīqa*) of Shaykh al-Shadhili derives from his master, ʿAbd al-Salām ibn Mashīsh. And his method derives from his master, ʿAbd al-Raḥmān al-Madanī. It is traced back from master to master until the sequence derives ultimately from Hassan, the son of ʿAli ibn Abi Talib."

154. Surat al-Hashr 59:9.

155. Surat al-Ahzab 33:23.

156. Surat Al ʿImran 3:152.

157. Surat al-Baqara 2:275 and 282.

158. Surat Hud 11:43. This moment describes the fate of Noah's son, who decided for himself to climb up a mountain to avoid the flood, rather than join his father on the arc. Ibn ʿAtaʾ Allah cleverly uses this context to criticize those who go it alone, escaping to a mountain top in ascetic retreat.

159. With this teaching of the Prophet Muhammad, Ibn ʿAtaʾ Allah begins his short treatise, *The Sign of Success on the Spiritual Path*; see Appendix One.

160. This passage offers commentary on Ibn ʿAtaʾ Allah's aphorism number 114; see Victor Danner, *Sufi Aphorisms,* 40 "When the forgetful man gets up in the morning, he reflects on what he is going to do, whereas the intelligent man sees what God is doing with him."

161. Surat Al ʿImran 3:101, and Surat al-Talaq 65:3.

162. Surat Yusuf 12:64.

163. Surat al-Hajj 22:41.

164. For a fascinating discussion of Maliki jurists' approach to the complex and socially incendiary topic of "commanding what is right," see Michael Cook, *Commanding Right and Forbidding Wrong in Islamic Thought* (Cambridge University Press, 2000), chapter 14.

165. Surat al-Furqan 25:63.

166. This story is told of Abu Hafs al-Haddad.; see note 95.

167. Surat al-Ahqaf 46:31, Surat al-Anfal 8:24, and Surat al-Shura 42:47.

168. Surat al-Hujurat 49:12.

169. Surat Hud 11:113.

170. This passage echoes another work of Ibn ᶜAtaᵓ Allah, *The Sign of Success for Behaving on the Spiritual Path*, which urges common people to keep the company of Sufis and saints and advises them on how to comport themselves with modesty in their presence. See Appendix One.

171. Surat al-Furqan 25:20.

172. Surat al-Nur 24:32.

173. Surat al-Saff 61:4.

174. Surat al-Nur 24:30. Ibn ᶜAbbad expanded upon the importance of this concept, "lowering one's gaze," in a more direct and literal fashion in his commentary on Ibn ᶜAtaᵓ Allah's aphorisms noting that vision incites passion, and cautioning Sufis to guard their gaze. In contrast, Ibn ᶜAtaᵓ Allah here gives "gaze" a more metaphorical meaning of self-concern. The two interpretations are complementary. See Ibn ᶜAbbad, *Mawāhib al-Ilāhīya*, 90-91.

175. Surat Ghafir (Muᵓmin) 40:19, and Surat al-ᶜAlaq 96:14.

176. Surat Ya Sin 36:77.

177. Surat al-Raᶜd 13:43.

178. Surat Hud 11:6.

179. Chapter Two is devoted to this point in its entirety.

180. Surat al-Talaq 65:3.

181. Surat al-Zumar 39:36.

182. Surat Al ᶜImran 3:173.

183. Surat al-Qasas 28:7.

184. Surat al-Muᵓminun 23:88.

185. Surat Yusuf 12:64.

186. Surat al-Rahman 55:60.

187. Surat al-Aᶜraf 7:34.

188. Surat al-Naziᶜat 79:32.

189. See *Lataᵓif al-Minan*, 217-8 (corresponding to Roberts, *The Subtle Blessings*, chapter 8)

190. Surat al-Fussilat (Ha Mim) 41:53.

191. Surat al-Fajr 89:27-30.

192. Surat Yusuf 12:53.

193. Surat al-Qiyama 75:2.

194. Surat al-Maᵓida 5:122. This phrase is repeated also in 58:22 and 98:8, always describing those souls that are dwelling in gardens of paradise.

195. Surat al-Tawba 9:72.

196. Surat al-Hijr 15:40-42.

197. Surat Maryam 19:93.

NOTES TO CHAPTER TWO, INTIMATE CONVERSATION,
AND CONCLUDING PRAYER

1. Surat al-An°am 6:14.

2. Surat Fatir 35:15.

3. Sufis and other Muslim intellectuals commonly attributed this maxim to the Prophet Muhammad, though sometimes it is attributed to °Ali rather than Muhammad. However, it is recorded as a hadith in the canonical collections of that genre. See Annemarie Schimmel, *The Mystical Dimension of Islam* (Chapel Hill: University of North Carolina Press, 1975), 189.

4. Shaqīq al-Balkhī (d. 809) was an early Sufi from the central Asian region of Khurasan. He was an advocate of absolute trust in God (*tawakkul*) for all material needs, and was one of the first Sufis to discuss mystical states in a systematic way.

5. Surat al-Balad 90:4.

6. Surat Saba 34:15.

7. Surat al-Qasas 28:24.

8. Ibn °Ata° Allah alludes to what his audience would already intuit: this incident of Moses requesting a little sustenance from God after watering the flocks of the marginalized women of Madyan comes (in the Qur°anic account of Surat al-Qasas) just before the incident of Moses conversing with God through the burning bush.

9. Surat al-Naml 27:62.

10. Surat al-Baqara 2:30.

11. Surat al-Baqara 2:148.

12. This exposition of the patterns of the wide-spread carpet is an extended commentary on one moment of Shaykh al-Mursi's *Litany of Light*, in which he prays, "O God, we beseech you for fear of you, hope in you, love for you, longing toward you, intimacy with you, satisfaction from you, obedience to the command from you, reclining on the carpet of contemplating you, gazing from you toward you, making invocation of you from you—There is no god except you! Exalted be you, O God, we have wronged our own selves."

13. Surat al-Anbiya 21:87-88.

14. Surat al-Baqara 2:185, and Surat al-Nisa° 4:28.

15. Surat al-Rahman 55:10-22

16. Surat al-Saba 34:15, and Surat al-Baqara 2: 172.

17. Surat al-Mu°minun 23:51.

18. See Roberts, *The Subtle Blessings*, chapter 8 for further interpretation about labor and self-interest.

19. The creation of humans and jinn (genies) are mentioned together in the Qurʾan. Just as human are sentient beings created from dust with solid bodies like clay, so jinn are sentient beings created from flame with non-solid bodies like smoke. On the creation and moral life of jinn in Islamic thought, see Sachiko Murata and William Chittick, *The Vision of Islam* (New York: Paragon House, 1994), 100-102.

20. Surat al-Dhariyat 51:56-58.

21. In saying "I have shown earlier how such rationalist views are null and void," Ibn ᶜAtaʾ Allah refers to earlier in this text, on page 311 (see note 121) where he refutes the Muᶜtazila, the rationalist moralists who dominated early Islamic theology. Most Sufis, as Sunnis from the medieval period, adhered to the Asharite theology that rejected their proposal that reason confirms revelation and instead claimed that all moral categories depended upon revelation, and considered the Muᶜtazila to be heretics. Here Ibn ᶜAtaʾ Allah echoes the common critique that the rationalists overemphasized human free-will and agency to the point of neglecting God's all-powerful will and determination. For an anecdote about Shaykh al-Shadhili arguing with Muᶜtazila scholars in Alexandria, see Douglas, *The Mystical Teachings of al-Shadhili*, 37.

22. The early Sufi, Ibrahim ibn Adham, enjoyed princely status and worldly authority before he renounced the world to pursue spiritual discipline. This status is symbolized in this story of his conversion and repentance by his hunting (a royal prerogative) and riding (a mark of social status). Ibn ᶜAtaʾ Allah notes his princely status in *Lataʾif al-Minan*, 207 (corresponding to Roberts, *The Subtle Blessings*, chapter 8) when explaining why al-Qushayri's famous *Treatise on Sufism* begins with Ibrahim ibn Adham. The parallel to the Buddha's story is not incidental, as Ibrahim ibn Adham lived in the city of Merv, which was an active Buddhist center in Central Asia before the population became Muslims.

23. Malik ibn Anas (d. 796 in Medina) was a jurist and "founder" of the legal school that came to dominate North Africa. All the Shadhili leaders adhered to the Maliki legal school, and the Shaykhs al-Mursi and Ibn ᶜAtaʾ Allah can be called Sufi-jurists. They conceived of Imam Malik not only as the founder of their legal system, but also as a founder of Sufism.

24. Shaykh al-Mursi makes a clever pun here, contrasting the meaning of two Arabic verbs that sound similar: *faqiha* means "to understand" while *faqaʾa* means "to pierce."

25. This is an example of the common practice known as *tabarruk*. People take a small object that has been associated with a revered teacher or saint, often from clothing or food, as a form of blessing or *baraka*.

26. This section acts as a commentary on his aphorism number 5; see Victor Danner, *Sufi Aphorisms*, 24 "Your striving for what has already been guaranteed to you and your remission in what is demanded of you are signs of the blurring of your intellect."

27. Surat al-Hujurat 49:12.

28. Surat al-Rum 30:40.

29. This is another example of Ibn ᶜAtaʾ Allah continuing to compose Sufi aphorisms in a pithy, rhyming style, even in the context of a discursive prose work. The aphorism in Arabic is *ka-mā infarada fīkum biʾl-khalq waʾl-ījād, ka-dhālika huwa al-munfarid biʾl-rizq waʾl-imdād.*

30. Surat al-Rum 30:40.

31. Surat al-Baqara 2:60, and Surat al-Sabaʾ 34:15.

32. Surat al-Muʾminun 23:51, and Surat al-Baqara 2:172.

33. Surat Ta Ha 20:132.

34. Surat al-Shuᶜaraʾ 26:214.

35. Surat al-Baqara 2: 238, Surat al-Nisaʾ 4:103, and Surat al-Hajj 22:78.

36. Surat al-Baqara 2:45.

37. Surat al-Tawba 9:72 and 34, and Surat al-Jumuᶜa 62:11.

38. Surat al-ᶜAnkabut 29:45.

39. Surat al-Baqara 2:197.

40. Sura Ta Ha 20:131.

41. Surat al-Nahl 16:97.

42. Surat Ghafir (Muʾmin) 40:57.

43. Surat al-Shuᶜaraʾ 26:36.

44. Surat al-Baqara 2:189.

45. Surat al-Talaq 65:2, and Surat al-Jinn 72:16.

46. Surat al-Maʾida 5:65.

47. Surat Hud 11:6.

48. Surat al-Anbiyaʾ 21:18.

49. Surat Bani Israʾil (al-Israʾ) 17:70.

50. See *Lataʾif al-Minan*, 218 (corresponding to Roberts, *The Subtle Blessings*, chapter 8).

51. Surat al-Rahman 55:10, and Surat al-Jathiya 45:13.

52. Surat al-Talaq 65:12.

53. Surat ᶜAbasa 80:31.

54. Surat al-Dhariyat 51:22.

55. Surat Ya Sin 36:78.

56. Surat al-Rum 30:27, and Surat al-Fussilat (Ha Mim) 41:38.

57. Surat al-Dhariyat 51:58, Surat al-Rum 30:40, and Surat al-Mulk 67:21.

58. Surat al-Hijr 15:21.

59. Surat al-Munafiqun 63:8.

60. The word for soul, *nafs*, is of feminine grammatical gender, and is therefore rendered here as "her." The gender is preserved in the translation of this poem because it is integral to the force of the poem, which compares the seductive soul to a seductive woman. This comparison is continued in the poetic quotation that follows, which cites the beloved women of pre-Islamic Arabic poetry, like Lubna and Suᶜda.

61. Surat al-Zumar 39:36.

62. Surat al-Maᶜida 5:1.

63. Surat al-Aᶜraf 7:172.

64. Surat al-Rahman 55:9.

65. Surat Al ᶜImran 3:179.

66. Surat al-Ahzab 33:8.

67. Surat al-Tawba 9:105.

68. Arabic poetry in pre-Islamic times always began with such a lament for the beloved who has decamped and left with her tribe. The ruins of their previous abode force the poet to stop and weep over lost days of love. See Michael Sells, *Early Islamic Mysticism*, introduction.

69. Surat al-Anbiyaᵓ 21:30.

70. See Ibn ᶜAtaᵓ Allah's aphorism number 6; see Victor Danner, *Sufi Aphorisms*, 24 "If in spite of intense supplication, there is a delay in the timing of the gift, let that not be the cause for your despairing. For He has guaranteed you a response in what He chooses for you, not in what you choose for yourself, and at the time He desires, not the time you desire."

71. Surat al-Maᵓida 5:4.

72. Surat al-Tawba 9:111. Abu Muhammad ᶜAbd al-Mālik al-Marjānī or al-Murjānī (d. 1299) was a Sufi from the early Shadhili community in Tunis. From this mention of his name, followed by an honorific phrase for the deceased, Victor Danner has dated the compo-

sition of *The Book of Illumination* to the last decade of Ibn Ata'illah's life; see *Ibn ʿAtaʾ Allah's Sufi Aphorisms*, 13. For anecdotes about al-Marjani, see Douglas, *The Mystical Teaching of al-Shadhili*, 220 and 230-231.

73. Surat al-Dhariyat 51:22.

74. In Egypt under the Pharaohs, funerary practice was to bury the dead facing West. Among Muslims in Egypt, the practice is to bury the dead facing toward Mecca (which for Egyptians would be toward the East).

75. Surat al-Hujurat 49:10.

76. Surat Maryam 19:25. Date fruits are often taken as symbols of nourishment given freely without labor.

77. In this extended analogy of living free like birds, Ibn ʿAtaʾ Allah draws not only on the Prophet's teaching, but also on the saying of Shaykh al-Shadhili: "By God, the sustaining power of the divine is sent down upon me and I see its channels running in me and through me, like a fish gliding through the water or a bird soaring through the air." See *Lataʾif al-Minan*, 73 (corresponding to Roberts, *The Subtle Blessings*, chapter 1).

78. This is an aphorism that is not found in Ibn ʿAtaʾ Allah's famous Book of Sufi Aphorisms: *Lā budda laka min al-asbāb wujūdan, wa lā budda laka min al-ghayb ʿan-hā shuhūdan.*

79. Surat al-Ahzab 33:4.

80. Surat al-Zakhraf 43:84.

81. This is Ibn Ata'illah's aphorism 2; see Victor Danner, *Sufi Aphorisms*, 23, who translates it as "Your desire for isolation, even though God has put you in the world to gain a living, is a hidden passion. And your desire to gain a living in the world, even though God has put you in isolation, is a comedown from supreme aspiration."

82. This is a commentary on Ibn ʿAtaʾ Allah's aphorism number 17; see Victor Danner, *Sufi Aphorisms*, 26 "He who wishes that at a given moment there appear other than what God has manifested in it, has not left ignorance behind at all!"

83. Surat al-Aʿraf 7:20-21.

84. Surat Bani Israʾil (al-Israʾ) 17:80.

85. Perhaps this incident in his early life prompted Ibn ʿAtaʾ Allah to compose his aphorism number 25, "No search pursued with the help of your Lord remains at a standstill, but any search pursued by yourself will not be fruitful"; see Victor Danner, *Sufi Aphorisms*, 28.

86. A beautiful example of the Sufi genre of intimate conversation with God (*munājāt*) is the conclusion of this work, as well as the con-

clusion of ᶜAtaᵓillah's *Kitab al-Hikam*; see Victor Danner, Sufi *Aphorisms*, 64-69.

87. Sumnūn (d. circa 900) was a famous early Sufi in Baghdad. He was known to others as "The Lover" (al-muḥibb) but he called himself "The Liar" (al-Kadhdhāb) He considered love superior to knowledge, and developed a special spiritual method that centered on selfless and absolute love. See Renard, *Ibn ᶜAtaᵓ Allah*, 124.

88. Surat al-Tawba 9:75. For details on this incident, see ᶜAlī ibn Aḥmad al-Wāḥidī, *Asbāb al-Nuzūl* (Beirut: Dar al-Kutub al-ᶜIlmīya, 1991), 145-146.

89. Surat al-Baqara 2:200.

90. Surat Yunus 10:88-89.

91. Surat al-Qasas 28:68. For Shaykh al-Shadhili's interpretation of this phrase, see Douglas, *The Mystical Teachings of al-Shadhili*, 181.

92. Surat al-Qasas 28:24.

93. Surat al-Aᶜraf 7:189.

94. Maᶜrūf al-Karkhī (d. 815 in Baghdad) was an early Sufi master who was one of the first to discuss the importance of love. He asserted that God's love for beings was a gift that could never be deserved or acquired.

95. Surat Fatir 35:32.

96. Surat al-Shuᶜaraᵓ 26:89.

97. Surat al-Anᶜam 6:94.

98. Surat al-Duha 93:6.

99. Surat al-Hadid 42:7.

100. Surat al-Tawba 9:103.

101. Along with Mālik ibn Anas, who is credited with founding the Maliki school of law, three other great jurists are credited with founding legal methods that are still commonly in use. Abū Hanīfa (d. 767) was the earliest and relied on reason and custom to arrive at legal decisions. Al-Shāfiᶜī (d. 820) was a great theoretical jurist and championed the use of Prophetic traditions to curb the use of reason. Al-Shafiᶜi, Abu Hanifa and Malik are considered by Sufis to have had mystical leanings and contributed to the growing pious acetic movement that became Sufism. Aḥmad ibn Ḥanbal (d. 855) was more suspicious of the use of reason and more dogmatic than practical in his approach to law. In this anecdote he appears as a narrow-minded legalist who challenges the Sufis' claim to practicing virtue that is deeper than obedience to mere rules. This story champions the Sufi, Shayban the Shepherd, over the jurist ibn Hanbal. A similar story is told about the Sufi

al-Shiblī. "Once a man asked al-Shiblī, 'How much alms is due on five camels?' The Sufi answered, 'One sheep is the required amount due, but among us Sufis, all the camels belong to God!' The man asked, 'By what principle do you make that decision?' Al-Shiblī replied, 'By the example of Abu Bakr, when he brought out all his wealth and said it all belongs to God. Whoever gives away everything he owns is following the leadership of Abu Bakr.'" Zarruq, *Qawāᶜid al-Taṣawwuf*, 28-29.

102. Mention of the word trust (*amāna*) alludes to the primordial covenant between God and all human souls before their material being on the Day of Destinies.

103. Surat Fatir 35:28.

104. Surat al-Nahl 16:27, Surat Al ᶜImran 3:7, and Surat al-Kahf 18:114.

105. These short phrases come from the "Litany of Shaykh al-Mursi," as preserved in its entirety in *Lataʾif al-Minan*, 249-257 (corresponding to Roberts, The Subtle Blessings, chapter 10). In particular, these phrases are preserved on page 253, in the passage beginning with "O God, who gathers people on the day in which there is no doubt (*Allahuma, yā jāmiᶜ al-nās li-yawm lā rayb fīhi*)..." This prayer is also known as "The Litany of Light," as translated into English by Douglas, *The Mystical Teachings of al-Shadhili*, 78-91 (for these phrases, see 84).

106. Surat al-Takathur 102:8.

107. Surat al-Shuᶜaraʾ 26:79.

108. Surat al-Furqan 25:67.

109. Surat al-Nahl 16:66.

110. Surat al-Talaq 65:3.

111. Surat al-Munafiqun 63:8.

112. Surat Al ᶜImran 3:139.

113. Surat al-Baqara 2:172.

114. Surat al-Mudaththir 74:4. An account of al-Shadhili's dream vision is also reported in by Ibn Sabbagh but with the terms knowledge, belief, faith, love and submission in a different order; see Douglas, *The Mystical Teachings of al-Shadhili*, 135. Ibn ᶜAtaʾ Allah relates his own experience of understanding this phrase, after hearing a teaching of Shaykh al-Shadhili: He said, "Whoever believes in God is kept safe from all things, and whoever submits to God rebels against God only minimally; if he rebels he asks pardon from God and when he asks pardon, God accepts his request." Ibn ᶜAtaʾ Allah writes, "The moment I heard this, I understood the meaning of Divine Speech, *And your clothing keep pure.*" See *Lataʾif al-Minan*, 76 (corresponding to Roberts, The Subtle Blessings, chapter 1).

115. Surat Ta Ha 20:97. Here the Qurʾan relates the words of Moses as he rebukes the Israelite tribes while destroying the idol of the golden calf that they had built to worship.

116. Surat al-Anᶜam 6:76.

117. Surat al-Ḥajj 22:78.

118. Surat al-Shuᶜaraʾ 26:77.

119. Ibn Sabbagh reports that these anecdotes about alchemy are recorded in slightly different narratives; see Douglas, *The Mystical Teaching of al-Shadhili*, 138.

120. Surat al-Kahf 18:7.

121. Al-Ḥasan al-Baṣrī (d. 728) was a pivotal figure in the Muslim community after the reign of the first four Caliphs. He was a preacher, jurist and ascetic moralist who preached fear of God and suspicion against worldly power. He practiced hunger and voluntary poverty as virtues and critiqued wealth as a distraction from the divine presence. Sufis see him as an early spiritual master who lived before the term "Sufi" gained currency. Al-Hasan al-Basri befriended story-tellers (*qaṣṣāṣ*) who told popular tales of the Prophets, embellished with details from Jewish tradition and Near Eastern folk culture. Purists in the Muslim community were dubious of such popular stories (which became known as *Isrāʿīlīyāt*) as sources of scriptural knowledge. This suspicion of story telling forms the background to this incident told about al-Hasan al-Basri.

122. Surat Hud 11:6.

123. Surat Rum 30:47.

124. Surat al-Anbiyaʾ 21:18.

125. Surat al-Hashr 59:9.

126. Surat al-Ahzab 33:19.

127. Surat al-Tawba 9:75.

128. Surat Muhammad 67:38.

129. Surat al-Tawba 9:34.

130. The wording of this *hadīth qudsī* in *The Book of Illumination* differs in small details from its accepted wording as it is produced in other works on hadith.

131. This parable is comparable to the parable of Jesus in which a master gives his servants money to test them and see how they serve him; see the Gospel of Matthew 25:14-30.

132. Surat al-Anᶜam 6:141.

133. Other medieval works by masters of the Shadhili community pursue the subject of sacrificing one's soul, such as a small work by Shaykh Ahmad Zarruq, *Sulūk al-Ṭarīq idha fuqida al-Rafīq* (Traveling

the Path When You Have No Companion) which exists in three rare manuscripts. For commentary, see Scott Kugle, "Master Without a Master," *International Journal of Religion* (forthcoming).

134. Surat al-An^{c}am 6:141.

135. Surat al-Hajj 22:11.

136. The passage (from this point through the next five paragraphs) consists of text not included in the published versions of *Kitab al-Tanwir*. This alternate ending has been found in manuscripts of the text, housed in the archives of al-Qarawiyyin in Fes, Morocco (Officially "Bibliotheque de l'Université Quaraouyine), primarily from number 1356, with verification from number 1353 (which has only slight differences in vocabulary due to orthographic similarities), with additional consultation of numbers 1364 and 1833. It is not unusual for texts written and copied by hand to have different, abridged endings. Part of this alternate ending, from Shaykh al-Mursi's teaching "Those who remain unruffled and content..." through the poetry, is duplicated in *Lata'if al-Minan*, 207-8 (corresponding to Roberts, *The Subtle Blessings*, chapter 8).

137. Douglas has translated the entire litany of al-Shadhili, known as "The Noble Litany and the Mighty Veil," including the passage from which this phrase comes: "We ask Thee to grant us deprivation of all but Thee, and such a sense of sufficiency with Thee that we may be conscious only of Thee; and such a kindness toward us in both [conditions] that Thou knowest to be befitting for one who has become Thy friend. Clothe us with outer garments of majesty, which befit our souls and moments. And makes us bondservants of Thine in all circumstances." Douglas, *The Mystical Teachings of al-Shadhili*, 67.

138. Surat al-An^{c}am 6:76.

139. Surat al-Rahman 55:29.

140. Surat al-Dhariyat 51:22.

NOTES TO APPENDIX ONE

1. Vincent Cornell, *Way of Abu Madyan: the works of Abu Madyan Shu^{c}ayb* (Cambridge: Islamic Texts Society, 1996), also includes a detailed biography of Abu Madyan and translation of his major prose compositions and poems.

2. Cornell,*Way of Abu Madyan*, 182.

3. There was a Sufi master in Gujarat named Aḥmad al-Maghribī, who had taken intiation with Abu Madyan's followers and spread his ideas to Western India. The Madyani lineage may have spread along

the routes of coffee trade from Yemen to India, through the agency of Sufis who were merchants.

4. Cornell, *Way of Abu Madyan*, 146.

5. Cornell, *Way of Abu Madyan*, 163-165. The published text upon which this translation is based is Ibn ᶜAtaᵓ Allah, *ᶜUnwān al-Tawfīq fī Ādab al-Ṭarīq* (n.p.: Dar al-Kitab al-Nafis, 1987).

6. Surat Bani Israᵓil (or al-Israᵓ) 17:1.

7. See *Lataᵓif al-Minan*, 182 (corresponding to Roberts, *The Subtle Blessings*, chapter 6) where Ibn ᶜAtaᵓ Allah cites the same poem with the addition of a prior couplet that specifies the name of the poet's beloved as "Zahrā."

8. Ibn ᶜAtaᵓ Allah quotes a hadith here without acknowledging that it is attributed to the Prophet Muhammad: *inna al-tāᵓib min al-dhanb ka-man la dhanb lahu.*

9. Ibn ᶜAtaᵓ Allah's aphorism number 95; this translation reproduces that of Danner, *Sufi Aphorisms*, 37. In this commentary, Ibn ᶜAtaᵓ Allah quotes his own Wisdom Sayings and those of Abu Madyan; in this way Ibn ᶜAtaᵓ Allah reveals his affinity for and deep debt to Abu Madyan, who initiated this genre of pithy Wisdom Sayings among North African Sufis.

10. Abu Madyan's Wisdom Sayings have been gathered in a collection entitled, "Intimacy of the Recluse and Pastime of the Seeker," and translated into English by Vincent Cornell, *Way of Abu Madyan*, 116-149. I have not been able to locate this exact saying among them: *ruᵓiyat maḥāsin al-ᶜabīd wa al-ghayba ᶜan masāwīhim dhālika shayᵓ min kamāl al-tawḥīd.*

11. Danner, *Sufi Aphorisms*, 42. This is aphorism number 128.

12. Abu Jahl was the most obstinate opponent of the Prophet Muhammad and his uncle, and the Qurᵓan announced that he was destined to be burned in the fires of Hell, as revealed in Surat al-Masad, chapter 111 of the Qurᵓan.

13. This couplet acts as a commentary upon Surat Al ᶜImran 3:31: *Say, if you love God then follow me that God might love you and forgive your faults, for God is the forgiving One, the One who cares.*

14. The Night of Destiny (*laylat al-qadr*) is one of the holiest nights of the Islamic devotional calendar, commemorating the Prophet Muhammad's receiving the Qurᵓan as revelation. It comes on one of the last odd-numbered nights during the month of fasting, Ramadan, but Muslim scholars have never agreed on which exact night it might

be. This ambiguity only heightens the excitement for Muslims, as it combines a sense of immediacy with an indeterminacy, forcing Muslims to suspend their sense of routine and certainty in order to be receptive to the elusive divine presence.

15. Ibn ᶜAtaʾ Allah's Aphorism number 156; see Danner, *Sufi Aphorisms*, 46.

16. Ibn ᶜAtaʾ Allah quotes a hadith without acknowledging it as a hadith: *Inna-mā al-aᶜmāl biʾl-niyāt*. This is the hadith judged by al-Bukhārī to be most important and thus placed first in his canonical collection of hadith reports.

NOTES TO APPENDIX TWO

17. ᶜAbd al-Raḥmān Jāmī, *Nafaḥāt al-Uns wa Ḥaḍrāt al-Quds* (Tehran: Intisharāt Iṭlāᶜāt, 1373 AH), 613.

18. Michael Sells (trans.), *Approaching in the Qurʾan: the Early Revelations* (Ashland: White Cloud Press, 1999), 202.

19. Surat al-Ikhlas 112:3.

20. Surat al-Nur 24:35. The masculine grammar of the noun light (*nūr*) is clearly displayed in Surat al-Anᶜam 6:122 which mentions light and immediately replaces it with the masculine pronoun *huwa*.

21. See Colby, *Subtleties of the Ascension* (Fons Vitae, forthcoming).

22. Surat al-Hijr 15:29. For a discussion of the grammatical gender of the noun "spirit," see Sells, *Approaching in the Qurʾan,* 183-197.

23. It is provocative to speculate whether a Sufi master like Ibn ᶜAtaʾ Allah would employ such images if he were living today. Because slaves are no longer a part of our social world, this translation uses "servant" for the Arabic *ᶜabd* rather than "slave." Both meanings are possible, but only the former will resonate with contemporary readers. Ibn ᶜAtaʾ Allah praises "servanthood" as an ideal state of human virtue, and it would be hard for us in our current social order to imagine "slavery" as an ideal state.

24. See Omid Safi (ed.), *Progressive Muslims: on Gender, Justice and Pluralism* (London: Oneworld, 2003) for compelling arguments on the urgency and ethical necessity of "gender justice."

The tomb of ᶜAlī al-Wafāʾ (d. 1405) within the confines
of a mosque standing within the view of that of Ibn ᶜAtaʾ
Allah (d. 1309).

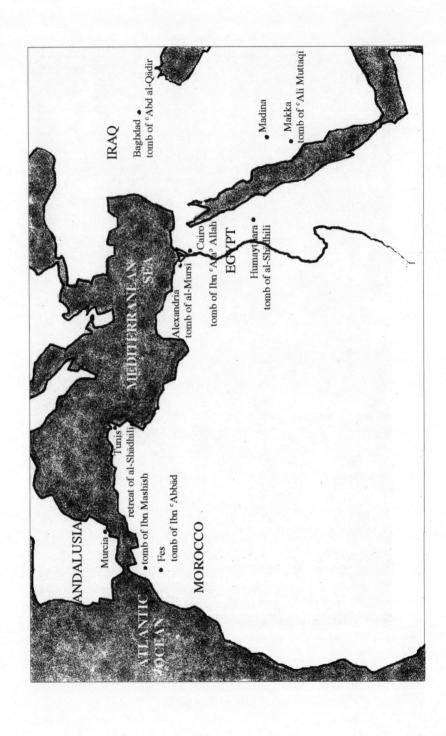

Adab: "proper respect." The systematic cultivation of outer comportment and inner character so that one can treat the other with deference, humility and respect.

Amāna: "a trust." Goods that are placed in trust with someone and must be relinquished safely at a later time. In Sufi discourse, the soul is considered "a trust" which God grants to each person for safeguarding but which must be inevitably handed back.

ᶜAql: "reason." The faculty of thought through which one can discern the ultimate outcomes of different means and judge the importance of these outcomes.

Asbāb (singular *sabab*): "causes of an effect." In this context, it implies means to achieve an end, specifically worldly means to achieve a livelihood. These are also called *ẓawāhir* (singular *ẓāhir*), or the "outwardly apparent" means of livelihood through interconnected networks, *wasāʾiṭ* (singular *wāṣiṭa*), of cause-and-effect relations which are, in inward reality, given directly by God.

Asmāʾ (singular *ism*): "names." The names of God that denote the divine qualities or virtues. In Islamic tradition, there are ninety-nine names of God extracted from the Qurʾan and used in worship and invocation.

413

Bashariya: "human nature." Characterized by both inner nobility and outer frailty. Humans were created with a needy nature, driven by an inner heat (*harāra*) that fuels their instincts and urges (*gharīza*), giving rise to craving and selfish ego.

Basīra (plural *basā'ir*): "insight." Spiritual insight into the nature of reality that comes through the heart's vision. It is closely lined with wisdom and contrasted to outward sight (*basra*) of the eyes' vision.

Dhikr: "calling to mind." Remembering the presence of God and divine qualities. Also the ritual practice of meditation, whether in silence, with recited formulas or with musical accompaniment.

Dīn: "religious path." This concept is more complex than just "religion," as commonly translated into English. It means obligation, responsibility, leading life in a moral way in order to give back the soul in submission to God. The Qur'an offers this meaning (in Surat Al °Imran 3:19): *Truly the religious path (dīn) of obligation in God's regard is submission to divine will (al-islām). The people of the book did not contradict [this path] except through envy of each other. Any who deny the signs of God, surely God swiftly calls them to account. Therefore if they dispute with you say, I have submitted my whole self to God and likewise those who follow me.*

Fadl: "bounty." Something received from the generosity of another that one does not deserve.

Fahm: "understanding." In Sufi discourses, understanding is contrasted with thinking; understanding is illumination in the heart given by God to comprehend God (*fahm biʾllah ʿan allah*), whereas thought is more limited to the operations of reasons and leads to speculation rather than certainty.

Fanāʾ: "vanishing." The spiritual condition of passing beyond the self and letting it fade from view. Often translated as "annihilation" or "obliteration." The result is *baqāʾ*, that spiritual state of "remaining" beyond selfishness, subsiding with God.

Fiqh: "understanding through reason." Especially understanding religious teachings through systematic application of reason. As a technical term, *fiqh* means jurisprudence or deducing a system of laws from the teachings of the Prophet. Ibn ʿAtaʾ Allah contrasts this conventional *fiqh* with real understanding of religion, *al-fiqh al-ḥaqīqī*, that comes with wisdom and virtue rather than with only reason and law.

Faqīr (plural *fuqarāʾ*): "impoverished one." In Sufi circles, this means one who embraces poverty voluntarily. It could be characterized as refusing ownership of goods and qualities, or perhaps more subtly as refusing to cling to such ownership.

Ḥadīth: "report." News about the teachings of the Prophet Muhammad through his sayings, doings, and spiritual states (*aqwāl wa afʿāl wa aḥwāl*).

Ḥaḍra: "presence." Specifically the divine presence of God. In North Africa, the ritual circle of *dhikr* meditation is known as the *ḥaḍra*, because it reminds those participating of the constant presence of God.

Ḥāl (plural *aḥwāl*): "state." One's spiritual state or condition in a particular moment, which is liable to fluxuation and change in the fleeting moment of the present time. Through different spiritual states (and by not clinging to particular states) one can be present with God.

Ḥāsid: "jealous." The tempter or Satan, who is jealous of the nobility granted to human beings.

Ḥijāb (plural *ḥajaba*): "separation." Physically a veil or curtain that separates one from another. Spiritually, anything that causes separation and alienation between beings and their sustainer.

Ḥikma (plural *ḥikam*): "wisdom." The human quality of knowing deeply and acting aptly, specifically acting in accord with divine will. *Ḥikma* also refers to a literary genre of "wisdom sayings," like aphorisms or maxims that are concise yet profound.

Ḥizb: "litany." A long formulaic prayer or invocation, recited at a particular time, often composed by a Sufi master for those who follow him. This is complemented by a *wird*, a shorter formula for meditation.

Ḥukm (plural *aḥkām*): "command." A message from one in authority that commands respect and obedience. The voice of God in the Qurʾan offers commands (enjoinders and prohibitions) as well as information, advice, parables and narratives about the Prophets. One type of command in the Qurʾan is the command to obey the command of the Prophet, giving rise to the discourse of Islamic law.

Iblīs: "devil." Proper name of the archangel who rebelled, refusing to bow down to the primordial human being created from clay, thereby becoming the tempter of human beings in the world (see *Shaytan* below).

Iḥsān: "doing good. " Acting in ways that are good, beautiful, sincere and wholesome toward the self and others. Along with submission (*islām*) and faith (*īmān*), these are the three dimensions of acting morally on the religious path (*dīn*, see above) taught by the Prophet Muhammad.

ʿIlm: "knowledge." In general, knowledge that comes from external learning. Specifically knowledge of religion passed on from teacher to student through traditional sources and reasoned discourse. People who bear such knowledge are respected as *ʿulamāʾ*. Contrasted to *maʿrifa* (see below), which is unmediated and intuitive.

Imām (plural *aʾimma*): "leader." This refers to the true leaders of the community by their righteousness, especially to ʿAli ibn Abi Talib, the nephew and son-in-law of the Prophet Muhammad. Shiʿa idealize him

417

both as the spiritual and political leader of the community, along with his direct male descendents. Sufis also idealize him as the spiritual leader of the community, along with the saints who inherit their spiritual values from him.

ᶜIrfān: "really knowing." The systematic cultivation of intuitive comprehension (see *maᶜrifa* below, which is derived from the same root). Another name for *taṣawwuf*, or Sufism.

Islām: "submission." The act of submitting oneself to the truth or to reality, so as to be at peace. In religious terms, submitting to the will of the divinity as known through one's own nature and experience. In devotional terms, submitting to the teachings of the Prophets. In communal terms, submitting to the teaching of the Prophet Muhammad.

Istislām: "resignation." The inner quality of submission in terms of the character virtue that brings it into effect, beyond the outer act of submission.

Īthār: "selfless giving." Giving without any expectation of benefit or giving others precedence over the self. The furthest extent of this virtue is self-sacrifice.

Karama (plural *karamāt*): "miracle." Specifically a miracle granted to saints in order to help others, rather than a miracle granted to Prophets to establish the truth of their prophetic mission.

418

Kasb: "earning." In Islamic discourse, the emphasis is on making a living through rightful earning, *kasb al-yamīn*. Beyond finances, one "earns" merit and acquires blame as the consequence of one's deeds, intentions and attitudes.

Khalīfa: "vice-regent." An authoritative representative who carries out the will of another. Specifically it refers to the righteous leaders of the Islamic community after the death of the Prophet Muhammad. In later Sufi communities, it refers to one designated the representative of a saint, who can transmit the saint's teaching and initiate disciples into the saint's community.

Khidma: "service." Serving others is the outer dimension of the Sufi path, which means both helping others meet their needs and respecting others by placing their needs before one's own

Kufr: "denial." Disavowing what one knows is actually the truth. In an outward sense, *kufr* is denying the truth of Islam as a religion. In an inward sense, it is denying the true nature of God and asserting another power as partner, such as the ego itself.

Maᶜrifa: "knowledge." Intimate experiential knowledge apprehended through intuition or spiritual taste, rather than knowledge as known by sensory perception or reason. One with such knowledge is called an *ᶜārif*.

Maᶜṣīya: "rebellion." Especially against the commands of God through persistent sin.

Maḥabba: "love." Implies an agapic desire of affection, intimacy and trust more than an erotic love or passion. This kind of love is also known as *ḥubb* and *wadd*.

Malakūt: "celestial realm of power." A level of the cosmos beyond the material world, or *mulk*. Forces of divine determination in the *malakūt* empower the material world to work according to its natural patterns.

Maqām: "station." A place of standing, referring to a certain spiritual situation in which one persists for a time, before moving on to another. The Sufi path is understood to consist of a journey from station to station in hopes of growing nearer to God.

Muᶜmin: "believer." Ibn ᶜAtaᵓ Allah means a Muslim believer who accepts not just the existence of one God and a Prophet, but specifically Muhammad as a prophet, the Qurᵓan as a divine message, with ritual, legal and communal obligations.

Munājāt: "intimate conversation." Specifically with God, as a form of prayerful petition and loving communion.

Mutajarrad: "one who leaves aside work." A recluse who has renounced worldly means and lives in isolation in order to worship and meditate (as contrasted with *mutasabbab* below). This isolation is not necessarily from human company but rather from relationships of working and earning. Also called *mutaᶜabbid*, an ascetic devoted only to worship.

Mutasabbab: "one who works to earn a living." One who struggles to support the self and dependent family through secondary material means (see *asbāb* above).

Muṭmaʾina: "tranquil." Quality of the tranquil soul, *al-nafs al-muṭmaʾina*, that is submissive toward divine reality, resigned to divine decrees, and therefore can rise to intimacy with God.

Nafs: "self." The self is often translated into English as "soul." It is the seat of self-awareness and the means through which the spirit (see *rūḥ* below) animates the body. The *nafs* could be of several kinds, depending upon its spiritual purity; the Qurʾan specifies three kinds of *nafs*, the one commanding to evil, the one that blames, and the tranquil one.

Qaḍāʾ: "eternal decree." The decree of destiny, decided before time and immutable. Often paired with *qadr*, the decree of empowering, that allows a specific action or event to happen in the world. Later Sunni theologians, like Abū Ḥāmid al-Ghazālī draw a distinction between the two, with "eternal decree" being more immutable and more removed from the realm of time and contingency.

Qiyāma: "the raising up." The day of resurrection when the dead will be raised to stand in the presence of God in judgement.

Qur³ān: "ever-recited recitation." According to Islamic belief the Qur³an is Divine Speech, the discourse of God's speaking, as transmitted to the Prophet Muhammad through the intermediary of the Angel Gabriel; see *waḥī* below.

Rizq: "provision." The means of livelihood, like food, shelter and clothing, that are provided by divine "apportioning" (*qisma*) to every person and every living being.

Rubūbīya: "lordship." God's incomparable quality of being *rabb*, lord and master of all things who nurtures and sustains their lives.

Rūḥ: "spirit." The force of life that animates the human body, breathed into it by God at the moment of its creation. In a mysterious way, it represents the one link of continuity between God and human beings, having been breathed from one into the other.

Ṣaḥāba (singular *Ṣāḥib, Ṣaḥābī*): "companions." The companions of the Prophet Muhammad in the early Islamic community are those who saw and heard him during their lifetimes.

Salaf: "those who came before." The followers of the companions of the Prophet and the earliest generations of Muslims, known as the "pious ancestors" (*al-salaf al-ṣāliḥūn*).

Sālik: "seeker." Literally, this means one who is on the road traveling, but metaphorically it means one who has undertaken a spiritual journey to reach a distant goal.

Shahwa: "lust." Selfish desires of all kinds, but especially those linked to bodily appetites.

Shar^c: "religious law." The ritual customs, moral norms and legal limitations given by a Prophet to the religious community that follows him. Islam acknowledges that God sent many Prophets to different communities, and therefore religious laws are plural. In reference to the specifically Islamic law, the word *sharī^ca* is often used, based on the same root, meaning "the wide and well-established path."

Shayṭān: "tempter." Refers to both a single figure, like Satan in English, and also to a host of smaller figures or forces of temptation, from stray thoughts to egoistic impulses.

Ṣidq: "sincerity." The basic component of morality and consciousness of God. In the Shadhili community, constantly sincere orientation toward God, *ṣidq al-tawajjuh*, is considered the essence of the Sufi path.

Sirr: "secret." The inner reality hidden within appearances. In Sufi discourse, it refers to the inner core of the human heart, the conscience, which when purified can act as the dwelling point of the divine presence.

Ṣuḥba: "companionship." In Sufi communities, this refers to the way of sitting in the company of others; it spans the distance from respectful audience, giving and receiving gentle advice, to cultivating friendships, to pursuing intimacy and love as spiritual training. As Ibn ᶜAtaᵓ Allah has said, "Companion-ship is the form and respect (*adab*) is its animating spirit."

Sunna: "example." The example of the teaching and behavior of the Prophet Muhammad, upon which the *sharīᶜa* is based.

Taᶜrīf: "making known." Taking upon oneself the means to come to right knowledge of something or someone.

Taklīf: "making obligatory." Taking upon oneself the responsibility to perform obligatory actions.

Taqwā: "wary consciousness of God." Often translated as the "fear of God" or awe. It is one of the most praised human qualities in the Qurᵓan, and maintaining it is one of the primary goals of Sufism.

Taṣrīf: "dealing or interacting." God's way of dealing with created beings by interacting with them through benefit or harm, for the apparent vicissitudes of reality are actually the consequences of the actions of God. Ibn ᶜAtaᵓ Allah's points is that apparent calamities open windows of knowledge, leading from insight to certitude. We can phrase this differently and say "suffering disappointment is opening insight."

Tawakkul: "trust." Specifically entrusting to God all of one's affairs.

Tawba: "repentance." Sincere remorse for wrongdoing, combined with outer action to ask forgiveness from those who have been wronged as well as conviction to not commit the wrong again. In Sufi communities, "repentance" means leaving worldly ambition and taking an oath of allegiance to a spiritual guide to pursue a higher spiritual aspiration.

Tawḥīd: "making something one only." Affirming and establishing the singular divinity of God (*ithbāt al-ilāhīya liʾllah*) through word, deed and attitude.

ʿUbūdīya: "servanthood." The spiritual state of being a servant to God and thereby serving other people and the created universe.

Waḥī: "inspiration." Specifically inspiration of a linguistic kind, in which a Prophet "hears" the Divine Speech of God, absorbs it into consciousness, and transmits it as an oral discourse to others. This whole process is called *tanzīl*, or "sending down" of a message from God. The message itself is called *kitāb*, often translated as "book" but better understood as "message," which highlights its inherently oral nature of hearing, reciting and transmitting.

Walī (plural *Awliyāʾ*): "friend and representative." Those who are so close to God as to become an intimate friend of God and thereby act as authoritative representative. Often translated in English as "saint."

Wujūd: "being." The reality of existence, not just of a single being in isolation, but as a particular "knot" of the holistic web of being that is sustained by the being of God.

Zuhd: "asceticism." Renouncing the world by minimizing one's dependence on worldly means. Also known as *nask*.

E

W

Z